Voicing the Void

Muteness and Memory in Holocaust Fiction

Sara R. Horowitz

STATE UNIVERSITY OF NEW YORK PRESS

Published by
State University of New York Press, Albany

© 1997 State University of New York

Rozewicz, Tadeus; *The Survivor and Other Poems*. Copyright © by Princeton University Press. Reprinted by permission of Princeton University Press.

Printed in the United States of America

For information, address State University of New York Press,
State University Plaza, Albany, N.Y., 12246

Production by Cathleen Collins
Marketing by Fran Keneston

Library of Congress Cataloging in Publication Data

Horowitz, Sara R., 1951–
    Voicing the void : muteness and memory in Holocaust fiction / Sara
R. Horowitz.
        p.   cm. — (SUNY series in modern Jewish literature and
culture)
    Includes bibliographical references and index.
    ISBN 0-7914-3129-0 (alk. paper). — ISBN 0-7914-3130-4 (pbk. :
alk. paper)
    1. Holocaust, Jewish (1939–1945), in literature. 2. Jewish
fiction—History and criticism. I. Title. II. Series.
    PN56.3.J4H67 1997
    808.83'9358—dc20   95-51818
                                                                        CIP

10 9 8 7 6 5 4 3 2 1

Contents

Acknowledgments   *vii*

1   Introduction: The Idea of Fiction   *1*

2   The Figure of Muteness   *33*

3   Voices from the Killing Ground   *47*

4   The Mute Language of Brutality   *71*

5   The Reluctant Witness   *95*

6   Muted Chords: From Victim to Survivor   *109*

7   The Night Side of Speech   *157*

8   Refused Memory   *181*

9   The Chain of Testimony   *217*

Notes   *227*

Bibliography   *245*

Index   *265*

Acknowledgments

As this book took root in the grounds of jagged remembrance, I was drawn to the interplay between the spoken and the unspoken, the told and the untold. I remain stunned by the terrible journey of the authors treated here, first in experience and later in memory. I have tried to remain true to their voices and their silences.

Many friends and colleagues gave generously of themselves, reading, discussing, challenging, suggesting. In particular, I would like to thank Lawrence Langer for his continued encouragement, and for his generous and attentive readings of early and later drafts of several chapters. Geoffrey Hartman's sympathetic readings of portions of the manuscript and his sharp editorial eye impelled me towards clarity and precision.

I thank also Nancy King and Jean Pfaelzer for sharing their thoughts on several chapters; Sarah Blacher Cohen, Alan Mintz, James Young, and Yael Zerubavel for support and encouragement; Berel Lang, for nuanced and challenging questions; David Kraemer and William Cloonan for sharing with me works then unpublished; Jonathan Richler for careful reading and much cheer. At the earliest stages of this project, I was nourished by the careful attention of Edward Engelberg, Murray Sachs, and Edward Kaplan, to whom I am indebted.

I am especially grateful to Ida Fink, who read sections of this manuscript, for extensive and illuminating conversations over nes-café and sweet pastries in Holon, Jerusalem, New York and Boston, and for friendship. I thank also Ilona Karmel for generously opening her thoughts and home to me.

My journey into the voicelessness of trauma and bereavement bears the traces of personal loss. In remembering the void I re-member myself. I dedicate this memory work to my parents, Frances Wiener Horowitz and Morris Horowitz, *Faygel bat Noah ve-Hannah u-Moshe ben Yisroel Shrage ve-Sarah Faygel, zichronam livracha*, whose absence has been a deep and steady presence in my life.

Introduction

The Idea of Fiction

I remember at one time
poets used to "poeticize"
it is still possible to write verses
it is also possible to do many other
    things
                    —Tadeusz Rozewics

Although it claims a vast and growing readership, Holocaust fiction goes against the grain. In the ongoing critical discourse about the Holocaust and its representation, the status of imaginative literature as a serious venue for reflections about historical events comes repeatedly under question. Holocaust fiction is seen by many readers as—at best—a weaker, softer kind of testimony when compared to the rigors of history, or—at worst—a misleading, dangerous confusion of verisimilitude with reality. Louis Begley, in reflecting on the connection of his novels to his personal experience as a child survivor, succinctly articulates what many readers find most problematic about the idea of Holocaust fiction: "To separate what is true from what is not would be like trying to unscramble an omelet" (Fein C10). But the word "fiction" as a synonym for "lies" poses it antithetically to truth and reflects negatively on the expressive possibilities of a particular literary form when applied to the world of actual events.

The present study presumes fiction as a serious vehicle for thinking about the Holocaust. The trope of muteness, predominant in Holocaust narratives of all sorts, functions in fiction deliberately and explicitly to raise and explore connections and disjunctures among fictional constructs, textual omissions, and historical events. Writers of Holocaust-centered fiction, like Begley, speak enigmatically of the fictionality of their work, simultaneously resisting and embracing this generic categorization. While diminishing the historical authority of their work, fictionality frees them from adhering to a certain kind of exactitude or fidelity, in order to attain a different kind of exactitude. The complexities of Holocaust fiction figure importantly not only in the critical discourse about the Holocaust but also within the fictional works themselves. The unravelling of these considerations are central to my exploration of muteness.

In a letter to the *New York Times Book Review*, Art Spiegelman takes great pains to insist that his cartoon opus, *Maus I* and *II*, not be classified as "fiction" on the *Times* "best seller" list: "to the extent that 'fiction' indicates that a work isn't factual, I feel a bit queasy." Originally serialized in successive issues of *RAW*, an avant garde commix magazine edited by Spiegelman and his wife, Françoise Mouly, *Maus* utilizes humanoid animals to depict the life and times of Vladek Spiegelman, Art's father and a survivor of Auschwitz. Two separate but intertwined narratives unfold: Vladek's story of suffering and survival in the past and Art's story of his troubled relationship with Vladek in the present, which, by the end of *Maus*, also becomes past.

Spiegelman's Holocaust book blurs the boundaries of genre in multiple ways. The commix format mixes narrative with graphic representation in the progression of line-drawn panels, utilizing a medium Spiegelman describes as "without pretensions to art"[1] (Dreifus 34), to enact a "modest" genre of Holocaust art, born of history, remembrance, and comic strip drawings. Graphically, *Maus* alternatively presents itself, on the one hand, as transparent vehicle for representing the past, replete with diagrams of hideouts and detailed sketches of barracks and bunkers and, on the other hand, as self-consciously contrived artifice, with self-referential depictions of Art in the act of drawing.

In addition, within the parameters of the commix, *Maus* shifts ground constantly between biography and autobiography: Vladek's autobiography, Art's biography of his father, Art's autobiography, the father's and the son's biographies of Vladek's wife Anja. As Vladek's autobiography, *Maus* depicts the survivor speaking his remembrances into a tape recorder, whose transcript the son faithfully reproduces in the vehicle of the comic strip. As Art's biography of Vladek, *Maus* repeatedly represents the son's agonizing over the aesthetically and ethically appropriate ways to represent his father, the Nazi genocide, and the historical and contemporary milieux. As Art's autobiography, *Maus* interposes the constant presence of the tape recorder mediating between father and son, an emblem of the Holocaust memories that come between them and also constitute the plane of their relationship. As Anja's biography, *Maus* offers spare and fragmentary traces of her life in conversations between her husband and son, whose remembrances clearly shape and perhaps distort her representation. Absent but repeatedly evoked are Anja's missing journals, represented as straightforward memoirs written with the intent of informing her son about her life.

Fidelity to his father's personal history and careful and exhaustive research into the visual aspects of camp topography and shelters (including archival photographs and sketches by Holocaust victims and survivors)[2] clearly indicate that Art Spiegelman saw his role at least in part as Vladek Spiegelman's biographer, not as a roman-à-clef graphic novelist. "As an author I believe I might have lopped several years off the 13 I devoted to my two-volume project if I could only have taken a novelist's license while searching for a novelistic structure." Spiegelman's protest to the *New York Times* claims a neat distinction between invention ("a novelist's license"), not factually reliable, and artistry ("a novelistic structure"), pressed into service of facts.

The artistry of Spiegelman's work rests not only on the dramatization of Vladek's history but on a contemplation of the conditions of its writing/drawing. The self-conscious portrayal within the comic of the cartoonist himself, at once author, narrator, and character—depicted in the act of gathering information, transmuting it into the text and graphics now in the hands of the reader—signals to us that Spiegelman is no naive raconteur. Instead, an awareness of the complexities of memory, narrative, trauma, representation, and perspective informs the work. Indeed, *Maus* repeatedly lets us know that what we read is not objective historical record but Vladek's story, his experiences and recollections. The words of Art's mother, Anja, are pointedly missing; after her suicide, Vladek burned the journals she had written in the hope that someday her son "will be interested by this." Moreover, other survivors in *Maus* have different memories. Spiegelman's narration permits us to contemplate the way that Vladek's story takes shape: not in some "pure" unmediated realm, but in the space between two people, the teller and the listener, a father and a son. *Maus* takes shape as much because Art wants to listen as because Vladek wishes to speak; it thereby takes in the contours of their complicated filial relationship.[3]

The space of the told story is framed by untold stories: Anja's stories, missing entirely except through the prisms of her husband's and her son's memories. In Art's recollection, Anja's love smothers and her suicide wounds. In Vladek's recollection, Anja appears weak and dependent. He repeatedly saves her sanity and life both before and during the war. Anja's muteness in *Maus* (and, presumably, in the life of the author) is thus triply reinforced: by her suicide, by the experiential and emotional gulf separating her from her son while alive, and by the postmortem destruction of her journals. Alongside Vladek's apparently open and unimpeded testimony is Anja's absent narrative. Her radical muteness undershadows Vladek's loquaciousness, reminding the reader that for every survivor's story that is spoken and heard, another's remains unvoiced, forever lost. Thus, Vladek's told and Anja's untold stories are companion pieces, whose unsettling symmetry is underscored by Art's final accusation to each parent in *Maus I*: "Murderer" (159) to Vladek; "You *murdered* me, Mommy" (103), to Anja.

If death radically and irretrievably truncates Anja's narrative, Vladek's is curtailed no less abruptly. Vladek's story of atrocity and survival ends with an account of his reunion with his beloved Anja, not long after liberation. "We were both very happy, and lived happy, happy ever after," he tells his son and then immediately asks him to stop the tape recorder. Deliberately cut off from Vladek's account is everything that happens next: Anja's suicide, his own incessant nightmares, the destruction of her memoirs. Then, as though to counter his imposed happy ending, his denial of continued loss, he calls Art by the name of his firstborn son, Richieu, murdered in childhood by the Nazis. Thus, beneath the chronological account that Vladek tells Art, and that Art depicts and retells, remains an unspoken past—unspoken, perhaps, because it is not past but still jarringly alive for Vladek. The omnipresent tape recorder, mediating between Art and Vladek, Art and his artistry, Art and the reader, accompanies the telling from beginning to end. Vladek's past becomes testimony by virtue of being spoken, heard, recorded, retold. Art bears witness for the witness. In this context, Vladek's switching off the tape recorder is particularly significant. It marks the end of the movement by which experience becomes testimony; it marks also the boundaries of testimony—events, emotions, and memories that, shrouded in muteness, are unavailable for testimony, at least directly. Anja's destroyed notebooks are the cognitive and psychological equivalent of Vladek's termination of the recording sessions. Art Spiegelman's artistry resides in making these absences felt, their resonances recognized if not understood.

While Spiegelman deliberately pushes against generic conventions in *Maus*, his letter to the *New York Times* clearly indicates one boundary whose blurring he resists. At least for the purposes of the *Times*'s rudimentary categorization, Spiegelman insists that history be neatly and conclusively marked off from the unreliable "fiction." In the *Times* letter, Spiegelman distinguishes between artistry, something he deems acceptable within the parameters of a true account, and fiction, something antithetical to truth, set unambiguously outside the pale of history. "If your list were divided into *literature* and *nonliterature,* I could gracefully accept the complement," he writes [emphasis mine]. Literature implies a serious aesthetic project, not necessarily a fiction. Spiegelman willingly acknowledges a seriousness of purpose and a measure of aesthetic success: "perhaps if there can be not art about the Holocaust, then there may at least be comic strips" (Dreifus 34).

What are the connections between lies and fiction, and between the lies of fiction and the truths of testimony? In discussing the constructed nature of autobiography, Barrett Mandel notes, "Language creates illusions that tell the truth . . . language constantly makes the discovery of truth possible because all language is rooted in human being and culture, so that even lies are anchored in being and contain the possibility of their own revelation" (63). Art Spiegelman's insistence on the nonfictionality of *Maus* rests on several points: that the events of the Shoah can be adequately represented in language and graphics, that they can be successfully transmitted to those not part of the Nazi genocide, and that the artifice of animation notwithstanding, *Maus* tells a truthful story. Strategies of narration and transmission ("a novelistic structure") do not impinge on the truthfulness of testimony.

Spiegelman correctly assumes that his choice to depict various categories of people as cartoon animals is responsible for the *Times*'s categorizing his work as "fiction." In fact, Spiegelman's graphic choices amplify the verbal narration, providing a constant reminder of the politics of genocide, the powerfulness of some, the helplessness of others, beyond the vagaries of individual personalities and perceptions. For Spiegelman, the iconographic choices—depicting Jews as mice and Germans as cats, for example—indicate the implied limits of representation, disallowing an interpretation that construes Germans as victims rather than perpetrators. The complexities of trauma and memory, too, may be adequately integrated into the fabric of testimony, as Spiegelman depicts the lasting effects of victimization on his father many years later. Some of Vladek's most annoying traits—misplaced wiliness, suspicion, manipulativeness—may well have been factors in his and Anja's survival. At the same time, Anja's radical muteness and Vladek's selective gaps denote the limits of representation and the consequences of trauma, at least for these survivors' stories.

Thus, Spiegelman's protest to the *Times* asserts a distinction between artistry and fictionality. Similarly, filmmaker Claude Lanz-

mann objects strenuously to references to his opus *Shoah* as a mere
"esthetic" project whose truth claims might be diminished in discussions of cinematic techniques of the sublime. "How do you dare to talk
about esthetic?" he demanded of a participant at a Yale University
seminar ("Seminar" 97). At the same time, like Spiegelman, Lanzmann
acknowledges the function of the artist's eye and hand. *Shoah* witnesses the Jewish catastrophe not by reproducing reality but through
carefully planned juxtapositions and staged segments; the film, Lanzmann asserts, is "not at all representational" ("Seminar" 97), not really
documentary, "more of a novel than an essay" (Gussow C13). Critical
reception of Lanzmann's film affirms the alliance of "art" with history.
Shoah has been described as "absolute proof that the historian is also
an artist" (Vidal-Naquet 111), as "a work of art" (Felman 206) whose
truth value surpasses those of feature films and docudramas, cinematic equivalents of literary fiction.[4]

Clearly both Spiegelman and Lanzmann have produced a work
outside the conventional boundaries of both art and historical writing.
Lanzmann's film uses no archival footage from the Nazi era. Rather
than exposition or off-camera commentary, the filmmaker allows his
complex story to unfold through a montage of disparate and discontinuous interviews with willing and unwilling subjects, visual imagery,
personal reflections, staged and spontaneous scenes. He develops, in
essence, a filmic equivalent of Spiegelman's *novelistic structure* in which
"real" witness and participants "play themselves" (Gussow C13). Both
Lanzmann's and Spiegelman's projects are "art," then, not because
they are products of the liberated imagination; both remain wedded
to a testimonial commitment, an emplotment already "given," if not
yet known. Both works are termed "art" in that they are cognitively and
emotionally effective and affecting, and make choices unconventional in
traditional historical or biographical narratives. Like Spiegelman,
Lanzmann relies not only on survivors who can fluently if painfully
articulate their memories; he also recognizes and conveys the testimonial possibilities present in moments of muteness. Both artists intrude
on their works; neither pretends to scientific objectivity of the disin-
terested researcher, yet both share and explicitly assert a commitment
to truth. Neither for Spiegelman nor for Lanzmann does artistry soften
or prettify the implications of the events they uncover and reveal;
rather the artistry resides in the meshing of disparate fragments into a
cognitive, psychological, and ethical whole that unsettles the viewer. In
other words, the artistry is not merely an overlay on already known
facts, but itself constitutes and interprets. Indeed, Lanzmann refers
to his film as "pensée . . . thinking" (Gussow C15).[5]

Spiegelman's and Lanzmann's respective projects challenge the boundaries between art and history. Where these boundaries blur, they imply that one can think better or at least differently about the events of history. The point is not so much to learn the facts directly from the mouths of survivors as it is to break down the cognitive and emotional barriers that keep the past safely in the past for listeners, readers, and viewers. The Shoah is still present in Spiegelman's and in Lanzmann's representations—in the relationship between parents and children, or between living Poles and dead Jews, or between Holocaust survivors and exilic landscapes. Most importantly, both Spiegelman and Lanzmann structure their works so that the reader or viewer becomes not so much a listener to a story, a memory, but a witness to ongoing acts of remembering, of reliving.

Both artists, however, take great pains to distinguish their own work from fiction. Echoing Spiegelman, Lanzmann insists that "[t]he truth kills the possibility of fiction".[6] One can imagine, of course, ways in which the softening of such categories as art, history, and fiction might be used to deny, falsify, or domesticate the events of the Nazi genocide.[7] (Indeed, sadly, one need not merely imagine.) As Spiegelman points out to the *New York Times*, "The borderland between fiction and nonfiction has been fertile territory for some of the most potent contemporary writing. . . . It's just that I shudder to think how David Duke . . . would respond to seeing a carefully researched work based closely on my father's memories of life in Hitler's Europe and in the death camps classified as fiction." In a sense, however, when Spiegelman disputes the best seller list's classification, suggesting that the *Times* "consider adding a special 'nonfiction: mice' category to your list," he is deliberately disingenuous to make clear that this story is not to be dismissed as invention.

Spiegelman's facetious solution to such "problems of taxonomy"—the creation of a new category, "mice"—underscores the inadequacy of conventional generic boundaries with regard to Holocaust testimony. Unable or unwilling to respond to the deeper issues that underlie Spiegelman's challenge with an open-ended exploration of such "problems of taxonomy," the *Book Review* editor complies with Spiegelman's request, relying on prior institutions of classification for the cartoon book: "The publisher . . . lists it as 'history, memoir.' The Library of Congress also places it in the nonfiction category. . . . Accordingly, this week we have moved *Maus II* to the hard-cover nonfiction list. . . ."[8] The murky terrain between fiction and history remains untrammeled.

What Spiegelman calls a problem of "taxonomy" characterizes fictional representations of the Holocaust. Spiegelman's discomfort with the categorization of his work as fiction marks a particular discomfort for writing about Auschwitz after Auschwitz, a discomfort that intrudes on all aesthetic projects but particularly those not developed by survivors themselves. The ongoing critical conversation about Holocaust writing probes the limitations and propriety of its aesthetic representations. Following Theodor Adorno, critical discourse interprets his much cited statement about the barbarism of poetry after Auschwitz to mean, variously, that one should not write lyric poetry, any poetry, any fiction, any "literature," or anything at all in wake of the Holocaust, unless or even if one is a survivor of the Nazi genocide. Broadly speaking, there is a high degree of discomfort with the idea of an aesthetic project built upon actual atrocity, as well as a proprietary sense of what belongs properly to the domain of the historian. Within these rough parameters, a special category emerges—that of *témoinages*, or witnessing—to contain survivor testimony of all sorts. For survivor writing, a literature of testimony develops that encompasses not only autobiography but fictional autobiography and imaginative literature, as well as poetry. The actual experiences of the writer, whether represented or transfigured in the work itself, anchor and validate the writing. The closer the writer to what Primo Levi refers to as "the bottom"—those murdered by Nazi genocidal practices—the more the work could be construed as itself being a part, a trace, a fragment of the atrocity or at any rate of the survivor's memory or psyche. Thus, while Jerzy Kosinski's novel *The Painted Bird* was controversial for its grotesque and possibly gratuitously violent depictions when it was first published, the purported confluence of the author's own childhood experiences and the novel's boy protagonist's fictional experiences helped to ensure the book a place in what has evolved into a "canon" of Holocaust writing.[9]

Like Spiegelman's faithfully rendered and imaginatively constructed commix, fiction of the Holocaust inhabits a space beyond conventional categories, mixing *témoinages* with invention. For example, Ida Fink's short story collection, *A Scrap of Time*, and her longer work, *The Journey*, are categorized by the Library of Congress as "fiction." Yet although the author does not dispute the category, she also asserts that the events described in both books "really happened."[10] Similarly, Louis Begley resists generically categorizing his autobiographically inspired novels, *Wartime Lies* and *The Man Who Was Late*. Indeed, the title of Begley's first novel, *Wartime Lies*, suggests the complexities of the issues. The "wartime" lies are the invented names and histories necessary to the survival of a young Jewish boy during the years of the Nazi genocide. Moreover, they refer also to the unmaking and remaking of the self—the internalization of the lies, the erasure of true

and assumption of false identities—resulting from that struggle to survive, and finally to the novel itself, a "lie" (or a fiction) about a childhood
(and the loss of childhood) during the war. Ultimately, the novel challenges the conventional understanding of truths and lies. The novel
disrupts the conventional ethical evaluation of lies as evil and truth as
good; in the context of the Holocaust, the truth could cost a survivor his
life. Some lies (such as those Begley's boy lives out) become themselves
the truths of one's existence; some events become knowable through
their fictions.

The novel charts a young, Jewish boy's loss of voice, agency, and
identity—the price exacted by survival—as it recounts the experiences
of Maciek, whose first-person account comprises most of the narrative.
Under the guardianship of his aunt Tania, Maciek survives the war by
assuming and shedding a series of false identities and histories. Intermittently, an unnamed adult narrator intrudes to comment upon the
action, human suffering and survival.

The Shoah disrupts and ultimately destroys Maciek's childhood,
ineluctably wiping his early years from memory. Before the war, the
child has begun to transact "pacts" and "bargains" with the adults in his
life. As Maciek begins to mature, his assertions of will, enacted through
food, sleep, and toilet habits, evolve into linguistic negotiations. When
the war propels his family into hiding, however, Maciek becomes
utterly reliant upon Tania to survive. To keep their Jewish identity
secret, Tania instructs him on how to speak, look, and move, and even
which emotions to display and which sins to confess before taking holy
communion. She drills him in German and rehearses him in a sequence
of fabricated life histories. He learns to wipe out of his speech all traces
of Jewishness. He accepts his aunt's authority, repeats and obeys her
instructions. In the sequence of boarding houses, cellars, and farms
they inhabit, "One had to talk, one could not always talk about books,
one had to be ready to talk about oneself. Which self? The issue was the
limit of one's inventiveness and memory, because the lies had to be
consistent—more consistent, according to Tania, than the truth" (95).
Reversing his prior movement toward independence, he learns to sub-
sume his will to Tania's, to substitute his voice for hers.

> She said it was lucky we had not forgotten for a moment we
> were Catholic Poles. . . . We would make ourselves very small
> and inconspicuous, and we would be very careful not to get
> separated in the crowd. If something very bad happened and
> she was taken away, I wasn't to try to follow: it wouldn't
> help her and I might even make things worse for both of us.

If possible I should wait for her. Otherwise, I should take
the hand of whatever grown-up near me had the nicest face,
say I was an orphan, and hope for the best. I shouldn't say I
was a Jew, or let myself be seen undressed if I could avoid it.
She had me repeat these instructions and told me to go to
sleep. (126)

The narrative presents Maciek as predominantly mute; when he
does speak, his own voice is displaced by that of Tania or other adults.
As bearer of Tania's ventriloquisms, Maciek is doubly mute, since
Tania's voice, too, becomes the vehicle for others' desires. "Tania's speech
and gestures . . . were never without purpose. That purpose was to conceal and please, to concentrate attention on what might gratify the listener and deflect it from us. I played the supporting role" (154). Thus,
Maciek and Tania do not merely tell wartime lies; they surrender the
agency of voice in order to become, for others, desired objects. For
Maciek, less skillful than his aunt, the strategy calls down the condemnation of others, who see in his speech acts evidence of "weak character . . . my habit of insinuating flattery. . . . always to be trying to make
oneself liked . . ." (96); his "habit of smiling when there was nothing to
smile about. . . . had to be because I was a little hypocrite" (100). Taken
together, Maciek's clumsy and Tania's more polished performances
underscore the loss of voice and erasure of identity of the Shoah victim, as substitution for or as prelude to the radical silence of death.
    These voices are extinguished solely because they are Jewish
voices. In expunging all traces of identity from Maciek's speech, Tania
insists on only one linguistic shard of Jewishness:

> . . . she would teach me what every Jew must do when his death
> is near: cover his head, with only his hands if necessary, and say
> in a loud voice, *Shema Yisrael, Adonai elocheinu, Adonai echad.*
> Hear, O Israel, the Lord thy God, the Lord is one. That was a
> way for a Jew not to die alone, to join his death to all those that
> had come before and were still to come. (71)

In Tania's rendition as recollected by the narrator, both the transliter-
ation of the original Hebrew verse and its translation into English contain an error in the words *eloheinu*, "our God"; in the narrator's translation "our God" becomes "thy God," underscoring Maciek's separation
and alienation from Jews, from Judaism, and from his Jewish self.
    Only as a non-Jew may the boy live; he can, however, die into
Jewishness. That one regains Jewish voice and language only at the
point of death, the ultimate extinction of voice, underscores the narra-

tive's network of symbolic associations. The narrative symbolically conflates darkness and muteness with Dante's hell, "that place mute of all
light . . ." (68), symbolically linking voicelessness with hopelessness,
moral emptiness, anguish, and death, and light with life, voice, truth,
and agency.

Enforced muteness represents both the source of trauma—for
Maciek, the Shoah itself—and, at the same time, the lasting effect of
trauma for the adult who was the child Maciek (but no longer goes by
that name). Ostensibly narrated in the first person by the child himself,
the narrative turns out to be only the most recent in an ongoing
sequence of ventriloquisms, this time of the adult survivor who displaces onto the mute child an imagined childhood: "our man has no
childhood that he can bear to remember; he has had to invent one"
(181). Like Tania's voice, however, the survivor's voice doubly affirms
Maciek's muteness.[11] For while the adult appropriates the narrating "I"
of the child's autobiographical narrative, in actuality the child's muteness extends into his adult life. For the novel opens and closes with a
man who also has no voice. Like the child, this man constitutes a witness only in the limited sense that he sees, he has seen, and he understands—but he does not bear witness. His profession indeterminately
described as one who teaches "how to compare one literature with
another" or "a literary agent with a flair for dissident writing," the
man "reads" or enables others to read "texts bearing witness against
oppression and inhumanity" (1). Yet, while retaining "the power to
grasp meaning and to remember," he does not himself bring testimony,
does not speak out of his own experience. Even the child's autobiographical narrative—seemingly that missing testimony—turns out to
be another kind of wartime "lie," attesting to the absence of narrative,
the muffling of testimony that itself constitutes a kind of testimony of
extreme victimization and ongoing trauma.

In *Wartime Lies*, Begley's autobiography is at many degrees fictionalized—by the tempting but unconfirmed implication of factual
coincidence with the author's life, by the disquieting play of Maciek's
"real" story against the multiple invented lives he puts forth, by the
adult narrator's admitted invention of even that "real" story, and by the
suggestion of conflicting and non-narrated life stories for that adult.
These multiplying layers of fictionality indicate something of the complexities of Holocaust survivor narrative. Indeed, the impossibility of
locating within *Wartime Lies* an "actual" story against which to measure the lies implies that something of the actual experience of survival remains always outside narration, accessible only in the interplay
between the unstated and the various versions of survival.

As Philippe Lejeune observes in discussing the "autobiographical pact," "The deep subject of autobiography is the proper name" (20). Autobiographical memory asserts the continuity of the experiencing ego through self-schema, which gives a sense of consistency between past experience and present life narrative.[12] Moreover, autobiography asserts a continued relationship not only between self and memory but between self and world; as Herbert Leibowitz notes, the autobiographical "'I' cannot be conjugated without the world outside of it" (5).

What constitutes autobiography under conditions that preclude owning one's "proper name," conditions that prohibit consistency between the life lived and the life narrated, conditions wherein the "world outside," if brought together with the conjugating "I," would annihilate it? The events recollected and recounted by the autobiographical subject who is a Holocaust survivor challenge the deep conventions of the genre; fictional autobiography and autobiographically inspired fiction provide a means to explore the nature of this challenge, as well as the events and repercussions responsible for it.

From Spiegelman's willingness to concede to the appellation "literature," and from the manifold references to Lanzmann's film as "art," it is clear that for those disturbed by the idea of a fiction of the Holocaust, "literature" or "art" may be distinguished from "fiction" by the question of invention, the departure from what Hayden White has termed "the discourse of the real." The sentences Vladek recalls uttering during the war years may not match exactly what he said, word for word. Spiegelman did not quote verbatim from the extensive taped conversations with his father, but rather selected key words around which he built the dialogue that appears in *Maus*. Nonetheless, to the best of their abilities both father and son remain faithful to what actually occurred. Spiegelman's technique then is one of distillation and condensation, not invention; he reduces Vladek's long statements to their essence. Fiction, as Spiegelman points out, takes different liberties.

To protect their respective projects from the kind of assaults mounted by historical deniers, and to assert the truth claims of their work to an uninitiated readership, Spiegelman and Lanzmann insist upon the "nonfictionality" of Holocaust art. For Spiegelman and Lanzmann, the easy conflation of "fiction" with "lies" threatens the integrity of their respective projects and the credibility of Holocaust representation. An illustration of the prevalence of this easy elision of "lies" and "fiction," an article entitled "History versus Fiction" published in a journal of Holocaust studies aimed primarily at educators defines the "fiction" under discussion as "the abiding tendency to either deny the Holocaust's magnitude, or to deny it ever occurred at all"; such overlaying of "fiction" (or lies) on "history" (or truth), the article goes on, emerges from "the promiscuous intellectual climate today."[13] To distinguish their work from the lying art of fiction, both Spiegelman and Lanzmann take great care to make visible the autobiographical, biographical, and historical boundaries of their works, and their refusal to invent facts or events. In their works, the absence of the unrepresented past is felt through the presence of remembering survivors rather than through invented scenarios. At the same time, both Lanzmann and Spiegelman acknowledge that, by innovatively manipulating their respective media to contain the story of the destruction of the Jews of Europe, they have produced something different from conventional historical documentation—Spiegelman's "novelist's license," Lanzmann's description of *Shoah* as "more of a novel than an essay." Like Spiegelman's droll suggestion of a new category for "nonfiction: mice," Holocaust fiction also suggests the need for an expansion of categories, for new classifications, new "taxonomies."

Lanzmann's description of his filmic works as *pensée* is most apt in conceptualizing the work of Holocaust fiction. In *Shoah*, Lanzmann explains, "real people . . . play themselves" (Gussow C13) in particular settings and juxtapositions not merely to dramatize a history already known and documented but to suggest new connections between people and events. In many works by survivors of the Nazi genocide, the liberties of fiction enable their authors to contemplate and express what could not be arrived at as well otherwise. It is not a matter of presenting the historian's work in a manner more emotionally or intellectually accessible to a broad reading public, but of representing one's own or another's experiences in a way that opens up complicated questions regarding atrocity, memory, history, and representation. In his discussion of memory and history, Pierre Vidal Naquet observes that "the historian . . . can not, however, say *all*, and what he can no doubt *least* communicate is death as it was experienced by the victims. . . ." (109). While Vladek Spiegelman lives long enough to transmit his remembrances to his son, most victims of Nazi atrocity did not live out the war. Only an imaginative leap reveals what might have been their story, simultaneously reproducing and revoking the radical muteness genocide imposes.

Ida Fink's "A Spring Morning," for example, begins with a casual restaurant conversation during which a Polish petty municipal official relates to his friends what he witnessed as the local Jews were marched off to their deaths. An eyewitness, he recollects that a Jewish man crossing the bridge over the Gniezna River "with his wife and his children for the last time in his life" likened the dirty river water to the color of beer. "Listen to this: Here's a man facing death, and all he can think about is beer" (39). The eyewitness's remark evokes a banal comment—"Maybe the guy was just thirsty, you know?" (40)

The narrative then switches focus and point of view; the ensuing interior monologue recounts the actions and emotions of the Jewish man, now dead, from the moment he rises on the morning of his death, through his stunning realization that he has "overslept his life," his desperate attempt to save his toddler by urging her to run from the line of doomed Jews toward a church, her fatal shooting, and finally, his last moments—carrying his child's corpse to his own death at the mass grave in the forest.

Thus, Fink's story presents two narrations of the day's event: one possible but inadequate, rendered by a surviving eyewitness, the other impossible but revealing, told from the point of view of its murdered victim. Fink's story makes clear that without the fiction—without the narrator's imaginative intercession into historical reality—the murdered man's life, fate, and feelings, the tragic indignity and the superfluous cruelty of his suffering would remain untold, and hence unknowable, consigned by his death to a radical muteness. Worse yet, the space left empty by the absence of his story would be filled, instead, by the narrative of someone whose Aryan ancestry leaves him safely outside the circle of victims whose march to death he watches impassively. "Thanks to him and to people like him, there have survived to this day shreds of sentences, echoes of final laments, shadows of sighs of the participants in the *marches funèbres*, so common in those times," (39) the narrative notes, not without irony. An unnamed narrator then steps in to interrupt and to contest the spoken story with which "A Spring Morning" begins and to supplement the available shreds, echoes, and shadows of sighs with the unspoken story of the dead man. From what possible vantage point might the narrator have witnessed the events narrated? If he were among the victims marching toward mass slaughter, then—like the murdered father—he would not be able to narrate the death of the child and parent. If a bystander, he would remain outside the experience of victimization. To call the imagined interior monologue "lies" and the eyewitness report "truth" would go against the ethical movement of the story. "A Spring Morning" explores the retrieval of impossible narratives, giving voice to stories consigned to muteness. Measuring the available eyewitness report with the interior monologue, we find that here the more "factual" account eclipses the truth. For it is the absent story made present by radical imagining that confronts the mass murder that has occurred.

Unlike Spiegelman, Fink embraces the ambivalences of fiction that make possible particular types of telling. Implicit in the development of representations different from, but complementary to, the labor of the historian is the presumption that the Holocaust will not remain outside the boundaries of aesthetic representation. Yet the conjunction of fiction with the historical events of the Holocaust has made both readers and writers uneasy since the earliest works appeared. Spiegelman's discomfort with the category of "fiction" occurs within a long history of discomfort not only with Holocaust fictionality but with aesthetic projects generally. May one speak at all of an aesthetics of atrocity? To pose the question so baldly is to appear either disingenuous, uninformed, or already committed to a response. Whether framed explicitly, or simply assumed, this question underwrites, and sometimes overdetermines, critical discussion of poetry, fiction, theater, and film that focuses on the experiences and reactions of victims and former victims of Nazi atrocity. In the decades since the war, readers have, by turns, repudiated the literary discourse as, at worst, misleading lies giving ground to historical revisionists, at best, unseemly and irrelevant; diminished its "soft" ways of knowing in favor of the hard facts of historical accounts; gingerly and apologetically analyzed its texts; seized upon its texts as unmediated historical documentation; revered it as sacred, or as a sublime "dreaming back."[14]

Notwithstanding his own corpus of Holocaust-centered novels, Elie Wiesel asserts an essential incompatibility between fiction and the concentrationary universe: "A novel about Auschwitz is not a novel, or else it is not about Auschwitz."[15] What has the discourse of literature to do with the systematic program of atrocity and mass murder we have come to call the Shoah, the Holocaust, the Churbin? Even the Holocaust survivors who transmute their memories into fiction and poetry regard their own work with ambivalence.

Wiesel's comment, like Spiegelman's request to classify his cartoon book as "nonfiction: mice," cuts to the heart of the conventions by which we categorize and define literary kinds. In counterpoising "novel" against "Auschwitz," the Holocaust novelist—if he is not to refute his own work—suggests that between the poles of chronology and invention, "fiction of the Holocaust" is different from either. Other writers of "Holocaust fiction," like Wiesel, assert that what they recount, if not *true*, is also not *not true*. Moreover, writers like Ida Fink find that a conventional memoir or historical accounting denies them the means to utter certain types of truths.

The critical discourse on the Shoah generally, and on the value of Holocaust literature specifically, has shifted and evolved—shaped and reshaped by successive encounters with the Holocaust writing, by the publication of new material and innovative literary genres and modalities, by changes in literary criticism and theory generally, and by ongoing conversations among philosophers, historians, and literary critics. Despite these changes, readers continue to argue—often vehemently— about the significance of imaginative literature in thinking about the Holocaust, about whether one *should* write, read, and seriously consider literary representations of the Shoah.

Three fundamental questions underlie the critical concerns about Holocaust literature. (1) Should one read (write) imaginative literature, rather than "straight" history, about the unimaginable, the concentrationary universe? (2) If so, how should one evaluate and understand this literature? (3) Is there a literary mode best suited to represent what has so often been termed unrepresentable? Theodor W. Adorno's oft-quoted dictum, "Nach Auschwitz ein Gedicht zu schreiben, ist barbarisch"—"To write poetry after Auschwitz is barbaric"—("Engagement" 125), has been echoed by others who, for differing reasons, fear that the transmutation of historical atrocity into imaginative literature necessarily entails a trivialization and betrayal of the real events of the Holocaust. In their respective fields and across disciplines, historians, historiographers and philosophers probe the cognitive and moral limits of representation of the Shoah, poetry and—especially—fiction have come to represent a special case that by definition may exceed the boundaries of ethics and propriety.[16]

Despite the spate of Holocaust-related publications in recent years, the growing audience for popular and scholarly books and films about the Shoah, the burgeoning of Holocaust studies courses on college campuses, and the establishment of new Holocaust museums and monuments, the questions regarding art and atrocity stubbornly resist resolution. Novelist and Shoah survivor Aharon Appelfeld wonders, ". . . horror and art. Can they coexist?" ("After the Holocaust" 83). The problem lies not only with fictional modality but with writing generally, with telling, with narrative. Notwithstanding his own novels, screenplays, and essays drawn from his experiences as a survivor, Arnost Lustig embodies the same paradox as Wiesel when he asserts, "To write of Auschwitz-Birkenau as it was—no one will do" ("Auschwitz-Birkenau" 393). At the heart of Holocaust narrative resides an essential contradiction: an impossibility to express the experience, coupled with a psychological and moral obligation to do so. Former victims of the Nazi genocide frequently express a deep ambivalence about their own Holocaust-centered writing—an ambivalence inscribed in the very unfolding of their narratives. As Maurice Blanchot observes in *The Writing of the Disaster*, "the disaster de-scribes."

Survivors such as Wiesel, Fink, and Begley develop in practice a poetics of atrocity that contains these ambivalences, working both within and beyond the pale of writing. The critical discourse of Holocaust studies mirrors this ambivalence as it limns the limits of memory and representation, with particular reservations about the confluence of art and atrocity that comprises Holocaust fiction. If not barbaric, as Adorno warned, the literary imagination after Auschwitz is said to domesticate, to trivialize, and to falsify what it seeks to represent.

The moral weight of Shoah writing—its testimonial function—and the massive catastrophe to which it testifies, contribute to a reluctance to read Holocaust narratives as "mere" art—that is, as imaginatively generated and artfully structured rather than historically determined, transparent texts. The horror Adorno expresses at the intersection of art and atrocity lingers in critical discourse decades later, despite the emergence and recognition—even by Adorno himself—of powerful literary treatments of the Shoah. Historians and philosophers often separate out the literary from other forms of narrative that seem less problematic. Thinking about the Holocaust has broadened to include the voices of many methodologies and disciplines, and the resultant ongoing conversations has deepened the way we understand the events and our own reflections. Nonetheless, over the years the place of literary studies and imaginative representation has remained shaky.

One reason that literary texts come to constitute a special category within studies of the Shoah is that, more than other forms of narrative representations, literature foregrounds its own rhetoricity. In fiction and poetry, language is acknowledged and explored not as a transparent medium through which one comes to see reality but as implicated in the reality we see, as shaping our limited and fragile knowledge.

Precisely the strength of this literary way of knowing, however, disquiets many readers. For example, in his 1970 *The Exile of the Word*, André Neher criticized Holocaust literature as an artificial construct, which, like the arguments of Job's comforters, falsified through interpretation. If one can confront the Holocaust at all, Neher insisted, one must do so outside of art and literature.[17] Fully two decades later, Berel Lang opens his excellent *Act and Idea in the Nazi Genocide* by first privileging historical writing and then undermining imaginative writing connected with the Shoah: "It seems obvious to me that anything written now about the Nazi genocide against the Jews that is not primarily documentary, that does not uncover new information about the history of that singular event, requires special justification" (xi). On the other hand, "Wherever it appears, literary representation imposes artifice, a figurative mediation of language, and the contrivance of a persona—that is, a mask—on the part of the writer . . . artifice tends to become conceit, and the writer's intervention . . . draws attention away from the subject itself."

Both Neher's and Lang's critiques of literary representations of the Shoah center on their sense of a moral obligation to remember and tell the events truthfully, to transmit historically accurate testimony. The artifice of art—the literary form, generic conventions, metaphors—construed as a thing apart from the events narrated, imposes an unwanted (because unreliable, untruthful) structure that occludes rather than reveals lived experience and historical memory. Literature is thus viewed as implicated in the narratological constraints inherent to writing about the historical events—problems for which the Shoah serves as a test-limits case—and, at the same time, as a special case, judged particularly problematic even when other forms of narrative are not. This critique of literary representations of the Shoah is exemplary rather than exceptional; it constitutes the fulcrum for much of the discourse about the Holocaust. Appelfeld recollects being admonished repeatedly, "Keep literature out of that fire zone. Let the numbers speak, let the documents and the well-established facts speak" ("After the Holocaust" 83).

Subsequent thinking about the Shoah develops and interrogates the ongoing and complex discussion about the nature of history, historical truth, and historical relativism, and the variegated shapes of memory, in the context of the Nazi genocide. A collection of essays gathered under the aegis of Saul Friedlander, *Probing the Limits of Representation: Nazism and the "Final Solution"*, follows two separate threads of argument that are then explicitly brought together. First, discussion centers on the difficulties and dangers inherent in representing the Holocaust in historical and literary narrative. Does the destruction of European Jewry remain singularly beyond our ability to describe, absorb, and understand? Here, too, imaginative literature poses a special case; citing Theodor Adorno, Friedlander questions the appropriateness of aesthetic forms to represent utter devastation. The second discussion focuses on the debate between traditional and "new," postmodern historicism and the moral and intellectual implications of each. Can one recover (as modern historians affirm) an objective truth by rigorously scrutinizing documents and interrogating witnesses? Or (as postmodernists assert) does one inescapably interpret—and thus shape—the very history one seeks to document as a necessary part of the documentary process? And if so, how may one speak of a "pure" and objective historical truth by which to measure competing interpretations? Both of these discussions consider the relationship between actual events and the narratives produced to recover or reconstruct them. Central to the project is an attempt to reconcile the testimonial endeavor associated with Holocaust studies—the search for documentable facts and proof—with the postmodern insight that the opacity of both events and language make historical events inaccessible.

Paradoxically, the very strength of the aesthetic modes in approaching the inaccessible and inarticulable evoke disquietude. To the extent that literary narrative substitutes language for world, or symbol-making over bare chronology, it uneasily evokes the linguistic mechanisms that facilitated the enactment of the Final Solution. In several essays, most notably those contained in *Language and Silence*, George Steiner probes the erosion of literature and of language itself, warped in service for the Nazis. He notes, "Gradually, words lost their original meaning and acquired nightmarish definitions. *Jude, Pole, Russe* came to mean two-legged lice, putrid vermin which good Aryans must squash, as a party manual said, 'like roaches on a dirty shelf'" (142).[18] The flourishing of atrocity among a highly literate people particularly disturbs Steiner, undermining his trust altogether in the literary endeavor. From the perspectives of literature, philosophy, and history, Lawrence Langer, Hannah Arendt, and George Mosse similarly caution against the comforting but falsifying rhetoricity that helps us to "feel better" without enabling us to "*see* better" (Langer, *Versions* 12). In different contexts, each notes the close links between emotionally manipulative but ultimately empty tropes and the Nazi reliance on a language laden with metaphor and abstraction, a language designed and successfully utilized to facilitate genocide.[19]

Ironically, the sense of the uniqueness of the Holocaust, its historical unprecedentedness, propelled both Shoah survivors and later thinkers toward imaginative literature, myth, and symbolic representation. But, according to Theodore Ziolkowski, imaginative literature mythifies the Holocaust, lifting "the historical event . . . out of its causative nexus." The extensive critical discussions of Holocaust literature compound the problem for Ziolkowski by distancing the reader still further from the history. "Instead of confronting the Holocaust, these [critical] writers, like Plato's artist, actually confront a literary reflection of the Holocaust" (683). However, reflections and representations constitute the only knowledge available to anyone not part of the concentrationary universe. Even the site of atrocity—transformed into what French historian Pierre Nora terms *les lieux de memoire*, the places of memory—does not offer a transparent medium for viewing what occurred there. Historical narrative also depends for its reconstructions upon language and narratology.[20] The bare chronicle toward which Lang aspires is impossible to attain outside of its rhetoricity.

Nonetheless, as writers and readers measure the stuff of literature against the authority of history, many echo these reservations. The comingling of fact with fiction, reality with artifice, memory with imagination, seemingly undermines the pursuit of truth, so vital to witnessing: of knowing exactly *what* happened in that night world, *to whom*, *by whom*, and *how*. Between verisimilitude and veracity yawns a wide gulf. The suspension of disbelief integral to the reading of fiction runs counter to the exacting demands one places upon testimony: might not one end in a suspension of belief altogether? For many readers share Art Spiegelman's sense of Shoah fiction as a dangerous enterprise, one that adds nothing substantial to our understanding of those events but instead gives fodder to the historical revisionists who deny that the events of the Holocaust occurred at all. Taken to its extreme, fictional representation of the Holocaust appears to some readers to make a fetish of language. Unlike a bare chronology, which aspires to the facts as such, the literary text—in avowing its own artifice, rhetoricity, and contingent symbol-making—threatens to shift and ultimately destroy the grounds by which one measures one set of truth claims or one historical interpretation against another. This fear is expressed perhaps most pressingly by critics of postmodernism, who fear, like David Hirsch, that its "radically skeptical mindset" (24) and its focus on language games and *jouissance* finally efface historical distinctions, precluding ethical thinking.[21]

In the current critical discussion, the facticity of history is frequently said to speak for itself, even if in a manner made more complicated by our growing consideration of the complexities of historical writing. Literary representation remains suspect, its particular attributes seem particularly problematic. The truth claims of historical writing has been linked with an antirhetoric or a pretense to transparent and unadorned rhetoric.[22] Often the "facticity" of historical accounts is contrasted with imaginative representations, and the latter requires justification. Critical readers who find themselves moved by particular works or constellations of works often seek to define a mode of Holocaust writing whose special attributes approximate (or counterbalance) "pure" representation.

In *Versions of Survival*, Lawrence L. Langer explores the different "versions" of survival that survivors evolve, in his analysis, as much to assuage guilt or reaffirm values as to retrieve the truth about what has happened. According to Langer, "Every narrative about the deathcamps includes an encounter between fact and memory, persuasive horror and the will to disbelieve" (4). Thus, we encounter not merely reflections, but flawed reflections of this night world. In *Holocaust Testimonies*, Langer examines the implications of the taped testimonies gathered under the aegis of the Fortunoff Video Archives for Holocaust Testimonies at Yale University, distinguishing these raw, oral testimonies from written sources, both historical and literary. As the survivor burrows deeply into the "ruins of memory" (a phrase Langer borrows from Ida Fink), details of living and dying under Nazi rule come through—details often censored in a more processed account.

According to Langer, two chronologies emerge in the Yale videotapes. One moves linearly through time, reflecting the survivor's active memory and asserting continuity with the pre-Holocaust past and the normalized present. The other loops endlessly into the past. "[S]eized by memory," the witness reexperiences grief as raw, immediate, and ongoing, "normal" life notwithstanding. Out of these chronologies come two conflicting rhetorics—of love and hope, and of anguish and despair.

The trajectory of Langer's writing on the Shoah has led him to critique the constructed and inauthentic nature of more polished forms of memory. "When literary form, allusion, and style intrude on the surviving victim's account, we risk forgetting where we are and imagine deceptive continuities" (45). Langer's critique points to ways in which not only literary but also historical texts frequently assert such "deceptive discontinuities." Historical writing, Langer explains,

> assembles the important data of experience, and it makes them accessible to an audience, the awareness of whose consciousness is a premise of the historian's efforts. A major source of despair for [survivors'] humiliated memory is the almost totally *excluding* effect of its revelations. . . . Thus this is not history as we ordinarily understand it . . . (109)

Embedded in Langer's analysis is the suggestion that we need to rethink all categories of writing if they are to absorb the diverse and complicated memories that emerge in oral testimony.[23]

At the same time, Langer's analysis of the divergent strands of narrative in survivor testimony also breaks down certain distinctions between authentic and constructed testimony. Survivors "construct" their memoirs, seeking to articulate memories so horrible as to lie almost beyond the pale of recollection, to express the amalgam of emotions—grief, elation, triumph, despair—at having survived, and to piece together a life afterwards.

Although Berel Lang's critique argues pointedly against fictional treatments of the Nazi genocide, his thoughtful analysis nonetheless points unintendedly to a discourse that might include the manifold forms of testimony, including memory, history, and literature, and construes fiction as something other than lies. Lang insists, first and foremost, that the Holocaust generate a "moral discourse—discourse not about moral issues, but *as* moral" (xii). Drawing on aesthetic theory, he argues against much of what currently constitutes the discourse about the Shoah, not only literary representations but also "the abstraction of theory or explanation" that "proposes to *think* rather than to feel or imagine" the events of the Nazi genocide (xii).

In delineating what would comprise such a "moral discourse," Lang draws on distinctly Jewish narrative traditions: midrash (interpretive narratives of biblical texts) and the Passover Haggadah (the ritual telling of the Exodus at the *seder*). Lang alludes to two sets of midrashim, one about the exodus and liberation of the Israelites from Egyptian slavery, the other about receiving the Torah at Mount Sinai. In one midrashic version of the revelation, all Jewish souls throughout time, past and present, gather at the foot of Sinai to receive God's word. In a similar gesture, the Haggadah enjoins all *seder* participants to acknowledge themselves as personally present at the exodus; the liturgy castigates the "wicked son," who asks "What is all this work for *you*?" for excluding himself from the collective experience. By acknowledging one's own presence at those significant moments, Lang explains, each person who speaks of those events is enabled thus to "tell himself" (xiii); in other words, telling (or writing) of those events entails not something external to the speaker and the listener (the writer and the reader), but rather, as Lang elaborates, a convergence of "writer, text, what is written about . . . and reader" (xii).

As in the instances of Sinai and the exodus, Lang asserts, "the presence of all Jews is also fixed within the events of the genocide" (xiii). The events of the Shoah, narrated from a perspective analogous to the narration of the exodus at the Passover *seder*, would be literally, rather than merely metaphorically, true, according to Lang, because the Nazis "willed [all Jews] to extinction" (xiv). In invoking midrash in the context of the Nazi genocide, Lang suggest a narrative of presence rather than of absence as the precondition for a moral discourse about the Nazi genocide. He situates this perspective in Jewish collective memory, as (re)constituted by midrash.

In actuality, Lang's "proposal that each Jew should tell the story of the genocide as though he or she had passed through it" (xiv) occupies a space between history and imagination, or, perhaps more correctly, a space inhabited by both history and imagination. Lang explains, "in retelling the Nazi genocide, the narrator tells himself not only as a speaker in the present but also as a character of the narrative, living in the text recited" (xii). However, the narrator, present in his or her own narration, was not necessarily *actually* present at the events narrated, a discrepancy that grows more pronounced with the passage of time. As at the seder, one must imagine oneself back into history in order to make history present, in order to acknowledge one's own presence in history. By calling the possibility of such a narration "literal," and by linking Shoah discourse with midrash, in spite of his suspicion of the discourse of Shoah fiction, Lang moves toward a way of thinking about "Holocaust fiction" as a mode similarly at the interstices of history and imagination. As a mode of interpretive *narrative* (rather than discursive commentary), midrash represents both truth and fantasy. Utilizing invented or interpolated characters and events, and multiple versions of the same episodes, the contradictory truth claims of diverse midrashim are seen traditionally not as competing but as concurrent.[24] To refer to our own presence at these seminal events as "literally" true would be to use the term "literal" in a way we do not usually understand it. A bare chronology of the forty years of desert wandering would not, after all, include us, nor does the text of the Torah record our participation in the multiple listing of names, tribes, and census-taking. If, as midrash asks, we place ourselves at the Red Sea and at Sinai and speak out of a narrative of presence, we do so through an act of imaginative interpolation. Holocaust fiction similarly asks the reader to understand it as "literally" true in a way we would not ordinarily use the term.

Both midrash and the seder liturgy invoke a relationship between the fixed and the changing, or the codified and the spontaneous, which approximates the paradoxical rigidity and fluidity of memory that Primo Levi discusses in *The Drowned and the Saved.* More than a mere plurality of interpretation, midrash posits contradictory and even transgressive meanings, which, while preserving canonical texts as such, read them against the grain, opening up a creative, interpretive space. Similarly, the traditional seder combines ritualized recitations of a codified text with the immediacy of performance and the invitation to elaborate the telling beyond the script of the Haggadah. In each case, the political and personal ideologies of readers and participants[25] are brought into active engagement with the collectively recollected history.[26] Midrash functions to fill textual gaps in Torah—missing transitions, conversations, events. In so doing, midrash itself produces gaps that in turn require interpretive narrative and the active participation of a reader who must "write himself." So, too, Holocaust fiction intercedes to fill in cognitive and psychological absences in history and memory, while itself also reproduces gaps—tropologically configured as muteness—that require of readers not distance but moral and emotional engagement.

Like the rabbinic fantasies of midrash, Holocaust fiction opens up a moral discourse different from, but contiguous with, the discourses of history or philosophy. Aharon Appelfeld sees an "unmediated relationship, simple and straightforward, to those horrible events" (91) as precondition for a kind of Holocaust literature through which the writer and reader, to use Lang's term, "writes-himself" (xii). When Louis Begley likens separating "what is true from what is not" in his fictional narratives to unscrambling an omelet, he is not merely pointing to the dispersal of autobiographical detail within the matrix of fictional invention. Begley's comments about his own work suggests ways in which a fictional life can be constructed to reveal something truthful—about the fragmented self under siege, about memory, about trauma—that may otherwise elude expression. Similarly, Jorge Semprun's novel *The Long Voyage* draws attention to issues that shape, and may even impede, the transmission of testimony—the receptivity and stamina of the listener,[27] the utter discontinuity between the concentrationary universe and the "normal" world outside, the effect of atrocity on the narrating subject. As midrash interposes itself in textual gaps, speaking where the Torah does not, Holocaust fiction claims the space of what remains unuttered in other modes of narrative, offering a vehicle to express, think through, and sometimes resolve complexities that underlie the critical discourse.

I am suggesting a critique of what I consider a false opposition between historical and literary discourse as a means to recovering the real.[28] Neither midrash nor the Haggadah restricts historical memory to the confines of a bare chronology. Instead, fanciful, conjectural, nostalgic, and transgressive narratives are interpolated into canonical texts. These later writings too become codified but structurally avoid closure. In this way, history is brought into the present through personal and collective acts of imagination. This comingling of discourses opens up a mode of access to what Saul Friedlander refers to as the "irreducible core" or "psychological residue [that] seems to defy the historian" ("Final Solution" 25)—that should comprise the focus of a moral discourse about the Shoah.[29] Here the value of imaginative literature to the growing discourse on the Shoah emerges. The self-critique imbedded in literary reconstructions of the Shoah draw attention to narrativity and to writing, rendering them visible rather than transparent. Instead of simply deflecting our attention away from the events toward

rhetoricity, the self-conscious artifice that characterizes literary reconstructions of the Holocaust insistently frames questions necessary to a
moral discourse. Semprun's novel, for example, explores the nature of
memory, both personal (the survivor's) and collective (ours), the role of
personal and collective paradigm (self-schema and history) in recon-
structing what happened, and the crucial but incomplete function of
language in reporting what is remembered.[30]

The critical discourse on Holocaust literature asks, in the second
place, what shall constitute the poetics of atrocity, the critical lexicon and evaluative criteria? The literature of the Shoah, Nelly Sachs
notes, can be written "only/with one eye ripped out." In *The Holocaust
and the Literary Imagination*—one of the first major works to treat literature of the Holocaust—Langer begins to develop what he terms "the
aesthetics of atrocity," an aesthetics emerging from close readings of
poetry and fiction. At the same time, he signals what proves to be a frequent and continuing concern with the propriety of critical discourse
itself.

That traditional critical apparatus may be at best, irrelevant and
at worst, callously out of touch with the import of Holocaust-centered
texts, has been of ongoing concern to many readers. A full decade after
the publication of Langer's book, in a 1985 introduction to Primo Levi's
If Not Now, When, Irving Howe still feels the need to apologize for the
seemingly "incongruous, even trivial" concerns of literary criticism
brought to bear on Levi's writing (14). The events of the Holocaust
become construed as a sacred domain, requiring a sacrilized canon and
hermeneutics. Howe's difficulties exemplify an uneasiness that per-
sists even now. The reader of Holocaust literature continues to traffic
between conflicting loyalties. Questions of morality and "authenticity"
displace discussions of literary technique and narrative strategy, as
though a truly "genuine" work would read itself. Repeatedly, readers
hesitate to assess the works as "literature," as products of the literary
imagination, presumably because to do so would diminish the significance of its substance.

If, as Sachs asserts, one *writes* Holocaust texts with only one eye,
one also *reads* them with one eye, the other trained, as it were, on the
event itself. At issue is not simply the stylistic competence of a particular writer but also the truth, authenticity, and morality of the writing,
its connection with the philosophical, political, metaphysical implications of the Nazi genocide. Since its earliest incursions into this bleak
terrain, the critical discussion of Holocaust-centered texts has evalu-
ated an artistic as well as a moral vision, asking not only whether the

writer has successfully represented the events narrated but also whether these events have been trivialized or exploited. While early critical works concentrated on evaluating the seriousness or authenticity of Shoah fiction, by the early 1980s a shift in critical focus had taken place. While the judgment of individual works continues, readers discuss the uses and abuses of memory, the ideologically differing underpinnings of all representations of the Shoah, popular culture, and the position of the reader.

As the central event of our century, the Shoah precipitates a moral and epistemological crisis. Like all thinking about the Holocaust, Shoah literature thus grapples with the implications of the Nazi genocide for its victims, its witnesses, its perpetrators, and for Western culture. The high stakes involve the ethical, psychological, and perhaps even the physical survival of Jewish, Western, and German cultures. For this reason, some early readers of Shoah fiction were disquieted by ambivalently delivered "messages" or "lessons." Irving Halperin, for example, in *Messengers from the Dead: Literature of the Holocaust* (1970), criticizes both Tadeus Borowski, Polish survivor of Auschwitz and author of the short stories collected in *This Way to the Gas, Ladies and Gentlemen*, and Jakov Lind, Austrian Jewish survivor and author of the short stories collected in *Soul of Wood* and of several novels, because fictional characters in their works offer no "spiritual resistance" and "pathologically hate the victims they betray." Similarly, in *The Resonance of Dust: Essays on Holocaust Literature and Jewish Fate*, Edward Alexander includes only

> writers who seemed to me primarily concerned with the relationship between the Holocaust and the course of Jewish history, the fate of the Jewish people. I have . . . excluded those writers for whom the destruction of European Jewry affords primarily a stunning example and ultimate revelation of man's inhumanity to man, or the occasion for apocalyptic excursions in thought and in literary mode. (xviii)

Alexander opposes the two categories—the specifically Jewish and the universal interpretations of the Shoah—as mutually exclusive. Moreover, in his formulation, a concern with Jewish history and fate provides the only grounds for an ethical discourse. Any other vantage point stands callously outside the catastrophe. Thus Alexander's reading responds to the implicit ideological position of the writers, rather than to the literariness of the works.

The critical ambivalence about literary projects in the context of the Shoah results in a narrowing of the definition of "Holocaust literature" even as the number of published works multiply. In response to Adorno's pessimism about the future of literature after Auschwitz, the literary history of the Shoah charts an ongoing argument about the "best," most effective, most appropriate, most truthful or authentic narrative form, an argument consistently posed against other, lesser literary forms, as though allowances may be made, if at all, only on a particular and a provisional basis. The variegated opinions on this reflect the differences in viewing the way a particular critic views the Holocaust, Jewish experience, literature, its relation to history, along with, perhaps, a temperamental preference for a particular literary mode.

For example, in *The Gates of Horn*, Harry Levin praises David Rousset's *The Other Kingdom*, a detailed analysis of the political infrastructure of "l'univers concentrationnaire" (the concentrationary universe) based on Rousset's first-hand observations and his memories as a survivor. Levin sees Rousset's narrative as exemplary for its authenticity and lack of embellishment: "A first-hand reminiscence of the concentration camps, such as David Rousset's is bound to be far more impressive than any fictitious approximation" (459). In contrast, Barbara Foley finds that the retrospective of the memoir imposes upon the Holocaust an unwanted telos, resulting in "an inadvertent parody of the conventional journey toward self-definition and knowledge." Similarly, the conventions of realism import "ethical humanist resolutions" incommensurate with the "totalitarian horror" of the Shoah, while the fantastic evades its historical immediacy, producing instead a "grotesque portraiture of . . . metaphysical evil" (333). For Foley, then, only inherently nonteleological genres can successfully represent the Holocaust. Thus, according to Foley, more than any other form, the diary resists imposing order and sense on the events described.[31] To a lesser extent, the "pseudofactual novel," a fictional mime of the diary doubly removed from the events described, imitates its resistance to telos.[32] For Hamida Bosmajian, by contrast, all documentary genres— including memoirs, diaries, pseudofactual and realistic novels—fail to genuinely address historical consciousness and self-evaluation. The day-by-day account of the diary renders "the outrageous . . . part of the daily routine" (23), while the retrospective autobiography expresses primarily the survivor's desire for relief from guilt.[33] The reader remains emotionally and cognitively outside the events described, ethically unimplicated in the horror.

In Levin's assessment, in "authentic" memoir where realistic narration adheres closely to events witnessed and experienced, language and literary form do not come between the reader and the events of history. In actuality, however, the Rousset narrative relies on the paradigms of literature—particularly the surreal and the absurd—to convey what he fears eludes conventional representation. While Levin sees in Rousset's narrative a straightforward reminiscence, Rousset himself repeatedly invokes not realism but the grotesque world of Alfred Jarry's Ubu plays. For Rousset, the lusty and amoral Ubu serves as antecedent and correlative to desire and despair in the extermination camps. To convey to the reader both the nature of the camp's social structure and the quality of his personal experience there, Rousset's writing veers from straightforward, sociological narrative toward a less conventional style. His translator notes that Rousset's narrative "departs from accepted idiom and syntax and even logical sequence. The bleak chaos of the camps called for a style as bleak and chaotic as itself" (Guthrie, 20). Foley's analysis acknowledges the constructed nature of retrospective autobiographical and fictional genres, which shapes the way events are recollected, condensed, and interpreted. Foley sees the diary as both a piece and a proof of history. But the diary, no less, invokes generic conventions that deliberately and incidentally shape and convey its writer's interpretation of the events described.[34]

Contemporary critical discussion about the Shoah shifts in scope and methodology. Critics "read" not only the literary texts opened up by the early writing of Langer, Alvin Rosenfeld, Sidra Ezrahi, and others but also popular representations, memorials, museums, documentary and feature films, and visual art. At issue are the connections among ideology, public memory, the making of history, the writing (and reading) of texts.[35] Contemporary critical approaches consider ourselves as historically situated readers of texts, viewer of films, listeners to testimony, visitors at memorials, teachers or students of the Holocaust.[36] The titles and subtitles of books and articles, where words such as "memory," "change," and "legacy" predominate, reflect the growing acknowledgment of the intimate linking of past, present, and future through the recovery of things past.[37] These studies have refined and complicated our ideas about the Nazi genocide and its implications for us now.

At the same time, they reflect a movement away from imaginative literature as subject matter, and precisely—and paradoxically—at a moment when there is a renewed appreciation for "the work of art" as such, for "literature as theory," for the novel as a discursive vehicle for thinking.[38] As I see it, the early discomfort regarding the confluence of fiction and history and of literature and atrocity continues to inform the contemporary critical discourse, diminishing the evaluation of literary projects.[39] In some sense, the muteness contained in literary representations of the Shoah finds some replication in the critical discourse about these representations. In an important way, however, fiction embodies complicated ideas about the Shoah, often anticipating by many years questions that emerge in theoretical discussion.

More than anything else, this extended critical debate makes apparent the ongoing discomfort in the face of literary treatments of the Shoah. Ultimately, to the extent that individual works succeed in representing the Holocaust, they do so despite their generic limitations. Moreover, they succeed by acknowledging these limitations in an inherent self-critique. Tropological muteness is an instrumental part of the enactment of such a critique, by means of which fiction thinks through not only what has been said but also what has been omitted.

The present focus on the figure of muteness offers a means to navigate this disturbing literary landscape. The alternating shifts between language and silence, between meaning and meaninglessness, in literary reflections of the Holocaust, propel us both into and beyond the texts. This oscillation bears on our understanding of the Shoah, its literary representations, and the critical discourse which follows. The present study explores the way Holocaust-centered literature functions as narrative—how the telling (writing) of the catastrophe shapes and informs subsequent knowing (reading) of the catastrophe. Thus, we examine the phenomenon itself by interrogating the literary structures that struggle to contain (that is, both to hold and to hold back) the Holocaust, measuring the Holocaust against the continuum not only of history but of literary history. The trope of muteness is central to the idea of Holocaust fiction, to the way imaginative representations of the Shoah address linguistic, ethical, and metaphysical concerns.

The chapters that follow explore the trope of muteness and its multiple functions in Holocaust fiction. "The Figure of Muteness" introduces the trope of the mute witness by means of a close reading of Jorge Semprun's novel, *The Long Voyage*. A memory novel—that is, a novel as and about memory—Semprun's narrative shifts intermittently from the narrative present, the long boxcar voyage to Buchenwald, into a recollected past and also a recollected future. The narrator, attempting repeatedly to describe the Buchenwald of experience and memory, discovers that a linguistic barrier separates him from anyone who did not also experience the unreal reality of the concentrationary universe. Even the camp site, the charred crematoria still piled with corpses, cannot help the witness to testify. Frustration leads the narrator to a resolution of silence. Thus, reading Semprun's narrative on the impossibility of testimonial narrative links the trope of the mute witness to the crises in language, memory, and meaning that characterize much Holocaust fiction.

The third chapter, "Voices from the Killing Ground," contrasts the self-conscious, self-doubting voice of survivor writing such as Semprun's with the seeming confidence of ghetto writers. While memoirs and fiction by survivors frequently question the nature of memory, language, and representation, the diaries, chronicles, and essays written in the shadow of death—in ghettos, in hiding—rely on the power of testimony to affect readers, bring about change, and stave off oblivion. In survivor writing, the trope of muteness shapes the work from within; by contrast, in ghetto writing, muteness intrudes as an external silencing force against which the writer struggles. In addition, the ongoing witnessing of Nazi atrocity coexists with the cognitive and emotional constriction of trauma. Ghetto writers evoke literary conventions and historical precedents in order to hold fast to religious, political, and cultural belief systems that give meaning to their suffering and connect them with their imagined audience. However, as destruction becomes inevitable and Nazi duplicity exposed, even the voice of the ghetto wavers and begins to approximate survivor writing.

In survivor writing, the trope of muteness functions as an index of trauma, which both compels and disables testimony. The mute witness of Holocaust fiction lives out this paradox, standing both in and out of language. The fourth chapter, "The Mute Language of Brutality," examines the most concrete variation of the figure of muteness, the aphasiac, through a close reading of Jerzy Kosinski's novel *The Painted Bird*. The writing of Kosinski, Charlotte Delbo, Primo Levi, Piotr Rawicz, and others utilize muteness to explore the struggle of the survivor/writer to devise a vocabulary that can carry the vision of the atrocity. Chapter Five, "The Reluctant Witness," examines the ways in which the mute both *stands for* and *bridges* the linguistic and symbolic poverty of the writer's own testimony, who (like the mute character) similarly cannot easily tell what she or he knows. Muteness thus connects also with the author's search for a credible, authentic voice, and to an impossible striving for sheer, unmediated representation. Fictional characters who cease speaking through will or compulsion, and narrators who repudiate or truncate their narrations, are central components in narrative strategies designed to express and negotiate crises in memory and credibility and at the same time navigate the intense and complicated emotions evoked by Holocaust testimony.

In Elie Wiesel's fiction, muteness takes on multiple meanings. Chapter Six, "Muted Chords," sets Wiesel's thematic exploration of human and divine silence against the development of these motifs in Jewish sacred and Western literary traditions. For Wiesel, muteness is the condition of the survivor, a mark of abandonment by God and at the same time a mark of human agency. In Wiesel's fiction, victims use silence to resist the Nazi death machinery, and survivors remember the dead by emulating their ultimate speechlessness. In addition, muteness signifies a radical interrogation of abstract concepts—whether religious or secular—that may falsely assert meaningfulness in face of the void.

In some survivor writing, the interrogation of speech and rhetoric enacted through tropological muteness deepens into a more general distrust of language and literary discourse. The seventh chapter, "The Night Side of Speech," examines the coaptation of the German tongue to the Nazi purpose. In the fiction of Jakov Lind, André Schwarz-Bart, and George Steiner, for example, linguistic ambivalence signifies not the difficulties of survivor testimony—the consequences of torture, trauma, and death—but the verbal evasiveness of the bystander and the collaborator with atrocity. Lind's short story "Soul of Wood" traces the encroachment of Nazi jargon into everyday German, exposing the death-bringing disjuncture between rhetoric and reality which forever taints that language. For this reason, the motif of the lost (or muted) language informs the works of Lind and Jean Améry, for example, who write in an acquired, exilic language, and of Paul Celan, whose self-conscious discomfort with his native language approximates the exile that marked his life.

Ultimately, however, the German language does not singularly bear the burden of atrocity. Chapter Eight, "Refused Memory," examines the function of the literary imagination itself in constructing Nazi ideology and practice and in evading ethical responsibility. Because the propagandist and the literary artist tap comparable forces in language, myth, and psyche, after the Shoah the symbolic imagination itself becomes suspect. In *The Ogre*, for example, Michel Tournier alternately constructs and deflates complex symbolic equivalences for the Nazi era, revealing the intimate link between the rhetoric of abstraction and the perpetuation of violence. The novel's critique of language encompasses literary structures and the symbolic imagination, culminating in a radical displacement of meaning. In addition, the protagonist's hyperverbiage constitutes an equivalent of muteness, an excess of language which denies memory and testimony.

Finally, the ninth chapter, "The Chain of Testimony," explores textual muteness in the fictional narratives of Ida Fink. Within the context of testimonial fiction, gaps and ellipses signify an absent testimony at once knowable and unknowable. Through these textual gaps, which are not devoid of but redolent with meaning, the narratives explore the functions and limitations of memory and narrative in the construction of Holocaust testimony. In Fink's complicated play of tenses and lacunae, telling and nontelling become intermingled, providing a narrative resolution of the crisis of representation.

2

The Figure of Muteness

Welches der Worte du sprichst
du dankst
dem Verderben.

[Whichever word you speak
you thank
destruction.]

—Paul Celan

The desire to fix the facts of the Holocaust, for once and for all, grows more urgent as the event fades further and further into the past. While time erodes the remnants of brutality and extermination, survivors of Nazi genocide push against the limits of language and imagination to revisit—in mind or in body—the deathcamps that once constituted their nightmarish world. With eyewitnesses still among us willing to probe and share their memories, we struggle to see that landscape with some clarity of vision. But as grass and shrub reclaim the Nazi deathcamps, as a generation of war criminals and collaborators, heroes and survivors ages and dies, the Nazi program of genocide and atrocity still strains belief. Despite a mounting body of historical and fictional narrative, photographs and films, relics and statistics, paintings and monuments, the Holocaust defies our best efforts to know—defies the survivor's best efforts to tell.

When the narrator of Jorge Semprun's novel *The Long Voyage* leads a pair of French women through Buchenwald two days after liberation, he is a privileged witness. Unlike survivors who, in later years, revisit deathcamps grown bucolic with the passage of time, Semprun's narrator feels no need for words and stories to evoke his experience. Both he and the camp bear physical evidence of the reign of atrocity that has just ended. He need not speak for he can point—or so he believes. In his first attempt to reveal to an outsider the "totally *un*natural world of the prison of death" where the "unreal and the absurd became familiar" (69), Semprun's narrator conducts a private tour of Buchenwald for two "incredible girls" from the French Mission.

> The big square where they had held roll call was deserted beneath the spring sun, and I stopped, my heart beating. *I had never seen* it empty before, I must admit, *I hadn't ever really seen* it. *I hadn't really seen* it before, not what you call '*seeing.*' . . . *I saw* this scenery, which for two years had been the setting of my life, and *I was seeing* it for the first time. *I was seeing* it from the outside, as if this setting which had been my life until the day before yesterday was now on the other side of the mirror. (70)

> "But it really doesn't seem all that bad," one of them said just then. (71) [italics mine]

Amid unburied corpses and gaunt survivors, the narrator quickly discovers that disclosure has already become impossible. The Buchenwald he experienced no longer exists. What remains of it scarcely ruffles the visitors. Two days after liberation, the Holocaust has already become history, no longer present, no longer accessible. The narrator's personal experience, too, has become history, and he cannot communicate it to anyone who has not shared it. Moreover, as that experience recedes in time, he finds that he himself must struggle to connect with it. Now a survivor rather than a victim, the narrator views Buchenwald with different eyes. Emptied of its terrible action, the deathcamp remains forbidding only in memory—a memory at odds with what he sees. The repetition of *seeing* and *seen* underscores the disparity between what was and what is. The "unreal"—normalized for him during his two year incarceration—has once again become unreal, unfamiliar. Expecting to shock the women—who had heard "that it was horrible, absolutely appalling" (70)—the narrator finds himself shocked, not by the horror but by its absence.

While the narrator couples what he sees with what he remembers, the women mistake the little they see for the complete picture. Their complacency prompts the narrator to put forth a real effort to evoke for them the world he remembers. If the empty square leaves them unimpressed, no matter. The narrator has at his disposal something more potent—more potent, too, than any story he could relate.

> *I take* the girls to the crematorium by the small door, the one leading directly to the cellar. . . . *I show them* the hooks from which the men were hung, for the crematorium also served as a torture chamber. *I show them* the blackjacks and the clubs, which are still there. *I explain* to them what they were used for. *I show them* the lifts which used to take the corpses to the second story, to directly in front of the ovens. . . . *I show them* the row of electric ovens, and half-charred corpses which are still inside. *I hardly speak* to them, merely saying: "Here you are, *look* there." It's essential for them to see, to try and imagine. . . . *I take* them out of the crematorium into the interior courtyard surrounded by a high fence. There *I say nothing, I let them look.* In the middle of the courtyard is a pile of corpses a good twelve feet high. A pile of twisted, yellowed skeletons, their faces hideous with terror. (74) [italics mine]

In the deserted square there remains only the echo of atrocity; in the crematorium complex awaits atrocity itself. The narrator relies upon the real gore—ovens, torture implements, putrid bodies—to speak on its own behalf. As the repetitive sequence of verbs indicates, the narrator intervenes less and less as he closes on the grotesque corpses. "I take. . . . I show. . . . I show. . . . I explain. . . . I show. . . . I show. . . . I hardly speak. . . . Look. . . . I take. . . . I say nothing. . . . I let them look." As the girls see more, the narrator says less, first explaining, then hardly speaking, finally saying nothing. While the narrator's words can represent the Holocaust, he implies, the hideous skeletons *are* the Holocaust. Before the mass of twisted corpses, the narrator no longer acts as guide, no longer shows. Face to face with atrocity, the girls can look for themselves.

But what they see, horrifying as it may be, does not help them understand his experience. The French women see a reality different from the one that the narrator shows.

> Looking at these wasted bodies, with their protruding bones, their sunken chests, these bodies piled twelve feet high in the crematorium courtyard, I'm thinking that these were my comrades. I'm thinking that one has to have experienced

their death, as we have, in order to look at them with that
pure fraternal expression. . . . It was stupid to try and
explain to them . . . these dreadful, fraternal dead need no
explanation. They need a pure, fraternal look. (75)

Faced with the anonymous mass of bodies, the narrator measures
what he sees against what he remembers. Once again, he becomes
aware of the barrier that experience erects between those who have
been part of the deathcamp ("we who have survived"), and those who
have not. He brings the women to his Buchenwald, but they encounter
a different one. Where they see only putrid physical remains, the narrator sees comrades. Where they see only dehumanized corpses, he
sees fellow sufferers. In the short time since liberation, the bodies have
transmuted from a part of a functioning deathcamp to a remnant of a
defunct one. Like his words, they can represent but not *be* the Holocaust. What he offers as unmediated reality turns out to be yet another
historical artifact. Even at the dark core of Buchenwald, as yet unsan-
itized and unbeautified, the Holocaust remains inaccessible to those
who have not suffered through it. While the survivor's memory reani-
mates the "fraternal dead," the women flee in horror and disgust.

The sight of his dead comrades, more accurate and more authoritative than any description the narrator could render, does not convey
to the women the "unreal" reality of Buchenwald. That failure convinces him of the futility of sharing his memories. It accounts, in part,
for his subsequent resolve "never again" to speak of his experiences in
the deathcamp. The reactions of the women to the camp itself—first
complacency, then disgust—indicate to him the reception that awaits
any stories he could tell.

. . . I might risk seeing the people around me who had con-
sented to hear me, even if only to be polite, grow weary and
bored and then die, sliding softly off their chairs, plunging
into death as into the almost stagnant water of my story, or
else I might see them slowly going mad, raving mad perhaps, refusing any longer to bear the complacent horror of all
the details and detours. (199)

Yet the novel itself constitutes precisely these "details and detours" that
the narrator resolves to keep to himself. Sixteen years after liberation,
the fear of oblivion outweighs the fear of inadequacy. Allowing his comrades to be forgotten entirely seems far worse than evoking their memory imperfectly. The narrative weaves back and forth in a fractured
chronology that centers on the narrator's boxcar ride to Buchenwald

but reaches deeply into past and future. Like his encounter with the nurses, the novel as a whole reveals his inability to bridge the gap between survivor and nonsurvivor. However, in describing his failure, the narrator gives an accurate measure of that gap. If we cannot truly enter into the "unreal" world of the deathcamps, we can at least know by how much it exceeds our worst imaginings.

Semprun's narrator moves from words to bones to silence and finally back to words, to the stories that together constitute his narrative. The stories reveal to us not so much the survivor's world as the process by which the survivor struggles to remember, to recount, and to bear witness. The novel, which begins as a record of the Holocaust, turns into a study of a survivor's attempt to pull together the strands of memory and weave them into the fabric of narrative. The narrator's efforts echo Semprun's own search for a fictional voice. In contrast to his narrator, however, Semprun cannot point to bodies, cannot walk through the roll call square, cannot visit the deathcamp. Even more than his narrator, who has at hand the physical remnants of disaster—cold, hard "facts"—the author is thrown back upon language and imagination to carry his vision. Neither author nor narrator can successfully write the catastrophe; they can write only of their struggle to do so. But if the narrator—who buttresses a factual account with hard evidence—despairs, what of the author? What of Semprun himself, also a concentration camp survivor, who marshals to the service of his memories a fictional narrator, a fictitious memoir, a fictionalized reconstruction of the deathcamp? And what of the reader, who seeks to extract from the literary construct a representation of and a meditation on this most intractable of subjects, the Nazi genocide?

D o history and literature collude or collide in reconstituting what David Rousset terms *l'univers concentrationnaire*—the concentrationary universe—the death-dominated landscape of the Third Reich? How can the literary imagination convey, much less explain, the unspeakable, unimaginable terrors of the Nazi program of atrocity and extermination? And what place has imaginative literature alongside the fact-bound reconstructions of historical accounting? Like history, fictional responses to the Holocaust strain against the limitations of language and of credulity. Like history, fiction struggles to absorb the event and to wrest from it a meaning. The narrativity of fiction mimics and intermittently displaces history. But its breach with the factuality of history places fiction at seeming cross-purposes with the allied acts of testimony and memory—the moral center of Holocaust narrative. Measured against that factuality, how can fiction render an account worth reading?

For this reason, the body of fiction associated with the Holocaust and its residue is a fiction at odds with itself, with history, and with the very idea of a fiction. The conjunction of historical consciousness and literary imagination yields up a highly self-conscious, self-doubting amalgam of works. In aspiring first to represent, then to mediate, then to interpret the catastrophe, the works traffic between historical time and the mythic structures through which we make sense of the world.

The present study traces the figure or trope of muteness in fictional responses to the Holocaust. The idea of muteness in fiction is exemplified concretely by the frequency of mute characters, structurally by the predominance of gaps and textual ellipses, and thematically by an overriding concern with language, silence, speech, muteness, writing, and blankness. In addition to providing a meaningful point of entry for exploring Holocaust fiction, the focus on muteness serves also to illuminate the implicit conversation among works of fiction, personal and collective history, philosophy, and literary theory. The trope of muteness is linked to the complicated and allied acts of testimony, memory, and interpretation, which inform all post-Holocaust reflections, fictional and historical alike.

Muteness expresses not only the difficulty in saying anything meaningful about the Holocaust; it also comes to represent something essential about the nature of the event itself. The radical negativity of the Holocaust ruptures the fabric of history and memory, emptying both narrative and life of meaning. Muteness instanciates a consistent movement of displacement—geographic, historical, linguistic, symbolic—that characterizes both the event and its subsequent reflections and depictions. Ultimately this movement centers on a displacement of language as such which aspires, finally, to silence. A tension between this silence which speaks the rupture and the narrative forms which attempt now to represent, now to bridge it, lies at the heart of Holocaust fiction. To write the Holocaust into the continuum of world history, Jewish history, and literary history disrupts the continuum; it effaces, shatters, or alters our interpretation of what comes before and after.

Navigating between historicity and fictionality, this study takes as its point of departure the pivotal presence of mute characters in Holocaust fiction and the related motif of the untold or truncated story. Hovering about the periphery, or featured in the center of widely divergent narrative styles and fictional modes, the mute character figures with surprising frequency and in many variations: congenitally aphasiac, war-shocked, feeble-minded, mutilated. Some—effectively if not technically mute—emit no more than a stream of unintelligible babble, animal sounds, or lunatic ravings; others consciously decide to refrain from speech; still others find themselves forcibly cut off from the languages they can speak.

Holocaust fiction puts into words what customarily remains outside the flow of historical narrative: the sufferings, resistances, aspirations of the individuals ravaged by genocide. Their lives and experiences are left out of historical accounts because the condition of genocide renders the individual subject unable to articulate his or her own experience (we cannot narrate our own death) and because this particular death is unspeakable. The Shoah places upon language demands that overwhelm the expressive potential of ordinary language. As Holocaust texts absorb points of view and subject matter conventionally omitted, there is a disintegration and reconstitution of texts, linguistic forms, and symbolic orders.

For this reason, Holocaust fiction enacts a kind of muteness in the very midst of an ongoing narrative. The absent, truncated, or incomplete telling helps unfold the ambivalences and ambiguities that shape not only the way we read Holocaust fiction but also the way we think about the Holocaust itself. Many of the complexities treated in this study are reflected in the contemporary critical discourse surrounding Holocaust studies generally. The questions that repeatedly arise in critical readings of Holocaust fiction—for example, the unrepresentability of the Holocaust, the inappropriateness of cojoining aesthetics and atrocity, the unreliability of memory, the falsifying demands of generic conventions—are not merely concerns prompted *by* the fictionality and rhetoricity of literary works, not merely a critical overlay. Rather, these complications are already present as self-critique in the fictional narratives; they configure and inform the fabric and texture of the works themselves.

In examining the role of muteness in fictional responses to the Holocaust, we begin to explore the nature of the discontinuities—both literary and historical—that characterize a catastrophe of such magnitude. For the frequent instances of narrative muteness echo at other levels of text. They resonate in the discontinuous plot and chronology of some fictional narratives, in the deflated rhetoric and peculiar lacunae of others. We see their stylistic refraction in opaque prose, in a halting, stammering style, or in a hyperfluency that simultaneously tenders and denies all possibilities of meaning. The present study connects these instances of textual muteness with explicit discussions of silence, language, and literary discourse, discussions occurring both within the imaginative text and elsewhere. In a body of literature that enacts testimony, this preponderance of nonspeaking characters, incomplete stories, and non-narrated narration suggests an ambivalence toward speech, language, and writing that must shape the way we read the texts that contain them. To what may we attribute this paradoxical use of mute characters and texts to render testimony?

The frequent instances of textual muteness express a loss of faith in the mimetic and interpretive possibilities of narrative and language. Can one successfully speak (or write) the Holocaust? Can the desired memory be retrieved, put into words, shared? Can the desired testimony be delivered? Rather than arguing for or against the unrepresentablity of the Holocaust and the appropriateness of imaginative literature, the present study examines the self-critique of fictional works which acknowledges both the articulateness and the muteness—the remembering and the forgetting—of Holocaust testimony. As the fiction of Ida Fink, Jorge Semprun, and Elie Wiesel attest, and the memoirs of Primo Levi and Charlotte Delbo affirm, Holocaust writers *simultaneously* succeed and fail in the act of retrieving buried or suppressed Holocaust memories and transmuting their details into testimonial narrative. Thus, instead of merely undermining memory, the recurrent instances of muteness in Holocaust writing *simultaneously* mimic, undermine, and promote memory. The eyewitnesses of Holocaust narrative worry about the accuracy and effectiveness of their testimony; they evolve narrative forms that anticipate, strategize, and represent their worst fears about the audience reception (will readers believe, care, act?), the representability of the event, and the potential for trivialization, domestication, or falsification of what happened.

In addressing these questions, the present study explores the broad theme of linguistic displacement as it unfolds in literature of the Holocaust—a theme that embodies speech and silence, language and writing, and, finally, meaning and morality. The following chapters examine primarily fictional narrative written from a retrospective stance—fiction that looks back on historical time in an attempt to represent, contain, integrate, and interpret a devastating event. The authors write under the shadow of those terrible events and their harsh implications for the human spirit. They write out of a deep conviction that the historical fact of Auschwitz, and the atrocities perpetrated by the Nazis from 1933 to 1945, have significantly affected the world we inhabit. In that sense, all of them—as all of us—are survivors. Today, we struggle to uncover the facts, to understand them, and to retrieve from them some meaning.

Because of this, these post-Holocaust narratives manifest—explicitly and implicitly—a tripartite concern with the acts of testimony, interpretation, reconstruction. As testimony, the works engage in memory and narration in order to reconstitute and describe, as best as one can, a terrible past and a lost world. Here, as in historical narrative, the testimonial impulse strives to call by name victim, survivor, bystander, collaborator, and perpetrator. In *The Long Voyage*, for example, Semprun's protagonist struggles with the pain and compulsion of memory after "long years of willful oblivion."

> I have to speak out in the name of things that have happened, not in my own name. The story of the Jewish children in the name of the Jewish children. The story of their death on the broad avenue which led up to the camp entrance, beneath the stony gaze of the Nazi eagles, surrounded by the laughter of the SS, in the name of death itself. (162–63)

Semprun's narration conflates historical and literary discourse in the moral imperative to stand witness. His fiction echoes the insistent push—found in diaries, memoirs, documentaries, and other fictional works—to speak a terrible truth.

In addition, as interpretation, the fictional works trace not only the facts but the implications of the Holocaust for those who come after. These works measure the destruction wrought by the catastrophe— an irrecoverable destruction of human life and entire communities, and a subsequent foreclosure of the possibilities of meaning. Like a black hole, the Holocaust swallowed up the structures—philosophical, theological, and humanistic—by which we order our lives. In plumbing the depths of loss—for the victims, for survivors, and for the human spirit—the interpretive thrust of these Holocaust-based narratives insists upon the rupture engendered by an event disconsonant with what comes before and after. Charlotte Delbo speaks this rupture when she reflects, in *The Measure of Our Days*, upon her experience at Auschwitz and her life afterwards. "I do what one does in life, but I know very well that this isn't life, because I know the difference between before and after" (258). Delbo's writing grapples with an historical moment that seems to stand outside of historical time; having survived the death camp, she can no longer orient herself. She struggles not to bridge but to limn the depths and breadth of the rupture.

As reconstruction, these works attempt the difficult task of bridging the rupture and rebuilding the shattered paradigms of meaning. In his poem "The Survivor," Tadeusz Rozewicz seeks "a teacher and master" to guide him in the painstaking piecing together of a splintered world.

> let him restore to me sight hearing and speech
> let him once again name things and concepts
> let him separate light from dark. (7)

The poem expresses a yearning, characteristic of this body of literature, for the restoration of order, significance, and values—a restoration
both demanded and blocked by the experience of survival that opens
and closes the poem ("I am twenty-four/led to the slaughter/I survived").
In order to fashion new mythic patterns and literary forms capable of
containing the trauma of the Holocaust and comforting the loss, Holocaust-centered narratives mine collective memory, private reflections,
and imaginative revisitations. The painful visions and revisions of
catastrophe provide a source whence to extract the "lessons of the Holocaust"—difficult lessons that probe the limits of human behavior and
human history. More lucid than comforting, these writings shape the
way we "take," or read, the Holocaust. At the heart of the reconstructive
effort lies a search for a moral center, a means of using past catastrophe
for future regeneration, past suffering for future understanding. Motivated by the possibilities of still greater destruction and irretrievable
losses, the works point toward the moral accountability necessary to
avert another catastrophe, perhaps of greater magnitude. They explore
the intermeshing of political, psychological, social, and symbolic dimensions of the disaster, insisting on the need to couple comprehension
with moral choices and moral actions.

Testimony, interpretation, reconstruction: corresponding roughly
to past, present, and future, the three acts follow one another not as
progression but as transgression. In the main, Holocaust-centered
narratives acknowledge at least partial failure on all three counts.
Tensions and contradictions both within and among each of these
three functions undercut the possibilities of success. For although it
privileges testimony, Holocaust fiction holds suspect the very fabric of
that testimony, memory and language. In retrospect, inconceivable
atrocity seems just that—inconceivable—and the survivor doubts his
own recollections. "If I remember correctly—and I don't believe this
memory has been reshaped in my mind— . . ." (48) Semprun's narrator
introduces one episode. While the inadequacy of language to represent the Holocaust has become something of a cliché in critical discourse focusing on representing the Holocaust in narrative, the cry
"No words!"—or something similar—comes up repeatedly in survivor
narratives. Holocaust writing calls upon a common vocabulary to refer
to events outside the experience of most readers—a shared lexicon
with no shared referents. Delbo, for example, complains that she has
at her disposal only clichés—that she must use ordinary words such as
fear, hunger, and *fatigue* to describe extraordinary conditions. Thus,
these works embody a deep skepticism that they cannot deliver the
testimony they promise.

In addition, to the extent that narratives succeed in overcoming linguistic limitations, they lend to the Holocaust a sense of coherence, betraying the insistence on rupture that informs the works. The works struggle, then, both to integrate into and to exclude from the continuum of history, literature, and meaning an event that both begs and refutes interpretation. As such, they reflect simultaneously desire and frustration of desire to reconstruct the paradigms of meaning shattered by the Holocaust. The opposing pulls within the texts of speech and muteness, of words and silence, also mark a more general discomfort with established patterns of rhetoric and broad literary structures, the very means of reforging the lost paradigms of meaning. The selfsame memories which invite—even impel—reconstruction also inveigh against it.

If the fear of linguistic and imaginative failure mark literary representations of the Holocaust, there lurk also fears of a different nature. The conflicts within the narratives indicate a concern not that these narratives will not work but that they will work all too well. The concentrationary universe, set into motion through a mingling of political, psychological, and historical forces working through language, myth, and symbolic form, asserts not the weakness but the power of the literary imagination—power not merely to describe but to reinscribe. The narrative silences reflect a wariness to call forth afresh the disaster—to invoke it by naming, by rendering too apt a description. The lacunae reflect, as well, an awareness that the power of artistic creation, once unleashed, moves out from the domain of its creator. Once written, literary work transmutes immediately into literary artifact, which accepts the multiple and divergent projections of a varied readership. The artist stands helpless to control the meanings imputed to the work and the uses put to it. The inability to control, or at least to direct, meanings mocks the sense of moral engagement that motivates the dredging up of painful memories and disquieting visions. That this literary activity may prove futile is foreshadowed in the recurrent presence of the survivor whom no one heeds and who finally falls dumb. That meaningful testimony may prove impossible is augured in the many retellings of a Nazi taunt: that, were the Jews miraculously to escape, survive, and tell their tale, no one would listen.

Thus, a sense of inevitable failure dogs Holocaust narrative, which varyingly proves ineffective, too effective, or simply besides the point. This failure—and the strategies evolved to mitigate it—connect strongly with the contradictory pulls of language and silence explored here. The present focus on speech, text, and meaning—and their absence—makes us aware that even "realistic" narrative is artifice, is imaginative recreation. This flaunted artifice shoulders a burden that seems more than the literary form can contain, more than language can represent, more than the imagination can muster. The disparity between factuality and narrativity becomes more apparent, catching the texts in a double bind. Without narrative, history remains unknowable; but when narrative displaces history, the real events become inaccessible. The representations which constitute our sole means of recovering the Holocaust also distance us from it, because they refract the event through a lens that inevitably restricts, recasts, and reinterprets what we see. Like Semprun's French girls we risk mistaking the remnants of catastrophe for actual catastrophe. Because of this, the *writing* of the disaster becomes as much the subject of the works as the disaster itself. Born not of aesthetics but of agony, this textual self-referentiality does not diminish the importance of historical moments. Instead, as we will see, it points insistently to a particular set of historical moments whose horror defies our best ways of knowing. In this light, the focus on muteness, mimesis, and interpretation take on a particular urgency and poignancy, reflecting the impossible desire to stand both inside and outside of language in order to grapple with the Holocaust.

The recurrent moments of muteness in Holocaust fiction work deliberately to train our attention on the interplay between the spoken and the unspoken, the recollected and the forgotten, the included and the omitted—not only in fictional, but in *all* Holocaust testimony. Rather than setting up a false opposition between fictional and historical writing, then, the present study examines how the more self-conscious discourse of fiction reshapes and complicates our reading of nonfictional Holocaust narrative generally.

This exploration of forms of muteness in Holocaust narratives resonates in interesting ways with some of the concerns of contemporary literary theory. In contemporary critical theory and practices, the interplay between the spoken and the unspoken has increasingly come into focus, as background gains the foreground and margins, the center. The postmodernist emphasis on the fragmentary nature of writing and the gap between the actual world and its linguistic representations, as well as the postcolonialist consideration of the condition of exile and the situatedness of the colonized speaking out of and against the culture of the colonizer, find resonances in the discourse about the Shoah. I would suggest that we inclusively term the present critical discourse post-Holocaust. The events of the Nazi genocide, paradoxically occurring both within and against Western culture, ultimately challenge—and perhaps disable—the confident and unimpeded transmission of that culture's knowledges, ideologies, and values. The desire to confront—and sometimes to occlude—the implications of the Holocaust for Western civilization, for Jewish culture, and for Western notions about Jewish culture (and by extension, that of all cultural others) has to a large extent triggered postmodern and postcolonial movements.

The present study explores the way Holocaust-centered literature functions as narrative—how the telling (writing) of the catastrophe shapes and informs subsequent knowing (reading) of the catastrophe. As juncture of literary and historical texts and contexts, Holocaust narrative raises a discomforting set of difficulties for the reader. The present focus on displacement—of both language and meaning—offers a means of tacking between the linguistic and metaphysical concerns of this uneasy and self-conscious melding of experience and imagination. The concerns addressed here reach across traditional disciplinary boundaries. It is to be hoped that this study, in its turn, feed into the multidisciplined discourse, which, from under the shadow of this bleak era, seeks some small illumination.

3

Voices from the Killing Ground

Tief
in der Zeitenschrunde,
beim
Wabeneis
wartet, ein Atemkristall,
dein unumstössliches
Zeugnis.

[Deep
in the time-crevasse,
by the
honeycomb-ice,
there waits, as a breath-crystal,
your unimpeachable
testimony.]
— Paul Celan

"What madness is it that drives one to list the various kinds of Jews who were destroyed?" Rachel Auerbach asked herself in "Yizkor, 1943," as the Nazis systematically liquidated the Warsaw Ghetto. Written on the "Aryan side" of Warsaw, Auerbach's lament for the ghetto Jews represents one piece of a vast project to document Jewish life and its brutal destruction. The "madness" that drove Auerbach to document the struggles of the Warsaw ghetto compelled countless others to write, to record, and to preserve a record of Jewish life and Jewish deaths.[1]

More than forty years later, in *The Drowned and the Saved*, Primo Levi explains that because the dead cannot tell their own story, survivors like himself "speak in their stead" (84). The stories of those who perished, however, reach us not only "by proxy" through the survivor. They also comes to us directly in the words of some of those who perished. From across the years, diaries, chronicles, even vast archives are unearthed on the killing grounds of the Third Reich. Written privately or in concert with others, thousands of pages of diaries and chronicles survived the murder of their authors. While memoirs and fiction written later by survivors self-consciously question the nature of memory, language, and representation, these earlier works claim for themselves a powerful and direct testimonial form. The trope of muteness shapes later works from within, figuring an internal set of complexities; by contrast, it intrudes on the earlier body of writing as an external silencing force against which the ghetto writers do battle.

Two recurrent images inform survivor narratives, figuring so frequently in fiction, prose, diaries, memoirs, and poetry that they may be considered type scenes. In the first, the victim of Nazi atrocity resolves to survive the genocidal assault in order to testify against the perpetrators and on behalf of the victims. In the second, the survivor of Nazi atrocity struggles with the impossibility of fulfilling that oath. The survivor—the former victim—testifies, but no one believes, understands, or pays attention. Or, overwhelmed by painful memories and the formidable work of testimony, the survivor remains silent. These two type scenes frequently occur within the same narrative. Juxtaposed, they illustrate the testimonial struggle of the survivor to impart a terrible knowledge—what Maurice Blanchot paradoxically describes as "the wish of all, in the camps, the last wish: know what has happened, do not forget, and at the same time never will you know" (82). Taken together, the two scenes also exemplify what Shoshana Felman has called "the crisis of witnessing."[2]

What precipitates the crisis of witnessing? The matter should be straight-forward: a horrible crime occurred in the presence of witnesses who later come forward to speak what they know. No reasonable person today doubts the facts of the Holocaust—doubts that Nazi genocidal practices were horribly and systematically enacted against women, men, children, the elderly, adolescents, who lived through and died under conditions of unspeakable atrocity. What in the nature of the Holocaust, language, memory, or witnessing, so complicates, then, the act of testimony?

When contrasted with the more familiar writing by survivors, the voices that emerge in ghetto writing sound strangely confident. If muteness at all figures in the works of the ghetto scribes (David Roskies's term), it does so primarily in response to external circumstances—the hermetic isolation behind the ghetto walls; the presence of spies and censors, the highly regulated flow of disinformation into the ghettos. The juxtaposition of spoken and unspoken recollections in survivor writing marks the massive trauma they experienced, as it configures the topography of memory: the sheer pain of remembered events, the need for survivors to move on, the difficulty in doing so, the utter incongruity of the "normal" world with "planet Auschwitz," the presumptuousness in speaking for the dead. The figure of the mute witness develops, then, as a post-Holocaust trope, rather than a predominant presence in ghetto testimony.

R ecent thinking on posttraumatic stress locates a species of muteness at the site and moment of trauma. Subsequent amnesia and aphasia reflect an already constituted belatedness that distances the victim from the events at hand. Indeed, Cathy Caruth's work on posttraumatic stress disorders situates the "enigmatic core" (3)[3] of the traumatic event in that it "is not assimilated or experienced fully at the time, but only belatedly . . ." (2). Clinicians and researchers describe the effects of traumatic stress in language that connotes absence. Variously described as an emotional "numbing" (Lifton),[4] "a void, a hole" (Krystal 114),[5] "a record that has yet to be made" (Laub),[6] massive psychic trauma has come to be understood as an event which, in essence, to use Dori Laub's words, "precludes its registration" and prevents the victim from being a witness to himself; by its nature, massive trauma results in cognitive constriction and flattening of affect, limiting what one can notice and feel. Given the multiple bereavements of family, friends, and community and the extremity of Nazi atrocity, Henry Krystal observes, for Holocaust survivors, "the nature of what is experienced . . . is so incompatible with the survival of the self that it is 'destroyed.' No trace of a registration of any kind is left in the psyche; instead, a void, a hole is formed" (114). The cognitive void occurs because of psychic mechanisms in the individual experiencing trauma and also because of the deliberate program of Nazi deception and disinformation which severely circumscribed what an individual could know with certainty at any point during the enactment of the Nazi genocide.

These ways of describing severe trauma are reconstructions of a moment of trauma already past from the perspective of the present (that is, the future, with relation to the events remembered). Total and partial amnesia, recurrent dreams and compulsive or inappropriate behavior (inappropriate, that is, with regard to the present, "normal" world) give retrospective evidence of a "primary repression," a kind of forgetting or nonregistration, already constituted at the moment of trauma.[7] Most frequently, such reconstructions are the only available access to the moment of trauma.

But the body of ongoing, concurrent witnessing to Nazi atrocity indicates also an active and conscious resistance to the cognitive and emotional constrictions. This contemporaneous witnessing gives us a more complicated and nuanced picture of what it means to live through—and even to die from—massive psychic trauma. Hence the paradox of ghetto writing: at the same time that the ghetto inhabitants became increasingly numbed to the brutal events that engulfed them, many noticed and documented that numbing; as their world literally grew more constricted—as Jews were concentrated in crowded ghettos whose physical spaces were subsequently further diminished—their writing expanded; as they were buffeted by rumors, lies, and hints of unspeakable events, many fought to sift through conflicting information to get at the truth. In a very real sense, ghetto writers did remain witnesses to themselves.

Dori Laub correctly observes that the impressive compendium of ghetto testimony was compromised by the isolation of the ghetto population from its intended audience, the unwillingness of the outside world to receive the testimony, the ghetto writers' ignorance of the Nazi plan and the unfolding of history, and "the inherently incomprehensible *and* deceptive psychological structure" of the Holocaust (80). Essentially, its "dimensions, consequences, and above all its radical *otherness* to all frames of reference" ensured that "There was therefore no concurrent 'knowing'" (84). To speak of the Shoah, however, as "*the event* [that] *produced no witnesses*" (80)[8] may be reading into the actual moments of trauma a belatedness not yet present.

What kinds of witnesses and what kinds of witnessing do the remnants of ghetto testimony situate at the moments of trauma? Moments, not moment, of trauma, because—unlike an auto or train accident and unlike the bombing of Hiroshima—the events of the Shoah endured over years, permitting its victims time to attempt to account for its causes, mitigate its effects, deflect its inevitability. For Laub, the radical destructiveness and "the very circumstance of *being inside the event* . . . made unthinkable the very notion that a witness could exist" (81). Based on his clinical work and research with Holocaust survivors for over two decades, Henry Krystal observes that the conditions of the Shoah diminished the victim's capacity to understand, respond to, and describe its effects. By its very nature, the enactment of Nazi atrocity led to a "progressive constriction of cognitive processes, including memory, problem solving, until a mere vestige of self-observing ego is preserved" (99–100). Lifton's work on *hibakusha* (radiation affected survivors of the atomic explosions in Japan) and shell-shocked soldiers distinguishes between the responses of "numbing," which blocks feeling, and "repression, which excludes or forgets an idea" (66); this important distinction enables us to acknowledge the aftershock of trauma without categorically precluding the possibility of witnessing. For, as we shall see in reading ghetto writing, that "vestige of self-observing ego" often suffices to adequately witness—that is, precisely, to notice, understand, and describe—its own deterioration, the destruction of family and community, even one's own dying.

While Laub and Krystal offer stunning illustrations of survivor amnesia, their research and therapeutic practices, of course, primarily consider the aftereffects of trauma, and the traumatic episodes only insofar as they are later inscribed in and by the survivor.[9] By contrast, the voices from the killing ground speak from the site of trauma in ways that must complicate our understanding of trauma and witnessing. In her work on the effects of torture on its victims, Elaine Scarry observes that just as "torture consists of acts that magnify the way in which pain destroys a person's world, self, and voice," so "acts that restore the voice become not only a denunciation of the pain but almost a diminution of the pain, a partial reversal of the process of torture itself" (50). As they notice and calibrate their emotional and cognitive responses to death and atrocity, the ghetto scribes witness from within the trauma.

Two of the most extensive sets of records, the *Lodz Ghetto Chronicle* and the Warsaw Ghetto *Oneg Shabbes* project, reflect collective efforts to record and understand the ongoing events. Within the pages of these collections, the writers sifted through the conflicting rumors and official information to determine the facts both for themselves and for future readers. "Who can render the stages of the dying people?" Auerbach asked rhetorically—the answer already contained in her own act of writing. Already then, ghetto writers saw their own efforts as resistance to an imposed muteness which sought to bury all traces of the murder victims. Against the Nazi attempt to relegate atrocity to a blank page of history—what Himmler referred to as the "unwritten and never-to-be-written page of glory"—Auerbach and others rendered the stages of living and dying under Nazi rule. Their words, filling the pages of diaries and chronicles, lining the margins of holy books, hiding encoded in deceptively innocent letters, chart the progress of annihilation. These words write the "unwritten page" of history from the vantage point of the murdered victims, restoring their voice after their death.

The *Lodz Ghetto Chronicle* is a comprehensive, day-by-day account of events in the second-largest ghetto of Nazi-controlled Europe, written steadily from January 1941 through July 1944. An official organ of the Archives of the Ghetto Eldest—part of the Jewish Ghetto administration—the *Chronicle* represents the joint efforts of approximately one dozen archive workers with unique access to important classified documents, including the internal records of the Jewish Ghetto administration and its correspondence with the German administration. With the exception of several extensive signed entries—primarily by Oskar Rosenfeld, Jozef Klementynowski, and Bernard Ostrowski—the personalities of individual contributors disappeared into unsigned contributions. Years later, we can read their words but cannot reconstruct their individual identities. In contrast, *Oneg Shabbes* was the code name for a project conceived and organized by Emanuel Ringelblum, working in secret and independently of the Warsaw Ghetto administration, the largest ghetto of Nazi-ruled Europe. The traditional "Oneg Shabbes," a Friday night gathering to celebrate the Sabbath with song and study (literally "enjoyment of the Sabbath"), provided a cover for Ringelblum's clandestine group. In addition to Ringelblum's *Notes from the Warsaw Ghetto*, which reflects his background as a social historian, the *Oneg Shabbes* includes over 100 volumes of reports, monographs, diaries, essays, and Nazi and ghetto documents. To give the *Oneg Shabbes* a "broad social base," Ringelblum deliberately solicited contributions from a heterogeneous group of ghetto inhabitants and incorporated private diaries. Unlike the *Chronicle*, individual contributions to the *Oneg Shabbes* often bear the names and recognizable viewpoints of their authors, leaving a tangible trace of many individuals who perished. Other writings from the Warsaw ghetto include the cryptic and abbreviated diary entries of Adam Czerniakow, Ghetto Eldest; the extensive diary of Chaim Kaplan, and the eclectic and enigmatic diary of Janusz Korczak.

As artifacts of ghetto life and as containers for narrative, these works impart a history separate from those of their authors. Their means of transmission, their physical condition and accessibility all tell us of the conditions under which they were produced and preserved. Ringelblum secreted the *Oneg Shabbes* material, along with his own notes, in sealed milk cans which he buried in the Ghetto. Although much of this material was recovered after the war, some of it was rendered illegible by water damage and portions have never been found. The Lodz Ghetto Archives, including multiple copies of the *Chronicle*'s approximately 1,000 issues, were hidden in batches in different parts of the ghetto. While the Germans discovered and confiscated one large cache, most of the material was retrieved after the war following the directives of the sole archivist who survived the Holocaust.

For most readers today, ghetto narratives come to us in diminished form: translated, edited, abridged, reproduced, sold in stores or through catalogues, sometimes remaindered. The distance between the object written and the object read marks the decimation and dissolution of Jewish communities by the events that the works document. One may travel to archives housing the actual diary—in New York, Jerusalem, Warsaw, Vilna—but most readers do not. With the exception of a few professional historians and scholars, readers rarely read these works in the original languages. And virtually no one consults original manuscripts. These geographic and linguistic limitations— ours, the readers', not theirs, the writers'—determine which works contribute to and which are excluded from our sense of the Holocaust.

Most of the *Oneg Shabbes* material and much of Ringelblum's own writing have never been translated into English. *Notes from the Warsaw Ghetto* represents only half of Ringelblum's original *Ksovim fun ghetto*. Ringelblum excluded journalistic writing from the *Oneg Shabbes*. So, while reportage by ghetto journalists exists in the form of feuilletons, it remains inaccessible to the reading public. Who we are as readers also determines which works become available to shape our ideas. For example, the Polish-Jewish culture, which informs much of the *Oneg Shabbes* archival material, feels alien to most Americans and Israelis: because the writing of an assimilated, marginal Jew, or of a Bundist, does not match the contemporary political and cultural climate, it rarely finds its way into translation. Later readers select works that affirm our sense of continuity or at least diminish the sense of discontinuity with the destroyed Jewish communities.

Moreover, reading these works we come up against pockets of inaccessibility. The style, idiom, and format of ghetto narratives place special interpretive responsibilities on us. Shimon Huberband's difficult handwriting, his idiosyncratic Yiddish, and the physical erosion his manuscripts have suffered make it impossible for us to read him clearly. The series of slim notebooks that form Adam Czerniakow's diary are often cryptic and so spare that we cannot fully recognize the events to which he refers. Janusc Korczak's writing is even more impressionistic, personal, and enigmatic. That we cannot ask Huberband to clarify, Czerniakow to elaborate, or Korczak to explain is a measure of our loss. However fragmented, the works must stand in for their authors. They must deliver the testimony that their writers could not complete.

These verbal remnants of catastrophe make our sense of the events more complex and encompassing. Their voices provide us with a counter-voice to Nazi propaganda. They corroborate and amplify other sources, adding to the body of verifiable facts about the Holocaust. Moreover, the cumulative effect and the particularity of the diaries and chronicles render a sense of how the writer lives through, one might also say "dies through," this catastrophic time. What falls inside or outside the boundaries of narration in ghetto accounts attests to a precarious situation, the difficulty of obtaining reliable information, and the nature of the events themselves.

Yet ghetto writing speaks with a strange confidence as it traces the progressive deprivation of property, livelihood, personal identity, and finally life itself. In the Lodz *Chronicle*, "The hand does not waver in writing this down. The hand is guided by a brain that reliably preserves all impressions of the eye and the ear" (363). By sharp contrast, in later years survivors fear that an insurmountable barrier separates those who have experienced the Holocaust from those who have not. A paradox informs survivor writing, much of which simultaneously insists that the readers *must* understand and *will never* understand what happened. Charlotte Delbo, for example, a French poet who survived Auschwitz, struggles against a language that, in her view, falsifies her experience. Her memoirs complain that ordinary words such as *fear, hunger, evil,* and *fatigue* fall short when used to describe extraordinary circumstances. The problem lies not only in the survivor's inability to speak the unspeakable; it lies also in our own inability—as nonparticipants—to imagine the unimaginable.

Ghetto writings, however, simply plunge the reader into the midst of daily life and death. The *Chronicle* discusses the waning supply of potato peels, a valued and expensive food in Lodz, sometimes available only with a doctor's prescription. Oskar Singer provides the "recipe" for a birthday "babka" his wife prepared for him: "Potato peels ground in the meat grinder, with ersatz coffee and a bit of flour—when done it looks like a deformed briquette" (461). Singer's birthday "delicacy" surpassed the ghetto staple—"ersatz food made of ersatz coffee, fried in a pan"—a bitter pancake that "epitomizes the bitterness of ghetto life" (463). The *Chronicle* also tracks the endless rumors about food supplies that radically swing the mood of the ghetto, and notes the build-up of excremental filth, the disease, and the death toll. "One lives in filth, one sleeps in filth, and one eats without observing the basic rules of hygiene" (261). There is a plea for a public laundry to save the ghetto from extermination. In Warsaw, Czerniakow also worries about laundry facilities, particularly after finding a "revolting louse" on his nightshirt (257). These detailed descriptions enable later readers to overcome the limitations of language, experience, and imagination, and understand what *hunger* and *filth* meant to ghetto dwellers.

The relatively unconstructed rendering of reality that unfolds in the diaries and chronicles yields a vision of Jewish life and death under the Nazis more varied than the one emerging from more idealized retrospective survivor accounts. Even in the shadow of destruction, and distorted by suffering, ghetto writing conveys a sense of the vitality and diversity of European Jewish life. There are competing ideologies and social differences. Huberband criticizes the raucous behavior of a distinctive group of young Gerer Hasidism and laments the "moral decline" of Jewish women. "Rarely did one notice a Jewish woman open her purse to give a groschen to a starving Jew," he complains (240). While Huberband disavows, "God forbid, a smear campaign of horrors against all Jewish women," his singling out of women for special scrutiny could reflect a gender-based view derived from pre-Holocaust times.

The Lodz *Chronicle* records approvingly the "ghetto's latest hit song" lampooning the newly arrived "yekes" or German Jews. "The song treats their ups and downs with good humor and tells of the *yekes*, forever hungry and searching for food, and the 'locals' who make fun of them and quite often take advantage of their naivete and unfamiliarity with local customs" (92). Ringelblum notes the ironic situation of both German and Polish Jews in the Warsaw Ghetto. The German Jews keep to themselves, speak of "unser Fuehrer," and await a German victory to take them back to their homeland (288). Polish Jews speak Polish more often than Yiddish, partly as "a psychological protest against the Ghetto—*you* have thrown us into a Jewish Ghetto, but *we'll* show you that it is really a Polish street"—and partly in "continuation of the powerful linguistic assimilation that was marked even before the war. . . ." (289) Such comments express the complicated and divergent sense of cultural identity that characterized the Jews of that time. They give us a sense not only of the destruction but of what was destroyed.

Rather than offering a heroic or idealized or nostalgic narrative, ghetto accounts critically evaluate the policy and behavior of colleagues and leaders. Ringelblum reveals how corruption and opportunism eroded the ghetto from within. The spread of typhus, for example, was abetted rather than contained by the sanitation squad that squandered the disinfection chemicals and blackmailed the more affluent "with the threat of ruining their linen, clothes, and the like" (218). Many ghetto sources condemned the disparity between economic classes—a disparity that often determined who would starve.

However, with rare exception, the *Lodz Chronicle* refrained from criticizing Rumkowski (the Eldest of the Jews) and his administration. Echoing Rumkowski's insistence on law and obedience, the *Chronicle* condemned smugglers and other dealers who disturbed the ghetto order. Survivor accounts, by contrast, note that the ability to "organize"—as it came to be called in the concentration camps—proved useful for survival. Unlike the Lodz chroniclers, Ringelblum was highly critical of ghetto leadership and often took issue with administration policies. He termed the Warsaw Ghetto Jewish Council a "den of wickedness and hypocrisy" (245) operating on the "Fuehrer principle" (164); Czerniakow, "a weak man" (316) who was "regarded as an idol" (164); Rumkowski, "extraordinarily ambitious and pretty nutty" (47), a man who "considers himself God's anointed" (48).

The *Lodz Chronicle*'s dispassionate tone carries over to its reports of Nazi brutality. As an official organ of the Ghetto Archives—potentially open to Nazi scrutiny—the *Chronicle* rarely mentions Nazis explicitly. In reports of murders, beatings, and humiliations, the passive voice predominates. Ghetto inhabitants "were shot," "were beaten," or "died" during an arrest. According to one entry,

> Abraham Dab . . . was shot in the shoulder at eleven o'clock this morning on Zaierska Street, near the vehicle gate of the Old Market. . . . Witnesses to the incident claim that the wounded man had been speaking with the sentry beforehand. It was obviously not possible to establish the substance of that conversation. (38–39)

Presumably—although the *Chronicle* does not say so directly—the sentry shot Dab. Why? The sentry's unavailability for questioning and unaccountability for his action—to the *Chronicle* writers, to the Jewish ghetto administration, and, by extension, to us—epitomize the legal powerlessness of the ghetto community. The report's bland tone reflects the chroniclers' idea of appropriateness in "the dry framework of a chronicle" (150). It also signals the precariousness of their situation. The circumlocution that ensures the continuance of the *Chronicle* lends a ghostly quality to what is reported, as though a disembodied menace were assaulting the ghetto. It also underscores our own need to read between the lines in ghetto documentation, to look for the unsaid within the said.

By contrast, Ringelblum's work contains fewer omissions, leaving less to the reader's intuition. He repeatedly identifies the agents of atrocity. Whether part of the German administration, the Jewish Council, the Jewish Police, or the office of the Ghetto Eldest, people bear explicit moral responsibility for their actions. To protect himself and his diary, he sometimes refers to Nazis by code: "They" or "Others" or the Hebrew for *lord and masters*, used ironically, to signify Nazi officials. More often Ringelblum and other *Oneg Shabbes* writers are openly critical of behavior they deplore. Not only the identity of the perpetrators but the moral outrage of the writers is less veiled than in the *Chronicle*. According to Ringelblum, "A simple Jew from a small town who went through fearful persecutions said there must be schools for torture in Germany. Otherwise, he could not understand where people could have learned such novel forms of torture" (63).

Despite Ringelblum's willingness to render moral judgment and attribute blame, his account also contains deliberate omissions. He does not mention Warsaw Ghetto resistance, choosing to leave an "incomplete" narrative lest his documents fall into the wrong hands. What Ghetto writers omit—as much as what they include—helps us to recall something of the conditions under which their writing took place.

The accuracy of ghetto accounts is also compromised by the Nazi's deliberate program of disinformation and deception. Of all ghetto writing, the *Lodz Ghetto Chronicle* enjoyed the most privileged access to documentary material. At the same time, the Lodz Ghetto was sealed off more hermetically than others: radios and outside newspapers were forbidden. The chroniclers relied upon their own reasoning to determine which information to trust. Generally they favored "official" information over the "rumors" that ran through the ghetto and disturbed its equilibrium. Yet in retrospect, those rumors often turned out to be more accurate than the information coming through official channels. As the chroniclers eventually learned, many rumors derived from illegal radios retained at great peril. Transcripts of radio broadcasts circulated, providing alternative communiqués to those officially sanctioned.

Communication from both Jewish and German sources told wildly conflicting stories. German officials continually assured the ghetto dwellers that they had nothing to fear from "resettlements." However, the suspicious array of personal items, identity papers, and other vital documents contained in the shipments of baggage arriving in Lodz for sorting, hinted at the fate of their "resettled" owners. At the same time, Lodz Jews received postcards from deported relatives, offering a "reassuring sign that these people are alive and able to work" (349). We now know that the Nazis forced their victims to write postcards which would arrive after their writers had been murdered. What appeared to be in the voice of "resettled" Jews was actually an act of Nazi ventriloquism that reinforced their muteness. Such trickery left the ghetto writers vulnerable to Nazi disinformation. The *Chronicle* cites a Gestapo report about the "labor" camp awaiting a series of "resettlements" from the ghetto. According to the report, this "gigantic camp," comfortably housing about 100,000 Jews, had been occupied by German nationals who "left the barracks in perfectly decent order, and even left their furniture for the Jews to use. The food supply at the camp is, apparently, exemplary" (145). This place so glowingly described is the deathcamp Chelmno.

Because chroniclers and diarists at once observe and share the circumstances they describe, their writings combine the studied "objectivity" of the historian with the indignation and despair of the victim. In 1944, for example, the *Chronicle* describes the desperation and degeneration wrought by hunger. Ghetto inhabitants poison themselves with rotten, decomposing potato peels "covered with fetid rubbish, excrement, and sweepings . . . undaunted by the obnoxious stench, the ghastly pestilence. . . . This is not simple hunger, this is the frenzy of degenerate animals. . . . This must not be, this cannot be" (479). The distance that the narrative asserts between observer and observed masks a more fundamental similarity between the "prosperous, ever so well-nourished bourgeois" who watches and the "degenerate animals" who "grub in this abyss of misery." The same conditions and the same murderous fate rule both. In Leyb Goldin's account of hunger in the Warsaw Ghetto, this distance collapses as he documents his own degeneration: "You feel that today you have fallen a step lower. . . . All these people around you, apparently, began like that. You're on your way. . . ."

This conflation of observer and observed suggests the impossible situation of a corpse delivering its own funeral oration or reciting Kaddish for itself. "Death lurks in every chink, every little crack," Ringelblum wrote (272). The increasing morbidity and mortality rates printed regularly in the Lodz *Chronicle*, and the unmanageable accumulation of unburied corpses noted there and in other sources, portray the ghettoes as cemeteries in the making. By 1942, Ringelblum saw the Jews as "*morituri*—sentenced to death" (320) and waiting out that sentence. In all the ghettoes, the increase in suicides reveals the mounting despair. As the Lodz and Warsaw archivists write obituaries for their colleagues, the distance between the writer and his subject narrows. This merging of observer into observed, of mourner into mourned, culminates in the truncation of the narratives themselves. Death or deportation overtook the diarists and chroniclers, as entire ghettoes were liquidated. With few exceptions, the end of narration attests to the writer's death.

T he abundance of ghetto writing stands in marked contrast to the silence immediately following the war. What prompted this writing in the shadow of death? It could not have been easy to find the stamina and resources under such overwhelming circumstances. In addition to the hunger and grief that sapped their energy, ghetto inhabitants faced shortages of pen, ink, and paper. In Lodz, frequent electric power cut-offs at the end of the work day made reading difficult. And yet, Ringelblum asserted, "Everyone wrote" (OS 386). By his account, what remains today represents only a small sample of the actual diaristic output in the ghettoes. At the same time that writers saw themselves transformed into "90 percent your stomach and a little bit you," as Leyb Goldin described himself (425), they were documenting that metamorphosis. They would write even at peril. Ringelblum observed, "The drive to write down one's memoirs is powerful: Even young people in labor camps do it. The manuscripts are discovered, torn up, and their authors beaten" (133). What was it that fueled and sustained this documentary urge?

On a personal level, the act of writing often provided the writer with a means to persevere through difficult times without giving way to despair. Against an onslaught deliberately designed to dehumanize the ghetto inhabitants, writing preserved their identity, reminding them that they were thinking, autonomous human beings. For private diarists as for archivists, writing allowed the "little bit you" to prevail over the "90 percent . . . stomach," if only provisionally. Ringelblum proclaimed in his notes, "Let it be said that though we have been sentenced to death and know it, we have not lost our human features; our minds are as active as they were before the war" (299).

Many of the Lodz and Warsaw Ghetto archivists drew from earlier training—as historians, economists, writers, researchers. Working in a professional capacity asserted a sense of inner continuity which fortified them. In a discussion of a special Soup Kitchen for the Intelligentsia— "a sort of club where these people who once were something meet for the midday meal"—the *Chronicle* attributes the Kitchen's success to its "special atmosphere." The Kitchen's elegant service and intellectual clientele maintain an illusion that things had not radically changed, meager rations notwithstanding (29). By providing professional stature, meaningful work, and a proper office, the Lodz Ghetto Archives similarly reminds its compilers of who they had been. On a more concrete level, the Archives also provided them with proper work documents and a supplemental food allocation. By writing, the chroniclers could establish the illusion of distance between themselves and those worse off, which mitigated their own sense of degeneration. The man who spoons spilled soup from a filthy staircase and the boys who grub for rancid potatoes stand in sharp relief—if only temporarily—to the person describing them. Even when this distance collapses, the act of writing reasserted one's dignity. As Goldin struggles to distinguish hungry humans from scavenging animals, his very ability to narrate—to assert, "we are not animals"—proves his humanity.

On a collective level, the chroniclers and diarists regarded their work as active resistance against the Nazi plan. Ringelblum believed that an explicit account of ghetto atrocity, smuggled out and brought to the attention of ordinary people, would put an end to slaughter. Even Germans, he assumed, would be horrified by the extermination of Jews. ". . . if the German populace knew about it, They [Nazis] would probably not be able to execute the mass murder" (292).

When annihilation seemed inevitable, ghetto writers saw their work as evidence that would be available to future readers. Their writing would preserve a tangible record of their suffering for a world that would otherwise not know what occurred. By naming names, the writing would rescue the memory of the victims from oblivion and call the perpetrators to the judgment of history. In addition, the writing would counter falsified documentation produced by the Nazis. Ringelblum and Czerniakow described staged newsreels filmed by the Nazis in the Warsaw Ghetto. "Every scene is directed" (Ringelblum, *Notes* 271). Today, those films survive but so does the testimony that undermines their authenticity. For Ringelblum,

> one thing is clear to all of us . . . we have fulfilled our duty. . . . Nor will our deaths be meaningless, like the deaths of tens of thousands of Jews. We have struck the enemy a hard blow. We have revealed his Satanic plan to annihilate Polish Jewry, a plan he wished to complete in silence. We have run a line through his calculations and have exposed his cards. . . . (295–96)

The refusal to accept the condition of muteness was equated by Ringelblum and other ghetto writers with effective resistance and collective, if not individual, survival.

Implicit in the chronicles and diaries is the vision of a posterity resembling the writers. Huberband evokes an unbroken chain of Jewish tradition linking his contemporaries with their spiritual ancestors and descendants. He sees religious Jews engaged in a holy struggle to maintain an ordained way of life, risking their existence to save sacred books and ritual objects, to obtain kosher meat and poultry, to retain traditional garb and beard. In a report on clandestine visits to the mikveh (ritual bathhouse), forcibly shut down, he elaborates:

> We imagined vividly the sight of our forefathers in Spain—how they rescued Torah scrolls, how they prayed with a *minyan* in secret cellars, due to fear of the Inquisition. They certainly never imagined that their descendants would find themselves, four hundred years later, in a much worse situation. . . . (201)

For women denied access to the mikveh, "the problem of the purity . . . became as serious as it was in the days of the ancient Roman edicts against Judaism" (195). By identifying with other historic moments—the Inquisition, the Roman era—Huberband claims a direct link with the ancestral past and asserts the continuity of Jewish history in adversity. Through analogy, he offers a source of courage and a rationale for optimism: just as Jews (and Judaism) survived previous crises, so their descendants would survive the Nazi onslaught. The ghetto Jews compete with, and perhaps surpass, the merit of their ancestors. Moreover, just as Huberband recalls, respects, and retells the actions of his ancestors, so future generations will find his experiences meaningful. In Huberband's formulation, narrative outlasts death. The religious idiom employed here and throughout his writing anticipates that his readership will resemble the people he describes: Torah-literate Jews who will understand both the terminology and its significance without explanation.

Other ghetto writers similarly envisioned an audience in their own image. They anticipated the outrage of a future reader—an outrage based upon shared values and a common idea of civilization. Generally, they remain untroubled by the suspicions that plague survivor reflections—that these shared values and this civilization were killed by the Holocaust, or that they brought on the Holocaust. Amid the rubble, the ghetto writers trusted that their words would have the ring of authority, would be believed, would be adequate. They portrayed Nazism as a form of temporary insanity overtaking at a specific and bounded historical moment. As time goes on, however, the ghetto writers show a dawning sense of their own breach with the past. Still, they imagine this breach healed when the war ends. With a German defeat, sanity would reassert itself.

Survivors, on the other hand, fear the rupture is radical and the madness permanent. Although they have outlasted the Nazi program of extermination and can speak in their own voices on their own behalf, they often speak with less assurance than do ghetto writers. In the aftermath, they no longer count on a postwar restoration of "sanity" or "normalcy." In survivor narratives, the posterity envisioned by the ghetto writers has already arrived, and it appears unwilling to bear the "legacy" of the Holocaust. The next generation, Primo Levi notes, finds the Holocaust "distant, blurred, historical" (198). In Levi's experience, the audience whose empathy and outrage the ghetto writer counted on, instead "judge with facile hindsight, or . . . perhaps feel cruelly repelled" (78) by survivor accounts. Like the ghetto writers, Levi insists, "We must be listened to" (199). Unlike them, he is less certain that his voice will be heard; and if heard, understood; and if understood, effective. *The Drowned and the Saved* attests to Levi's despair that "The experiences that we survivors of the Nazi Lagers carry within us are extraneous to the new Western generation and become ever more extraneous as the years pass" (198). While most ghetto writers anticipated judgment and justice when "the world" finds out what has been done to them, survivors acknowledge that little happened when the world found out. In fact, the world may have known more than ghetto writers suspected.

The problem lies not only with posterity ("the world") but with survivors themselves—their ability to remember and represent extreme events that defy belief and expression. Levi blames the "fallacious" nature of memory, too fluid or too rigid to be entrusted with the burden of testimony. He describes memory as, on the one hand, "not carved in stone" (19) and, on the other hand, "fixed in a stereotype . . . crystallized, perfected" (24) by either infrequent or too frequent invocation. The unreliability of memory, the inadequacy of representation, and the indifference of posterity problematize the role of the witness and the nature of testimony for Levi. Other survivors too wonder whether the sense of mission that fueled ghetto writing has been betrayed. Delbo reflects back on her desire to survive Auschwitz in order to bear witness, "the voice promulgating the ultimate count. . . . Here I am. . . . My voice gets lost. Who hears it? Who knows how to heed it?" (257) Ultimately, survivors know from personal experience and from the retrospective of history what ghetto writers could only suspect: the magnitude of the catastrophe. "Normal" to all appearance, the world after the Holocaust remains abnormal, profoundly altered by the events. This is seen in the continued impact of the past on the present—in the personal or interior lives of former victims, and by their sense of "civilization" and "culture"—the audience to which ghetto writers once appealed—as complicitous with their victimization.

Ironically, then, while ghetto writers could not know whether they would survive—and most did not—their works reflect greater confidence than the testimony of survivors. Because they had not yet experienced the worst, had no intimate knowledge of the concentrationary universe, ghetto writers were more certain of their ability to describe all that occurred to them and around them. In space and time, the distance from Lodz to Chelmno, or from Warsaw to Auschwitz, is short but crucial. Former victims, having survived the marches and the deathcamps, having learned the ruthlessness and comprehensiveness of the Nazi genocide, remained silent for years after—silenced by loss, by the experience of atrocity, by the rupture that proves irreparable.

The ghettos, of course, were a prelude to the extreme conditions of the death camps. Anonymous, decomposing corpses piled up unburied in ghetto cemeteries; death became an everyday sight in the streets. Overexposure to death, coupled with starvation and exhaustion, numbed the ghetto dwellers emotionally, just as it later numbed the *musselmanner* of the camps, those who had given up all human response, all hope. The *Chronicle* wonders about the "populace's strange reaction" to tragedy:

> Is this some sort of numbing of the nerves, and indifference, or a symptom of an illness that manifests itself in atrophied emotional reactions? After losing those nearest to them, people talk constantly about rations, potatoes, soup, etc.! It is beyond comprehension! Why this lack of warmth toward those they loved? (255)

Ringelblum reports "Extraordinary slackening of kinship ties" where family members betray one another to curry favor and gain privilege.

But in the midst of ghetto horror there still remained a semblance of the life the ghetto dwellers once knew: schools, synagogues, jobs, commerce, culture. Although deportations and deaths had begun to fragment families, many remained intact, even if stressed. Oskar Singer celebrated his 1944 birthday with his wife, children, and sister. Some people still had adequate shelter, garden plots, window boxes (in which to cultivate vegetables), and access to toilets. The excremental filth described in the *Chronicle* does not compare with the filth of the camps. There inmates were often forbidden to use latrines and had to use the same bowl for food, chamber pot, washbasin. Despite their suffering and privations, ghetto inhabitants could maintain some measure of dignity and autonomy. In Lodz, workers mounted hunger strikes to protest inadequate or unequal food distribution, brutal and humiliating treatment by foremen, intolerable working conditions. Although placed in a situation designed to humiliate and dehumanize them, the ghetto dwellers still had names, not numbers. And the Lodz and Warsaw archivists could work steadily on their important projects. Amid disease, starvation, and increasing deportations, ghetto inhabitants could assert some control over themselves and their bodies.

G hetto narratives, then, trace the writers' struggle to understand what was going on, and to devise strategies for survival. The accounts look to history and literature for ways to respond emotionally and pragmatically to the Nazi onslaught. If literary and historical models ultimately do not answer these challenges, they temporarily shore up a sense of connection with the past—with a lost normalcy—and promise, by analogy, the continuity of Jewish life and the eventual return to normalcy. The *Chronicle* asserts that ". . . a Jew is a fatalist . . . he consoles himself with the knowledge that he has already suffered greater losses and ordeals and somehow survived them too . . . while we wait for a better tomorrow. Such is our mentality!" (244).

With some ambivalence, the *Chronicle* calls up the archetypal wiliness of the Jew to ward off catastrophe. On the one hand, the *Chronicle* reiterates Rumkowski's blaming ghetto discord on "Jews [who] were . . . too clever by half" (111). On the other hand, the *Chronicle* notes with pride instances where "our Jews found a way to cope" with—that is, to thwart through trickery—German regulations, just as the literary Jew maneuvers against stronger opponents by relying on wits. When Nazi law made civil marriage illegal, for example, the Lodz Ghetto administration found ways to circumvent the regulation and perform legally recognized marriages. The archetype of the Jewish trickster evokes an admixture of Jewish pride and anti-Semitic stereotype. In any case, the strategy proved ineffectual against an enemy whose programmatic deceptions were more tricksterly and sinister than could be imagined.

Similarly, both Huberband and Chaim Kaplan evoke historical precedents that make ghetto suffering meaningful. For them, martyrdom functions as a form of spiritual resistance, maintaining the integrity of the murdered and inspiring those who remain. Whether or not his reading of history is correct, with respect to his own era Huberband erred. Not Judaism but Jews—more broadly defined than ever before and dissociated from any belief or practice—were to be eradicated.

Ghetto writers frequently compared their situation with the medieval Jewish city. Rumkowski viewed Lodz as an autonomous Jewish city-state and himself as its representative and negotiator. Thus, he wanted Lodz to become indispensable to the economic well-being of the German body politic, whose leaders he saw as reasonable men who would honor their word. "The plan is work, work, and more work! . . . I will be able to demonstrate, on the basis of irrefutable statistics, that the Jews in the ghetto constitute a productive element. . . ." (*Chronicle* 115). Rumkowski's plan, as well as his rhetoric, implicitly accepts the Nazi definition of Jew as commodity, as thing which will not be disposed of so long as it remains useful. For us, Rumkowski's reiterated equation of "work" with "life" and "peace" has uncomfortable overtones. Although the Eldest could not have known, it resonates with the slogan above the entry gate at Auschwitz: "Arbeit Macht Frei."

In retrospect, the paradigmatic, autonomous Jewish city-state which informed Rumkowski's decisions was irrelevant to the Nazi plan to eradicate all traces of Jewish life from Europe. At best, his administration succeeded in delaying, but not commuting, the death sentence. As ghetto conditions worsened and salvation became increasingly unlikely, some ghetto writers sensed the bankruptcy of such a model, and the unprecedented desperation of their own situation.

As conditions worsened, as the ghetto sensed more and more the Nazi purpose, ghetto writing began to take on characteristics of survivor accounts. This evolution can be seen in Ringelblum's rejection of historical precedents. In November 1940, Ringelblum—like Rumkowski—saw ghetto life as "returning to the Middle Ages. . . . The Jews created another world for themselves in the past, living in it forgot the troubles around them, allowed no one from the outside to come in" (82). This formulation casts the Jews as active agents and beneficiaries of ghettoization. That the Jews did not "create" the ghetto, that they were powerless to prevent the "outside" from coming in, does not figure in Ringelblum's assessment. However, by June 1942, Ringelblum rejects such comparisons. "To my mind . . . all this search for historical analogy is beside the point. History *does not* repeat itself. Especially now, now that we stand at the crossroads, witnessing the death pangs of an old world and the birth pangs of a new. How can our age be compared with any earlier one?" (300).

As Ringelblum comes to realize, the Nazis deliberately lulled ghetto dwellers into outmoded strategies of survival that later proved futile. For example, the rich, ongoing, and diverse cultural life in the ghettos took the edge off despair. These voices, now perceived as spiritual and cultural resistance, attest to the tenacity and resilience of the ghetto dwellers under impossible conditions. Had the Nazi goal been anything short of total annihilation, their inner strength would have helped them endure. But the Jews were death-bound whatever they did. According to a November 1941 report from a high-level German official in Warsaw, the German Ghetto Administration deliberately permitted the Jews "maximum freedom . . . in so-called cultural activities." The Jews "have theatres, variety shows, coffee houses, etc. The Jews have opened public schools and to a considerable extent developed the trade school system." The report credits the ghetto's administrative and cultural autonomy with producing "a certain reassurance which is necessary if their economic capacity is to be exploited for our purposes. . . ." According to the report, "The Jews are waiting for the end of the war and in the meantime conduct themselves quietly. There has been no sign of any resistance to date" (Czerniakow, 402).

The ghetto writers themselves may have played unwittingly into the German scheme. The *Chronicle* distinguishes between the activities of its Archives and the work of a new research department. On orders from German officials, the department created assemblages of dolls and puppets illustrating Eastern European Jewish customs and types for display outside the ghetto. To the chroniclers, it was obvious that the Germans intended these exhibits to arouse anti-Semitism.

> . . . the figurines and groups depicting the traditional life of Eastern [European] Jews were intended for an exhibit which was to serve as a sort of museum of East European Jewry in Litzmannstadt. We stressed that this department had been formed not at the suggestion of the Chairman but by order of the Ghetto Administration and that the ghetto made a point of remaining aloof from this department, not approving of the direction in which it was moving. (348)

Was the work of the Archives also envisioned by the Nazis (who examined its premises and condoned its activities) as an exhibit documenting an exotic but defunct civilization? In retrospect, every form of resistance short of armed combat may have played into Nazi hands.

Discovery of Nazi duplicity came too late for most ghettos to mount a full-scale, active armed resistance. As this realization hits the ghetto writers, they feel indignant at being tricked. They bitterly resent their leaders' futile policy of appeasement and fear that their own writing has been compromised unknowingly. Their strident, confident voices had been muted by Nazi disinformation, in ways the writers had not realized. According to Ringelblum,

> Whomever you talk to, you hear the same cry: The resettlement should never have been permitted. We should have run out into the street, have set fire to everything in sight, have torn down the walls, and escaped to the Other Side. . . .

Now we are ashamed of ourselves, disgraced in our own eyes,
and in the eyes of the world, where our docility earned us
nothing. (326)

As ghetto writing shifts into the mode of survivor memoir—for example,
after the destruction of the Warsaw Ghetto when Ringelblum writes
retrospectively about the *Oneg Shabbes* activities—the tone becomes
increasingly bitter and cynical about the possibilities of survival and
testimony.

A tragic irony informs our reading, an irony born not out of the
writer's artistry but out of our own position in history. We know
how the story ends even before we begin reading. With rare exceptions,
the ghetto writers perished, along with their entire communities. While
they continued to hope for the best, we know the worst. We have
learned the relentlessness of Nazi atrocity and the thoroughness of
genocide. Because we know more than the ghetto writers, we read their
narratives with a conflict of emotions. Their hopefulness both soothes
and disturbs us. On the one hand, ghetto writing appeals to us because
it asserts traditional patterns of meaning we may like to retain—civilization, martyrology, human dignity. On the other hand, through the
testimony of survivors—those who have come close to "the bottom," as
Levi says—we see those patterns as significantly, if not irretrievably,
ruptured.

In writing fiction, survivors deliberately play upon the tragic irony
that, in some sense, undermined their efforts. The author, the audience,
and sometimes the narrator, know more than the characters who struggle to survive, blind to what history holds in store. Jurek Becker's
novel, *Jacob the Liar*, illustrates the sense of betrayal the Jews felt
when the ghetto was liquidated despite their best efforts for survival.
The plot turns on the imposed silence within in the ghetto walls with
respect to incoming news. Newspapers from the outside world were
forbidden, radios were confiscated. Because the isolated Lodz Ghetto
thirsts for—but only rarely obtains—reliable information, Jacob goes to
great risks to pierce the wall of muteness that keeps ghetto inhabitants ignorant and in despair. At first sneaking into Polish-only latrines
to read the scraps of newspaper placed there for hygienic purpose,
Jacob finally generates his own "news," which he attributes to a nonex-
istent radio.

The fabricated news is configured not so much to represent reality
as to match the contours of the ghetto dwellers' hopes. As Jacob feeds

his fellow Jews a series of "broadcasts" predicting an imminent Allied victory and hasty liberation, the ghetto suicide rate drops. Like Rumkowski's policy, and like the various forms of cultural and spiritual resistance, Jacob's good news keeps the ghetto dwellers hopeful and cooperative. The novel presents Jacob's activity as a form of resistance to enforced muteness, a resistance whose efficacy and meaningfulness the novel ultimately challenges. The novel ends with the ghetto's liquidation. The narrator—sole survivor of Jacob's transport—learns what the author, a Lodz Ghetto survivor, and the reader have known all along: that fabricated broadcasts prove no match for history. The confabulated narrative of hope that Jacob produced for the ghetto masked but could not ultimately displace the narrative of destruction. Neither the hopes of the ghetto nor the regrets of the author nor the wishes of the reader can alter the ending of the story. The narrator feels betrayed by his own eagerness for Jacob's false comfort, by his own acquiescence in the silencing of truth.

I n a private manuscript prepared for his family, a survivor of Mengele's medical "experiments" at Auschwitz warns,

> Be very, very careful, for we are prone to forgetting fast. That which our ancestors suffered in Egypt today has become only a few minutes' hasty reading of the Hagada in anticipation that the matzos dumplings are to appear on the table as soon as possible.

Rather than transmitting meaning, ritual retelling can empty the story of meaning, can render it mute without actually silencing its voice. Many survivors share the fear that the Holocaust will suffer in the retelling, that it will come to future readers as a prepackaged "event," that the public has grown tired of reading the Holocaust, and that nothing will change. In the seder ceremony, "remembering" ancestral suffering may turn into a kind of forgetting.[10]

The Haggadah, however, contains not only the story of the Israelites' deliverance from oppression, but the story of descendants who transmit the story. So absorbed are they in the telling that they continue until the call for morning prayers. As participants in the seder, we too take our place in an unbroken (if diminished) chain of transmission. If we cannot—as the Haggadah commands—see ourselves as though personally liberated from Egypt, that very inability serves to remind us of our own distance from slavery and, consequently, to remember both oppression and deliverance. How do we hear—and then tell—the stories of the Holocaust in a manner that will stave off forgetfulness? How do we take up the burden of testimony without denying the Holocaust a real place in our memory and our thoughts? The written shards of ghetto life offer us a means not of reconstituting the entire story of the Holocaust, but of thinking it. Though disparate, taken together they help us to look at the Holocaust not as an Event but as a series of daily events, experienced by people whose writing survived the destruction, and people whose writing was destroyed, and people who did not write at all. In combination with survivor testimony, they recollect a painful and terrible past in a way that neither domesticates nor falsifies.

4

The Mute Language
of Brutality

You whom I could not save
Listen to me.
Try to understand this
    simple speech as I would
    be ashamed of another.
I swear, there is in me
    no wizardry of words.
I speak to you with
    silence like a cloud or
a tree.
    —Czeslaw Milosz,
    "Dedication"

In *The Painted Bird*, Jerzy Kosinski utilizes the perspective of a mute protagonist to put words to something usually kept outside the boundaries of language: the experience of a self undone by atrocity, told from the perspective of the undone self. As an object of ongoing atrocity, the protagonist's narration comes from outside the linguistic system, outside of the self-defining and world-defining power of words.

A grotesque turn of the picaresque, *The Painted Bird* traces the desperate meanderings of a six-year-old Eastern European boy during the war years. Entrusted in 1939 by his anti-Nazi (and hence, endangered) parents to the care of "a man traveling eastward" (1), the boy—whose name remains undisclosed—soon finds himself alone and on his own in a hostile, dangerous countryside. He wanders from village to benighted village, seeking shelter from the harsh elements and refuge from SS roundups. With the fair-haired local peasants, who regard his ominously dark complexion with superstitious as well as political fear, he strikes a series of shaky alliances. He survives all peril but emerges at the war's end deeply scarred psychologically and unable to speak. The boy's loss of speech forms the structural and symbolic center of the novel, while its recovery constitutes the novel's ambiguous and much-debated ending.[1] These two events focus our attention on the significance of speech and language in the novel as a whole.

In her work on torture and its effects, Elaine Scarry observes that "its resistance to language is not simply . . . incidental or accidental attributes" of atrocity but an inherent constituent of its transaction (5). "World, self, and voice are lost," Scarry notes, "or nearly lost, through the intense pain of torture. . . ." (35). Scarry's insistence on seeing as an integral component of torture the enforced muting of the narrating subject reinforces the observations of clinicians and researchers working with posttraumatic stress. From his therapeutic work with Shoah survivors, Henry Krystal comes to understand living through extreme atrocity as "so incompatible with the survival of the self that it is 'destroyed.' No trace of a registration of any kind is left in the psyche; instead, a void, a hole is formed" ("Integration" 114). By its nature, the intense pain of atrocity works against the possibilities of its being placed into words.

Scarry's work also suggests something more: that the muteness of the survivor is not merely the aftereffect of atrocity. Destroying the victim's voice is its desired outcome, its aim. "The goal of the torturer is to make the one, the body, emphatically and crushing *present* by destroying it, and to make the other, the voice, *absent* by destroying it" (49). The silencing of the victim affirms that the perpetrator possesses all the power, and the victim none. As Michel Foucault observes, ". . . speech is no mere verbalization of conflicts and systems of domination . . . it is the very object of man's conflicts" (216).

In *The Painted Bird*, Kosinski makes of muteness itself a witness to the conditions that imposed it. By the emplotment of the novel, the internal monologues of the speechless boy, and the imagery which stands in where the boy's language falters or his cognitive abilities fail, Kosinski gives the "void" a frame, so that its contours may be explored. Julia Kristeva sees in the "ruptures, blank spaces, and holes" of language and narrative "the sign of a force that has not been grasped by the linguistic or ideological system. . . ." (165). In considering the boy's speechlessness not only as the aim and effect of atrocity but also as a speech act—the only one possible under the sign of genocide, Kosinski also frames the boy's muteness, so that its edges and boundaries define a topography different from the muteness of perpetrators. In limning the boy's speechlessness, Kosinski works toward a poetics of atrocity.

If Walt Whitman, in a moment of artistic uncertainty beside the ocean of life, hears "peals of distant ironical laughter at every word I have written,"[2] what of the poet who lives beneath the shadow of the factories of death? A tension permeates this body of literature, born of the conflicts and contradictions inherent in the writing. From this ironic tension emerges the mute witness, with his silent testimony whose muteness echoes both the victim's terror at the moment of experience and the author's frustration years later. As victims, Kosinski and poet Nelly Sachs, for example, struggled with aphasia brought on by their encounters with atrocity during the Third Reich.[3] As authors, they—like many others—refrained from setting into print their recollections of the concentrationary universe until years after the war's end and their own liberation. Like the narrator of Semprun's novel *The Long Voyage*, they seem to have decided "never again to talk about this voyage. . . . at least a long period of silence, years of silence about this voyage" (105) to the deathcamp, discouraged, they tell us again and again, by the enormity and impossibility of the task.

In an "Afterword" to *The Painted Bird*, Kosinski explains that he wrote the novel in order "to examine 'this new language' of brutality and its consequent new counter-language of anguish and despair" (256). Yet, notes George Steiner in *Language and Silence*, for what Kosinski attempts to describe, "The right speech [is] . . . often a close neighbor to silence" (21). Thus, at the center of his search for a "new language," Kosinski places a mute boy, the nameless protagonist of *The Painted Bird*.

As Kosinski's narrative unfolds, language functions not so much as a means of communication but as a way of marking difference, an exclusionary tool by which one calibrates social acceptability and worthiness for living. For the boy, language becomes the emblem of difference, a difference that is negatively valenced. The peasants whom the boy encounters regard all difference with fear, mistrust, and hostility. For this reason, the boy's aphasia comes as no surprise; by the time he loses the power of speech in Chapter 11, he has already learned to be wary of words, to consider them carefully, and to mete them out parsimoniously. Early on, he discovers that his urban, educated speech pattern sets him apart from the peasants and their regional dialects—a dangerous distinction under the circumstances. His first guardian mutters constantly "in a language I could not quite understand" (3); the peasants in the second village where he seeks shelter speak "in a dialect unknown to me" (14). All his efforts to communicate meet with frustration and rejection: "I tried to tell them something, but my language and the manner in which I spoke it only made them giggle" (15) The boy's perception of his own difference from the peasants comes out of this growing sense of linguistic difference. Later on, he finds himself under the dubious protection of a farmer who orders him to "display my urban language" to the "convulsed" amusement of the local peasantry (85). But for those in hiding from the German forces during the Nazi era—fugitives who desperately needed to blend in—marks of difference were no laughing matter. Often Jews whose physical appearance could "pass" as Aryan feigned muteness lest their Jewish (or otherwise foreign) accent give away their displacement and their cover.[4] The boy, for all his tender years no less hunted than his elders, realizes the danger inherent in his every utterance.

While the boy is not necessarily Jewish, the otherness implied by his linguistic difference links him with the Jew, who signifies the Other. For the peasants, the boy observes,

> were people of slow, deliberate speech who measured their words carefully. Their custom required them to spare words as one spares salt, and a loose tongue was regarded as a man's worst enemy. Fast talkers were thought devious and dishonest, obviously trained by Jewish and Gypsy fortune tellers. (85)

The peasants see Jews as slick, fast-talking entrepreneurs, possessors of a keen and dangerous linguistic ability with which they manipulate others but which, in turn, gives them away. When a Jewish girl found by the peasants after her escape from a sealed freight car bound for an extermination camp "babbled in a language no one could understand" (106), the boy finds the similarity more than a bit unnerving. Although neither Jew nor Gypsy, the boy is constantly mistaken for both. The boy goes into hiding because of his parents' political, rather than racial, legacy. Of course, anti-Nazi activists had their own good reasons to watch their words—but for content rather than accent; Bruno Bettelheim recalls a saying current during the Nazi era: "Lieber Gott, mach mich stumm, dass ich nicht nach Dachau kumm" (85) [Dear God, make me mute, so I don't go to Dachau]. But in the case of the Jews and Gypsies, not *what* they said but the very act of speaking betrays them. For his own safety, then, to mask his difference, the boy begins to measure his words, just as he later shaves his head to eliminate his telltale, Gypsy-black (or Jewish-black) hair and attain a measure of invisibility. In a sense, muteness becomes his vocation.

The boy's inappropriate speech also marks discontinuity with his past—a linguistic discontinuity that signals his removal from sources of security, identity, and order. His subsequent muteness—the somatic manifestation of wordless horror—embodies the rupture that atrocity works in his life—a rupture severing him from his past, from his family, and from possibilities of meaning. In the second half of the novel, the boy attempts to interpret the significance of that muteness and to make sense of the other disasters that befall him. His speechlessness brings with it an immediate sense of meaninglessness which continues to plague him for the rest of the novel. When the boy loses his voice, the best system of meanings he has been able to construct collapses. The boy drops the heavy missal at a local Corpus Christi procession, incurring the violent wrath of the peasantry. Ritual torment devised by the boy's current "guardian"—a sadistic farmer who suspends him by his arms for hours on end, dangling within reach of the vicious and deadly jaws of the farmer's dog—leaves the boy too weakened to bear the missal as charged. As the boy crumples beneath its weight, so does the ordering principle he has imagined governing his universe—"the ruling pattern of the world . . . revealed to me with beautiful clarity" (131).

This pattern centers on accumulation of "indulgences"—prayers that "have an immediate influence" on one's life. Seeking to understand and control the chaotic and painful events of his life, the boy amasses "days of indulgence" in the eyes of the Lord, by an almost constant recitation of these prayers in the months preceding Corpus Christi. He concludes that his own heretofore ill fortune resulted from a deficit in some heavenly account.

> I saw in my mind the unending heavenly pastures full of bins, some big and bulging with days of indulgence, others small and almost empty. Elsewhere I could see unused bins to accommodate those who, like myself, had not yet discovered the value of prayer.
> I stopped blaming others; the fault was mine alone, I thought. I had been too stupid to find the governing principle of the world of people, animals and events. (132)

For the boy, religious worship amounts to formulaic speech with magical powers. He sees prayers as strings of words—whose sense does not concern him—which must be recited aloud (or at least muttered) to be effective. Meaning inheres not in the word, but in the act of utterance. Just as earlier the peasants react not to what the boy says but to his manner of speaking, here the boy concerns himself with the form (and formality) of prayer, rather than its contents. Desperate to make sense of his world, the boy predicates his system of meanings on mean-inglessness. In his imagery, the prayers themselves turn into hollowed-out objects, empty of meaning themselves, but capable of filling the empty and unused receptacles that await them. For months the boy frantically recites high-scoring prayers continuously, "almost seeing their pile constantly rising until some of the saints, stopping on their strolls through the heavenly pastures, look approvingly at the flocks of prayers soaring up from earth. . . ." (134). In the boy's imagination, spoken words become concretized and tangible; however, they do not increase in meaning. Instead, in their meaninglessness they displace their utterers. The saints tend "flocks" of prayers, not of people. While the boy thinks he has acquired divine and kindly foster parents, his vision rehearses his own abandonment.

The hollowness of that vision, and its true import for the boy, become clear to him on Corpus Christi. Because on that day "the bodily presence of the Son of God would make itself felt in the church more than on any other feast" (141), he confidently fights his way past the hostile peasants to reap the rewards of his diligence. Asked unexpect-edly to serve as altar boy, the boy feels relieved, reassured, certain of his salvation.

> A hot wave swept over me. I looked at the sky. At last someone up there had noticed me. They saw my prayers lying in a huge heap like potatoes piled high at harvest time. In a moment I would be close to Him, at His altar, within the protection of His vicar. This was only a beginning. From now on a different life would begin for me. I had seen the end of terror that shakes one until it squeezes the stomach empty of vomit, like a punctured poppy pod blown open by the wind. (142)

In the boy's anticipation of success, the full pile of prayers contrasts with the stomach emptied by terror. But when he drops the missal, the emptiness (for him, the inefficacy) of the "indulgences" becomes linked with the emptiness of terror. Not only words but utterance itself proves meaningless. Before the crowd of peasants, already vengefully distrustful of the "Gypsy vampire," seize him roughly and attempt to eject him from the Church, the boy gives out "an involuntary shout" (144). This last sound to emerge from his throat for a long time effec-tively empties him of words just as "terror . . . squeezes the stomach empty of vomit." Once outside the Church, carried by the peasants and fearing the worst, he finds he cannot utter a single syllable. "I wanted to cry and beg for mercy, but no sound came from my throat. I tried once more. There was no voice in me" (145). When both word and utterance become emptied of meaning, he becomes empty of word and utterance. The divine betrayal and human cruelty, the cumulative terrors he has experienced since parting from his parents, prove too horrible for expression, even by a scream. The prototype for that terror stricken, betrayed muteness lies earlier in the novel in the boy's recollection of a bombing he witnessed long ago near his parents home: "Only one old woman came up from the dark pit . . . when her toothless mouth opened to speak she was suddenly unable to utter a sound" (75). As the boy notes, regarding mutes, "There were not very many of them and their absence of speech made them seem very much alike" (147). The boy himself later acquires a friend, a *doppelgänger* known only as the Silent One, whose significance we shall later examine. The boy's loss of the power of speech, and his concomitant loss of faith in language's ability to bestow meaning, anticipates a turning point—one of several—in his conception of the cosmos and in his system of values.

From the church the peasants hurl the boy deep into a large, full, and foul manure pit—a brackish baptism into a silent, unremittingly sadistic world. Interestingly, Lena Wertmuller uses this same fetid plunge—an apt image for the sordid world that the Nazis created and termed "anus mundi"—as one of the crucial events in her film *Seven Beauties*. In Wertmuller's film, Pedro, a "failed anarchist" incarcerated in a concentration camp as a political prisoner, rebels against the cruel Nazi regimen. Unlike the boy, Pedro "becomes a symbol of strength and freedom in this pointless race toward the barracks and the latrines" (329). SS machine guns kill him, "the brown liquid closing in on this free man's body" (330). Although Wertmuller portrays Pedro's action with more than a hint of cynicism—Pasqualino, the wormlike protagonist of the film, earlier terms rebellion "a meaningless suicide . . . they would have shot us in the guts. . . ." (273)—she admires Pedro's moral courage and unvanquished spirit much as she fears its futility. Such rebellion has become increasingly difficult, even impossible, Wertmuller suggests, in a world where the Pasqualinos, and not the Pedros, survive. And survive Pasqualino does, just as Kosinski's boy survives his ghastly experience. Unlike Pedro, the boy neither enters nor emerges from the excrement a free being, capable of moral choices. Rather, he emerges into a moral chaos out of which he tries to forge a new order.

Only upon his emergence from the cesspool does the boy fully grasp what has befallen him. "Suddenly I realized that something had happened to my voice. I turned to cry out, but my tongue flapped helplessly in my open mouth. I had no voice" (146). As irretrievably lost as his voice, his faith in the church, in a benevolent ruler of the universe, in prayer, collapses, leaving a void he knows not how to fill. He puzzles, "There must have been some cause for the loss of my speech. Some greater force, with which I had not managed to communicate, commanded my destiny. I began to doubt that it could be God or one of His saints" (147). Not long afterward, he begins to piece together a new schema, a new cosmic hierarchy. Not the God of the church but some malevolent deities control the world. Since the church claims speech—"indulgences" and the Word that was God—as its domain, the true masters must claim speechlessness, with the boy's muteness a sign of his election: "The Evil Ones were interested in me at last. To train me in hatred they had first separated me from my parents, then . . . robbed me of my speech. . . ." (165). And, indeed, in the confusion that immediately follows the war, his muteness endears him to black marketeers and other members of the underworld who "regarded my being mute as an asset which ensured my discretion when I carried out my missions" (246). But, although the boy links speech with church morality and impotence, and muteness with evil and power, the narrative itself resists these categories of meaning.

While the boy struggles to interpret and to find meaning in muteness, the narrative suggests that the foreclosure of speech also forecloses the possibilities of meaning and interpretation. Indeed, the boy's interpretations of muteness seem so absurd that they impel the reader past them and toward what the boy experiences, observes, registers and records. As we turn repeatedly from the narrator, who interprets, to the narrative, which leaves pending the interpretive act, we encounter afresh the rupture engendered by the Holocaust, and the impossibility of closure with the trauma of atrocity.

In one sense, the boy's muteness represents just another of the many mutilations that occur as gratuitous cruelties in *The Painted Bird*, similar in that respect to a brutal episode in Piotr Rawicz's novel *Blood from the Sky*. In the Rawicz novel, a young boy in a besieged ghetto sticks out his tongue to express his utter disdain for a Nazi roundup unit. Incensed by the child's insolence, the SS punish him by cutting out his tongue. This ghastly action signals the start of a gory massacre of small children discovered hiding in a makeshift classroom—all under the eyes of the unprotesting Jewish narrator. In both Kosinski's and Rawicz's accounts, the mutilations serve to represent atrocities far more brutal than those depicted and to mark, through the silence of the protagonist, the helpless silence of ghetto and concentration camp victims. In *The Painted Bird*, the boy must watch—sometimes unwillingly participate in—a series of horrible mutilations performed upon both people and animals. In rapid sequence, he witnesses the incineration of a friendly squirrel (chapter 1), the application of hot pokers as "treatment" to a child's gangrenous leg (chapter 2), the gouging of eyes (chapter 4), the mauling to death of feeble-minded woman, the pecking to death of a bird by its flock (chapter 5). Although Kosinski has been criticized for the excessive cruelty in his works, even a casual reading of accounts of the Nazi era reveals that actual events surpassed Kosinski's fiction in cruelty and ferocity. More important, for our purposes, Kosinski does not insert scenes of cruelty gratuitously. These scenes, interwoven into a cohesive backdrop, imprint themselves onto the consciousness of both the boy and the reader. The cruelty to animals comments upon and amplifies the treatment of humans and shapes the way the boy perceives the world and himself. In addition, they enable Kosinski to circumvent the reader's psychic numbness and to force the reader to react constantly to the raw material presented.

In *Notes of the Author on "The Painted Bird," 1965*, Kosinski explains his use of this textual device, the "natural subplot" whereby he establishes a parallel between human and animal action. Kosinski cites, as an example, the blinding episode in the miller's house (chapter 4). Along with the plowboy whom he suspects of carrying on an affair with his wife, the miller brings home a tomcat for his estrous female cat. The feline "courtship" and copulation create a sexual undercurrent that the miller wishes to exploit—he hopes it will force his errant wife and her lover to betray their suspected liaison. Here, notes Kosinski, this device is "double used," by the miller and by the author. In this way, by presenting images and then representing them in analogous forms, the author creates a system of symbols in the novel, pointing toward "the unstated behavioral and psychological analogy between character and animal" (18). In the final analysis, the analogy repeatedly breaks down in Kosinski's narrative because the actions of man and beast do not balance out. In Kosinski's narrative, the animals do not behave "bestially" in the way that the people do. The animals rarely inflict pain; in fact, they do so only upon human instigation—as when the sadistic farmer incites his dog to kill the boy or when another farmer hitches two strong horses to choke a third, maimed horse. While the peasants surpass the beasts in cruelty, the dumb, tormented animals function as alter egos of the mute boy. They correspond, as well, to the other silent victims who people the periphery of the novel—those sealed in the freight cars that cross the countryside, those whose ashes send "cold sweat" pouring down the boy's back (111).

Even before losing his ability to speak, the boy sees himself as a dumb animal, victimized with no possible appeal. Early in the narrative he befriends a squirrel who releases him from his loneliness. When a gang of older boys, for their amusement, capture the squirrel, pour gasoline over it and ignite it, the boy can only look on helplessly at his friend's anguish. Not long afterward, when the boy himself becomes the victim of a boisterous crowd's cruel idea of entertainment, he chooses the image of the squirrel to describe himself: "I hopped around like a squirrel while he continued whipping me" (15). In this way, the boy develops for himself a private set of symbols drawn from his encounters with animals. As he unconsciously begins to identify with them, speech becomes superfluous. Thus when he finally becomes mute, he completes the identification. But the significance of the animal imagery goes beyond the immediate experience of the boy, beyond what he can see or know. For—and herein lies the novel's dramatic irony—Kosinski (and his reader) recognize allusions that the boy does not.

Underlying Kosinski's novel, grounding it in time and place even while the narrative reaches toward the mythic dimension, hints of the historical reality seep through. As private and limited as is the boy's vision (appropriate to his age like the children's perceptions in Ilse Aichinger's novel *Herod's Children*), it still offers enough information for the reader to locate it historically, to fill in what the boy leaves out. Like Rawicz in *Blood from the Sky*, Kosinski moves back and forth between vagueness and specificity. While Kosinski situates his protagonist in an unnamed Eastern European country (reminiscent of the antihistoricity of Rawicz's epilogue), in the "Afterword" to *The Painted Bird*, Kosinski discusses a particular country

> in which most of the extermination camps had been located . . . between 1939 and 1945 only a million people had died as the result of direct military action, but five and a half million had been exterminated by the invaders. Over three million victims were Jews, and one third of them were under sixteen. These losses worked out to two hundred and twenty deaths per thousand people, and no one would ever be able to compute how many others were mutilated, traumatized, broken in health or spirit. (254)

Thus Kosinski's boy does not wander through mythic time and place but through a particular historic moment in a particularly brutal country. The "mutilated, traumatized, broken in health or spirit" occasionally make their way into the boy's narrative: the Jewish girl, raped and torn apart after her escape from a freight car, the small boy hurled by his parents from another freight car and found broken and bruised by the peasants who steal his shoes and clothing and then leave him to die. More often, however, the victims are represented in the novel symbolically, primarily through the agency of dumb, victimized animals.

When the boy finds an emaciated, maimed horse abandoned by its owner, he coaxes the horse to walk to the nearest village on its broken leg. "I spoke to him about the warm stable, the smell of the hay, and I assured him that a man could set his bone and heal it with herbs" (82). After protecting the limping animal from a pack of hostile dogs, the boy restores it to its grateful owner, who decides to kill it. The farmer's two healthy horses, hitched to a rope that will choke the invalid one, "looked with indifference at the victim." For his part, the boy feels guilty of a deception, of complicity in the horse's death. "I stood wondering how I could save his life, how I could convince him that I had no idea that I would be bringing him back to the farm for this" (84). Under the Nazi regime, people, too, were coaxed to their death with sweet and alluring false promises. The scene evokes the atmosphere of the concentration camp, tinged with death and guilt.[5] The indifference of the healthy horses to the plight of the maimed one echoes the peasants' lack of remorse for their treatment of the boy and other fugitives.

While the dumbness of the maimed horse links him with silent victims, unable to speak out on their own behalf, the dumbness of the two strong horses associate them with the silent collaborator, unwilling to speak out on anyone else's behalf. To make the parallel with the concentrationary universe more complete, the boy learns that the owner plans to use the horse meat for food, and "a hide for tanning, and bones for medicinal purposes" (83), a reminder of the way the Nazis stockpiled and utilized every possible part of their victims' bodies—gold teeth, hair for blankets, skin for parchment and lampshades, ashes for fertilizer. The use of an animal analogue to Nazi atrocity does not evoke the unbearable horror that repels the nurses in Semprun's *The Long Voyage* when faced with the putrid corpses in the crematorium courtyard; neither does it call up psychic numbness as does actual film footage of skeletons, living and dead, both before and after liberation. Kosinski's narrative moves from the animal to the human, inducing a cumulative effect. The boy later hears the "strange tales" of the concentration camps:

> . . . after leaving the train the Jews were sorted into different groups, then stripped naked and deprived of all their possessions. Their hair was cut off, apparently for use in mattresses. The Germans also looked at their teeth, and if there were any gold ones they were immediately pulled out. (99)

The reader feels that the event described has occurred before repeatedly; it resonates with the fate of the mutilated horse.

When a group of peasants discover a Jewish child flung, the boy surmises, from the train by the child's parents, the narrator projects onto the anonymous Jewish child the same feelings as he does onto the horse.

> When he was tossed out of the train his parents or his friends no doubt assured him that he would find human help which would save him from a horrible death in the great furnace. He probably felt cheated, deceived. He would have preferred to cling to the warm bodies of his father and mother in the packed car, to feel the pressure and smell, the hot tart odors, the presence of other people, knowing that he was not alone, told by everyone that the journey was only a misunderstanding. (102–3)

The boy ignores his own resemblance to the child—receiving false assurances from now-distant parents. The other child's physical resemblance to him poses an actual threat to his own safety; he fears lest someone associate him with these damned people on account of his black hair and then turn him over to the Germans. Thus, the boy disowns a kindred spirit and rejoices at his death. "Although I regretted the boy's tragedy, at the bottom of my mind lurked a feeling of relief that he was dead" (103). Here too, the boy's inner betrayal of the other child evokes the bitter choices (or nonchoices) of the ghetto and concentration camp, where people sometimes survived by denying (and dooming) friends and family.[6]

Most chilling of all in this succession of brutality, no humane feelings emerge to temper the unrelenting cruelty. The indifference with which people view the suffering of animals reflects the sangfroid, even merriment, with which they regard human anguish—an association especially significant in evoking a system that "exterminated" Jewish "vermin" by means of an insecticide.[7] Notice the cumulative effect of three sequential scenes. The partisans' shooting of a friendly stray dog and the horse owner's behavior toward the doomed horse resonate in the boy's encounter with a detachment of German soldiers. The first two animal scenes render the third all the more painful, poignant, and hopeless.

> I felt now like the mangy dog that the partisans had killed. They had first stroked his head and scratched him behind the ears. The dog, overwhelmed with joy, yapped with love

and gratitude. Then they tossed him a bone. He ran after it, wagging his scruffy tail, scaring the butterflies and trampling the flowers. When he seized the bone and proudly lifted it, they shot him. (76)

When the farmer approached the horse to check the position of the noose, the cripple suddenly turned his head and licked the farmer's face. The man did not look at him, but gave him a powerful, open-handed slap on the muzzle. The horse turned away, hurt and humiliated. (84)

A few of the soldiers surrounded me. They pointed at me, laughed or grew serious. One of them walked up close to me, leaned over, and smiled straight in my face with a warm, loving smile. I was going to smile back when he suddenly punched me very hard in the stomach. I lost my breath and fell, gasping and groaning. The soldiers burst into laughter. (114)

While the boy does not share the fate of the two animals, his sense of their humiliation deepens his own, and the depiction of their deaths suggest that the boy, too, may be murdered. When the boy's squirrel goes up in flames, the village boys responsible "looked on, laughing" (6). The peasant women who torment Stupid Ludmila "to the accompaniment of raucous laughter and loud encouragement" only "looked on calmly" as one woman deals Ludmila "the final deadly blow" (54). *Lebensunwertes Leben* [life unworthy of life]—Jews and Gypsies, for example—managing to escape SS actions looks in vain for "human help which would save him from a horrible death. . . ." (102). At the hands of the peasants such unworthy life would receive only further humiliation and torment. In Kosinski's narrative, the peasants rape these victims, steal their meager possessions, and finally kill them or turn them over to the Germans for extermination. Understandably, the boy concludes that

the more harm, misery, injury, and bitterness a man could inflict on those around him, the more help he could expect. If he shrank from inflicting harm on others, if he succumbed to emotions of love, friendship and compassion, he would immediately become weaker and his own life would have to absorb the suffering and defeats that he spared the others. . . . What mattered was that a man should consciously promote evil, find pleasure in harming others, nurturing and using the diabolical powers granted him by the Evil Ones in a manner calculated to cause as much misery and suffering around him as possible. (158)

If speech typically distinguishes man from lower forms of life, the boy loses his power of speech in part because speech has lost its humanizing purpose.

Rather, in Kosinski's narrative, speech invites and incites atrocity—illustrated not only by the boy's experiences, but by the central image of the novel, the painted bird. The novel's title refers to a sadistic diversion devised by one of the boy's "protectors," bird-catcher Lekh. To ward off recurrent despair, Lekh selects one of his birds and, with "stinking paints of different colors," he paints "its wings, head, and breast in rainbow hues . . . more dappled and vivid than a bouquet of wildflowers" (49). Released to rejoin its flock in the center of the forest, the bird soars

> happy and free, a spot of rainbow against the backdrop of clouds, and then plunge[s] into the waiting brown flock. . . . The painted bird circled from one end of the flock to the other, vainly trying to convince its kin that it was one of them. But, dazzled by its brilliant colors, they flew around it unconvinced. The painted bird would be forced farther and farther away . . . one bird after another would peel off in a fierce attack. Shortly the many-hued shape lost its place in the sky and dropped to the ground. (50)

Like other animal-human analogues in the novel, the bird's experience echoes and anticipates that of the boy.[8] Virtually identical with the rest of the species, the bird is set apart by physical difference ("rainbow hues") arbitrarily applied. While the bird perceives itself as part of the flock, the look-alike flock sees him as an interloper threatening the integrity of the group. They ward off his approach in order to ensure the purity of the flock. The boy, too, initially seeks out the companionship of his species; like the bird he is set apart from a homogeneous (fair-complexioned) group by the arbitrary marking of coloration (his dark hair and eyes). Unlike the bird, the boy survives because he recognizes finally the difference that the peasants assert between himself and the group.

The link between the painted bird image and the human experience impresses itself on the boy immediately, and subtly, in a way he can neither articulate consciously nor analyze but which shapes his narrative and the images he subsequently chooses to describe himself and others. Later on, he makes the association even more explicit: "I suddenly felt like Lekh's painted bird, which some unknown force was pulling toward his kind" (241). Ironically, this association comes to the boy not when he lives among the peasants but when he rejoins his parents after the war. In the chapter where he first introduces the painted bird, the boy recounts the fate of Ludmila, a feeble-minded, primitive and lusty woman, the object of Lekh's passion, who seduces the men of the village. Lekh's songs feature her as a "strange colored bird flying to faraway worlds, free and quick" (48). The bird, identical in every way but color, pecked to death; the boy, different linguistically and physically, tormented and treated as dangerous; the woman, savage, insane, hypersexual, brutally killed by the other women: the three images taken together define the Other. They link up with images in anti-Semitic propaganda of the Reich and with racial thinking generally; they seem to threaten the integrity and survival of the group and of the individuals who comprise it. As such, they mirror the Nazi obsession with racial purity and fear of racial contamination.[9]

The boy forfeits his power of speech as he forfeits his ability to define himself. Like Sartre's idea of the European Jew, defined from without by the anti-Semitic attitudes of others, the boy configures his identity in reaction to the responses of the people he encounters. Unable to define himself, he cannot tell his own story. Initially, his sense of himself derives from his feeling of attachment to his parents—a feeling that rapidly erodes. In the very first sentence of his narrative, he awaits them anxiously, "expecting my parents to come for me any day, any hour" (3). Before long, however, while still at the hut of Marta, his first guardian, his certitude wavers. "I wondered whether my parents would ever find me again" (9). Fleeing Marta's burning hut, lost and alone, he appeals in his crisis to his parents.

> I believed that now I would meet my parents in the ravine. I believed that, even far away, they must know all that had happened to me. Wasn't I their child? What were parents for if not to be with their children in times of danger? (12)

The response, appropriate to an abandoned and frightened six-year-old child, also reflects the way in which victims of Nazi persecution denied evidence of their own deadly situation, clinging fiercely to a belief in some sort of imminent salvation. In Ladislav Fuk's *Mr. Theodor Mundstock*, the protagonist blandly assures his friends that "there aren't any transports going to Lodz and aren't going to be any" (2). He himself draws comfort from his preparedness for the ordeals of the concentration camp; ultimately, however, he meets with a fatal and freak accident before even boarding the transport train. The boy in Kosinski's novel cannot hang on to his denial for very long: "Just in case they [parents] should be coming near, I called out to them. But no one answered" (12). Thus, he must confront "The monstrous idea that my parents were not here, would not be here. . . ." (13). When next he finds himself frightened and alone, not the memory of his parents but that of his second protectress, Olga, comforts him: "I remembered the two things, which according to Olga, were necessary for survival without human help" (27). In fact, he transfers his hope of some magical assistance from his parents to Olga: "I had nothing to fear. Some unknown force, either from above or within myself, was leading me unerringly back to old Olga" (32).

As Olga displaces the boy's parents in his emotional construct, the externally imposed definition of self that she represents displaces the nascent authentic self developing in the boy at home. Much of what he brings with him into exile causes him pain. The fables and children's rhymes he has preciously memorized presumably earned him praise at home; they are traces of a former order and way of being. When he recites them for the peasants, they pour burning vodka down his throat and laugh at him. Their physical power over the helpless boy gives Olga and subsequent protectors the ability to define him. They do so in terms of their own projections, based on deep fears of death and disintegration. Marta tells him that disease comes "from a pair of black eyes set close to a hawk nose. Such eyes, known as Gypsy or witches' eyes, could bring crippling illness, plague or death" (7). Olga confirms this, elaborates: "Such a darkling as I, possessed by this evil spirit, could be recognized by his bewitched black eyes . . . I could stare at other people and unknowingly cast a spell over them" (18). The boy begins to absorb the way others perceive him, seeing himself through their eyes and adopting their definitions. He takes great care not to stare directly at anyone, lest he cause their death. Told later in the narrative "that my black hair would attract lightning" (57) to his host's farm, he blames himself when lightning does, in fact, strike. "I believed that my hair had attracted the lightning to the barn and huts. . . ." (60). In *Difference and Pathology*, an exploration of the functions and mechanisms of stereotyping, Sandor Gilman explains what underlies these projections and the boy's acceptance of them. "The group is embodied with all the positive associations of the self. . . . The Other is therefore both ill and infectious, both damaged and damaging. . . . the image of the dangerous Other serves both as the focus for the projection of anxiety concerning the self and as the means by which the Other defines itself" (120–30). Through the relationship of the peasants to the boy, Kosinski's novel explores in microcosm the stereotyping and scapegoating that characterized the racial thinking of the Third Reich and that culminated in the extermination camps, designed to neutralize the dangerous Other and protect the German body politic.

Because of his youth and powerlessness, the boy readily yields over to adults the power to shape his identity. Like the nameless monster of Mary Shelley's *Frankenstein*, the unnamed boy molds his self-perception to fit the fears of those who surround him. As in the case of the monster, the inability to put forth one's own story places one at the mercy of the projections of others. To give voice to one's story is to generate meaning; to listen to another's story is to affirm the other's autonomy. Shelley's monster gains the sympathy only of those few who do not first see him, prejudge him, and silence him. The boy's muteness leaves him storyless like the monster and convinced of his own monstrousness. This storylessness reflects the peasants' refusal to hear in him the authentic voice of the Other. It marks, instead, their insistence on judging him solely by the measure of his difference. The black magical abilities projected onto the boy also reflect a line of Christian theology that equates the Jew with the anti-Christ, endowed with powerful and dark satanic powers.[10] The peasants tell the boy that "the Lord was using the Germans" to punish the Jews" (99) who

> had to perish by fire, suffering the torments of hell here on earth. They were being justly punished for the shameful crimes of their ancestors, for refuting the only True Faith, for mercilessly killing Christian babies and drinking their blood. (100)[11]

In *The Informed Heart*, Bruno Bettelheim suggests that this fear of the Jew's mythical, magical power to inflict great harm enabled the SS to define their own murderous activity as self-defense. Maintaining this vision of the Other is predicated upon excluding the voice of the Other. When the boy encounters SS men in their glittering uniforms, he no longer believes in his own perceptions. Instead, he internalizes the Nazi view of him, and sees himself through their eyes as a dirty subhuman. "I felt like a squashed caterpillar oozing in the dust. . . ." (119). Blank to the point of anonymity, this nameless being puts forth no words of his own.

C losely linked with the power of speech, eyes also figure importantly in the novel. Muteness and speech are complexly interwoven with blindness and sight, because to witness implies both to see (to be an eyewitness) and to speak (to bear witness). The perpetrators of the Nazi genocide could not see Jews as people like themselves; they did not witness against atrocity while it was occurring, nor later. Survivors, on the other hand, initially silenced by what they have seen, bear witness both by speaking out and remaining silent. Survivor muteness witnesses; it constitutes a form of testimony, uncovering a trace of what was endured. In the context of Holocaust testimonies, muteness is not merely as the absence of speech, its polar opposite. Rather, muteness comprises a speech act whose context, (non)speaker, and frame enable us to interpret it. In *The Painted Bird*, muteness is coupled with belated utterance just as blindness is coupled with belated insight.

The narrative focuses on the boy's dark eyes because, like his unusual and unsettling speech pattern, their color marks him as Other. Their presumed power of bewitchment valences this Otherness. In addition, like speech, eyes are crucial to the boy's subsequent role of witness. An early blinding episode prefigures the boy's muteness and amplifies its significance. In a graphic and gory scene, the miller—another of the boy's "protectors"—gouges out the eyes of a plowboy, rumored to be carrying on an affair with the miller's wife. The scene resonates with the blindings in both *Oedipus Rex* and *King Lear*—associations that bear on our understanding of the boy's curious role of mute witness.

The imagery and sequence of action in the blinding scene of the novel resembles the progression of the parallel scene in *King Lear*, a confluence that Lawrence Langer has also noted.[12] The deliberate vengefulness of the perpetrator, the drawn out interval that separates the loss of the first eye from the destruction of the second, sustain the horrifying effect of both scenes, a connection Kosinski makes explicit through the confluence of language and action. "Out, vile jelly! / Where is thy lustre now?" (3,6:83–84), cries Cornwall, and he steps on Gloucester's eyes. The miller steps on the plowboy's eyes, leaving "only a crushed bit of jelly. . . ." (38). An air of illicit sensuality, of adultery, pervades both scenes: Gloucester betrayed by his bastard son Edmund, butt of Gloucester's off-color humor at the start of the play; the miller responding to his wife's adulterous betrayal. The miller transgresses an unspoken code of hospitality when he assaults a guest; Gloucester admonishes Cornwall, "You are my guests: do me no foul play, friends. . . . I am your host: / With robbers' hands my hospitable favours / You should not ruffle thus. . . ." (3,6:31,39–41). In evoking Shakespeare's bleakest play as a touchstone, Kosinski implicity compares the tragic visions, suggesting that the boy's world is far bleaker. Blind Gloucester describes his sightless world as "all dark and comfortless" (3,6:85). The boy in Kosinski's novel tries to imagine a happier fate for the plowboy: ". . . if only the eyeless could still see through their memory, it would not be too bad. . . . Who knows, perhaps without his eyes the plowboy would start seeing an entirely new, more fascinating world" (39). Quite to the contrary, however, as King Lear bemoans and the boy later learns, "A man may see how this world goes with no eyes" (4,6:154). One is reminded of the lines of Nelly Sachs, as she struggles in her poetry with the memories of her concentrationary experience: "This can be put on paper only / with one eye ripped out" (387).

Oedipus's blind seer Tieresias indicates to us that one may see *better* with no eyes, for the dazzle of appearances cannot then blind one to the truth. The boy's muteness correspondingly renders him a far better, more accurate witness, for he—like the speaker of Milosz's poem—has "no wizardry of words" to distract the reader from his truth. Unlike Cassandra—fierce and uncompromising seer of harsh reality, never credited by her listeners—Kosinski claims credibility for his protagonist by having him say nothing at all. An inverse Cassandra, then, the boy absorbs all, reveals nothing. Fascinated by the detached eyeballs of the plowboy and dissatisfied with the limitations of his own vision, the boy imagines he can claim the plowboy's lost sight as his own.

> Surely they [the eyeballs] could still see. I would keep them in my pocket and take them out when needed, placing them over my own. Then I would see twice as much, maybe even more. Perhaps I could attach them to the back of my head and they would tell me, though I was not quite certain how, what went on behind me. Better still, I could leave the eyes somewhere and they would tell me later what happened during my absence. (38)

When the miller upsets the boy's plan by crushing the eyeballs underfoot, the boy realizes the fragility of vision. The boy intuits the connections between vision, destruction, and memory and commits himself to the role of witness. "I made a promise to myself to remember everything I saw; if someone should pluck out my eyes, then I would retain the memory of all that I had seen for as long as I lived" (40). Even without the loss of one's vision, the world the survivor knows vanishes everywhere except in memory. Seeing and remembering must precede narrative; thus, the boy observes sharply and remains mute. Aharon Appelfeld who, like Kosinski, wandered alone as a child hiding from Nazi roundups in Eastern Europe, similarly uses a young orphan as the central consciousness of his narrative *Kefor 'al ha'arets*. That child's "eyes registered each sight, so that when the time would come he would be able to relate them in his own language, though he did not know then that only he would be the faithful witness. . . . Only he, in his innocent attentiveness, could piece together image to image" (61). In each case, witnessing/seeing makes possible an eventual witnessing/testifying. Kosinski's narrative itself seems shrouded in silence, with few instances of direct dialogue. The novel offers us what the boy sees, as though through the lens of some hidden camera, without narrative commentary or interpretation. "Do not begrudge us oracles from birds," Oedipus urges the seer (1. 310); the words could well be directed toward Kosinski. The blind seer interprets things, the mute boy records them.

The link between blindness and muteness also touches upon a moral dimension of the Holocaust—the willful ignorance and complicity of the bystander to atrocity. What one pretends not to see, one need not protest. In that brutal scene where Cornwall gouges out Gloucester's eyes, Shakespeare never suggests that Cornwall's moral vision predominate. The theatergoer cannot imagine Cornwall as Gloucester's moral peer. The reactions of characters within the play echo our own sense of order violated, of justice breached. So great a sense of moral outrage does Cornwall's cruelty evoke that one servant actually rebels against him. Another servant expresses the audience's moral indignation and condemnation of Cornwall when he proclaims, "I'll never care what wickedness I do / If this man come to good" (3.6:99–102). Despite Gloucester's torment within the play, then, Shakespeare's drama affirms a moral code that the audience recognizes. However, when Kosinski's miller brutalizes the plowboy, the narrative refrains from judgment. Here, the servant—the nameless boy—watches the attack in silence, until finally, he clears away the bloody evidence. Like collaborators with Nazi atrocity (who later protested that they were "following orders"), the boy fulfills the demands of his job, averts his eyes from the bloody evidence, and ascribes all to duty. "It was my duty to keep the room neat and the floor swept. As I cleaned, I kept away from the crushed eyes, uncertain what to do with them. Finally I looked away and quickly swept the ooze into the pail and threw it in the oven" (39). Kosinski's youthful protagonist has neither the power nor the maturity to take moral responsibility for what he witnesses; however, the adults in the novel do no better. The ovens in which the boy incinerates the remains of the plowboy's eyes evoke the deathcamp crematoria.

Neither blind like Gloucester nor deluded like Lear, Kosinski's boy, like Cordelia, sees truly and becomes speechless. Cordelia, too, shuns speech; to her father's ill-conceived questions she replies, "Nothing, my lord" and then, yet more curt, "Nothing" (1,1:89.91). Her reticent presence interrupts speech, interrogates language which can be abused, misused, manipulated. Her silence speaks less eloquently, but more accurately, than her sisters' hyperbolic language, although Lear initially does not understand the difference. Ultimately Lear values her reticence, straining to hear the words that he imagines her mute lips to utter. He addresses her still corpse: "What is't thou sayst? . . . Do you see this? Look on her, look, her lips. . . ." (5,3:723–25). Cordelia's silence reveals a grim truth to her father: that they cannot escape the misery he has wrought. Her innocence, her goodness cannot, ultimately, shield her from a treacherous and untimely death. This harsh indictment of cosmic injustice so unnerved British audiences that a bowdlerized version of the play substituted a happy ending for Shakespeare's tragic one; Samuel Johnson found the play's "instances of cruelty . . . too savage and shocking" to be performed: "I was many years ago shocked by Cordelia's death, that I know not whether I ever endured to read again the last scenes of the play till I undertook to revise them as an editor" (223–24). Such delicate sensibilities could not survive even the opening scenes of Kosinski's novel; what would Johnson say to Kosinski's assertion that "real events had been far more brutal than the most bizarre fantasies" ("Afterword" 254).

The boy's muteness facilitates his function as scapegoat, repository for society's repressed passions and forbidden desires, ritually slaughtered to purge the guilty and restore them to innocence. It strengthens his association with nameless victims of Nazi atrocity, killed to preserve the racial "purity" of Germany. In a different context, Robert J. Lifton describes the muteness that afflicts some survivors of mass catastrophe as a type of "symbolic death" (65), and the link between silence and death has been noted by others.[13] In Kosinski's novel, the series of symbolic deaths that the boy undergoes take on a ritualistic character,[14] underscoring his role as scapegoat. In one instance, the boy repeatedly dangles dangerously above the fatal jaws of the fierce dog Judas. The boy symbolically reenacts a type of private passion play in which he simultaneously assumes the role of both Christ (hung by his arms from a wooden beam, menaced by Judas) and anti-Christ (outsider, putative Jew). If the boy consistently evades death, he pays with the death of animal surrogates, closely identified with him. He sleeps at the bottom of the bird cage from which Lekh extracts the birds to paint, and in the hutch, with the rabbit he is later forced to skin alive. An elderly German soldier, relic of a kinder era, spares his life by "simulating [his] execution" (78) with two gunshots. The carpenter leaves the boy in the center of an open field during thunderstorms, as though to propitiate some angry deity. These symbolic deaths allow the boy to represent those who did not survive. It is their deaths that his silence signifies; his muteness legitimizes his testimony as theirs, not only his own.

The boy's recovery of the power of speech at the novel's conclusion represents a symbolic rebirth corresponding to the death that his muteness symbolizes. To judge by earlier episodes of rebirth in the novel, one may not be too sanguine about his prospects. The inconclusive and ambiguous terms of his recovery have left readers confused and divided.

> I opened my mouth and strained. Sounds crawled up my throat. Tense and concentrated I started to arrange them into syllables and words. I distinctly heard them jumping out of me one after another, like peas from a split pod. (250)

Like the brutal episodes of the narrative, the boy's words are "arranged" but not assigned meaning. The image of words "jumping out" of the boy "like peas from a split pod" convey the eagerness with which he speaks. The image also evokes the earlier figuring of "terror that . . . squeezes the stomach empty of vomit, like a punctured poppy pod blown open by the wind" (142). The confluence of imagery leaves unresolved whether the boy's words of testimony redeem him from silencing terror or merely empty him. This ambiguity is reinforced by the presence of the Silent One, another unnamed boy who, unlike the protagonist, can speak but refuses to do so. The Silent One's muteness marks a deliberate decision:

> It was known that he could speak, but at some stage of the war he had decided that there was no point in doing so. Other boys tried to force him to speak. Once they even gave him a bloody beating, but did not extract a single sound.(227)

In a sense, they are one; that Kosinski intends them as such may be surmised from his reference elsewhere to the protagonist as the Silent One (*Notes* 17). Similarly, having reconciled himself to aphasia, the protagonist muses, "It mattered little if one was mute; people did not understand one another, anyway" (249). The Silent One consciously manifests the same dynamics that act upon the less reflective, younger protagonist. Doubtless, the two young survivors have seen similar horrors; doubtless, they share a common, tortured path. By the war's end, they both arrive at the same deadly code of vengeance that the protagonist acquires from his Soviet mentor.

Attempting to implement this code impels the Silent One to break his long-maintained silence, prefiguring the protagonist's recovery. To avenge a humiliating and painful beating, which the protagonist suffers at the hands of a local peasant, the Silent One secretly throws a railroad switch, killing a trainload of people as the train hurtles over a cliff. The two boys rejoice over this mass slaughter, for the brutal peasant is presumed to be on board. Soon after, the boys realize that the peasant was not on that train. The Silent One's resolve momentarily breaks: ". . . he fell down on the grass and cried as though in terrible pain, his words muffled by the ground. It was the only time I had heard his voice" (237). Broken with cries of pain, his silence metamorphoses into muffled, inaudible sounds. The earth swallows his words before they can reach the ears of even his dearest friend. Since only pain exists, these inarticulate anguished sounds will do; they are all the communication one needs.

On the other hand, the protagonist's own recovery seems more encouraging:

> . . . the phone rang insistently again and again.
>
> I pulled myself out of bed and walked to the table. I lifted up the receiver and heard a man's voice.
>
> I held the receiver to my ear, listening to his impatient words; somewhere at the other end of the wire there was someone who wanted to talk with me. . . . I felt an overpowering desire to speak.
>
> . . . I began to recite words and sentences. . . . (250)

The boy's assurance of a listener overcomes his earlier conviction that "It mattered little if one was mute." Unlike the Silent One, who mutes his bitter words and resumes a life of silence, the protagonist speaks "loudly and incessantly . . . convincing myself again and again and again that speech was now mine and that it did not intend to escape through the door which opened onto the balcony" (251).

Here, Kosinski utilizes analogous images or scenes to achieve a cumulative effect. The mock-recovery of the Silent One, the protagonist's alter ego, must be taken as an alternative to his own—as a second, and equally plausible, conclusion that Kosinski provides the novel, as though Shakespeare had Cordelia simultaneously live and die. Taken together, these two resolutions of muteness comment on the fate of the survivor. Over and over, the protagonist has proven his adaptability; thus his recovery, in one sense, may be expected. However, his scars run deep, and the speech he recovers is not the same as that which he lost, for he incorporates into it all that he has seen and endured. He speaks "like the peasants and then like the city folk, as fast as I could, enraptured by the sounds that were heavy with meaning, as wet snow is heavy with water. . . ." (251). Unlike the indulgences which are empty of meaning, the boy's regained words are full of meaning. However, with his power of speech, the boy does not recover the sense of wholeness with which the narrative began. He has grown in dreadful knowledge, and his words—which we never learn—reflect the rupture of his world as surely as do the Silent One's cries of despair. Kosinski narrative thus thwarts the impulse to seal off the anguish with false reassurances.

The first published edition of *The Painted Bird*[15] contains an epilogue describing the boy's future in third-person narrative, corresponding to the third-person prologue (both in italic), retained in the later edition, which briefly offers his background. Although the epilogue gives the novel a symmetry missing in subsequent editions, the openness of the ending in the later edition renders the narrative unresolved, deliberately ambiguous. The restoration of speech and the moment of healing with which the narrative closes do not neutralize the rupture, symbolized by muteness. For Kosinski would have the reader confront the Holocaust, confront it without tidy resolutions. The movement from mute observation to undisclosed speech provides no promise of a world left intact; all the challenges expressed through the boy's prior muteness stand unrefuted. The boy's sounds, "heavy with meaning," call upon the reader to pit himself against the absence of words, to try again and again to approximate the boy's truth, and to imagine its frightening implications.

5

The Reluctant Witness

A man deflects his testimony;
for what really cries in him,
he keeps silent, sometimes
for his own good.
                    —Haim Gouri

In Peter Morley's documentary film, *Kitty: Return to Auschwitz*, Kitty Felix Hart returns to the concentration camp where she had been incarcerated thirty-three years earlier. Against the backdrop of present-day Auschwitz, Morley films Hart's struggle to describe her experiences there to her adult son who accompanies her. Hart participates in Morley's film for both a public and a private purpose. She returns to Auschwitz in 1978 so that the camera, in filming Auschwitz, will refute those who claim that the Holocaust "never happened," and so that her son, in visiting Auschwitz, will know and understand what his mother endured. She comes to Auschwitz in order that the place of atrocity may bear witness to that atrocity. But the peaceful scene laid before her belies the violence of her memories. At best, the present camp can serve as a silent prop for her own incursions into the realm of remembrance. At worst, its silence and pastoralism refute what she knows to be true.

Because the verdant serenity of present-day Auschwitz misrepresents both personal and historical memory, Kitty realizes she must not only present but represent the camp for her son and for the camera. What Kitty shows her son and the camera does not measure up to the ferocity of her own testimony. Struck by the contrast between what was and what is, she begins to recount anecdotes and incidents, to pile up the everyday details of atrocity, to use words and stories to compensate for what her son and the camera cannot see. The camp holds a set of locales that trigger her memory. As she reaches each setting, Kitty describes her first night in Auschwitz, the metal bowl that served her as both soup dish and chamber pot, the diseases that ravaged the camp, the selections. Her words and stories engage her son's—and the viewers'—imagination. "You have to imagine," she urges again and again, "You have to imagine." At each new vista her voice grows more rapid, more emotional, more frantic—and more marked by a Polish accent which was barely discernable earlier in the film. Standing in the central court-yard—the one used for the grueling roll call—she tells her son to picture it bare, without vegetation. "You have to imagine, there was no grass here. Here was only mud. If there were grass," she adds, "we would have eaten it." Kitty not only supplements but competes with the cam-era's vision, ultimately displacing the celluloid images with verbal ones drawn from her own memory. As she plunges into the depths of Holo-caust memory—or, more correctly, as memory overtakes her—the past claims its place in the present through the shift in her speech pattern.

The film builds upon this contrast between script and setting, and the reactions of the onlooker—Kitty's son, and by extension, our-selves, the viewers—to both. Unlike the narrator of Jorge Semprun's novel, *The Long Voyage*, who ushers the liberators through courtyards that still bear the sights and stench of charnel, Kitty leads her son—and Morley's camera—through a deathcamp grown bucolic, where grass covers the courtyards, the train tracks, the roads. Unable to simply point to the carnage she remembers, Kitty recognizes early on that the Auschwitz she shows her son does not measure up. She real-izes that her stories must compensate for what her son cannot see, and what Morley cannot film, because it no longer exists. Her words must trigger his—and our—imagination; her telling must link past with present, must bridge seeing and knowing. Like Semprun's two French nurses, Kitty's son is sympathetic, concerned, well-inten-tioned—and entirely of another world. His discordant reactions to Kitty's stories mark the chasm separating eyewitness from listener. Unable to easily assimilate what his mother tells him, he has palpable difficulty picturing the Auschwitz of Kitty's memory, and picturing the mother he knows in that Auschwitz. For example, after seeing seemingly endless rows of crude latrine holes, and listening to Kitty's description of the hordes of women fighting for access to them, he exclaims, "And you had no toilet paper!" "Toilet paper!" she responds, incredulous. His inability to grasp what she tells him and to respond appropriately reveals the distance between their worlds and experiences—a distance that separates past from present, deathcamp from memorial, and survivor from all others, however well-intentioned.

In Morley's documentation of life in the deathcamp, Kitty's son stands in for the viewer. He represents those of us who come after the Holocaust, and his reactions anticipate our own. What he sees, Morley allows us to see; what he hears, Morley allows us to hear. Despite the vividness of what Morley calls Kitty's "word pictures . . . more horrific than any photo,"[1] the viewer—together with Kitty's son—struggles with myriad emotions: disbelief, incomprehension, awkwardness, sorrow. These reactions illustrate to viewer and to Kitty alike the difficulty in bearing witness. That Kitty tells a "true" story—a nonfiction one drawn from her own store of memories—and that she tells it to the most sympathetic of listeners—a son, an audience eager to learn—does not free her from the impossible burden of creating credible narrative out of incredible circumstance. Word pictures notwithstanding, we are ultimately gainsaid what Maurice Blanchot elsewhere refers to as

> . . . the so called dignity of knowledge: that ultimate propriety which we believe will be accorded us by knowledge. And how, in fact, can one accept not to know? We read books on Auschwitz. The wish of all, in the camps, the last wish: know what has happened, do not forget, and at the same time never will you know. (Blanchot 82)

To validate her own knowing, to anchor her own memory, Kitty searches the deathcamp grounds for some remnant of the old Auschwitz, her Auschwitz. Poking with her son in the ashy soil over the remembered site of a mass grave, she unearths a fragment of a bone. Triumphantly she holds up the fragment for her son and for Morley's camera. When narrative fails, eyewitness turns archaeologist. She has found an artifact, a remnant, a trace of the old Auschwitz corresponding to the language-trace that constitutes her stories. Auschwitz the park contains and conceals Auschwitz the deathcamp, just as the Third Reich's policy of secrecy once contained and concealed the final solution. The peaceful landscape, which lies through silence, yields up its secrets grudgingly and only in fragments. Yet the traces—physical and linguistic—work against the erosion of time (the encroachment of nature, the lifespan of the survivor) and human agency (the Reich's policy of secrecy; the historical revisionists who, in part, motivate Kitty's participation in the film). Taken together, bits of bone and bits of narrative bring the viewer closer to some sort of knowing, however incomplete.

The narrator of Semprun's *The Long Voyage* recalls his first attempt—two days after liberation—to reveal to an outsider what it

was like to live in a Nazi deathcamp. Kitty Hart revisits Auschwitz
thirty-three years after liberation with her adult son. Considered
together, these two incursions into the memory of the survivor, one fictional and one historical, reveal the difficulty of communicating to nonparticipants what the survivor saw and felt during the Holocaust. Both
for Kitty and for Semprun's narrator, conventional narrative—simply
telling the story—seems inadequate. What they see and what they
remember, what they show and what they tell, collide. Their sympathetic, eager listeners grow incredulous, uncomprehending, repulsed—
or plainly miss the point. These two survivors sift through the physical
remains of atrocity looking for something to anchor their memories, to
validate their recollections. But as they search for more effective means
to communicate what they have experienced, as they search to transcend language, they repeatedly fall back on narrative to make their
story heard, understood, and believed.

Kitty Hart's difficulties typify the struggles of the Holocaust survivor who wishes simply to bear witness, to tell a story at once personal
and collective. Kitty's points of failure—moments when, despite her
efforts she senses that her words have not been fully understood, that
the places of memory, *les lieux de mémoire*, have not adequately testified
to remembered atrocity—exemplify the trope of the mute witness. What
does it mean, to testify? From testis (witness) and fie (make), the act of
testifying constitutes the making of the witness. Much as the witness
produces testimony, testimony produces the witness. The limitations
of language, memory, and imagination come between survivors and the
testimony they strive to deliver, impeding the making of the witness. In
this specific sense, the Holocaust remains—to invoke the phrase used by
Dori Laub and Shoshana Felman—"an event without witness." In survivor writing and in theoretical discourse, the Holocaust has been
repeatedly figured as "without witness" because survivors repeatedly
tell us in the midst of testimony—as Kitty Hart does—they cannot find
the words, images, and narrative forms that can convey their experiences accurately. Primo Levi complains that "our language lacks words
to express the offense, the demolition of a man" (*Survival* 22); Charlotte Delbo reflects, similarly, "Words do not necessarily have the same
meaning" (264). Arnost Lustig refers to two former concentrationees
who once worked at the crematoria at Auschwitz-Birkenau: "What they
saw is silenced by the limits of language" ("Auschwitz-Birkenau" 399).

In addition, the Holocaust has been described as "without witness" because, with rare exception, the victims of Nazi genocide perished. In their absence, others attempt to speak for them ("in their
stead," says Levi), approximating the voices of the dead. However, as

Levi notes, "we, the survivors, are not the true witness" (*Drowned* 83). The unavailability of "the true witness" for testimony constitutes in itself a kind of testimony, but one easily misconstrued, misinterpreted, or ignored. Lyotard, to illustrate this potential, begins *The Differend* with the following:

> You are informed that human beings endowed with language were placed in a situation such that none of them is now able to tell about it. Most of them disappeared then, and the survivors rarely speak about it. . . . How can you know that the situation itself existed? That it is not the fruit of your informant's imagination? Either the situation did not exist as such. Or else it did exist, in which case your informant's testimony is false, whether because he or she should have disappeared, or else because he or she should remain silent. . . . (3)

Thus, we lack, as Levi explains, the testimony of "the complete witnesses, the ones whose deposition would have a general significance" (*Drowned* 84). The death of the victims of necessity forecloses the possibility of a testimony of genocide experienced first-hand.

Further, the Holocaust remains "without witness" because its few survivors must attest to living through (one might say dying through) a set of conditions that, in a sense, approximated death. The extremities of atrocity inflicted in concentration camps, in Gestapo beatings, in the ghettoes, indeed in all parts of the concentrationary universe worked to annihilate the self. Reflecting on his own experiences at the hands of the Gestapo in Belgium, Jean Améry states,

> The tortured person never ceases to be amazed that all those things one may . . . call his soul, or his mind, or his consciousness, or his identity, are destroyed when there is that cracking and splintering in the shoulder joints. . . . Only through torture did he learn that a living person can be transformed so thoroughly into flesh and by that, while still alive, be partly made into a prey of death. (40)

Atrocity unmakes the self, unmakes the world, and thus undoes the very possibility of coherent testimony. "Whoever was tortured, stays tortured," Améry observes, decades after his liberation from Auschwitz (34). Impossibly, the self unmade by atrocity is called upon to narrate its own unmaking, its own inability to narrate. To articulate one's own unmaking from first-hand experience gives it the lie, presenting a coherent self not unmade, and thereby mitigating the radical negativity of the Holocaust. In other words, the unmaking of the self works against the making of the witness that constitutes testifying.

Further, what the available evidence points to remains, in some sense, beyond belief, even as one believes the veracity of its account. Charlotte Delbo, a survivor of Auschwitz and other deathcamps, opens her three-volume account of suffering at the hands of the Nazis, *Auschwitz and After*, with the following enigmatic disclaimer: "Today, I am not sure that what I wrote is true [vrai]. I am certain it is truthful [véridique]" (1). In literary representations of the Shoah, survivors frequently signal to readers that they feel unequal to the task. The brutal nature of Nazi persecution can scarcely be credited even by those who have themselves experienced it. Soon after his release from Belsen, one man confessed,

> Even I, after more than a year there, cannot talk about it without feeling as if I were making it all up. Either that, or telling a dream that someone else had dreamed.[2]

This disbelief, this distrust of one's own memory characterizes virtually all concentrationary accounts. Arnost Lustig remarks, "Once I was a prisoner here. Why do I feel the same way as those who were never here, never saw Auschwitz-Birkenau?" ("Auschwitz-Birkenau" 394). From the retrospective of survival, the survivor cognitively recognizes the memory as accurate and, moreover, externally verifiable. The experience of the Shoah, however, radically ruptures the continuum not only of history but of personal memory, so that the self who remembers—a self situated in a world returned to "normalcy"—cannot recognize its identity in the self remembered, cannot emotionally own the events remembered.[3] In this light, survivor writing simultaneously insists upon the necessity and impossibility of narrating the Holocaust, thus enacting both testimony and nontestimony at the same time.

Finally, when we—who have not personally seen nor experienced the Nazi genocide—read or hear survivors recount, we inevitably frame the radical unfamiliarity of their world in terms of our known, familiar world. In so doing, we domesticate it, diminishing the horror those stories contain. Thus the real events remain unread or unheard, precluding in another way the making of the witness.[4]

The survivor answers a psychological and moral impulse to recount what he or she has seen and experienced in the concentrationary universe, to relate what he or she knows to be true. Burdened with an intractable, intransmissible testimony, survivors—like Kitty and Semprun's narrator—wish to be heeded. And, like those two witnesses, the survivor comes to this task with the reluctant drive of the ancient mariner. To tell the story risks distortion and half-truths; yet not to tell it condemns the victims to obscurity and the event itself to oblivion—a betrayal of a different nature.

Like the theorists who later read their works, survivors of the Shoah acknowledge the unrepresentability of the events they strive to represent. Lustig, for example, despairs of his ability to accurately recall and portray what happened:

> It is not in one's power, even if one thought of nothing else since leaving Auschwitz-Birkenau, to recall more than a fraction of what was, what happened, how four million died there. ("Auschwitz-Birkenau" 394)

Moreover, like Kitty and other survivors, Lustig finds our vocabulary too anemic to contain the relentless brutality, so that the experience itself defies description. Delbo despairs of imparting any knowledge of her experience to readers who have not shared it, since all words at her disposal—words such as *faim, peur, froid, mal, amitié* [hunger, fright, cold, evil, friendship]—exist for the uninitiated "as though these words were weightless" (264). Paradoxically, the diarists and chroniclers trapped in wartime ghettos or those hiding perilously outside the ghetto walls, write with greater assurance. They worry that their writing will not find its audience in the free world but remain confident that their words would speak forcefully and unequivocally on their behalf. In their painstakingly detailed description of Jewish life and death under Nazi domination, one sees clearly what starvation, filth, and fatigue meant to them. Years later, however, survivors saw all too clearly that neither those voices nor their own had the shattering effect, the moral thunder, they had expected. Levi's writing, for example, becomes increasingly pessimistic about its own usefulness. The posthumously published collection of essays in *The Drowned and the Saved* undermine even the cautious certainties of *Survival in Auschwitz,* his first volume. Delbo, too, concludes, "All their words are frivolous. All their words are false" (264).

Against these limitations—of language and of imagination—the survivor struggles to give text and context to fragments of remembered atrocity so that the reader or viewer can know what occurred. Novelists encumber the act of testimony, so that witnessing carries with it a residue of nonwitnessing. To enter into a testimonial pact with such a witnessing—to agree to hear it and in turn to witness the witness—one realizes that no act of testimony is ever complete and sufficient to contain the remembrance of atrocity; the irretrievable losses of family, community, and world; the presence of genocide even decades later.

The theoretical discourse about Holocaust testimony poses the alternative of speech to silence, the one implying faith in the functions of narrative, chronology, and remembrance, the other implying an overwhelming rupturing of the narrating self, of language, of memory. Fictional responses to the Shoah, however, often envision a kind of testimony that is at once both speech and silence, as different from everyday narration as it is from traumatized silence. Fiction writers develop strategies to acknowledge without acquiescing to the limitations of narrative, and to incorporate without becoming identical with muteness.

Consider the cautionary epilogue to Piotr Rawicz's novel *Blood from the Sky*, the fictional memoir of one survivor's experiences:

> *This book is not a historical record.*
> If the notion of chance (like most other notions) did not strike the author as absurd, he would gladly say that any reference to a particular period, territory, or race is purely coincidental. (316)

Rawicz's disclaimer counters the explicitly historical context of the novel, set in "An average-sized town in the Ukraine. July 12, 194-" (8) with besieged ghettos, six-pointed yellow stars, crematoria, and other icons of the Nazi regime. Reminiscent of the prologue to Twain's *The Adventures of Huckleberry Finn*,

> Persons attempting to find a motive in this narrative will be prosecuted; persons attempting to find a moral in it will be banished; persons attempting to find a plot in it will be shot. (10)

the contradiction that the marginal inscription poses to the central body of writing suggests an ironic displacement of meanings. Just as the marginalia subverts the text that precedes or follows, so the text itself subverts the interpretations through which a culture knows and creates itself and its history. When Twain wrote, for example, slavery had long since disappeared as an issue; but what Huck sees on the river and along its banks suggests something sinister about human nature that Emancipation did not shift. However, Rawicz's epilogue disturbs in a way that Twain's warning does not. Twain's prologue aims its dual-pronged subversion at his own text and at its reader; Rawicz's epilogue erodes historical context as well. The epilogue, which seemingly effaces what comes before, suggests that the Holocaust did not occur, at least not as recorded. As such, it works against the imperative to testify, which informs this and other Holocaust writing. By its negation of historicity—*"This book is not a historical record"*—the epilogue also sets into opposition historical and fictional narrative, undermining the reliability of fiction as a means of representing the Holocaust.

Rawicz deliberately destroys the illusion of truth that the novel creates. This tension between writing and effacement informs the narrative as a whole. The novel utilizes the device of the found manuscript: the autobiography of Boris, a Jewish survivor of Third Reich ghettoes and prisons. The narrator of the novel edits, comments upon, censors, and summarizes portions of the manuscript, deciding what all other readers should read. The voice of the eyewitness is partially muted by its first reader, who mediates it for all others. We read an expurgated version of the manuscript that comprises the novel, replete with editorial commentary. The interaction between the two sources of narrative—Boris, whose voice comes first, and the narrator, who has the final say—becomes a way of thinking through the problematics of Holocaust writing in general and Holocaust fiction specifically. How does a survivor gain credibility when writing about an incomprehensible, incredible event? The narrator—anticipating perhaps our own hesitations—measures how much should be known, proscribes how it should be told, and, finally, judges the teller. The resulting narrative touches upon the difficulty of trusting any version of the Holocaust. At best, Boris's autobiography as presented in the novel offers a private, isolated view; at worst, a bowdlerized one. Considered together, narrative and epilogue offer a mixture of vagueness ("any reference to a particular period, territory, or race is purely accidental") and specificity ("in the Ukraine. . . . July 12, 194-"), which simultaneously establishes and undermines the centrality of language, reading, and writing in witnessing the Shoah.

In every telling about the Holocaust, the novel suggests, there exists also a not-telling, which inscribes the limitations of one's ability to tell and one's ability to know. On the one hand, the narrator/editor dissociates himself disdainfully from the narrator/author (Boris) and his manuscript; on the other hand, the novel places the fictional narrative in the pseudofactual context of the found manuscript, thus authenticating it. These opposing pulls make it difficult for the reader to place herself and to know how to take the narrative. What sort of knowledge regarding the Shoah does the novel offer? In the body of literature associated with the disaster, Blanchot writes,

> . . . we say nothing except insofar as we can convey in advance that we take it back, by a sort of prolepsis, not so as finally to say nothing, but so that speaking might not stop at

the word—the word which is, or is to be. Spoken, or taken
back. We speak, suggesting that something not being said is
speaking. . . . (21)

Similarly, evaluating his own attempt to "bear witness," Primo Levi
writes, "I have done so, as best I could, and I also could not have done
so; and I am still doing so. . . ." (*Drowned* 83). The epilogue to Rawicz's
novel unbalances the testimonial thrust of Boris's memoirs; the novel
illustrates how Holocaust narrative simultaneously says and unsays,
confirms and denies, says *by* unsaying, confirms *by* denying.

Through the double perspective of Boris and his "editor," Rawicz
anticipates and directs the reader's reaction to the brutal events that
the novel documents. Like Kitty's son and Semprun's nurses, the editor
of Boris's manuscript stands in for the reader. "It was not without faint
repugnance that I handled Boris's papers" (138), he confesses. As both
reader and (re)writer of the found manuscript, he illustrates the
ambivalent, ambiguous bond linking the writer and reader of literature
of atrocity.

The intimate and open recollections of victims of atrocity evoke
fear, shame and revulsion in addition to disbelief. Levi senses this
judgment

in the eyes of those (especially the young) who listen to his
stories and judge with facile hindsight, or who perhaps feel
cruelly repelled. Consciously or not, [the survivor] feels
accused and judged, compelled to justify and defend himself. (*Drowned* 78)

To an account of horror, the reader responds with an amalgam of contradictory emotions—sympathy coupled with indifference, simultaneous
identification with and revulsion toward both victim and victimizer.
For the writer of Holocaust fiction, finding the properly "weighted"
vocabulary represents only part of the struggle. For in succeeding in
describing the experience of victimization, the survivor risks alienating
the very reader whose comprehension and empathy was sought. A cat-
aloguing of the details of atrocity ultimately may distance the reader,
differently, but as overwhelmingly as an absence of any detail whatever. A pile of emaciated, putrefying corpses strikes us with horror, as
it did the nurses in Semprun's novel, but we have difficulty identifying
or empathizing with corpses. In fact, the Nazis anticipated and utilized this response. The systematic reduction of concentration camp
internees to walking corpses greatly facilitated their murder. The SS
could view the concentrationees as a different, inferior species, and

their execution as "extermination" of nonhumans.[5] As Robert J. Lifton points out in *Nazi Doctors*, the SS physicians who ran the deathcamps regarded the prisoners as already dead, and thus evaded an internal sense of responsibility for murdering them.

In *Death in Life*, Lifton, an American psychiatrist, describes his own "psychic numbness" while conducting a series of interviews with survivors of the bombing of Hiroshima.[6] Although the early interviews left him "profoundly shocked and emotionally spent," within several days Lifton noted a change in his own response.

> I was listening to descriptions of the same horrors, but their effect upon me lessened . . . and while I by no means became insensitive to the suffering described, a more comfortable operating distance between *hibakush* [explosion affected persons] and myself quickly developed. (10)

Convinced of its "normalcy" and professionalism, Lifton nonetheless views his response with suspicion.

> During my first few interviews in Hiroshima I felt overwhelmed by the grotesque horrors described to me, but within the short space of a week or so this feeling gave way to a much more comfortable sense of myself as a psychological investigator, still deeply troubled by what he heard but undeterred from his investigative commitment. This kind of partial, task-oriented numbing now strikes me as inevitable, and, in this situation, useful—yet at the same time potentially malignant in its implications. (26)

Psychiatrists and psychologists treating the aftermath of the psychic trauma inflicted upon the Holocaust survivor similarly observe that ". . . the concentration camp survivors . . . provoke a variety of emotional responses such as guilt and anxiety or disgust, because of the threat implied to our denial of death or cowardice" (Krystal, 29). In a discussion of the proliferation of "Holocaust courses" on college campuses, historian Paula Hyman points out that readers may be "motivated less by a healthy desire to understand the event than by a morbid fascination with pain and suffering" (109). In designing the U.S. Holocaust Memorial Museum in Washington, D.C., the museum planners strategized ways to simultaneously show and shield historical film footage graphically depicting Nazi atrocity. Sensitive not only to the difficulties museumgoers may experience coming upon such films without warning, and also of the potential of such footage to function as snuff films, the museum placed viewing monitors behind walls, making the films both part of and apart from the exhibition. In a similar way, survivor narratives often struggle not only against the limits of language but also against an anticipated set of responses to a narrative that is, precisely, powerful.

The need to shatter this "psychic numbness," to force a vision so linked to brutal experience upon a timid or naive or sadistic reader impels the writer of Holocaust fiction beyond memoirs and reportage, beyond history into the realm of the imagination. Of his own novels, inspired by the Nazi era, Rawicz says, "For myself, in what I write and think, I find that I am concerned less with the historical than with the psychological, the metaphysical, above all the ontological aspects."[7] Rawicz's deliberate and flagrant departure from historicity disturbs readers looking for a historically and ethically responsible treatment of the Shoah. Some readers protest the "abuse" inherent in fictional narrative when "myth displaces history and the survivor displaces the murdered millions."[8] But the displacements—of narrative, of voices, of history—in Rawicz's novel do not efface history; rather, they insist upon a witnessing that is cognitively and psychologically unsettling to the reader. Like Emily Dickinson, who advises, "Tell all the Truth but tell it slant / Success in Circuit lies" (248), Rawicz's narrator asks that one thinks through the world-shattering losses of the Shoah, rather than recite a chronology. But how does one discern truth in these circuitous trappings?

The discourse of fiction self-consciously addresses itself to the difficulties of Holocaust narrative: limitations of language, of imagination, of the reader. By compressing the distance between the Holocaust writer and reader, fiction breaks down the reader's defensive resistance to the ghastly events described. Jerzy Kosinski, in an "Afterword" to his novel *The Painted Bird*, explains:

> A fictional life . . . forces the reader to contribute . . . he actually enters a fictional role, expanding it in terms of his own experience, his own creative and imaginative powers. (258)

At the same time, Holocaust fiction remains acutely aware of its accountability to historical truth. By refuting passivity, fictional narrative does not permit the reader, in Blanchot's words, to "accept not to know." Instead, like the writer, the reader hangs caught between "know what has happened" and "never will you know" (Blanchot 82). This generates a certain tension, particular to works that take the Holocaust as their point of departure, where the fear of betraying the event becomes itself an integral part of the narrative.

Blanchot suggests that "It is upon losing what we have to say that we speak . . . just as we say nothing except insofar as we can convey in advance that we take it back" (21). In the Rawicz novel, Boris wonders, "Can it be . . . that our only real betrayal is the one we commit against silence?" (295). The central problem of Wiesel's novel *The Oath* stems from the protagonist's vow of silence the day his village was massacred. If, as Delbo says, "words have all faded since time immemorial. / Words lost their color long ago" (112), then everything written about that black era entails a sharp compromise and, of necessity, falls short. Like Kitty, who narrates on film a series of disjointed episodes, and holds up for the camera a chip of bone, the writer of Holocaust narrative remains aware of the fragmentary nature of testimony. One cannot speak all, nor can one speak for all. Like the fragment of bone, which—for lack of more complete remains—must represent the whole bone, the entire individual, and all the dead, a fragment of memory or narrative must stand for the Holocaust.

6

Muted Chords

*From Victim
to Survivor*

The Survivor

I am twenty-four
led to slaughter
I survived.

These labels are empty and synonymous:
man and beast
love and hate
friend and foe
light and dark.

Man can be killed like the beast
I've seen:
cartloads of hacked-up bodies
who will never be saved.

Concepts are but words:
virtue and crime
truth and falsehood
beauty and ugliness
courage and cowardice.

Virtue and vice have equal weight
I've seen:
a man who was vicious and virtuous.

I seek a teacher and master
let him restore to me sight hearing and speech
let him once again name things and concepts
let him separate light from dark.

> I am twenty-four
> led to slaughter
> I survived.
>
> (Tadeusz Rozewicz, 7)

T adeusz Rozewicz's 1947 poem, "The Survivor," inspired by his experiences in the Polish underground movement during its struggle
against the Nazi invasion, moves from seeming triumph to ironic
despair. While the protagonist of *The Painted Bird* struggles to survive,
as Kosinski explains in his *Notes*, "because he cannot do otherwise,
because his is a total incarnation of the urge for self-realization and
self-preservation" (16), Rozewicz's survivor questions the worth of survival. The poem's survivor cannot dismiss what he has witnessed, yet
he does not know how to absorb it. The poem focuses not on atrocity
itself—its depiction takes only one line—but on the moral chaos left in
its wake. The "hacked-up bodies" call into question all the survivor
wishes to believe in; they signal the devaluation of human life and
reduce moral "concepts" to mere "words," empty rhetoric. Witness to
events so searing that they blind him, Rozewicz's survivor becomes a
mute witness, deprived of "sight hearing sound." His inability to connect to the world on a sensory level serves as an analog for a corresponding inability to make moral distinctions. He remembers the
words—"man," "beast," "virtue," "crime," "truth," "falsehood"—but not
their sense. The intermingling of "light and dark" evokes the primeval
void—the tohu-bohu before the "beginning," before the "Word."

Like Kosinski's protagonist, Rozewicz's survivor has lost faith in
words. The paradigms that order his universe have been shattered.
With neither humanly nor divinely sanctioned values, he rejects the
value-laden language of abstract moral concepts. He seeks a "master" to
restore order to the chaos man has wrought—someone godlike, to distinguish light from dark, to infuse words once again with meaning.
Ultimately this divine task may prove beyond mortal ability; the shattered world, Rozewicz implies, may not be ours to piece together. Thus,
the poem ends as it begins, with the fact of survival—but a survival
burdened with a devastating knowledge, a knowledge that undoes all
other knowing.

Perhaps this is why Charlotte Delbo ends the first volume of her
trilogy, *Auschwitz and After*, with the following words: "None of us will
return. / None of us was meant to return" (113–14). Some scenes, some
events remain too devastating to integrate psychologically and cogni-

tively. Three decades later, Argentinean journalist Jacobo Timerman discusses the effect of atrocity on the tender bonds of family and filial connection. For Timerman, incarcerated more than thirty years after the defeat of the Third Reich by another anti-Semitic regime, the systematic torture of family groups in view of one another marks "the true end of the civilization I'd been reared in" (*Prisoner Without a Name* 149). The tender bonds of intimacy prove fragile in the face of such brutality; the personal and communal values associated with them fall apart:

> The entire affective world, constructed over the years with utmost difficulty, collapses with a kick in the father's genitals, a smack on the mother's face, an obscene insult to the sister, or the sexual violation of a daughter. Suddenly, an entire culture based on familial love, devotion, the capacity for mutual sacrifice, collapses. (148)

An encounter with atrocity on so massive a scale as the Holocaust—not one family, not several, but millions—rends the fabric of culture and faith. Whatever once held at the center of one's universe—God, man, political ideology, nature—holds no longer. More than the struggle against great odds for survival, the search for a moral center informs much of the writing by and about survivors of Nazi genocide. So much so, that some readers express concern that the psychological and moral struggle displaces actual events in post-Holocaust discourse. David Roskies, for example, observes, "Judging from these accounts, the real arena of struggle was not between Jews and the Nazi machine, but between Jews and their silent God" ("Holocaust" 210).[1] This seemingly off-center focus reflects a sad truth, one corroborated by survivor accounts: the ordeal of the victim of Nazi atrocity did not end, alas, with liberation from the camps.

For the eyewitness to bodies "hacked-up" by the Nazi machinery, the cognitive, emotional, and ethical struggles are not merely intellectual difficulties. As real as the hunger inside the camps, the angst of the survivor corrodes from within long after grass has hidden the railroad tracks leading to Auschwitz and Mauthausen. Henry Krystal concludes that religious faith "cannot withstand so massive an aggressive assault as was the destruction of European Jewry" (*Massive Psychic Trauma* 6). William Niederland remarks, "The survivors of a massive destructive assault suffer from social pathology related to the distrust and fear of man. Their basic trust in the beneficence of God, reasonable behavior of men, and causality in general has been destroyed" (Krystal 325). When the terms "man" and "beast" become, as Rozewicz puts it in his poem, "empty and synonymous," human language loses the capacity to assert ethical and spiritual values. Nazi victims witnessed the withering away of their own humanity under the extreme pressure of their situation—something even more disturbing to them than the bestiality of their SS tormentors. Shame and horror at behavior forced upon them often haunts them many years afterward.[2]

Along with physical pain, concentration camp internees often had to bear their own harsh self-vilification, their own sense of complicity—albeit unwilling—with the concentrationary universe. In *Night*, for example, Elie Wiesel recalls longingly eyeing the soup of his dying father in Buchenwald. Wiesel judges that covetous gaze harshly, concluding that he "did not pass the test" (114). In actuality, the young man does not snatch his father's soup bowl. On the contrary, he manages to obtain for him a second ration. Despite the filial devotion in deed, Wiesel blames himself for a moment's contemplation of treason.

> It's too late to save your old father, I said to myself. You ought to be having two rations of bread, two rations of soup. . . . Only a fraction of a second, but I felt guilty. (105)

When the protagonist of Ilona Karmel's novel *An Estate of Memory* accepts the position of *Anweiserin* to better her chances for survival, she feels she too has betrayed herself and her companions. Fighting to retain moral agency, the women in Karmel's novel form "makeshift families" and forge a code of behavior: act on behalf of "family" survival, for "us" rather than solely for oneself. This simple but difficult code unravels in the complexities of camp life, and Tola falls short of her own expectations. "What is it? Anything done for someone else is a sacrifice, a noble deed; but try to do the same thing for yourself and the sacrifice becomes a disgrace. Why? I too am someone; I've no contract for survival, I too am afraid" (342). As survivor recollections indicate, after liberation survivors frequently cannot reconcile what they have done with what they believe; they cannot integrate the self they inhabit with the behavior they recall.

Thus, it is not only the inadequacy of language that silences survivors. For what is one to do with this chilling and discordant knowledge of self and world? Elie Wiesel vowed to observe ten years of silence about the horrors he experienced before attempting to write about them. The protagonist of his novel *The Town Beyond the Wall*, also a survivor, deflects questions about the concentration camp. The protagonist of Semprun's *The Long Voyage*, a novel centering on the eight-day cattle car journey to Auschwitz, expresses a similar impulse:

I decided never again to talk about this voyage, never again to allow myself to be placed in the position of having to answer questions about this voyage. I knew, though, that this would not be possible, never to talk about it. But at least a long period of silence, years of silence about this voyage, God, that was the only way to survive it. Maybe later, when no one talked about it any more, maybe then I would talk about it. (105)

These survivors deliberately hold back their testimony. Under a strong compulsion to bear witness, they seem uncertain of what they wish to communicate.

In fictional narrative about victimization, death and survival during the Shoah, characters often feign muteness rather than give themselves over to hollow words. The protagonist of Karmel's novel, for example, ceases to speak once she accepts the position of *Anweiserin*, except for the most concrete uses of language—work orders and food demands. She "did not want to talk. Even to say 'No news' or 'Hot!' meant dressing up, slipping a makeshift face over what she felt was her true face now—something immobile and smooth, the lips' seam drawn tight" (375). Believing that her life struggles prove her less "good" than others, Tola's last shred of integrity rests solely on her refusal to mouth empty words. If there is a consistent message running through the bleak corpus of Shoah literature, it is the bankruptcy of language not only to render experience but to comment upon it in any meaningful way. The writers write against words, against concepts. Like Rosewicz's survivor, they resist naming things.

In particular, they resist naming abstractions—value-laden words whose simple meanings can no longer be trusted. Another Rozewicz poem speaks through the voice of a survivor who struggles to resume his life "after death." With difficulty, the survivor reconnects with ordinary speech, which had become meaningless in the concentrationary universe. Slowly he relearns concrete terms, words to represent such everyday objects as "table," "bread," "knife." He struggles to regain the vocabulary of ethical precepts. The more he repeats the loftier language, the less convinced he seems of its meaning: "man must be loved / I studied night and day / what must be loved / I answered man," he says early in the poem ("In the Midst of Life" 45). Later,

> . . . I repeated to myself
> human life is important
> human life is of great import
> the value of life

outweighs the value of all things
created by man
man is a great treasure
I kept repeating stubbornly (47)

Much as he yearns to reconnect with the humanizing notions he held
before "death," the speaker's stubborn and stiff repetition reveals his
posthumous (that is post-Holocaust) discomfort with these terms. The
code words of heroism, sacrifice, and glory—traditionally used to motivate and solace during times of war and crisis—ring false in the context
of the concentrationary universe. The devaluation of human life subverts
prior paradigms of meaning and reduces moral concepts to empty
rhetoric. The contradictory requirements placed upon language in Holocaust narrative—both to maintain and to bridge this rupture—generates
a reluctance to move beyond the realm of memory and representation.

The distrust of language and its ability to mislead, confuse, and
falsify did not begin with the concentration camp victims nor with the
infamous Nuremberg laws. Because of radical advances in the technology of killing, World War I marked a rupture between the military
ideals of heroism and the realities of large-scale, anonymous slaughter
on the battlefield. Ernest Hemingway captures this erosion in *A
Farewell to Arms* through the musings of a World War I volunteer:

> I was always embarrassed by the words sacred, glorious, and
> sacrifice. . . . I had seen nothing sacred, and the things that
> were glorious had no glory and the sacrifices were like the
> stockyards at Chicago if nothing was done with the meat
> except bury it. There were many words that you could not
> stand to hear and finally only the names of places had dig-
> nity. . . . Abstract words, such as glory, honor, courage, or
> hallow were obscene beside the concrete names of villages. . . .
> (143–44)

Like the speaker of Rozewicz's poem, Hemingway's volunteer shuns
words that seek to transcend rather than simply record historical events.
The seeming transparency of Hemingway's style responds to this disillusionment with rhetoric. He explains that his fiction reports without
commentary, refusing to interpret for readers who must "understand the
same way that they always do in painting" (*Moveable Feast* 75), without
the mediation of interpretive language, imposing false order on real
turmoil. Hemingway gives the illusion of dispensing with the mediation of language, mimicking as closely as possible actual events.[3]

The victim of Nazi atrocity shuns such rhetoric for an additional reason: it serves any master. The ghettos, the labor and death camps, the years of humiliating persecution have taught that Hemingway did well to reject such terms as "glory," "sacrifice," and "honor." For in the name of such lofty concepts, eleven million people vanished into the earth or up in smoke. If the proper terminology enabled the Nazis to "exterminate" the polluting "vermin" and infecting "germs," if Nazi slogans and speeches facilitated their grisly business, then language itself cannot emerge unscathed. In this appalling context, words, concepts offer scant comfort, their mitigating powers merely what Sartre calls "mauvaise foi" [bad faith]—comforting illusions that prevent one from confronting uncomfortable truths. By nature an ordering process, narrative imposes a logic, a significance on actions that have none. Although writers of Shoah literature must use language, they do so with a cynicism that perpetually puts the entire endeavor in question. The narrator of one of Ilse Aichinger's short stories begins, "My language and I, we don't talk to each other, we have nothing to talk about. What I need to know I know" ("My Language and I" 66).

The *crise de langage*, which burgeoned between the two World Wars, tapped into a self-conscious, self-doubting current already present in the literary tradition, a counterpoint to the confidently eloquent mainstream. The era of the self-assured, verbose Dickens was also the era of Poe; the era of Balzac, also that of Nerval.[4] What Ihab Hassan terms "invisible writing" (*Dismemberment* ix) became a significant literary mode in the nineteenth century, already suggesting that "ordinary discourse ceases to carry the burden of meaning" (13). The poets Mallarmé, Rimbaud, Blake, Valéry, and others "accuse common speech" (13); dissatisfied with the limitations of language and of literary form, they sought "to transcend themselves in a complex silence" (ix). They develop a reductive, self-repudiating literature addressing what Robert Martin Adams calls the "awareness of Nothing" (*Nil* 7); indeed, Rimbaud exemplifies this by ceasing to write at all after the age of nineteen. In some measure, this comprises the literary inheritance seized upon by writers of Holocaust narrative. The muted chords struck in the nineteenth century resonate later on in more somber tones.

Ultimately, the concept of the void expressed in the muteness of these literary models differs from the void in Shoah literature. Nineteenth-century symbolist poetry reifies the void in a search willingly undertaken by the poet. It connotes a refutation of the limits of empirical knowledge by the artist who transcends the constricting world of appearances for the richer inward journey, at once liberated and liberating.[5] The pure soul of the poet stands contrasted with the corruption of materiality and the falseness of appearances. For victims of Nazi genocide, however, the horrors witnessed and experienced disfigure and destroy the body whose materiality cannot be kept safely apart from the spirit it encases. In the nineteenth century, the poet Mallarmé seeks in the void a promise of transcendence, an escape from the material existence he disdains.[6] The victim of Nazi atrocity, by contrast, yearns for the mundane, corporeal existence truncated by the policies of the Third Reich. Threatened with physical removal from historical time, the Nazi victim seeks not transcendence but survival, and then testimony. When the Holocaust artist criticizes the bourgeois values that so disturbed the Romantic poet, it is not because—as the Romantics felt—those values cheapen and vulgarize life but because in some way those values incorporate, approve, even promote the devastation wrought by the Third Reich.[7] Hassan notes that the "reification of experience begun in the nineteenth century ends by imposing the muteness of language against which Sartre, Camus, Sarraute, and Robbe-Grillet struggle. All recognize that death compounds the futility of human life in a universe without pre-established norms. . . ." (140). The particular nature of death in our century—violent, impersonal, and massive—reaches its shameful denouement with the staggering number of corpses fed daily into the deathcamp crematoria.

Utilizing mute characters and narratives that oscillate between speech and silence, Wiesel's fiction critiques the "invisible writing" of the nineteenth century as an "ascetic silence that means the withdrawal from language" for its own sake (Cargas 49). The protagonist of *The Town Beyond the Wall*, imprisoned upon returning to his native town several years after surviving the Holocaust, once again undergoes torment at the hands of authorities. Forced to stand facing a blank prison wall for several days in succession, Michael encounters a sympathetic prison guard who tries to help him. Contrary to orders, the guard allows Michael to sit and talks kindly to him. Yet Michael cannot bring himself to trust this guard and to acknowledge the other's claim as humanitarian, as kindred spirit.

The guard speaks seductively and sensitively. He tells Michael, "I dreamed of becoming a poet. Expressing the inexpressible. Translating into words, into music, until silence. . . . Silence weighs upon me, too. . . . One day I will compose a great poem about the prisoners of silence" (149). The guard calls upon traditional sources of meaning in modern culture—literature, music—to attest to his own sensitivity. But Michael rejects this offer of friendship as a sentimental "trap." For the guard does not witness the destruction of the Jews; he witnesses only a literary tradition of prison poetry and fiction. He begins and ends in language, rather than in experience, and so never really sees the Jews of Michael's town whose destruction is enacted outside the boundaries of prison literature. Wanting to speak on behalf of the general category of "prisoners of silence," the guard does not incorporate into his vision the concentration camp and the social and political regime that established it. His implicit equation of the romantic prison of the French literary tradition with the concentrationary universe effaces historical difference, preventing a genuine confrontation with history and with the Shoah. Victor Brombert has noted the distinction between the "experience of prisons (where inmates affirm beliefs that predate their incarceration) and the radically alienating experience of the camps" (182), which precludes the former serving as symbol for the latter.

Holocaust narrative insists upon the meaninglessness not only of text but of history. In *The Writing of the Disaster*, Maurice Blanchot observes, "There can be this point, at least, to writing: to wear out errors. Speaking propagates, disseminates them by fostering belief in some truth" (10). There inheres in this bleak body of literature a fundamental mistrust of words and deflation of language. Tradition patterns by which one seeks to understand catastrophe, to place it in comprehensible context, fail here; these patterns collapse under the weighty demands that the concentrationary universe places upon them. The sheer magnitude of the event, the foreclosing of real options for the victim, precludes a meaningful tragic vision. Rozewicz, in "Precis," concludes,

> the question
> that the Danish prince
> put to himself
> I have passed over in silence
> it is too cruel and vulgar a joke
> for the man of today (100)

The arbitrary nature of Holocaust deaths often disturbs victims more than the idea of death itself. In Semprun's *The Long Voyage*, Hans rebels against dying merely because of the accident of his birth to Jewish parents—because of how he is seen rather than what he believes. He wishes to choose his own life and his own death. Over and over he repeats, "'I don't want to die a Jew's death. . . . I don't what to die merely because I am a Jew,' he refused, to have his destiny inscribed in his body" (178). He joins the Underground, dies his own death outside the deathcamp, his paltry victory the best one can hope for under the circumstances. His comrades investigate but never learn the details of his death; in that sense he shares in the anonymity of the other Jewish deaths, after all. Rather than heroic tales or dignified eulogies, Semprun's narrator can muster only a silent "pure, fraternal look" (76) before the piles of bodies that remain upon liberation of the camps. The anonymity, the severely circumscribed choices, the multitude of dead, stand in marked contrast to the dignity normally accorded the protagonist of tragedy.

Rather than tragedy in the classical sense, Holocaust-inspired literature resembles what Northrop Frye terms tragic irony. He sees its protagonist, the *pharmakos*, or scapegoat,

> neither guilty nor innocent. He is innocent in the sense that what happens to him is far greater than anything he has done provokes. . . . He is guilty in the sense that he is . . . living in a world where such injustices are an inescapable part of existence. The pharmakos, in short, is in the situation of Job. Job can defend himself against the charge of having done something that makes his catastrophe morally intelligible; but the success of his defense makes it morally unintelligible. (41)

The ironic mode dominates in literary representations of that era. Used ironically, culturally loaded words—Hemingway's "glory," "honor," "courage," for example, or Rozewicz's "virtue," "truth," "beauty"—contain their own negation, thereby signaling the collapse of a credible system of values.

Perhaps the writer who has survived Nazi atrocity speaks out, like Job, so that others will not speak out for him in a way that would deny what he knows to be true, would misconstrue the implications of the abyss that he has glimpsed. But language, patterns of rhetoric, have been "damaged" (12), as George Steiner notes in *Literature and Silence*, if not irretrievably, surely significantly. Judging by the body of Holocaust fiction, its writers overcome reticence only with deep misgivings. The protagonist of Piotr Rawicz's novel *Blood from the Sky* expresses this when he digresses from the narrative of his manuscript to pen an aside:

> Perhaps one day I shall try to capture this scene. If I do, a niggardly demon will do its best to rob me of every destitute word that might serve to describe the objects and human beings surrounding me here and now, so close and so tangible—human beings with whom I don't know what to do,

except love them. I shall have obstinately to snatch from this jealous demon every word that is even slightly appropriate, and it will be a harder battle than the one in which I have just gained victory. More shameful, too, like everything that serves to describe, to debase reality. (276)

In Elie Wiesel's Holocaust narratives, these word-consuming demons seem to lurk on every page, silently challenging every word he writes. In contrast to Kosinski's mute protagonist who struggles to speak but cannot, the mute characters of Wiesel's fiction consciously refrain from speech, as though muteness were their vocation. Wiesel's mutes point to what cannot be spoken, what must remain unuttered. Through them, Wiesel focuses on the interplay between expression and omission—the locus, in the words of Octavio Paz's "Poema a Roman Jakobson," which lies

> Entre lo que veo y digo,
> entre lo que digo y callo,
> entre lo que callo y sueño
> entro lo que sueño y olvido . . .
>
> [Between what I see and what I say,
> between what I say and what I keep silent,
> between what I keep silent and what I dream,
> between what I dream and what I forget. . . .]

Their silence comments ironically upon the verbiage of the characters who do speak; by their mute presence, Wiesel tries, paradoxically, to indicate to his reader what eludes him.

In discussions about his writing, Wiesel acknowledges that his narratives unfold about a silent center. Wiesel offers several explanations. Like other survivors, he complains of the paucity of vocabulary to render an accurate sense of the concentration camp.

> We all knew that we could never, never say what had to be said, that we could never express in words, coherent, intelligible words, our experience of madness on an absolute scale. . . . All words seemed inadequate, worn, foolish, lifeless, whereas I wanted them to be searing. Where was I to discover a fresh vocabulary, a primeval language? . . . [the language of the concentrationary universe] negated all other language and took its place. . . . ("Why I Write" 201)

In addition, the forbidding nature of his vision, its fearful truth, becomes compromised when put to language. "What kind of words? . . . Language had been corrupted to the point that it had to be invented anew, and purified as well. This time we wrote not with words, but against them. Often we told less—so as to make the truth more credible." Most of all, Wiesel suspects the very act of writing novels about the Holocaust, the possibility of betraying the dead by turning genocide into grist for literary mills. He asks, "How can one convince oneself—without feeling guilty—that one may 'use' such events for literary purposes? Would that not mean that Treblinka and Belsen, Ponar and Babi-Yar all ended in . . . words? That it was all simply a matter of words?" ("Art and Culture" 410). Suspicious of what gets lost in translating experience into language, Wiesel asserts that if he could "communicate a silence through silence I would do so . . ." The testimonial imperative, however, requires progression through language. While responsibility to the past ordains muteness, commitment to the future requires speaking. "I believe that speech can bring people together" (Cargas 6).

Over time and the progression of his writing, Wiesel develops a typology of silence. Wiesel draws upon the concepts of silence that inform Kabbalistic mysticism on the one hand, and the absurdist writers of twentieth century France—Camus, in particular—on the other.[8] He attempts to distinguish among modes and moods of muteness, just as one distinguishes among kinds of language. Most important to Wiesel is the experiential difference between the silences of the victim, the indifferent observer, and the perpetrator. "The silence of the victims was in a weird, unreal, way a constructive silence; it added something to our history. The silence of the accomplices was a destructive one because it destroyed our future" (Cargas 8). In articles, interviews, and essays, as well as in his fictional narrative, Wiesel vilifies "the whole outside world, which looked on in a kind of paralysis and passively allowed whatever was being done to be done" ("Eichmann's Victims" 511). In *The Town Beyond the Wall*, Michael is obsessed by the memory of a neighbor who peered silently through his window as the town Jews were rounded up and led to their slaughter. In *A Beggar in Jerusalem*, on the eve of the Six Day War the protagonist fears for the survival of the State of Israel, whose precarious isolation he likens to the Jews of Europe twenty-five years earlier, when even "the Vatican kept silent" (10). In the muteness of the onlookers inheres an evil as great as that of the Nazi perpetrators, and more hypocritical. Wiesel redraws the lines of complicity to encompass not only active collaboration with Nazi genocide but also the unresponsive spectator who did not protest. The silent onlookers to atrocity constitute, in Jorge Semprun's words, "simply another facet, but an equally interior facet, of the society which had given birth to the German camps" (161).

In Wiesel's narratives, the silent passivity of the victims transmutes into a silence of agency, when victims use muteness to resist their own or other people's death. In *The Town Beyond the Wall*, Michael recounts the story of a preternaturally silent child who does not utter a sound as Nazi militia repeatedly thrust bayonets into the haystack where he hides with his mother. Michael observes, "The hero of my story . . . is neither fear nor hatred; it is silence. The silence of a five-year-old Jew, Mendele." While acknowledging that the silence of the victims may have abetted their murder, Wiesel accords it also an uneasy sanctity. As it unfolds in Wiesel's narratives, the muteness of victims affords them a measure of human dignity in a setting designed specifically to rob them of both dignity and humanity. On a metaphysical level, Wiesel differentiates between "a healthy silence, Sinai, and an unhealthy silence, that of chaos before Creation." His fiction struggles with divine muteness in face of human agony, which comes to represent a kind of antirevelation that Wiesel counterposes to the divine revelation at Sinai.

If silence is the calling of the nineteenth-century poet, for Wiesel as for Rosewicz silence is simply the condition of the survivor. Rosewicz's poetry testifies to the destruction of transcendent meaning and philosophical values, and to a linguistic black hole that can be negotiated—if at all—only on the level of sheer materiality. If you do not respect the physical being of another person, he suggests in "The Survivor" and elsewhere, you have negated that person's spirit, and the very possibility of spirit in the world. Timerman's description of torture instantiates Rosewicz's contention: extreme torture shatters the intimate bonds of family and with it a coherent sense of self, civilization, and world.

For Elie Wiesel, steeped in Jewish texts and tradition, the rupturing of transcendent ethical meaning and of family connections are ineluctably linked. Classical rabbinic literature repeatedly casts the complicated bonds between God and Israel in metaphors of family relations, filial and marital. In his novels, Wiesel explores the implications of each of these relational metaphors on both the familial and the theological levels. In *The Gates of the Forest* the governing metaphor is parental, and in *A Beggar in Jerusalem*, spousal.

Wiesel writes an ongoing narrative of and as testimony. There are three aspects to witnessing in his writing: theological, humanistic, and narrative. All three components revolve around a silent, inarticulable center. On the level of theology, Wiesel depicts not merely a silent God but the abrogation of the ongoing conversation between Jews and the Jewish God. The Shoah does not fit neatly into a frame of reference shaped by Jewish texts, Jewish history, and the idea of a Jewish God.

On the human level, Wiesel focuses on the different silences of the dead victims, of bystanders, of perpetrators—silences of solidarity, denial, or affliction. Most urgent is his sense of obligation to the dead. He explains, "I am duty-bound to serve as their emissary, transmitting the history of their disappearance. . . . Not to do so would be to betray them. . . . And since I feel incapable of communicating their cry by shouting I simply look at them. I see them and I write. . . ." ("Why I Write" 203). On the level of narrative, Wiesel's writing interrogates its own sufficiency, pointing self-consciously to absences and inadequacies. He notes, "the concentration camp language negated all other language and took its place. Rather than link, it became wall. Can the reader be brought to the other side?" ("Why I Write" 201). These three components coalesce in the search for an ethical narrative, whether God-ordained or humanly ordered, linking past destruction to future action. Wiesel's writing expresses a persistent obligation to history, to posterity, and to the dead.

In his tripartite concern with theology, human relations, and communication, Wiesel measures traditional Jewish explanations of suffering against the challenge of the Shoah. Turning on a filial metaphor for God and Israel, this tripartite concern also informs Talmudic consideration of suffering in its most extreme form. In the most extensive discussion of suffering in classical rabbinic literature (Berachot 5a-b), the Talmud offers three possible explanations for human suffering. Suffering may come (1) as punishment for sin, or (2) as chastisement for the neglect of Torah study; once these two options have been dismissed, the rabbis understand suffering (3) as *"Yisurim shel ahavah,"* or "afflictions of [God's] love," modeled on father/son relations. A protracted rabbinic dispute ensues around the exceptional case, suffering that falls outside the limits of even this third possibility. "What is suffering of love? Any [suffering] that does not cause the neglect of Torah. . . . Any [suffering] that does not cause the neglect of prayer. . . ." Suffering so extreme as to disable the sufferer from studying Torah or from praying cannot be understood as "afflictions of love."[9]

In his insightful analysis of the extensive passage in Berachot 5a-b, David Kraemer sees in these two "neglects" a "breakdown in communication with God," which, by its very nature, cannot be "afflictions of love." Kraemer observes, "if you can't speak to God (prayer) or God won't speak to you (through study of Torah) then how can this be suffering of love?" (192)[10]

Thus, at its most extreme, suffering isolates individuals from one another and from God. Despite the impulse to absorb traumatic events into the continuum of Jewish history, classical rabbinic Judaism sees extreme suffering as characterized by the impossibility of communication, of relationship, of narration, of explanation. Moreover, to the extent that classical rabbinic Judaism views Torah study as antidotal to suffering—the passage in Berachot notes that "Anyone who engages in [the study of] Torah, suffering separates from him" (185)—extreme suffering obliterates the means of its amelioration, along with the source of ethical values and comfort (Torah and prayer).[11] To the extent that Torah study and prayer in Judaism form the nexus of community, their cessation enforced by suffering denies individual sufferers communal interactions that might serve to reconstruct those values. In essence, then, the Talmudic text envisions the possibility of suffering so radical that it engenders a rupture with what comes before and what might come after, removing the sufferer from the continuum of Jewish history, community, texts, and values.

Post-Holocaust literature critiques liturgy and scriptures as a nexus of Jewish meaning and language. In the religious sphere words— and the Word—prove an inadequate defense against the assault of the Shoah. In *Lamentations*, the prototypical Jewish response to national disaster, the prophet bemoans the destruction of Jerusalem, placing that catastrophe in a context that affirms divine justice and universal order: "Woe unto us, for we have sinned" (5:16). However, much of Jewish response to the Holocaust—the poetry of Paul Celan and of Jacob Glatstein, for example—condemns and finally erases the Jewish God. Celan calls God "die Niemandsrose" [the No man's Rose].

In Wiesel's writing, the Shoah is construed as that extremity of suffering that remains outside the bounds of "afflictions of love," in other words, outside the bounds of communication and explanation. The protagonists of Wiesel's narratives consciously refuse to pray or find themselves blocked from prayer. They are torn from routines of study and from communities of learning. In *Night*, the protagonist asks himself:

> Why, but why should I bless him? Every fiber in me revolted. Because He had thousands of children burned in his furnaces? Because He set into motion six crematoria, working day and night, Sabbath and holidays? Because in His great might He created Auschwitz, Birkenau, Buna and such death factories? How could I say to him: Blessed art Thou, Eternal One, Master of the universe, who chose us from among the nations to be tortured day and night, to see our fathers, our mothers, end up in the crematorium? Blessed be Thy Holy Name, Thou who chose us to be engorged upon Thine altar? (76)

The Yiddish poet Glatstein similarly links the extremities of suffering with the cessation of prayer and study, setting of a counter-revelation:

> We received the Torah on Sinai
> And in Lublin we gave it back.
> Dead men don't praise God,
> the Torah was given to the living.
> And just as we all stood together
> at the giving of the Torah,
> so did we all die together at Lublin. (68)

For Wiesel, the essence of the Shoah is a multifarious breakdown in communication, which his narratives paradoxically seek to communicate.

Wiesel's writing enacts an implicit dialogue with classic rabbinic explanations of suffering. In the passage in Berachot (5a-b) the rabbis stipulate that radical and inexplicable suffering may be understood as "afflictions of [God's] love" if and only if the sufferer accepts these afflictions in love, that is, "willingly." The Talmud later illustrates the possibility of extreme suffering lovingly afflicted and lovingly accepted with the example of Rabbi Aqiba, who rejoices in the opportunity martyrdom affords to worship God with his entire being (Berachot 61b).[12] Aqiba exemplifies the rabbinic urging to accept suffering with joy. However, the Talmudic text undercuts this acceptance by presenting a series of onlookers who question the meaningfulness of righteous Aqiba's extreme agony, culminating in the ministering angels who demand of God "Is this Torah and this its reward?"[13] In the account in Berachot, God answers the angels' protest by promising Aqiba "life in the world to come," thereby explaining away apparent injustice. In the Martyrology [*Eileh Ezkerah*], a medieval *piyyut* that has become part of the Yom Kippur liturgy, God responds by demanding that the angels curtail their words of protest and remain silent. "Another word and I will turn the world to water," God threatens. The articulation of suffering unjustified by either sin or love threatens to revoke not only the covenant binding God and Israel but the Noahide covenant guaranteeing the continuity of creation.

A Transylvanian rabbi in *A Beggar in Jerusalem* exemplifies the potentiality for joyful acceptance suffering, as exhorted in the Talmud, in the context of the Shoah. As the Jews in the rabbi's community line up for systematic slaughter at the hands of the SS, the rabbi tells them, "such is the will of God. We must accept it. . . ." (70). The rabbi's initial assurance of the transcendent meaning of his people's suffering resonates with the account of Aqiba's joy at martyrdom.

> We are going to die and God alone knows why, on whose
> account, and for what purpose; I do not know. But He
> demands our lives in sacrifice. . . . And so it is with joy—
> pure, desperate, mad joy—that we shall say to Him: "So be
> it. Thy will be done." (71)

But just as the Talmud undercuts the loving potential in Aqiba's suffering with the protest of the ministering angels, Wiesel's narrative
undercuts the rabbi's joyous acceptance by juxtaposing the victims'
humiliation, torture, and death.[14] The immensity of Jewish suffering, its
gross lack of proportion to any possible misdeed, shakes the rabbi's
conviction, puncturing his rhetoric of piety. The rabbi watches the Jews
obediently dig their own mass grave under the cool supervision of the
SS and begins to question God's purpose: "the God of Israel is today vio-
lating the law of Israel. The Torah prohibits killing the cow and her calf
on the same day; yet this law, which we have faithfully observed, does
not apply to us" (73). God does not merely remain mute in face of this
massacre, but seems to retreat, to renege upon earlier words of promise.

T he filial metaphor for the relationship between God and Israel,
   and its familial and theological implication for extreme suffering,
underlie Wiesel's novel *The Gates of the Forest*, whose youthful protagonist progresses through different kinds of muteness. An enigmatic
admixture of hasidic tale and war adventure, *The Gates of the Forest*
traces Gregor's struggle to survive, physically and spiritually, the Nazi
incursion into Transylvania. The novel follows the young fugitive from
his cave hideout in the forest to the peasant village where he masquerades as a mute orphan, then back to the forest where he joins a
group of Jewish partisans. Finally, a lapse of many years finds Gregor
in a New York synagogue, tormented by memories, a doubting and
alien figure among devout hasidim. Each of the novel's four sections
bears the name of a season. The progression from spring to winter suggests not the hope of renewal conventionally associated with the cyclic-
ity of nature but the indifference of those cycles to human suffering. In
each "season" Gregor encounters a spiritual mentor who ensures his
survival. The novel examines Gregor's continued efforts to understand
their enigmatic teachings and his fierce struggle to regain a moral center. For Gregor, the gates of the forest open onto a mysterious realm, a
vision both seductive and forbidding, comforting and threatening, a
metaphysical region as fearsome as Job's whirlwind. "Gavriel," Gregor's real name, means "man of God." During the Nazi era he abandons
the Hebrew name to conceal his Jewish identity, and also to signal

God's abandonment of the Jews. The novel marks Gregor's perilous journey to reconnect to that name and to language, which both mediates and corrupts experience.

Like the protagonist of Kosinski's *The Painted Bird*, Gregor lives a substantial period of time hiding out as a mute in the Eastern European countryside. While the unnamed protagonist of Kosinski's novel discovers he has lost his capacity to speak, Gregor voluntarily feigns muteness. Gregor's interlude among the Romanian peasants is a virtuoso performance of an art in which he has had practice. The novel opens with Gregor hiding out from SS hunters in a mountain cave, anxiously awaiting his father's long overdue return. Since his father's departure days, perhaps months earlier, Gregor has refrained from speaking. Obeying his father's instructions, he remains silent partly to remain undetected but mostly because he is alone. This first silent episode reflects the isolation of the victim. Despite the danger of discovery, this unstable suspension of speech breaks down as soon as someone wanders into Gregor's vicinity: "the waiting and the uncertainty were more than he could bear, and he was tempted to disobey: I am going to scream" (6). His father's failure to appear on the appointed day fills Gregor with foreboding and with a childish disillusionment with his father's power and trustworthiness.

> If he had not come, it was because he had changed; he must be in a world . . . where promises enclose emptiness.
>
> In the past Gregor had thought his father was all powerful and unshakable, clear-headed in a way that both comforted and terrified those who loved him, those who feared him. They all clung to him, to his words, to his vision. In his presence, they felt pure, strong, and invincible. He spoke little, but what he said had the ring and conviction of truth. He used to say, "Tomorrow will be a fine day," and the sun obeyed him. (6)

Gregor's irrational disappointment in his father reflects the fragility of familial roles and family structure in face of massive onslaught that Timerman speaks of when describing the tortures of the Argentinean prison. But Gregor's musing also evokes a theology, anticipating the survivor's arguments with God later in the novel; he assigns to his father godlike attributes: "all-powerful," "pure," "unshakable." Gregor's loss of faith in his father prefigures his loss of ritual faith and consequent abandonment of religious observance. The absence of Gregor's father is an early analog for the eclipse of God during the Holocaust.

The novel's first scene contains a revision of Genesis, a re-creation story enacted not with words but by their absence. The forest is a distorted Garden of Eden; the revised creation sets into motion a new world of inverse order. In imitation of the God of Genesis, who places Adam in a perfect garden, provides him with food, and prohibits eating a special fruit, Gregor's father places his son in a murderous forest, provides him with rations, and prohibits speech: "under no circumstances open your mouth or otherwise betray your whereabouts" (6). Like Adam, Gregor understands that the penalty for disobedience is death.

In his solitude, Gregor's experiences his forest sojourn, like Eden, as "outside time" (4), history, and language. In a parallel to the six days of biblical creation, Gregor counts his first six days in the forest: "His father had promised to come back in three days. Gregor had counted three days, and then three more days. After that he had stopped counting" (5). Like Adam, Gregor's resistance to transgression collapses at first temptation. Gregor calls out to the first stranger who happens by, then fearfully awaits retribution: "I disobeyed my father; I am going to be punished" (6). Like Adam, Gregor falls into historical time.[15] Living in history and living in language are yoked in this section of the novel. The stranger pierces Gregor's silent world with unspeakable stories of roundups and murders. Their conversation is punctuated by the sounds of freight trains with miserable human cargo cutting through the forest; the stranger alludes cryptically to the hideous events of the era—massacres, deathcamps, transports. The world is recreated in the image of destruction, as over the forest hover the ghosts of "Jews driven from their homes and transformed into clouds" (3). The world created by God in Genesis has been dismantled and displaced and divine order supplanted by genocidal efficiency.

In the primordial garden, Adam bestows names upon all the animals, as—in an act of imitatio deo—he partakes in creation. "Names played an important part in creation, didn't they? It was by naming things that God made them. . . . a name has a fate of its own" (9–10). In contrast, Gregor, like the narrator of Rozewicz's poem, refuses to name things, relinquishing even his own name for the safety of an alias. Expelled from Paradise for his transgression, Adam loses his name-giving power, and with it his godlike dominion over the universe. But only after Gregor rebels against his father's mandate of silence does he acquire the power to name. The newcomer is nameless: "My name left me. You might say that it's dead" (9). Plunged into a world where "millions of men live under false names; there is a divorce between man and his name" (9). In naming things, first God and later Adam inscribe the unnamed into the natural world order, the ongoing life flow. When Gregor names, he inscribes the named into the genocidal order. By renaming himself "Gregor," he gets to live out the war. In bestowing his Hebrew name, Gavriel, on the nameless stranger, Gregor inscribes his companion into Jewish history. Not long after, soldiers capture "Gavriel" and send him off to share the fate of other people with Jewish names.

Because utterance and naming prove deadly in Gregor's experience, he retroactively reinterprets the primordial creation of Genesis. Later in the novel, Gregor tells a young orphan living among the partisans, "If your father is dead, it means that God is unjust, that life is a farce. It means that God doesn't love man or deserve his love. . . . In the beginning God created man in order to kill him; he created him because he has no pity" (132). Since speech colludes with murder, all creation, all utterance, emerge not as life-giving but as death-dealing. The orphan's name, *Haim* (life) suggests that all survivors, indeed all living beings, live under a death sentence.

The God-like prerogatives of speech and naming bring an unwanted death-giving power. Gregor discovers that after a gestation of muteness the nature of speech has grown corrupt. Rather than linking him to the sacred through an imitation of Godly utterance, Gregor finds that "War had taught him to curse" (4). A sense of the death-bringing capacity of speech impels Gregor to accept the ingenious ruse of Maria, his family's former servant. Forced to return to her native village in Romania after the roundup of the Jews of Hungary, Maria agrees to shelter Gregor. Fearing his speech patterns will betray his Jewish origins, she orders him to "be dumb. . . . You must forget that you ever knew how to talk" (63). She passes him off as her feeble-minded, mute nephew, cruelly abandoned by his profligate mother. Freed from the painful and dangerous game of naming, Gregor eagerly assumes this disguise. "Gregor up gave speech. This was no sacrifice at all" (63). His muteness links him with the Jews whose ghosts hover in the skies in the guise of black clouds, clouds that "were making no sound" (4).

Gregor's muteness in Maria's village anticipates the continued indebtedness Wiesel expresses toward the murdered victims. Elsewhere Wiesel confesses, he "owe[s] nothing to anyone, but everything to the dead" ("Why I Write," 202) Already during the war, when Gregor's own survival is not yet assured, he senses that only with silence may he speak on behalf of the dead, to whom he already owes a heavy debt. Both his father and "Gavriel" risk their lives to save his; presumably they die, although Gregor cannot be sure. His silence represents a penance and a repayment; he senses that by remaining mute he best expresses a solidarity with his decimated people. In muteness,

Gregor again becomes a Jew, reconnecting with his Jewish name. "Without realizing it Gregor had been transfigured. The voice of Gavriel vibrated within him, regulating his breathing and giving depth to his silence" (83).

As a mute, Gregor's interaction with the villagers convinces him of the complicitousness of language in evil-doing. The narrative undercuts two sacred forms of speech—the confession of sin and the praising of God. Appearing as if from nowhere, Gregor quickly acquires a privileged status among the peasants, who see in his dumb innocence a mark of divine favor. They constantly seek him out and unburden themselves to his captive ears, certain that he can neither understand nor reveal the secrets they confide. The discordance between pious words mouthed publicly and covert sins harbored within appalls Gregor. One of the peasants tells him,

> Do you see those people . . . ? . . . Well, they're liars, every last one of them. How do I know? Because I'm a liar myself. My whole life is a lie. I lie to the priest, to my wife, to my friends. You're the only one to whom I don't lie. . . . To the others I lie continually. . . . how can I live without lying? (72–73)

Gregor's own silent posture leaves him feeling smugly superior, certain of his virtue. As the village's unofficial confessor Gregor becomes well acquainted with its seamy underside. He listens to their stories of lust, greed, pettiness, jealousy. Even in confessing truthfully to Gregor, the peasants speak dishonestly. They turn to Gregor rather than the priest because they are not genuinely repentant. The villagers' peccadilloes pale beside the sin that the priest confesses: he has betrayed a Jewish fugitive from Nazi persecution. Resisting the priest's exhortations to proclaim God's glory in face of wanton slaughter, the Jew blasphemes. In righteous indignation the priest expels the young Jewish man from his hiding place in the church. When the Jew falls into German hands soon afterward, the priest realizes he has caused his death. In the name of spiritual salvation, he has ensured an innocent man's physical death.

The travesty of the priest's action comprises Wiesel's criticism of church complicity with Nazi purpose. As Wiesel elaborates elsewhere, the vicious anti-Semitism of the Third Reich was nourished by centuries of Western Christian civilization. "A symbol of compassion and love to the Christian, the cross has become an instrument of torment and terror to be used against Jews," observes Wiesel.

> Christianity's role in the Holocaust should not be under-
> rated. The Final Solution was rooted in the centuries-old
> Christian hatred of the Jews. . . . The killings had taken
> place in a Christian setting. Protestant leaders applauded
> Hitler—as did their Catholic counterparts. Those who
> killed . . . felt no tension, no conflict between their Chris-
> tian faith and their criminal deeds. Twenty-two percent of
> the SS remained loyal to the church even while murdering
> Jewish men, women, and children. As for Hitler, he was
> never excommunicated. ("Art and Culture" 406)

In addition, the fugitive Jew's unwillingness or inability to pray links
him with the extremities of suffering in which even Talmudic sages
cannot see signs of God's love.

To the peasants, Gregor's muteness comes to represent both corruption and purity. The villagers forge a deep and complex psychological bond with him, as they bare their innermost yearnings and
their secret fears. "When they confided in him they seemed to be delivering themselves to the powers of darkness with which part of him
was somehow linked" (73). Through his blank and storyless persona, he
assumes the characteristics of a dreaded and inaccessible Other. He
functions as a demiurge before whom the villagers bring sin offerings.
In his muteness Gregor serves as a blank screen. Cleansed momentarily of their shadow selves, the villagers then see in the boy's blankness the purity of spirit to which they aspire. They make of him an
inverse scapegoat: Adamic innocence, before knowledge, before the fall.
The priest tells him, "You're lucky my boy; Satan's interested only in
intelligence" (86).

Through the villagers attitude toward Gregor and his "mother,"
Ileana, Wiesel critiques Christian anti-Semitism. The dual attitude of
the villagers toward Gregor echoes their feelings toward Maria's sister.
A sensual temptress in the collective memory of the village, Ileana represents for them both salvation and damnation. They spit on the
ground at the mention of her name, saying, "may she be cursed." Even
Maria calls her "a slut" with "a devil in her" (69). At the same time,
some proclaim her "a goddess" (76), "a saint" (108), "the most beautiful
among us, the one with the most generous, the most open heart" (109).
Richard Rubenstein observes that for Christian theologians, the presence of the Jew "enable[d] the Christians to lead a decent life. . . .
Unconsciously intuiting mankind's most demonic temptation . . . the
Christian often sought to ward off temptation by projecting it onto his

stereotype of the Jew" (21). In the collective projection of the villagers, Gregor and Ileana fuse into a representation of "the Jew." The historical silence of the Jew, representative of the Christian society that suppressed Jewish voices, blends with the willful silence of Gregor and the absence of Ileana.[16]

Gregor's meditation on and imitation of the scriptural Judas extends Wiesel's critique. The village schoolmaster calls upon Ileana's mute "son" to play the role of Judas in the annual school performance, a role no one else will agree to play. Set just after Christ's crucifixion, the play depicts the trial of Judas by his peers. The disciples call a series of witnesses to the betrayal and crucifixion of Jesus, and finally pronounce judgment upon Judas. Casting a mute in the role of Judas seems appropriate to the villagers who reason that such a traitor could say nothing in his own defense. The schoolmaster muses, "A silent Judas, there's something original for you, a Judas struck dumb by God! Moral: He who sins by his power of speech shall lose it" (89). The villagers rationalize that Gregor's preternatural innocence and gratuitous suffering protect him from guilty association with the vile character he portrays. This conflation of sinner and saint, of demonic and divine, emerges from the peasants' insistence on "interpreting" Gregor without "reading" him—that is, on projecting onto him their own narratives without knowing his. Gregor's muteness—response to present and representation of past anti-Semitism—makes possible their denial of his voice. The town penitent tells Gregor he is "the fruit of the union" between Ileana and "Our Lord"; "Gregor, do you realize that you might be the Lord's son? And that your illustrious father made you dumb so that you couldn't tell?" (78).

Through the weeks of rehearsals, the villagers behave toward Gregor with a special kindness and protectiveness, as though the mute had volunteered for a perilous and holy mission on their behalf. When performed, however, the play transmutes from a reenactment of history to a sacrificial ritual. When the actors accost Gregor in the final act with "Judas! Traitor!" (101), the bored audience rouses itself from torpor, urging the child-actors on to violence. As the peasants' cries build to a frenetic crescendo, Gregor reflects, "They haven't changed . . . I haven't changed. . . ." (103). The violent course of events in the Romanian village—a microcosmic representation for all of Nazi-occupied Europe—are, Wiesel suggests, at once timeless and time-bound. Judas, Ileana, and Gregor blend into one archetypal scapegoat, linked through muteness.

Just as the forest interlude of muteness in the first section of the novel contains a revision of the biblical creation story, Gregor's mute-

ness among the peasants in the second section offers a rewriting of
Christ's passion, wherein Judas Iscariot supplants Jesus Christ as
redeemer. As the crowd becomes increasingly agitated, Gregor becomes
trapped by muteness; the peasants demand, "He must be made to
speak!" (103). In response, Gregor stupefies the crowd by dramatically
regaining his power of speech. The peasants deem this inexplicable
"recovery" a miracle, a mark of divine intervention. They recant their
earlier condemnation of Gregor and his "mother." Once again he
becomes "our Gregor," "a saint" (108). They attempt to excuse their
rough treatment by explaining, "It isn't you we wanted to kill; you
know we love you, you know that. It was Judas who deserved to die.
Him! the traitor" (108). Insisting that "Judas is a saint, not me" (109),
Gregor demands that they beg forgiveness from Judas—"Only he can
forgive you." Elevating Judas to the role of Christ, Gregor extracts
from the peasants and their priest an admission that Judas "is the victim; not Jesus; he is the crucified; not the Christ" (109). Gregor wishes
to convey that in unleashing the unmerited hatred they bear Judas
onto Jews, they enact the crimes of which they accuse Judas.

Gregor intuits yet a deeper kinship with both Jesus and Judas.
Plunging into his role by method acting, he studies the character of
the archvillain as the Gospels depict him. Gregor feels troubled by the
texts he reads. The scriptural account of Judas's heinous betrayal
seems unconvincing and elliptical. Gregor cannot accept thirty silver
pieces as sufficient motivation for "Christ's best disciple and closest
friend" (94) to turn on his master. Searching for "other reasons, more
hidden" (94), Gregor concludes that the story of Judas's betrayal was
invented to exculpate God of any responsibility for the existence of evil.
"If Christians insisted that Judas had killed himself, it was to absolve
Christ of his own death" (95). Judas is, in a sense, Christ's Christ.

Although the peasants accept Gregor's revised narrative, although
they listen to the mute who speaks, they resist the voice of the historically silenced people. The peasants agree to restore Judas to his innocence and to beg his forgiveness. However, they withhold their
clemency from the people who had, for centuries, borne Judas's punishment. Prepared to accept a mythical Jew but not a real one, they slip
from Gregor's power as soon as he reveals to them his true identity.
When he begins to speak, Gregor also reclaims his original name:

> That I am not Judas you already know. And I have told you
> that I am not Ileana's son, either. All I have left to tell you is
> this: my name is not Gregor. I am a Jew and my name is a
> Jewish name, Gavriel. (111)

This final unmasking and revelation proves too much for the shocked peasants: "Make him dumb again! Cut out his tongue!" (112). They reassert their violent voice only by silencing him, reinscribing him into the destiny of the European Jew.

By uttering his Hebrew name "Gavriel," Gregor places his own victimization in the continuum of Jewish suffering. But in attributing Gregor's survival to muteness, Wiesel signals the end of one era in Jewish history and the beginning of another. Gregor's wagering on silence reverses the traditional Jewish reliance on words and on linguistic cleverness to see one through adversity. Jewish lore and Jewish history abound in stories of individuals, even entire communities, saved through the power of the spoken word. In *A Beggar in Jerusalem* Wiesel alludes to the danger of theological disputations for medieval Jewish communities.[17] When "a very learned Christian king"(49) demands that the Jews of his kingdom prepare a delegation of scholars to defend their faith publicly, the Jewish community worries more about the political strategy of speech acts than about philosophy and theology:

> what line should they adopt? Specifically: should this mission, so delicate, so heavy with consequence, be entrusted to the community's most pious or most gifted member? Should we pray for his victory or his defeat? Some said: We're not lacking in scholars known for their devotion and their knowledge; let them do their duty; our faith is at stake and it must be defended at all costs. Others, more moderate, adopted a more realistic stance: safeguarding our honor would be a fine achievement, but what about the vengeance of the king should the Jews outwit his priests? (50)

In much of Jewish literature, language figures as a means both of averting disaster and of coming to terms with it. David Roskies notes Sholem Aleichem's use of language, an idealized form of colloquial Yiddish, "as a protective shield, as a surrogate for action, and as a veritable code of survival" ("Sholem Aleichem" 54). Tevye, for example, can "literally talk his way out of expulsion" (64). In contrast, although Wiesel's Gregor momentarily stuns the frenzied mob by speaking out, he ultimately abandons himself to their violent will. Only the unexpected intervention of a nobleman sympathetic to the partisans delivers Gregor from a brutal death. Like most Jewish survivors of the Nazi era, he survives not by wit but by accident.

Further, Gregor's muteness implies that language has lost the capacity to interpose itself, to mediate a harsh reality—to function, in

Robert Alter's words, as "the last line of man's defense against a history gone wild" (*Defenses of the Imagination* 14). The self-deflating comic mode of Jewish literature takes the edge off despair, distancing one from the vicissitudes of history.[18] Roskies notes, for example, the three-part plot developed by Sholem Aleichem which ironically undercuts the omnipresent threat of pogroms:

> (1) the arrival of news from the outside world sends the isolated shtetl into a state of panic; (2) all normal activity stops as the entire shtetl prepares feverishly for the imminent event, but (3) when the truth is finally revealed, everyone is disappointed, duped or disgraced. (57)

In this configuration, language poses a false threat, subsequently neutralized through language. Wiesel mimics Sholem Aleichem's tripartite structure but with significant alteration. The threefold plot, repeated in Wiesel's writing, and in works of other Holocaust writers, consists of the following: (1) the arrival of news from the outside world drives the Jewish community into vehement and stubborn denial of the veracity of the news; (2) the community plunges frenetically into routine, insisting on maintaining "normalcy"; finally, however, (3) the inevitable truth intrudes, and everyone is killed or deported.

In *Night*, for example, Moshé the Beadle miraculously survives the mass slaughter of deported Jews deep in the Galician forest. He makes his perilous way to the narrator's Hungarian village of Sighet to warn its Jewish inhabitants to flee while they still can. The Jews take him for a madman; they pity him, but refuse to heed his warning. Wiesel quickly moves from Moshe's despair at being unheeded to a description of what ensues in Sighet:

> That was toward the end of 1942. Afterward life returned to normal. The London radio, which we listened to every evening, gave us heartening news: the daily bombardment of Germany; Stalingrad; preparation for the second front. And we, the Jews of Sighet, were waiting for better days, which would not be long in coming now. (5)

One and a half difficult years later, this optimism endures. In the spring of 1944, all agree that "No doubt could remain now of Germany's defeat. It was only a question of time" (6). Although, as the narrator notes, the Jews of his village could leave for Palestine instead of awaiting the German invasion of Hungary, Sighet Jews continue to ignore Moshé's desperate warning. With studied optimism, they await the ghettoization of Sighet and the subsequent deportation of its entire

Jewish population to concentration camps. Free to choose between false and true words, the Jews choose the security of words that comfort through lies. Here, unlike in Sholem Aleichem's narrative, the threat both conveyed and denied through language is ultimately borne out not in language but in deed. The bearer of truth responds with muteness. "Even Moshé the Beadle was silent. He was weary of speaking" (6).

In a similar manner, the protagonist of Aharon Appelfeld's *Tzili: The Story of a Life* offers a post-Holocaust recasting of one of Jewish literature's stock characters, the feebleminded but righteous silent sufferer. Tzili, the protagonist of Appelfeld's novel, bears a marked resemblance to Isaac Loeb Peretz's "Bontche Schweig," (Bontche the Silent) a resemblance that underscores the difference between their fates, and between Appelfeld's and Peretz's eras, separated by a century. Both Tzili, a young girl, and Bontche, a pious man, live out their lives in mute acceptance of the cruelties of others. Exploited and finally abandoned by their respective families, both remain sweet-tempered, although somewhat feebleminded. Their stories conclude quite differently, however—Bontche's with posthumous recognition and reward in the celestial court, Tzili's with a miscarried pregnancy and displacement after the Holocaust. Nevertheless, Tzili fares better than the rest of her family; her smarter and better educated siblings presumably perish during the war. Peretz's story attacks social ills and religious hypocrisy; Appelfeld's novel exposes the failure of eloquence and erudition—traditional, language-dependent Jewish means to success in a hostile environment.

In *The Gates of the Forest* the narrative initially associates language with killing. Gregor learns early on that "Words kill. At the beginning there is always the word. *Fire!* a lieutenant was calling out somewhere, and a line of men and women tumbled into a ditch. . . . Open your mouth and you may tumble Gavriel into his ditch" (147). To dissociate himself from the murderous capacity of language, the enigmatic stranger who disrupts Gregor's solitude in the forest chooses a language of riddles and lacunae. By his deliberate incoherence Gavriel makes of silence a speech act distinguished from the death-bringing Nazi utterances; Gavriel structures a language to "open my mouth and say nothing" (13). In contrast to the destructiveness of words, silence appears fraught with significance. While Gregor does not easily comprehend Gavriel's confusing manner of speaking, the latter's silences-in-language are linked not with murder but with dying innocently. Gavriel speaks of "the fragile and heart-rending silence of the children at the hour of their death" (21). But this initial dichotomy—language

and killing on the one hand, silence and victimization on the other—
soon breaks down. Despite the sanctified meaning inherent in silence,
Gregor senses that the Nazi war against the Jews has tainted silence as
much as it has language: "Silence has become heavy, weighted down by
the passage of time. . . . It even had a smell, the smell of torture, and it
spit blood, the odor of a prisoner who has been jeered and beaten and
left to die" (43). Gregor opts for muteness partly as an enactment of solidarity with the murdered victims. At the same time he realizes that
speechlessness also separates him from them and consigns them to
oblivion. Memory requires narrative, and narrative requires words.
With this recognition, Gregor assumes the testimonial paradox. Narrative is the sole means of keeping the dead in remembrance. Through
silence he commemorates their death, but only in language can he bear
witness. Early in the narrative, Gavriel tells of the death of Gregor's
father. He urges Gregor to continue talking about the man because
"As long as you go on he is still alive" (24). Gavriel's expertise lies in the
art of silence ("I can keep silent. That's what I do best" [13]); however,
he also knows the value of the proper word, the right story, and the
commitment testimony.

To illustrate to Gregor the work of narrative, Gavriel creates narratives. He contends that properly told, a story can speak a truth
beyond words. Through a parable about muteness Gavriel alludes to
the redemptive possibilities of language. He relates the tragic history of
Moshe the Mute. Moshe "had his tongue cut out. . . . He had the power,
by the use of words, to dispel darkness. That's why they cut out his
tongue" (24). The beadle of a small Eastern European synagogue,
Moshe of the story begins as one of the stock characters of Jewish fiction—the unassuming and unrecognized righteous man. As the story
unfolds, Moshe the Mute turns out to be the long-awaited Messiah
sent to redeem the people of Israel. As the Jews of Moshe's village come
under Nazi jurisdiction, Gavriel rails against the silence of the beadle
whose utterance could inaugurate the Messianic era. "You've no right to
be silent. . . . A single gesture, a word, an outcry; above all an outcry
from you can change everything" (48). But rather than the rarified,
preternatural utterance that would overturn the natural order and
bring an end to history, the beadle chooses the ordinary discourse of
domesticity. He marries and prospers, moving from eternity into history. Finally SS death squads round up the village Jews in front of
what will become their common grave. Moshe watches the carnage in
silence, having forgotten the messianic potential of utterance. As bearer
of the redemptive word, he could have reversed the story of Jewish
catastrophe; as a mortal speaker, he remains powerless. On a whim the

Nazis cut out his tongue. Thrust from the mundane world of discourse, he recovers his messianic identity and knowledge but can no longer utter the redemptive word. Gavriel explains, "They cut out his tongue and he became my friend. . . . Every man who has his tongue cut out becomes a friend of mine" (30). In Wiesel's writing, ethical commitment begins with the choice to side with the victim. From this perspective, words connote agency and belong to the aggressor.

Gavriel's story encapsulates Wiesel's complicated web of associations with speech and silence, and the oscillation of alliances between life and death forces and between spiritual redemption and oblivion. At first silence is presented as an index of innocent victimization, the emblem of those deprived of the ability to freely narrate (that is, to live out) their life stories. At its most extreme, silence symbolizes the dead, whose life-narratives have been truncated radically and irretrievably. In mimicking their silence one identifies completely with them. Indeed, as Wiesel observes in another context, dead victims and living former victims are interchangeable:

> If I am still here, it is because a friend, a comrade, a stranger, died in my place. . . . The system of *Lebensschein* in the ghettos and of *Selekzion* in the camps not only periodically decimated the populations, but also worked on each prisoner to say to himself: "That could have been me, I am the cause, perhaps the condition, of someone else's death." ("Eichmann's Victims" 515)

In *The Gates of the Forest*, Gregor himself remains alive only because others risk death to save him. His passivity and silence in the face of the frenzied spectators at the passion play is a complete identification with the dead. Wiesel elsewhere elaborates:

> To die struggling would have meant a betrayal of those who had gone to their death submissive and silent. The only way was to follow in their footsteps, die their kind of death—only then could the living make their peace with those who had already gone. ("Eichmann's Victims" 516)

Thus, in Gavriel's story about the mute Messiah and in the larger narrative of *The Gates of the Forest*, speechlessness memorializes the dead through an act of identity that both purifies but also condemns the living. In this configuration, silence connotes virtue but also powerlessness, or a power that, like the redemptive knowledge of Moshe the Mute, always comes too late. After immersing himself in muteness Gregor realizes its ambivalence. Gregor muses, "You are silent and around you everything is silent. . . . Wrong again! Silence, too, is a demon, stifling its mocking laughter" (25). In the village, Gregor's speechlessness creates a blankness that others interpret and exploit. The silence of the innocent facilitates the will of the aggressor, complicating its claim to pure virtue.

Against identification with the dead through muteness and passivity, Wiesel counterposes solidarity with the living through speech and action. In *The Gates of the Forest*, Gregor joins a band of Jewish partisans. Their active resistance to Nazi genocide suggests the possibility of an alternative to the dichotomization of language/murder and silence/victimization. In cooperating with the partisans, Gregor explores the potential for resistance through language. Just as silence commemorates the dead, Gregor believes that there exists a language that saves lives. Recollecting Gavriel's making of silence a speech act through narrative, Gregor constructs his language of resistance in storytelling. Hoping to find Gavriel, Gregor organizes a rescue mission with the partisan's leader, Leib, and his girlfriend Clara. Gregor and Clara pose as young lovers and recount their invented history to a crusty prison guard in hopes of winning his sympathy. They persuade the guard to help them locate a crafty Jew who has hidden in the prison. Hoping for information, Gregor participates in a vulgar, anti-Semitic conversation with the guard despite his repugnance. But Gregor's efforts to locate Gavriel trigger increased watchfulness among all the police and militia. As a result, Leib is captured and sent to his death. Thus, Wiesel suggests, whatever one does, one risks playing into the forces of genocide. Both the mystery of sanctified silence and the bonds of human speech prove fragile in collision with so massive an onslaught.

Moving from the situation of the victim to that of the survivor Wiesel continues his exploration of language and silence in *A Beggar in Jerusalem*. Set in Israel more than two decades after liberation of the camps, the novel focuses on the aftermath of the Shoah. Amid the religious and national excitement of Israel's victory in the 1967 Six Day War, the survivor confronts the searing implications of his own drastic experiences: the shattering of faith in both God and humanity, the vaporization of sources of meaning. By creating a composite narrative—a collage of realistic descriptions, surrealistic accounts, historical allusions, and rabbinic legends—Wiesel explores the possibilities for creating meaningful narrative out of the Holocaust. *A Beggar in Jerusalem* expands upon themes introduced but not developed in the final section of *The Gates of the Forest*: debilitating but incommunicable memories, anesthetized emotions, torturous questions, implausible theodicy.

In *A Beggar in Jerusalem* Wiesel conflates human and divine muteness, linking both to the absurdist movement in postwar France.[19] Working out the conflicting pulls of solidarity with living and dead victims, aspiring to reconstruct a shattered ethical and symbolic order, Wiesel is drawn toward writing that begins by assuming nothing (or nothingness) and moves from there to a reconstruction of values.[20] In *The Town Beyond the Wall*, Wiesel distills Camusian values into the sentence "Try to help others" (143). However, in *The Gates of the Forest*, Gregor finds even this modest goal beyond him. All of his attempts to rescue others, whether physically, during the war, or emotionally, afterward, are thwarted. His attempt to save Gavriel results in Leib's death; his attempt to comfort Clara in marriage years later is overwhelmed by the memories haunting each of them.

Like the writing of Shoah survivors, absurdist writing responds to the devastating events of World War II, to the inefficacy of language and ideas of civilization, and to the resulting moral upheaval. The most significant Western influence on Wiesel's thinking was Albert Camus[21] whose journals, essays and fiction refer explicitly and implicitly to the war against the Jews, to Nazism and to collaboration.[22] For Wiesel, the absurdist movement provides a framework for him to sort through his chaotic recollections and pained memories in the years immediately following his liberation from Buchenwald.[23] In *Le Mythe de Sisyphe*, Camus defines the absurd as the painful gap between man's desire for meaning and the silence of an indifferent universe. Wiesel directs the demand for meaning at God, who remains as mute as Camus's indifferent universe.

In Wiesel's novels the Holocaust deprives the victims of a sense of purpose and meaning; survivors want desperately to wrest from those terrible events some significance. Just as the biblical Job seems less distressed by his suffering than by its apparent meaninglessness, the victims of Nazi atrocity yearn to place their suffering into a comprehensible context. In a review of Kosinski's *The Painted Bird*, Wiesel locates the arbitrariness of the boy's victimization at the novel's tragic center. "Had his hair been blond and his eyes blue, this memoir would not have been written. And this is precisely what makes it so significant and so tragic: it was due to a joke, painful and absurd as it may sound" ("Everybody's Victim" 40). The juxtaposition of tragedy or despair with laughter is a characterizing feature of absurdist writing. The human quest for significance is incompatible with the terms of our existence; this incongruity provokes absurd laughter.[24]

Laughter, an alternative to muteness, wordlessly expresses but does not interpret man's absurd condition. In Samuel Beckett's *Happy Days*, Winnie, who is buried in sand first up to her waist then up to her neck, struggles against despair at the sheer meaninglessness of her life. She seizes upon whatever distraction the stark set provides. The bare stage is Beckett's visual equivalent of muteness and contrasts with Winnie's incessant outpouring of words. "How can one better magnify the Almighty by sniggling with him at his little jokes, particularly the poorer ones" (24). Although she will not admit it, Winnie herself constitutes one of the Almighty's "little jokes." Her incessant verbiage distracts her from the absurd, but cannot alleviate her despair.

> What would I do, what *could* I do, all day long, I mean between the bell for waking and the bell for sleep. . . . Not another word as long as I draw breath, nothing to break the silence of this place . . . save . . . a brief . . . gale of laughter . . . should I happen to see the old joke again. (18)

In Beckett's play language functions as an expression of the desire for meaning, and simultaneously as a coverup for its absence; silence— the bare stage, the gaps in Winnie's speech—expresses the meaninglessness that constitutes Winnie's true condition. Taken together, they comprise the "old joke," indexed by laughter, which is neither speech nor silence.

Like silence, absurd laughter is unsettling; it jostles one from complacency and bad faith. In Camus's novel *The Fall*, for example, laughter shatters the protagonist's sense of purpose and position, setting the fall into motion.

> I felt arise in me a vast feeling of power and, how can I explain it, of achievement, which swelled my heart. I stood up tall and was going to light a cigarette, the cigarette of satisfaction, when, at the same time, a laugh burst out behind me. (43)

The protagonist's arrogance contrasts sharply with the deflating effect of the laughter. Although the laughter has no particular meaning, the protagonist reads in it a judgment: "The entire universe began to laugh at me then" (86). The laughter fulfills the dual function of revealing and expressing the absurd, piercing the verbal shield of rhetoric.

In Wiesel's writing laughter connotes the space occupied simultaneously by speech and speechlessness. In *The Gates of the Forest,* Gregor associates the mysterious Gavriel with his laugh, the first sound he emits when they initially meet. When Gregor searches for Gavriel years later, he describes the laughter. From Gavriel, Gregor learns about Nazi atrocity, about the death of his father, about the withdrawal of God. Nonetheless, Gavriel asserts, "I'm listening to the war and I'm laughing" (7). For Camus, Beckett, and others, mortality unsettles human assurance of inherent significance; the brutal mass killings that Wiesel witnesses and represents in his novels does so even more strongly.[25] Gregor complains that Gavriel "talks so that I won't understand him and laughs so that I'll doubt his sanity [*raison*] and my own" (10). The French word "raison" is particularly apt; what Gavriel reveals through his incomprehensible words and eerie laughter—the workings of the concentrationary universe—boggles the imagination. Even the partisans, less sheltered than Gregor, can scarcely believe the stories Gregor repeats to them. Gavriel's revelation of systematic genocide threatens to unhinge Gregor's sanity (*raison*), and to rob him of a sense of purpose (*raison*). Gavriel's laughter reveals the abyss; hearing it permanently marks Gregor.

For Wiesel, laughter is the verbal equivalent of madness. The apparent senselessness of each hides a fierce truth abut human cruelty and suffering, death and divine absence. In *A Beggar in Jerusalem* laughter and insanity converge with the concept of "sick memory" ("la mémoire malade"). The three living Jews remaining in David's town after the Shoah are inmates of the asylum. They laugh convulsively during David's visit, decades after the war. The youngest explains to David the nature of their malady:

> Imagine the unimaginable. . . . Imagine my seeing this town without its Jews. . . . Just imagine that in my fantasies I find it empty of Jews and Jewishness, absurdly impoverished and criminally twisted and defamed. . . . Well do I know that these are the hallucinations of a sick and tortured mind, my own. . . . (24–25)

What the inmate asks David to imagine as the product of his imagination has, of course, already occurred. The inmate's words simultaneously mask and reveal the truth. His agonized vision is indeed the fruit of "sick and tortured" minds but not those of the asylum inmates. The inmate understands his memory as sick (malade) in the sense that he remembers falsely; in actuality, his memory is sick (malade) because it recollects evil (mal). For Wiesel, the events of the Shoah overwhelm conventional (sane) discourse. The language of the madman is the language of testimony; the madman displaces the sane witness, that is, one whose memory has not been "sickened" by history, and narrates more reliably.

Just as the narrative underscores the truth of the inmate's mad vision, when witnesses in the world outside the asylum speak the truth, they are taken for madmen. The sole survivor of a mass execution realizes he has been granted immortality in order to bear witness. The Nazi officer who commanded the executions warns him, "You'll speak, but your words will fall on deaf ears . . . they will refuse to believe you. They will not listen to you . . . you possess the truth, you already do; but it's the truth of a madman" (80).

While laughter is the mark of "la mémoire malade," it also represents an alternative to the inadequacies of both language (which distorts) and silence (which occludes). In *A Beggar in Jerusalem* the narrator retells an anecdote drawn from the tales of the Hasidic mystic, Rabbi Nachman of Bratzlav:

> Somewhere in this world, Rabbi Nachman of Bratzlav used to say, there is a certain city which encompasses all the other cities in the world. And in that city there is a street which contains all the other streets in the city. And on that street there stands a house which dominates all other houses on the street. And that house has a room which comprises all other rooms in the house. And in this room there lives a man in whom all other men recognize themselves. And that man is laughing. That's all he ever does, ever did. He roars with laughter. (30)[26]

In the anecdote Rabbi Nachman pares down human existence and civilization into one essential component: laughter. Both sense and nonsense, laughter rather than reason or philosophy constitutes the core of human existence. Elsewhere Wiesel explains Rabbi Nachman's "metaphysical laughter" as "Laughter that springs from lucid and desperate awareness, a mirthless laughter, laughter of protest against the absurdities of existence, a laughter of revolt against a universe where man, whatever he may do, is condemned in advance. A laughter of compassion for man who cannot escape the ambiguity of his condition and of his faith. . . ." (*Souls on Fire* 198). For Wiesel the suggestion of "metaphysical laughter" as a language outside of language offers redemptive potential, albeit one never actually attained. In *A Beggar in Jerusalem* the prophet Elijah, traditionally seen as harbinger of the Messianic era, explains that "laughter is itself a miracle, the most astonishing miracle of all" (33).

Just as laughter remains both within and beyond utterance, the figure of Rabbi Nachman of Bratzlav represents both the disruption and continuity of Jewish memory. Bratzlaver Hasidim—followers of Rabbi Nachman—comprise the only Hasidic group not to have established a dynastic line of rabbinic leaders to replace the founding rebbe. Rather than choosing a living successor, they consider the late Rabbi Nachman to be their rebbe in perpetuity. Contemporary Bratzlaver Hasidim continue to speak of Rabbi Nachman in the present tense. Bratzlaver faith and practice revolves then around an absent center in which they sense an overwhelming presence; Bratzlaver meaning emanates from a muteness saturated with significance.

Elsewhere Wiesel notes that the written record of Rabbi Nachman's teachings were compiled by Nathan, his closest disciple and scribe, whose life's work was "to collect the Rebbe's teachings, his table conversations, scraps of thoughts and sentences uttered here and there; his dreams, his moods, his anecdotes; absorb them all, then write them down, giving them continuity and form" (*Souls on Fire* 178). Nathan recorded his best recollection of the eclectic, enigmatic stories that Rabbi Nachman recounted, transmitting them to subsequent generations of Bratzlaver Hasidim. Echoing the conjunction of absence, presence, and meaning that characterizes Bratzlaver Hasidism, Rabbi Nachman's most significant and most esoteric text is known as *Sefer ha-Nisraf*, the Burned Book, destroyed in 1808 at Rabbi Nachman's instructions. Although the title refers to the book's destiny rather than its contents (which remain unread and unknown), the title registers uncannily with the fate of the Jews during the Shoah, whose book Wiesel endeavors to write.

Through the existence/nonexistence of texts that Rabbi Nachman did/did not write, Rabbi Nachman embodies for Wiesel the paradox that is at the core of Wiesel's own work: the conjunction of speech and silence. The figure of Rabbi Nachman is a key to Wiesel's writing, resonating with Wiesel's concerns about storytelling, despair and faith, continuity and rupture. Bratzlaver Hasidim, nicknamed "the dead Hasidim" or "the Hasidim of the Dead" because they adhere to their dead rebbe, emblemize both the Shoah dead and the survivors whose memories constitute a bridge between the dead and the living.

Central to Rabbi Nachman's thought is the paradox of faith: one must believe in God despite seeming evidence to the contrary. Rabbi Nachman focuses on the Kabbalistic concept of *zimzum*, the withdrawal of God from the universe to create both emptiness (where the created world will exist) and immanence. In the emptiness, described as a space devoid of divine presence, one may come to doubt God's existence. For Rabbi Nachman, neither rationality nor philosophical thought can answer questions of faith. Instead, the question provoked by the silence of God's withdrawal finds its answer in the "holy silence" of the believer.[27]

The depth and complexity of Rabbi Nachman's metaphysical struggle enable it to serve as a groundcloth for Wiesel's writing. In Rabbi Nachman, Wiesel finds "a zone of silence, a zone of darkness which I shall never pierce" (*Souls on Fire* 180). Wiesel transposes Rabbi Nachman's paradox of divine absence to God's withdrawal during the Holocaust, importing and elaborating Rabbi Nachman's concept of "holy silence," along with his rejection of systematic theological discourse. Wiesel observes that Rabbi Nachman "transmits his vision of the world by telling tales . . . rather than by enunciating theories" (175). The narrative method of Rabbi Nachman elucidates Wiesel's own choice to enact the work of testimony through fiction. Bratzlaver Hasidism underlies much of both *The Gates of the Forest* and *A Beggar in Jerusalem*—Gavriel's metaphysical laughter, Gregor's confession at the end of the novel to Gavriel who is at once dead and alive (mirroring the Bratzlaver practice of confession to Rabbi Nachman), the Jerusalem beggars who are in actuality mystical seekers (linked by the convergence of the Hebrew word for both "beg" and "seek"),[28] the telling of stories, the yearning for redemption that is always deferred. Rabbi Nachman's most famous story, "The Seven Beggars," a parable of exile, despair, and redemption, breaks off after the narrative of the sixth beggar. Neither the tale of the seventh beggar (said to symbolize the biblical David and the Davidic Messiah)[29] nor the resolution of the frame tale (which should end in redemption) exist; Rabbi Nachman left the story incomplete, telling Nathan he would not narrate the final sections.

The link between Rabbi Nachman's paradox of faith and the Camusian absurd is obvious, along with their shared suspicion of theoretical systems. This connection enables Wiesel to develop a discourse that connects Jewish mysticism with contemporary absurdism, conjoining past with present or theology with humanism.

In Wiesel's novels, the characters' struggles with muteness and with truncated accounts exemplify Wiesel's search for a narrative voice. In *The Gates of the Forest*, the partisans demand that Gregor repeatedly recount the details of their leader Leib's capture. Each time he does so the partisans listen to his testimony in hostile silence. Although Gregor relates his story confidently and coherently, in "the voice of the perfect witness," the partisans misconstrue his account. Not yet a survivor, and narrating events still fresh in memory to companions who share his experiences, Gregor discovers that already the act of testimony is complicated. Innocent of any actual betrayal, Gregor discovers that his story convicts him, distancing him from his listeners.

> The human voice brings people together and separates them. Brick by brick, stone by stone, the voice builds walls, a man knocks his head against them, it hurts; it no longer hurts. Eventually the voice becomes a prison. . . . The voice is a desert. Whoever is thirsty drinks his own blood. I am thirsty. I am burning. They don't even notice. (163)

Each successive retelling widens the gap between himself and his listeners, until he doubts the veracity of his own story. "Listening to his own voice, he found it false. This isn't the true story. . . . The more I talk the more I empty myself of truth" (163). Gregor's difficulty in finding the proper way to offer his testimony mirrors Wiesel's own difficulty. Any verbal recitation of experience involves distortion, omission, compression; words hide as much—or more—than they reveal. Gregor muses, "The repetition of the truth betrays it" (163).

Like many of his fictional protagonists, Wiesel finds that despite himself, in each retelling of the stories of the murdered Jews of Europe, he must repeatedly consign them to death. In a sense, testimony in Wiesel's works is always belated. The Jews have already died; no amount of speaking out now can effectively reverse the consequences of the absence of testimony then, the worldwide muteness about the Holocaust. In repeating the story of the murdered Jews, Wiesel re-enacts the powerlessness of the survivor to save the others. With each narration, he ushers them again to their death.

Disturbed by his inability to rescue Gavriel or Leib, Gregor longs to reverse the progress of historical events. In altering the facts as he constructs a fabricated account of the day just past, Gregor discovers that even art comes up against limits of representation. Like all Shoah fiction, Gregor's narrative is trapped in history, bounded by the events narrated. Try as he may to alter this ineluctable enchainment of events, Gregor's imaginative account is shaped by what he knows to be true. No matter how one tells the tale, at the end Leib must die, just as the multitude of other murdered victims repeatedly meet their deaths in Wiesel's narratives.

> He was back in the town . . . retracing the route he had followed the preceding days and trying, unsuccessfully, to correct some of his errors. . . . I never met Janos; I never asked

him to look for a Jew. . . . Too late. . . . as long as he talked,
he was safe. He would have liked to talk for days and nights,
but the events themselves carried him forward inexorably
and he their prisoner, had to submit. The end was rising up
to meet him; there was no way of delaying or circumventing
it. (162)

As he relates the story of Lieb's capture, Gregor discovers that the very
retelling so necessary to keeping the dead in remembrance must simultaneously send them to their death again and again. Gregor repays
his indebtedness to the dead by speaking on their behalf; in so doing,
however, he exacerbates his feeling of culpability. By the time he fin-
ishes narrating his grotesque fantasy of betrayal, he hopes the partisans will execute him.

Gregor's search for a way to speak "truthfully" not only of events
but of their psychological, ethical, and theological implications, reflects
Wiesel's search. To convey his feeling about the randomness of Leib's
death and his own feelings of complicitousness, Gregor begins to use
language in a different way. Conventional narrative—a "chronological
and coherent account" (161)—has succeeded only in alienating the partisans from Gregor: "my words have dug a ditch between us. I must now
build a bridge that they may share my shame as I share their silence"
(165). Gregor's "bridge" traverses the same path as the author: the creation of a fictional narrative that approximates but does not mimic
remembered experience. Gregor begins to narrate a strange tale of
guilt and betrayal. Using his two meetings with the anti-Semitic prison
guard as inspiration, he reconstructs the events preceding Leib's capture with "a grotesque interpretation. He and Janos were accomplices"
(171). Rather than defend himself against the partisans' suspicions,
Gregor constructs a story to fit their unspoken accusation and his own
feelings of culpability. To his surprise, Gregor discovers that this distorted fabrication unintentionally reveals a truth of its own. By imaginative invention, Gregor plumbs his own deep feelings of guilt, for Leib
is yet another person who dies while Gregor survives. The partisans
mistakenly accept Gregor's fiction as a literal account, a bare chronology of the events as they occurred. Only Clara "reads" Gregor's story
and grasps its emotional content. She criticizes her companions' understanding of Gregor's narrative, and by extension, readers of Wiesel's
narrative who read superficially or too literally. "You stop at words. . . .
You must learn to see through, to hear that which is unspoken" (174).

Like Gregor, Wiesel searches for an appropriate voice, a proper
mode of testimony. Like Gregor, Wiesel strives to speak in the voice of

"Gavriel"—the archangel who, according to the Kabbalists, represents the truth graspable by mortal man.[30] That voice "seemed to affirm and deny the conclusion: everything is true and everything is a lie" (9). Gavriel's voice, enigmatic and incoherent, embodies both silence and utterance. Through the unfolding of fictional narratives Wiesel similarly seeks a language that embodies the spoken and the unspeakable. In unraveling the limitations of even that language, Wiesel forcefully conveys to the reader the dimensions of the witness's dilemma. Instead of offering to his readers a meaning, Wiesel proffers his yearning for one.

While Wiesel speaks in a eloquent and straightforward voice in his essays, in his fictional words testimony takes the form of a complex and fragmented narrative that must be read as Clara "reads" Gregor's story. Indeed, many of Wiesel's novels focus on the telling of—and the listening to—stories whose simple, folklike surface opens onto a multistranded consideration of the Shoah.

In *A Beggar in Jerusalem* Wiesel utilizes multiple narratives within a larger narrative to explore the significance of storytelling. Even more than Gregor, David personifies the writer's vocation. His central activity is retelling legends and other stories that he has heard, seen, or invented. In one legend, a *maggid*[31]—a traveling mystical storyteller—explains to David that one must cloak one's deepest visions in an appropriate story. The right story can transmit meaning that cannot be contained in literal language.

> Remember that according to Scriptures we are supposed to be a nation of priests. What does that mean? Remember: once upon a time the high priest prepared and purified himself all year long to pronounce a single word—God's name— just once, in just one place: in the inner sanctum of the Temple, on the Day of Atonement. He who wishes to follow in his footsteps must learn to say the right word at the right time and in the right place. (83–84)

The *maggid's* exhortation embeds utterance in the context of anticipatory silence. The High Priest's pronouncement takes its shape from the silences that frame it. Like the Holy of Holies in which it is uttered, and like the Day of Atonement, God's sacred name is the fulcrum for transformative possibilities. As though anticipating the testimonial challenge David will pursue, the *maggid* begins to instruct David in the mystical act of storytelling.

The *maggid* construes storytelling as a discourse different from ordinary speech, which limits, distorts, or falsifies reality. While the structure and resonances of stories enable them to convey the multi-

textured fabric of human meaning, the *maggid* debunks other language-dependent systems whose literality, causality or reductivism
oversimplifies or constrains. He refutes both religious and secular
rhetoric. For example, the *maggid* refuses to carry proper identification
papers. Although arrested for lacking the necessary documents, the
maggid resists what he sees as the governmental imposition of an official identity—an identity of words on paper—which reduces the complexities of his existence to arbitrary terminology. He explains, "I know
who I am and where I come from; I told the police, but they didn't
believe me. They have greater faith in one little scrap of paper than in
a human being. Well I refuse to be like them." (82). What the *maggid*
does not need to explain are the words that would officially define his
existence on those documents: "Jew" or "foreigner." The reductivism
of the language of state as imprinted on identity papers inscribes Jewish destiny on their bearer. The rhetoric of state becomes the rhetoric of
death.

In addition, the *maggid* repudiates the false comfort of conventional religious discourse. The *maggid* interrogates Jewish texts and
measures them against his own experience in the world. When the
words of liturgy run counter to experience, he refuses to pray. He asks,
"how do you explain that of so many prayers, repeated by so many holy
and just men through so many centuries, not a single one has ever
been granted?" (84). The *maggid*'s questions challenge David's faith in
Jewish texts and Jewish authority, unsettling the young man's assurance that "everything that is written and transmitted must be true"
(84). Instead, the *maggid* attempts to construct a mode of discourse
that avoids the contingency of language, a discourse where "speech
and silence agree" (27); Wiesel encloses within the larger narrative
framework of the novel legends and parables of the *maggid* and of the
Jerusalem beggars who supersede him as storytellers. Through a multiplicity of philosophical stances and narrative voices that he succes-
sively adopts and undermines Wiesel aspires to the fictional equivalent
of the *maggid*'s storytelling.

Through the figure of Katriel, whose actual existence the novel
puts to question, Wiesel explores fiction as a provisional resolution of
the conflicting impulses toward speech and silence. Katriel, who associates silence with the tacit understanding of intimate companions,
expresses the limitations of representative narration. "I love silence. . . .
My father and I. . . . My wife and I . . . we can sit together whole
evenings without exchanging a word, and yet when we get up, we know
we have told each other all there is to tell" (108). David, by contrast,
associates silence with the Shoah dead and with the isolation of the sur-

vivor. Their debate on the merits and drawbacks of speech and silence functions as an indication of the author's internal debate. Katriel complains, "I don't like words! They destroy what they aim to describe, they alter what they try to emphasize. By enveloping the truth, they end up taking its place" (135). David counters, "they too are God's creation. Tell yourself that they possess an existence all their own. You prefer to feed truth with silence. Good. But you risk distorting it with contempt" (135).

Away from the protective circle of his family Katriel sees that like language, silence can be misconstrued, can be death-bringing. The men in his army brigade perceive him as an eccentric isolate; his silence discomforts them. Unable to engage in the small talk of camaraderie, he remains isolated until one of the soldiers accuses him, only half in jest, of promoting tension and unease: "It's your fault. . . . By your silence you've robbed them of their power of speech!" In the original French, the soldier's language links the silent platoon even more strongly with the Shoah dead: "Because of you they are as mute as tombstones" (143–44, translation mine). By assuming their muteness the soldiers become memorials for the murdered Jews of Europe. Anticipating battle, the association with destroyed ancestors augurs ill. Prompted by their reaction to him, Katriel begins to distinguish between the easy silence of intimate companions and the "silence which divides. . . . The kind of silence which . . . is creating hurt and bitterness among us" (106). Faced with the divisive effect of his own muteness, Katriel seeks to ally the integrity of silence with the expressiveness of words.

Resonating with the example of the *maggid*, Katriel turns to fiction, to storytelling. He explains his developing poetics of storytelling to his unit. From his father, a master storyteller, he learned "to measure myself against my words and to attune myself with their silence if not always the truth they conceal" (107). Like the *maggid*, Katriel finds that storytelling offers an alternative to the isolation of silence and the distortion of language, using words to convey a meaning beyond words. When Katriel recounts his father's tales, he subtly infuses them with a meaning of his own: "I am just repeating his words. But the silence within the words is my own (107). Katriel's creation of a language that neither distorts nor falsifies, and that incorporates a silence neither divisive nor death-bringing, mirrors Wiesel's ongoing narrative effort. Like Katriel who retells his father's stories, Wiesel too writes twice-told tales—his own rendering of biblical figures, Hasidic masters, Talmudic personages. Wiesel moreover discovers that in imitating the silence of Shoah victims one inevitably enacts the destructive silence of denial and the more malignant silence of collaborators. Similarly, Katriel moves from the sufficiency of intimate silences into an awareness of destructive ones.

> . . . not all silences are pure. Or creative. Some are sterile, malignant. My father can distinguish between them with ease; I only with difficulty. . . . I like silence to have a history and be transmitted by it. (108)

Through Katriel, Wiesel expresses his hope for a narrative that can meld together the truthful aspects of speech and silence. Ultimately Katriel's stories affect the soldiers on a profound level: "Something in Katriel's voice succeeded in focusing his comrades' attention. He spoke softly, as though studying a sacred text, as though he tried to pierce the wall between word and thought" (107).

Through Katriel, David comes to valorize storytelling as a form of testimony that incorporates, shapes, and directs silence without being itself silenced. Amid the contesting voices of living and dead, of celebration and mourning, David must maintain a delicate, if tenuous balance. Just as the Psalmist who, in setting his grief at the destruction of Jerusalem "above my highest joy" (137:6), allows for a happiness that does not imply forgetfulness, David begins to realize that, in testimony, the survivor's memory can meld together two seemingly incompatible realities without betraying either. The vision conflates history and literature, memory and imagination, narrator and author. Katriel/David's storytelling represents the author's own fiction writing as a means of bearing witness in a way that yokes past, present, and future without denying the historical rupture.

Through the activities of the storytelling beggars (or seekers) who gather nightly at the Western Wall in Jerusalem, Wiesel focalizes the narrative on the possibility of redemption after Auschwitz. Just as Katriel discovers in storytelling a mode that, by incorporating both speech and silence, enables testimony to take place both within and outside of language, the beggars enact a ritual to reunite an absent God with Israel, without denying the permanence of the rupture that divides them after the Shoah. Each night the beggars await the *Shekhinah*, the feminine aspect of the divinity. Each night they anticipate the Queen-Bride exiled from the godhead, whose eventual reunification with God, according to Kabbalists, will bring redemption and restore primeval harmony (Scholem 229–33): "Happy is he who unites his words and his silence with the silences of the Shekhinah, the divine presence which prowls about this place" (86). The figure of the Shekhinah conflates with *Malka*—"queen"—Katriel's, or perhaps David's, wife who is mistaken one night for the divine presence, and dubbed "the queen of madmen" (123). The narrative undercuts the beggars' mystical aspirations and their attempts at salvation. At the same time, the appearance of a woman who may be David's bride suggests that in the absence of divine redemption, one constructs redemptive moments in human encounters, in love, and in friendship. For Kabbalists, mundane acts bear metaphysical consequences. The uniting of the human bride and bridegroom both represents and brings about the unification of the Shekhinah and the Godhead, and God and Israel (Scholem 227).

In Wiesel's fiction, the inability to sustain loving relationships after the Shoah functions as a compass by which to chart the psychological effects of trauma on subsequent intimate relationships and as a metaphoric meditation on the alienation of God from humanity. As humans lose the capacity to feel God's love, they lose the capacity to love one another.

Wiesel shrouds all love relations after the Shoah with an oppressive and debilitating silence. Like Clara and Gregor, the lovers in Wiesel's novels stare mutely at one another, engulfed and separated by individual memories and losses. Wiesel's portrait of the fragility of love in the face of massive psychic trauma contrasts sharply with more optimistic writing that poses human love as ameliorative, even in face of atrocity. For example, in *Man's Search for Meaning*, Victor Frankl asserts that his love for his wife helped him to transcend the daily routine of Nazi brutality.

> In a position of utter desolation, when man cannot express himself in positive action, when his only achievement may consist in enduring his sufferings in the right way—an honorable way—in such a position man can, through loving contemplation of the image he carries of his beloved, achieve fulfillment. (58–59)

Quoting the Song of Songs, Frankl affirms that "love is as strong as death" (60–61). Wiesel's narrative interrogates the tropes of romantic love, which come to Frankl unbroken. In Wiesel's narratives, genocide compromises or destroys love.[32]

In Wiesel's writing, love that endures becomes a source of added suffering rather than a palliative. In *The Gates of the Forest*, during the war Clara swears undying love to Leib shortly before he is captured and killed. True to her word decades later, she affirms that Leib "is dead to the rest of the world but for me he is alive and I love him" (212). In a parody of Song of Songs, the love that extends beyond Leib's death makes of Clara's entire world a cemetery. The image she carries of her beloved represents a "resignation, to death" (213). Clara asks Gregor to "become Leib" (213) and marry her. After their marriage, she interposes her dead lover between herself and her husband. The marriage degenerates into an arena of silent suffering where "Hatred strikes a man dumb" (219). The muteness of the spouses reflects the toll that the Holocaust has taken upon their capacity to give and accept love, and to speak in its tropes.

Like Clara, the protagonist of *A Beggar in Jerusalem* finds that his haunted memory drives a wedge between himself and his wife, despite his desire to love her. For David, love evokes a difficult internal battle. "I look at my wife, I touch her and I love loving her, yet something in me shrivels and rebels" (205). Like Clara, David interposes between himself and his love the memory of the dead. The dead, forcibly silenced by their murderers, possess no voice of their own; only through the living can they make themselves heard. Thus, they intrude upon David's present relationships, appropriating his voice as their own. Malka's voice reminds David of his mother's, her eyes of Ileana, who sacrificed her life for him. David speaks to his dead mother. "[T]he silence, it is on your lips I find it and give it back. Wandering beggar or prisoner, it is always your voice I seek set to free inside me" (197). These associations paralyze David, distancing him from the woman he loves.

As countless dead interpose themselves between David and Malka, David reflects, "All of a sudden I realize that the sky is filled not with stars but with funeral candles" (145). David's loyalty to the dead prevents him from acting on his love for Malka. Rather than return home with her, he isolates himself. The stars transmute into memorial candles, into death itself, and finally into the "the eyes of death, the eyes of the dead stolen by death from the living" (145).

*T*he Gates of the Forest ends without resolving Gregor's unhappy marriage to Clara. In the anguish of ongoing bereavement, each survivor remains locked within his or her own circle of dead, isolated from one another. As years go by, the couple endures prolonged silences, each haunted by intense memories, yearnings for vanished connections to loved ones, community, belief system. On a psychological level Clara's and Gregor's relationship represents the continued feeling of loss that infuses the lives of survivors. Unlike the case of the biblical Job whose reconstituted family and sevenfold restitution of property perfectly displaces his sense of loss, even successfully reconstructed families and communities do not compensate survivors for what has been destroyed. On a theological level, the marriage between Gregor and Clara symbolically explores the relationship between God and Israel, metaphorically represented in classical Judaism as lovers or spouses whose union reenacts both creation and redemption but whose alienation signifies divine abandonment.

> Two embracing bodies; mystery dwells in their union; it is enough that a man and a woman give themselves to each other for God to confer his powers upon them and for the world to be once more out of chaos. Somewhere a man is looking with hatred and bitterness at his wife's tormented face; another night without sleep, without oblivion. God, my God, why have you forsaken me? (214–15)

In the degeneration of the couple's relationship which began in love but moves toward estrangement, Wiesel suggest an alienation between God and Israel after the Shoah. Because their suffering ruptures the bond of love between Clara and Gregor and blocks the possibility of communication, it cannot be understood as "afflictions of love." Gregor's relationship with Clara mirrors his relationship with God. Initially Gregor is in love with Clara, who withdraws into memories of Leib, the martyred lover of her youth. In the early years of marriage Gregor waits, sometimes patiently, sometimes fiercely, for Clara to become fully present to him. Ultimately Gregor finds that he cannot love an absence, that thwarted love "enters the magnetic field of hate" (219). Gregor repeatedly resolves to leave his wife but cannot bring himself to abandon her and his memory of who she had been for him. Instead, the couple live in a silence broken only by the most rudimentary utterances.

Simultaneously Gregor feels betrayed by God's abandonment of the Jews during the Shoah. "After what happened to us, how can you believe in God?" (194) he angrily demands of a hasidic rebbe in New York. Although he argues bitterly against God and against religious faith, he cannot bring himself to leave Judaism. Irresistibly drawn to the joyous hasidic worship, he nonetheless remains withdrawn from its song and celebration. Like his marriage to Clara, his relationship with God is characterized by alienation, silence, an absence of communion, but also by an unspoken yearning. Attenuated to the breaking point, neither relationship is wholly severed. As Gregor cannot take the final step of divorcing Clara, he also cannot renounce the covenant of God and Israel.

The novel ends with the simultaneous reinfusion of love for Clara and for God, effected through two acts of ritual worship: the donning of *tefillin* (phylacteries) and the recitation of the mourner's prayer, *Kaddish*. The nature of these two actions and their role in traditional Jewish practice point toward a restitution of the bonds of human and divine love for Gregor.

Traditional Judaism construes the act of donning (or "laying") *tefillin* as an affirmation of the covenant and as an act of loving intimacy. *Tefillin* consist of two leather boxes, each containing four biblical verses affirming the covenental and historical relationship between God and Israel. Jews[33] place one box on their forehead, the other on the left bicep, near the heart.[34] One wraps the end of the strap of the latter box around one's arm, then around one's finger like a ring of betrothal or marriage, reciting the following verses of Hosea:

> I will betroth thee to me for ever; and I will betroth thee to me in righteousness and in judgment, and in loyal love, and in mercies. And I will betroth thee to me in faithfulness: and thou shalt know the Lord. (Hosea 2:21–22)

Finally one wraps the strap around the hand and fingers, forming the letters of the name of God (Shaddai). The vow of betrothal in Hosea reunites the husband with his estranged wife. As constructed by the book of Hosea in an extended metaphor, the figure of the wife/harlot engaged with adulterous lovers conflates with the image of errant Israel engaged in idolatry. The husband/God withdraws, withholding h/His bounties, ostensibly to punish the sinful wife/people, but in actuality as an act of love that brings about the restitution of the bonds of marriage/covenant. Sobered by her aloneness, the wife renounces the false *be'alim* (that is, idols [plural of *Ba'al*] but also husbands).

In Hosea, the metaphor of the wife/harlot places Jewish suffering in a meaningful context—punishment for sin and, more importantly, a mark of divine love—something Wiesel's writing consistently and explicitly resists in the context of the Shoah. Nonetheless, the moment of *laying tefillin* constitutes Gregor's point of return both to Clara and to the Jewish God.

> Clara, will be astonished. "What?" she'll say. "You're going back to religion?"
>
> Clara. . . . She must be saying: He's gone; he'll never be back. No, Clara; I'm not going; I've decided to not to go. Wait for me; I'll be back. After the prayers, after the *Kaddish*. Let's resume the struggle. (225)

By ritually enacting the covenental betrothal, Gregor provisionally breaches the paths of communication ruptured by the extremities of suffering. The moment Gregor prays to God, he mentally envisions speaking meaningfully with Clara.

> He prayed in a low voice. The *Tefillin* were wound around his left arm. As soon as the prayers were over he would take the road home, the road of solid ground. He would say to his wife, "Sit down; I want to talk to you." (225)

After a long period of silence and withdrawal, Gregor reconnects to language, to the possibility of a language that, by containing suffering, reopens possibilities of love, communion, and consolation.

Finally, in the recitation of the *Kaddish*, "that solemn affirmation, filled with grandeur and serenity, by which man returns God his crown and scepter" (225), Gregor comes full circle. If, as the Talmudic argument suggests, the extremities of suffering rupture the possibility of communication with God (the ability to pray), that rupture need not be permanent. Through uttering the *Kaddish*, Gregor reverses the alienation born of afflictions too massive to be deemed "afflictions of [God's] love."

> He recited it slowly, concentrating on every sentence, every word, every syllable of praise. His voice trembled, timid, like that of the orphans suddenly made aware of the relationship between death and eternity, between eternity and the word. (225–26)

In Hosea, the husband/God initiates the restoration of love and language, out of a yearning for the beloved wife/Israel. In Wiesel's narrative, Gregor's yearning—for lost love, for lost faith—initiates the renewal of marital and covenental bonds.

Because the survivor cannot escape the duality of existence, survivor writing emerges as double—visible and invisible, articulate and silent. The simultaneous desire for speech and muteness reflects a notion of doubleness that resonates throughout Wiesel's novel. Caught between faith and despair, David aspires to convey both—and their intertwining—through storytelling. Like Jerusalem itself, a double city—"visible yet hidden" (11)—whose history contains successive destructions and rebuildings, the survivor's memory can encompass fragments of pain as well as of elation. By containing oppositions, nar-

rative enables the narrator (David), the author (Wiesel), and the reader
to transmit and absorb contradictory versions without having any one
version negate another. David muses:

> Victory does not prevent suffering from having existed, nor
> death from having taken its toll. How can one work for the
> living without by that very act betraying those who are
> absent? The question remains open, and no new fact can
> change it. Of course, the mystery of good is no less disturbing
> than the mystery of evil. But one does not cancel the other.
> Man alone is capable of uniting them by remembering. (210)

But the ambiguity, the multiplicity of visions in Wiesel's novels
undercuts any resolution tentatively offered. "While accepting ambiguity and the quest arising from it, the beggar at times would like to
lose his memory; he can not" (210). Each beggar has his own version of
historical catastrophe, his version of redemption. By drawing the reader
into first one version, then another, then another, Wiesel undermines
them all, forcing the reader to grapple with the unspeakable abyss.
Through the interplay of words and muteness Wiesel unsettles the
reader, taking on the function of Rabbi Nachman of Bratzlav's storyteller, the dual burden of *histoire* (history) and *histoire* (story) to
another storyteller.

Like Rozewicz's poem "The Survivor," Wiesel's fictional narratives focus not on representing atrocity but on challenging the reader to
think through the spiritual, ethical, and emotional implications. Prior
structures of meaning—faith in God, humanity, political ideologies—
cannot contain the extremities of human suffering and cruelty. The
trope of muteness, embodied in silent and unintelligible characters,
underscores the failure of language to mediate a harsh reality. At the
same time, Wiesel develops a poetics of silence through storytelling,
linking Jewish and Western textual traditions.

7

The Night Side
of Speech

... in this Lager ... the rubber truncheon was called
der Dolmetcher, the interpreter: the one who made
himself understood to everybody. ...
—Primo Levi, *The Drowned and the Saved*

O f all the weapons in the Nazi arsenal, the most deadly by far was the
spoken word. In view of the brutalities of the Third Reich, this bald
formulation may well strike one as a perverse overstatement. Yet the
obsession of Nazi leadership with public speeches and radio broadcasts,
with slogans and chants, with word coinage and euphemism, prevents
our dismissing it as mere intellectual construct. While the survivors of
l'univers concentrationnaire despair of ever finding vocabulary adequate
to their experience of horror, the Nazis did, in fact, develop the lexicon to
set this night world into motion and perpetuate it for over a decade. It is
not merely a question of orders given, of policies stated, of brutal purpose
put into words. The *Sprachregelung*—the language rules—of the Third
Reich interposed a linguistic barrier before the reality of atrocity; Nazi
jargon galvanized a nation, often overriding personal conscience. Fil-
tered through the screen of catchphrases and abstractions, the most
heinous acts acquired an aura of heroism.

Unlike Hemingway who deplored the use of empty abstractions to
mask what he perceived as the meaninglessness of wartime carnage
and suffering, the Nazis deliberately encoded morally reprehensible
acts in a vague idiom. The "simulated innocence of the Nazi language,"
as one linguist terms it (Esh 134), masked the structures of mass anni-

hilation with a veneer of respectability. For example, a seemingly
innocuous word for departure, *Abwanderung*, became the code word
for deportation to an extermination camp (Esh 156). Clichés and slogans increasingly permeated ordinary discourse, effectively blocking
critical thinking and inner accountability. A Hitler Youth leader,
explaining to a German film director the meaning of the Third Reich,
answered "Marching together."[1] In 1933, Hitler proclaimed the "whole
educational system, theatre, film, literature, the press, and broadcast-
ing . . . harnessed to preserve the eternal values which are part of the
essential nature of our people" (34). The Nazi party controlled every
medium of communication, staged massive public rallies as well as
smaller, local meetings. The encoding, abstractions, and circumlocutions that characterized Nazi Deutsch marked the discourse at all levels of society. In her analysis of the 1961 trial of Adolf Eichmann in
Jerusalem, Hannah Arendt notes Eichmann's proclivity for stock
phrases (36–55); Erwin Leiser points to the "accumulation of clichés" in
"non-political" films issued in Germany between 1933 and 1945 (19).

The Nazis infused the German language with banalities and pat
formulae designed sometimes to conceal but more often and more importantly to interpret their actions. The Nazi leadership developed a system
of expressions and symbols that imposed a pre-text upon actual atrocity,
an already articulated rationale that removed from a compliant populace
the burden of making moral choices. The purpose of the Nazi language
system, according to Arendt's incisive analysis, "was not to keep these
people ignorant of what they were doing, but to prevent them from equat-
ing it with their own 'normal' knowledge of murder and lies" (*Eichmann*
86). Consequently, she explains, "What stuck in the minds of these men
who had become murderers was simply the notion of being involved in
something historic, grandiose, unique . . . which must therefore be difficult to bear" (*Eichmann* 105). In his study of the elements of propaganda
in Nazi cinema, Leiser reaches the same conclusion: "Behind a statement like 'Wake up, Germany!' was concealed its opposite. The object
was to put to sleep conscience, independent thought, belief in freedom
and human dignity. . . . Moral values were annulled in the name of a new
morality. . . ." (9). Thus Nazi-Deutsch evolved a discourse whose utterances displaced actuality, a speech whose intention was muteness.

Nazi rhetoric discouraged clear, incisive analysis. During his trial,
Eichmann reverently recalls Himmler's "winged words"—words Eich-
mann's Israeli judges term "empty talk" (Arendt, *Eichmann* 105)—
which placed the Nazi war against the Jews in fuzzy heroic perspective.
Eichmann's own syntax was notably incoherent. The German-born
Israeli policeman responsible for conducting the interrogation remarks

that Eichmann's "German was hideous. At first I had a very difficult time understanding him at all—the jargon of the Nazi bureaucracy pronounced in a mixture of Berlin and Austrian accents and further garbled by his liking for endlessly complicated sentences which he himself would occasionally get lost in" (*Eichmann Interrogated* vi). For Eichmann, Nazi-Deutsch had effectively displaced other forms of discourse. It controlled his utterances as it constructed his reality. "Officialese [*Amtssprache*] is my only language" (*Eichmann* 48). Arendt astutely sees in Eichmann's speech a nonspeech, terming it a "mild case of aphasia" that was part of a larger cognitive disability:

> The longer one listened to him, the more obvious it became that his inability to speak was closely connected with an inability to *think*, namely, to think from the standpoint of somebody else. No communication was possible with him, not because he lied but because he was surrounded by the most reliable of all safeguards against the words and the presence of others, and hence against reality as such. (*Eichmann* 49)

Arendt portrays Eichmann not as an exceptional figure, diabolical or pathological, but as an altogether too commonplace Nazi prototype. In this light, Eichmann's linguistic disfunction has implications beyond his individual case. So bound up was Eichmann's reasoning with Nazi circumlocution—the substitution, for example, of the phrase "to grant a mercy death" for murder by gassing (*Eichmann* 108)—that he could not even comprehend the moral issues on whose basis he stood trial. The resultant camouflage was, of course, the intention of the language rules of the *Sprachregelung*.

The muteness of Shoah victims marks their helplessness. By contrast, the peculiar aphasia of Nazi-Deutsch is an enabling muteness, a muteness of agency. Simultaneously obfuscating and sufficiently clear to command action, Nazi-Deutsch constructs a reality while destroying the reality of its victims. In "Soul of Wood" Jakov Lind juxtaposes these two kinds of muteness through the contrasting figures of a mute Jewish boy and the Austrian collaborator who serves as his caretaker. "Soul of Wood" recounts the struggle of Wohlbrecht, a one-legged Austrian war veteran, to survive the Nazi occupation of his country, while sacrificing neither opportunity for material gain nor his own particular notion of honor. The story deconstructs Nazi-Deutsch by literalizing some of its idioms, exposing the use of meaningless verbiage to cover up harsh facts that the characters of the story prefer to avoid. During the progression of the narrative, Lind peels off successive layers of verbal construct that mask an abhorrent reality.

The story turns on the euphemistic expression "special treatment" ("Sonderbehandlung"). The opening sentence marks the overturning of both discourse and reality: "Those who had no papers entitling them to live lined up to die" (9). The narrative introduces a death world whose inhabitants live out a death sentence, which may on occasion be delayed and only rarely remanded. One is reminded here of Ringelblum's realization that European Jews, whether in camps or in ghettos, were "*morituri*—sentenced to death" (320). Because it is assumed, the death sentence need not be uttered; the absence of words of reprieve suffices to condemn the victims. Even life-saving language ("papers entitling them to live") affirms the regime's utter control over the lives and deaths of its subjects, reinforcing through omission the predominance of killing.

A former employee of deported Jews, Wohlbrecht first encounters the ominous term "special treatment" while negotiating the sale of their vacated apartment. Deeded the property as advance payment for hiding Anton Barth, their paralyzed son, Wohlbrecht deposits the boy in a deserted mountain cabin. Wohlbrecht assures the S.A. official interested in the apartment that young Anton Barth has been delivered to the St. Veith Insane Asylum. Without saying so explicitly, Wohlbrecht's conversation indicates that he knows of the asylum's use as collection point and extermination center for the physically and mentally incurable. The S.A. officer expresses satisfaction that the boy will receive "special treatment." Wohlbrecht protests this apparent contradiction of what he knows to be true. "What do you mean, special treatment? . . . He'll be liquidated good and quick." Wohlbrecht understands the literal meaning of "special treatment" as legitimate, curative medical attention, which conflicts with his knowledge of what actually occurs at St. Veith. The S.A. officer confirms Wohlbrecht's supposition about the killings at St. Veith. "Exactly, exactly. . . . They call it special treatment. A technical term" (44). This brief exchange initiates Wohlbrecht into Nazi Deutsch. The S.A. officer traces the linguistic source to a vague and nameless "they"—in German, "Man"—who, from a distance, confer meaning and approval on language and on action. In using "their" language, one deflects moral responsibility from oneself onto "them." The S.A. official does not deny the murderous reality hidden behind the term "special treatment." Both he and Wohlbrecht acknowledge what occurs at St. Veith. While Wohlbrecht initially says so outright, the S.A. officer uses a code to both say and not say what is already known.

Wohlbrecht's familiarity with Nazi jargon saves his life when he later finds himself an inmate of the asylum. There, he learns an entire lexicon of technical terminology, which expands into a network of disconnected abstractions. Only the victims remain outside the language system, and thus unaware of what will be done to them. Nazi idiom offers them the possibility of false hope, should the term be literally true. It keeps from them a full knowledge of Nazi plans and methodology, disabling resistance.

To ensure a compliant populace and to keep intact their own cognitive and moral constructions, the death-dealers thicken the verbal smokescreen. In a speech full of double entendre, the notorious Dr. Mückenpelz, head of the clinic, assures his patients that special treatment cures rather than kills.

> It has come to my attention that one of you, I prefer not to mention any names, I'm not even saying he is a member of your group, has been spreading rumours. The story has been going round—and believe me, it has no foundation whatsoever—that a disproportionate number of patients at St Veith's are dying a violent death. Gentlemen, please, take my word for it that is an untruth, not to say a lie. What we call special treatment in this institution—is just that. The patient is subjected to a special treatment to make him recover more quickly. The treatment is based on a new kind of drug which I myself have introduced here. In only a few hours' time amazing results are registered. Sometimes, in fact, it takes only a few minutes. Most of the patients react splendidly and an average of approximately sixty-two patients a day are treated with the new drug. If you should observe that a friend or acquaintance has not returned to the dormitory that night, it means that your friend may count himself among the fortunates, for he has been discharged from the institution. Because, due to the shortage of space, we send these lucky men home the very same day. That's cause for rejoicing—aren't all of us dying to get back to our loved ones again?—and not cause for worry. (52)

The sardonic humor, apparent to the reader but not to the participants in the scene, heightens the sense of menace that pervades the institution. The layering of disinformation, double meanings, and bald lies allows Mückenpelz to shift and control the meanings in the language he uses. His "cure"—death—is, after all, the only possible cure for the "diseases" he treats: racial degeneration, physical deformity, mental retardation, Jewishness. Mückenpelz's final sentence, which asserts that we are "all of us dying to get back to our loved ones again," resonates ominously with the fate of Wohlbrecht's Jewish employers who, the narrative notes earlier, "were going home to their parents and relatives who were also long dead" (10). The confluence textually links the murder of St. Veith patients with the murder of the deported Jews and the systematic genocide of the Third Reich.

The Jewish couple's ancestors lived and died in Odessa but they need go only as far as the "little Polish town of Oswiecim" to join them. The patients at St. Veith need not travel at all for special treatment; clinic doctors murder by pumping "fresh country air . . . into the patient's carotid artery" (53). Mückenpelz's deceptive address typifies the way Nazis used verbal reassurances to gain the cooperation of masses of people who might have otherwise become unmanageable. Successive promises and deals with the Judenrat, for example, bought the Nazis a more or less orderly and efficient evacuation of Jews from their scattered quarters to ghettos, and then to concentration and extermination camps. The Nazi language, notes one linguist, must be viewed as

> an instrument to implement a policy of murder and first of all to stupefy, to confuse and to deceive the victim, and to conceal from him the real meaning of the expressions used. We regard the Nazi-language, primarily, as one of the most important tools used by the Germans in the physical extermination of the Jewish people. It was not directed solely against the Jewish people. . . . (Blumenthal, "Nazi Vocabulary" 58)

In Mückenpelz's talk, not only the misleading lies but also the veiled threat keeps the asylum inmates in line. As in Jurek Becker's novel *Jacob the Liar*, the victims grasp at the flimsiest of explanations rather than acknowledge the horror in store.

The manipulation of the victims was only one function of the Nazi language. In "Soul of Wood," Lind focuses additionally on the perpetrators' efforts at self-exoneration and on the use of language to construct a matrix through which heinous acts appear heroic. As Geoffrey Hartman points out in a discussion of terror, "programmatic or collectively exerted terror requires that the executioners not only see themselves as idealists or enthusiasts, but also hold a massive conviction that they are either saving their victims . . . or purifying mankind of those who cannot be remade" (115). In Lind's story, Mückenpelz sees himself not as murderer but as reformer of the politically deviant, as purifier of society. His methodology denies actual atrocity by conforming with the figures and metaphors of Nazi-Deutsch. The doctor submits each patient to a battery of psychological examinations before delivering him over for special treatment. Following the murder Mückenpelz demands a

detailed written account of the patient's last minutes, including a confession of guilt and an apology to the Reich. For Mückenpelz, the
patient's acknowledgement of his social/political disease affirms the lie
articulated through Nazi jargon. By confessing and apologizing, the
patient illustrates that he no longer suffers from the disease and so
"special treatment" works. The patient's "recovery" asserts that the disease metaphor is not metaphor at all but a literal description of medical
reality. Thus, Mückenpelz explains to the physician who does the actual
killing that the medical record must show

> a real change in the patient prior to treatment, thus sub-
> stantiating our theory concerning sub-human enemies of the
> people, because otherwise, my good friend, our work would
> be based on a mere hypothesis. . . . It would be a downright
> crime against science if a German neurologist were unable to
> cure a patient's political hallucinations before subjecting him
> to the final treatment. (60)

However, in comparing Mückenpelz's address to the patients with
his instructions to the hospital staff, a discrepancy emerges. Mückenpelz explains to the patients that after receiving special treatment, a
sick person "recover[s] more quickly," often in "only a few minutes."
To the hospital staff he indicates that the "cure" precedes the treatment. The speech to asylum patients more deliberately hides the
essence of special treatment, whose true meaning becomes obvious in
the instruction to physicians. Now called "final" treatment rather than
"special," the term suggests the Final Solution. The slippage effectively
deconstructs Nazi-Deutsch and the medical metaphor of the cure. The
movement from "special treatment" to "final treatment" and then to
the unstated Final Solution indicates what Mückenpelz and the hospital staff already know but will not say: that they are engaged in murdering "undesirables."

One patient, diagnosed as an "incurable psychopath, Marxist"
sighs and mutters a single word—"criminal" (59)—before dying.
Although he cannot empower himself to escape death, by his utterance
he refutes the constructs of Nazi-Deutsch which make his death desirable and legitimate. However, Mückenpelz instructs the doctor administering the fatal injection to issue a more detailed—and completely
fabricated—account of the proceedings. The medical report should
include the following:

> The sick man gazed at me out of mute eyes and begged me to
> grant a last wish. He said: I beg your forgiveness, Doctor, for

having caused you and the Herr Professor so much work. I
realize of course that I have unconsciously sympathized with
the Bolsheviks all my life, but I tried to keep it secret in the
examination. May my death bring happiness and prosperity
to Germany. (59)

Mückenpelz retroactively silences the dying man, effacing his last
words and negating his perspective. The patient's accusatory language
is displaced by Mückenpelz's ventriloquized confession which accords
with the metaphoric conventions of Nazi-Deutsch. Mückenpelz's report
invents an execution scene that vindicates the punishment and marks
a restoration of order.[2] That the scene never actually takes place is of no
importance; what matters is the documentation. The paperwork reaf-
firms the predominance of language over reality. Similarly, a study of
Nazi-Deutsch notes the frequent use of the phrase *auf der Flucht
erschossen* to explain the deaths of some labor camp inmates; often, the
slave laborers were shot for sport right in the camp. The formulaic
explanation, while completely fictitious, linguistically justified the
shooting by fabricating an escape, earning the killer a reward for vigi-
lance (Blumenthal, "Nazi Vocabulary" 60).

Wimper, the doctor in charge of administering the lethal treatments, reacts with disgust to Mückenpelz's verbal juggling. He ridicules
its inflated rhetoric: "Science! Serving your fellow men! Professional
ethics! Saviours of humanity! A lot of phrases, cooked up by men like
Mückenpelz and mouthed by every fool!" (58). However, as a later
drunken conversation with Wohlbrecht reveals, Wimper possesses his
own set of abstractions whose rhetoricity, like the "winged words" Eichmann nostalgically recalls, blinds him to his own culpability.

When we say extermination we mean extermination and
when we say keeping the blood pure we mean keeping the
blood pure. If somebody's got an abscess, you cut it out. Jews
and Communists, Freemasons and clergymen, asocial elements and idiots are an abscess. It's got to be lanced. (67)

Wimper begins with an insistence on concrete language—"extermination"—which contrasts with Mückenpelz's figurative speech. However,
he immediately slips into the Nazi metaphors of racial purity, racial
degeneration, and disease. Like Mückenpelz, Wimper uses figurative
language to place his action in a context he finds acceptable, even lauda-
tory. While the syntax of Wimper's sentences indicates that he believes
he is stating matters as simply and as concretely as possible, the words
themselves indicate a pattern of thought as detached from actuality as

Mückenpelz's theory of reform. "Extermination" (Ausmerzen)—the least abstract of Wimper's terminology—is itself a metaphor that equates the murder of undesirables with squashing insects. Keeping the blood pure (Bluterhaltung) introduces a theoretical framework by which to evaluate particular actions that, in another context, would be deemed utterly criminal. By the time Wimper shifts to the abscess (Geschwür) metaphor, he no longer recognizes the undesirables as independent subjects. Rather, they signal invasion or infection of the body politic, and thus their removal constitutes sound medical practice. The "it" of the final sentence thoroughly objectifies the victims, so that their murder is no murder at all. Moreover, the progress from active verbs—"we say," "we mean," "you cut"—to the passive "it's got to be lanced" obscures agency and, thus, accountability. Despite the stated aspiration for precision and concreteness, which the declarative construct of Wimper's syntax affirms, Wimper will not utter the one precise term for what he does at St. Veith: murder. Thus, paradoxically, the Nazi lexicon multiplies in order to ensure silence about the killings—at St. Veith, in the ghettos, in the camps.

Taken together, the remarks offered by Mückenpelz and Wimper suggest not only a general connection between violence and abstraction but also the specific role of physicians in the Nazi biomedical vision and the function of that vision in facilitating genocide. The Nazi physician was crucial, not incidental, to atrocity. As both Mückenpelz's and Wimper's comments indicate, Nazi racial thinking expressed itself through metaphors of death and disease—metaphors concretized in killing centers. Jews, and others deemed unworthy of life (*lebensunwertes Leben*), were viewed as diseased organs to be amputated, or as vermin to be exterminated, for the well-being of the body. The programmed extermination of these people, no longer regarded as people, took this medical metaphor to its literal conclusion. Even the notorious and ghastly medical experiments performed in the concentration camp—and alluded to in Lind's story with Mückenpelz's vat of pickled genitals—represented not random acts of sadism that opportunistically exploited the helplessness of the concentrationee. Rather, they were intimately bound up in the Nazi biomedical vision, in the ideal of race purification, and in the vision of Jew as life-threatening. In this light, murder appeared life-affirming, saving the body politic, the German nation. Authorizing this "healing" and lending it legitimization was the physician.

In *Nazi Doctors*, Robert J. Lifton proposes a psychological model—the paradigm of "doubling," or the "divided self"—to help explain the coexistence of extreme cruelty and extreme decency in the same person.

The "healing-killing paradox" reached its most exaggerated form in the concentration camp, where the doctor's self split into two distinct entities—what Lifton refers to as the "Auschwitz" or "killing self," and the former or "healing" self. The healing self carried on the doctor's previous notions of decency and humane conduct, and his professionality. The Auschwitz self bore the brunt of the concentrationary universe and also shouldered the guilt. This second self did the "dirty work"—the killing, selections, medical experimentation—so that the healing self could keep a clear conscience. In addition, the ideological beliefs of the Auschwitz self enabled the Nazi doctor to see his murderous actions in a different light. The Auschwitz self constructed a network of meanings and significations designed to fend off feelings of culpability. Thus, the divided self performed a sort of psychological legerdemain, which allowed the doctor to override moral judgments and to call murder by another name.

The deterioration of language that pervaded the Third Reich fostered this psychological split. Not only Nazi doctors employed this linguistic tactic. Through Wohlbrecht, the primary consciousness of "Soul of Wood," Lind explores the divided self and its role in perpetuating Nazi atrocity among bystanders. For all his consternation at the obfuscatory term "special treatment," Wohlbrecht, too, uses muddled thinking and cluttered verbiage to cordon off the good from the bad self. Central to Lind's critique is not Wohlbrecht's repeated moral compromise but his steadfast refusal to acknowledge, even to himself, that any compromise has been made. For example, called upon by both Mückenpelz and Wimper to spy upon the other, Wohlbrecht finds a way to comply without admitting he is acting dishonorably. He reasons, "Drink wine, hear what you can hear, give an opinion from time to time; 'report' was a Prussian word that didn't have to be taken seriously" (65). For Wohlbrecht, language becomes a means to perpetually straddle moral issues. He neither joins the Nazi cause nor commits himself to work against it, thus he finds himself espousing conflicting views simultaneously, willfully unaware of the contradictions.

Even more illustrative of the "healing-killing paradox" is Wohlbrecht's "rescue" of Anton Barth. Compelled by a vaguely reasoned sense of honor but frightened by the possible consequences, Wohlbrecht both fulfills and abrogates his promise to Anton's parents. In secreting Anton in a secluded mountain cabin, Wohlbrecht faces real peril—indeed, his brother-in-law dies in the rescue effort. Once at the cabin, however, Wohlbrecht abandons Anton to certain death. Since the paralyzed boy is incapable of feeding himself, Wohlbrecht knows he will soon starve, despite the safe haven and modest provisions. Wohlbrecht maintains an incessant chatter as he carries Anton up the mountain, a hyperverbiage by which he avoids acknowledging the inevitable outcome of his partial rescue.

The muteness of the youth—he can only mutter a few barely comprehensible sounds—contrasts sharply with his guardian's prattle, calling attention to its freneticism and also its emptiness. Wohlbrecht's subsequent references to young Anton highlight the guilt he refuses to admit consciously. He tells an acquaintance that Anton is "just fine. And he eats like a horse. Yes, he's fine. I'm not worried about him, he's got his belly full" (49). At the same time, Wohlbrecht brags of the fine skeleton he has hidden away in the forest: "in the woods I got my skeleton, not my own, I was just talking, it's Toni's" (50). Just as Wohlbrecht both saves young Anton and condemns him to death, Wohlbrecht's words contain a version of a living and a dead boy. Pressed to explain the discrepancy, Wohlbrecht evades the issue with grotesque humor: "for a stiff he looks good and healthy. 'Cause he eats all day. You never saw such an appetite. One of these days he'll eat me too" (50). Embedded in Wohlbrecht's ludicrous explanation lies the guilty admission he refuses to speak (just as Mückenpelz's address to the asylum inmates reveals more about their fate than the professor would care to have them know). Thus, Lind links the speech of Nazi collaborators with willful omissions and with psychic distancing from atrocity. In Lind's later fiction, language becomes fragmented almost to the point of impenetrability;[3] not only the characters but even the reader can barely discern the issues at hand.

Appropriately enough, in "Soul of Wood," which focuses on the abuse and deterioration of language, the only surviving Jew cannot speak intelligibly. Born as a freak with a large head, a shriveled torso and shrunken limbs, Anton Barth gradually grows a body, but develops only minimal motor coordination. His paralysis leaves him virtually mute; only his parents and Wohlbrecht can understand the foghornlike sounds he emits. Unlike the other characters in the story, who speak constantly but avoid thinking very much, young Barth thinks continually but converses with no one. The narrative thus sets up an opposition between speech and thought. Barth's large, lashless eyes, paralyzed like the rest of his body, perpetually stare out at the world, but like the boy in Kosinski's *The Painted Bird*, he cannot share his observations. Speech, Lind indicates, used too often as a political tool, loses its power to communicate and to stimulate perception.

The progress of Anton Barth's aphasia moves in counter-direction to that of Kosinski's protagonist. While Kosinski introduces to us a normal, healthy boy rendered mute by his encounter with human cru-

elty, Lind's paralytic begins to speak (and to move) as he moves away
from people—and as the result of the "agonizing pain" (39) inflicted by
a charging stag that blunders into the cabin. The muteness of Kosinski's boy establishes a kinship with silent, victimized animals; Anton
Barth excitedly tells the animals gathering around him on the moun-
taintop, "You don't have to be afraid of me. A miracle just happened to
me. I can talk. . . . I can talk. . . . All I had was thoughts and a mouth
and eyes" (39). Barth joins a deer herd, exercising his new verbal ability only with animals. In view of the degeneration of speech among
humans, he has found the only means possible to safeguard his own
from corruption. To people he speaks only one word—his own name—
which he shouts over and over into the valley. Finally, Barth metamorphoses into a deer; after the war, he is found with hay in his mouth,
craving salt.

After the German defeat, a handful of Nazis and collaborators
come to claim him as "their" Jew. In order to acquit themselves of war
crime charges, they plan to pretend to have saved Barth at great personal risk.[4] When they demand his identity papers, Barth tells them,
"I'm a deer" (93). Once among people, he does not utter another word.
The motley collection of war criminals demand that Wohlbrecht sign an
affidavit attesting to their fabricated role in Barth's rescue. Once again,
language—this time the official documents—camouflages and recon-
figures reality.

The metamorphosis of human into animal is a recurrent trope in
Shoah fiction. The human who speaks only with animals or who imitates
animal (non)speech disassociates from a human discourse of cruelty.
Paradoxically, out of the unintelligible sounds and silences of animals,
emerge the human voices of victims whose humanity was denied by
their tormenters. Nazi jargon obscures the suffering of the victims,
which becomes visible again in tropes of animal talk. In Kosinski's novel,
the boy's muteness reinforces his identification with dumb animals and
their plight, the equivalence established by means of his aphasia. Ernie
Levy, the protagonist of André Schwarz-Bart's novel, *The Last of the
Just*, metamorphoses into a dog, barking, begging, and galloping around
a restaurant table.

Like Kosinski's animal dumbness and Lind's deer talk, Ernie's
barking expresses a profound sense of despair, a deep anguish. Ernie
"decide[s] to be a dog" (324) because of his family heritage and because
of his own experience under Nazism. The last of a dynasty of *lamed-
vov*—thirty-six holy men on whose righteousness the survival of the
world depends—Ernie[5] possesses a special sensitivity to human suffering. For the *lamed-vov*, transmuting into a dog is a trope for cosmic

despair in Schwarz-Bart's narrative. When "the spectacle of the world is an unspeakable hell . . . [o]ther Lamed-Vov, like Hecuba shrieking at the death of her sons, are said to have been transformed into dogs" (5). Ernie bears a burden far weightier than that of his predecessors: the misery and brutal murder of Jews in the Third Reich. Under such unprecedented conditions of atrocity, Ernie's wife warns that without an unshakable faith in God, "we'd all become dogs, like the Just Man of Saragossa, when God abandoned him for only one minute" (368). Ernie's barking thus incorporates both the suffering he witnesses and his loss of faith in a just and powerful God.

Ernie's canine metamorphosis encapsulates Jewish destiny at the hands of the Nazis. At a young age he learns that the Reich values dogs more than Jews. This realization begins when a rabidly pro-Hitler teacher explains to Ernie's class that any instructions issued to the class apply only to German students, not to their "guests," the Jewish children. Should the teacher wish to address these "guests," he will so indicate by prefacing his remarks with the name of an animal. Thus, he orders, *"Die Hunde, die Neger und die Juden austreten!* . . . Dogs, Negroes and Jews, step forward!" (250). When a gang of schoolboys ambush Ernie, "the beast a-borning rose to the little boy's throat, and he howled for the first time" (263). To stave off their attack, he growls menacingly and bites them, transforming himself into the creature of their rhetoric. Ernie's growling dog represents the beast they see in him—the beast within the Jew-hater, projected outward onto the body of the Jew and absorbed internally by Ernie.

Later, bound for Auschwitz, Ernie watches an SS guard order his dog to attack a Jewish woman: *"Man destroy that dog!"* (414). The death of Ernie's entire family in a detention camp in France and the atrocities perpetrated against the Jews of Europe pushes Ernie to rebel against God and the sacred heritage of the *lamed-vov* tradition.

> If it is the will of the Eternal, our God, I damn his name and beg him to gather me up close enough to spit in his face. And if . . . we must see the will of nature everywhere and in all things, I ask Nature humbly to make me an animal as quickly as possible. . . .
>
> Which is why, with your permission, I shall do everything humanly possible from now on to turn myself into a dog. (322–23)

Ernie studiously imitates "with all his heart and soul, the local manner of being a dog." He changes his name from Levy to Bâtard (mutt), grows a moustache that gives his face "the look of a poodle," and walks

with "a friskiness" (323). The abandonment of his Jewish name signifies
the rejection of his identity as Jew, the sloughing off of his "now rejected
Levy skin." For Ernie, becoming "a dog" implies an abandonment of
his *lamed-vov* mission and its constellation of values. As "a dog," Ernie
molds himself into the figure of Nazi rhetoric. In this guise, he insinu-
ates himself into French Catholic society, carousing in cafés and fine
restaurants while Nazi forces round up and murder the Jews of Europe.

In Schwarz-Bart's novel, becoming "a dog" signifies three discrete
and contradictory meanings: the righteous "Lamed-Vov . . . transformed
into dogs" in anguished solidarity with human suffering; the victim,
"Dogs, Negroes and Jews," barred from human discourse; and the collaborator, like the "dog" Ernie becomes, welcomed into the society of perpetrators. These elements coalesce in Ernie's final canine performance.

> First it was vigorous "arf-arf"s that he barked against his
> plateful of bones, then a spectacular tumble, after which he
> got up on all fours and, amid general hilarity, galloped
> grotesquely around the large table. One of the women threw
> him a bone, which he dug into, teeth flashing, in perfect
> mimicry. . . . Finally he springs at Mélanie on all fours, and
> tries to bite off a pretty chunk of flesh. . . . Finally Ernie . . .
> sits up, delicately pinches Mélanie on the cheek and barks in
> her face. . . . Laughter all around. Which stops suddenly
> when they see that Ernie is galloping around the table at a
> frantic, desperate rate and that tears from the depths of his
> drunken soul are running down his cheeks while he barks
> hoarsely, as if at death—barks, barks endlessly. . . . (324–25)

The scene begins as a celebration of hedonism and of the bestial side of
human nature, aspects foreign to the *lamed-vov* tradition and integral
to the forces Ernie joins. Midway through his canine performance, however, a change occurs; Ernie finds himself acting a different sort of dog
than he intends. At the moment when Ernie feels overwhelmed by the
depth of human suffering, he decides to "become a dog," because the
Nazi beast denies the subject experience of its victims. As part of his
doggish act, Ernie barks at Melanie and pinches her cheek. "[S]uddenly
feeling the extravagant sweetness of a human face between his thumb
and his index finger" (325) Ernie recoils as though burned. The sudden
contact jolts Ernie out of his unfeelingness into an exquisite sensitivity
to the other's humanness. The shock of human touch awakens him to
the communion of suffering that constitutes the domain of the *lamed-
vov*. He becomes again not the Nazi beast but "a dog with Jewish eyes"
(338) whose tears and anguished barking link him with the ancestral

lamed-vov, transformed to dogs at the sight of human misery. Ernie has come full circle, ready to resume his place with the doomed "dogs" rather than share in the bestial commonality of their enemies.

Official manipulation of language to marshal public opinion and direct behavior is not the exclusive hallmark of the National Socialist Party nor even of totalitarian regimes. One need not look far for manifestations of what Orwell calls "Doublespeak"; George Mosse cites the replacement of the title "Secretary of War" by the less bellicose-sounding "Secretary of Defense" in the United States ("Embourgeoisement")—a cogent but by no means unusual example of this sort of linguistic maneuvering. This universal proclivity—which normalizes atrocity and deflects individual accountability—helps explain how ordinary people commit acts of extraordinary cruelty. But the discrepancy between the appealing words and the gruesome reality, and the extent to which the rhetoric pervades the fabric of society in the Third Reich, represents a different order of magnitude. One study of Nazi-Deutsch begins with the assertion that, were a scholar with no historical knowledge of the era to analyze Nazi documents and contemporaneous newspaper articles, he might well conclude

> that the era in which it was created was one of comparative peace and tranquility, unprecedented in German history. The disingenuity suffusing this language, the criminal and even murderous motives which underlay it, can only be conceived by examining words, idioms and expressions side by side with the objects and situations they were used to describe and convey. (Blumenthal, "Nazi Vocabulary" 50)

Moreover, as dissident voices were stilled through murder, fear, or exile, only the voice of Nazi propaganda remained to gloss the activities in the Reich.

Because that voice spoke German and carried with it the resonance of German culture, many opponents of the Reich adjudged that language tainted, permanently perhaps, by its Nazi associations. For Germans whose life's work was intimately bound up with language—writers and actors, for example—the Nazi appropriation of their native tongue placed them in a particular dilemma. Some, like the protagonist of Klaus Mann's novel, *Mephisto*—a roman-à-clef based on the life of Mann's brother-in-law, opera singer Gustav Grundgens—capitulated to the Reich. Out of fear or avarice, these people added their voices to the swelling chorus of "Heil Hitler!" Others, like Klaus Mann's father, Thomas Mann, and Bertolt Brecht, chose exile, as much to preserve their language from corruption with Nazi-Deutsch as to save their own lives. To speak or write German in Germany was to mouth lies; only in exile could one maintain one's integrity as a German writer. In his poem "Deutschland," Brecht sadly acknowledges,

> In deinen Hause
> Wird laut gebrüllt Lüge ist
> Aber die Wahrheit
> Mus schweigen.
> Ist es so? (112)

> [In your house
> Lies are roared aloud.
> But the truth
> Must be silent.
> Is it so?]

Jewish writing frequently figures German as a lost language, preserved—if at all—in a rarified form by victims of Nazi atrocity. For Elias Canetti, only those who remained uncontaminated by the "terrible events" of the Reich preserved the purity and innocence of the German language. As a Jew, Canetti feels strangely beholden to the country that sentenced him to a dehumanized and brutal death. In *The Human Province* he asserts, "The language of my intellect will remain German—because I am Jewish. . . . I want to give back to their language what I owe it. I want to contribute to their having something that others can be grateful for" (53). He urges those who, like himself, safeguarded the German tongue from contamination through Nazi association to relinquish their charge politely and graciously:

> People will soon be looking for their own language, which was stolen from them and deformed. Anyone who has kept it pure during the years of utmost madness will have to hand it over . . . he now owes the Germans their language; he has kept it clean, but he now has to hand it over with love and gratitude, with interest and compound interest. (65)

In Canetti's curious formulation, the "people" in quest of their "stolen language"—people who were, themselves, speaking German in Germany during the years 1933 to 1945—somehow attain a neutral status, neither despoilers nor guardians of their native tongue. Canetti leaves unclear what exactly these "people" were doing at the time, and how they may be distinguished from the language-thieves. In *At the Mind's Limit*, Austrian Jean Améry, who fled the Nazis to Belgium and survived Auschwitz and Bergen-Belsen, notes, "In the years of exile our relationship to our homeland was akin to that toward our mother tongue. In a very specific sense we have lost it, too, and cannot initiate proceedings for restitution" (51). Unlike Canetti, Améry feels he cannot restore to Germany what he himself no longer possesses.

The trope of the lost language appears also in the writing of Paul Celan, whose poetry reflects both Améry's sense of disenfranchisement and Canetti's idea of guardianship. Celan's language, suffused with archaisms and obscurities, aspires to an uninterrupted link with a much earlier German—one that precedes the Reich by several centuries—thus neatly dissociating itself from Nazi-Deutsch. By inserting transliterated Hebrew words in some of his later poems he offers his German audience a language that excludes them, as German society excluded him during the Nazi era.[6] Like Canetti, Celan, as it were, returns the German language to the German people. Unlike Canetti, Celan makes them work for it. Despite its linguistic and conceptual difficulty, Celan's poetry offers its readers neither oblivion nor absolution from a guilty past. Although Celan eschews Nazi neologisms, *l'univers concentrationnaire* forms the nucleus of his works. In his Bremen speech of 1958, Celan insists:

> It, language, remained: yes, in spite of all. But it had to go through its own answerlessness, go through a terrible muteness, go through the thousand darknesses of death-bringing speech. It went on living, and gave birth to no words to describe what had happened; but it survived these events. Survived and came to light again, "enriched" by it all.[7]

Celan does not write in German to repay a debt nor to proffer a gift; rather, as one of his translators suggests, his German words pose "questions they could ask only in (and of) the mother tongue" (Felstiner, "Translating" 22). Celan's personal dissociation from a personal and literary Germanic heritage is emblemized by the romanization and orthographic transposition of his original (Germanic) family name, Ancel, into the anagrammatic Celan.

Precisely this linguistic "enrichment" ("angereichert") to which Celan refers in the Bremen speech leads George Steiner to conclude, "Everything forgets. But not a language" ("Language and Silence" 150). Nazi-Deutsch sounded the death knell of the German language, argues Steiner in his famous essay on the uses of German during the Reich.

> Use a language to conceive, organize, and justify Belsen; use it to make out specifications for gas ovens; use it to dehumanize man during twelve years of calculated bestiality.

Something will happen to it. Make of words what Hitler and Goebbels and the hundred thousand *Untersturmführer* made: conveyors of terror and falsehood. Something will happen to the words. Something of the lies and sadism will settle in the marrow of the language. . . . It will no longer perform, quite as well as it used to, its two principal functions: the conveyance of humane order which we call law, and the communication of the quick of the human spirit which we call grace. (143)

Not a willful forgetfulness but rather "only the most drastic truth" (151), Steiner cautions, can quicken the moribund language. Celan pursues this fierce and drastic truth, following language in its journey through "the thousand darknesses of death-bringing speech," perhaps paying with his life for the harrowing voyage.[8]

Other writers found the language of the Third Reich utterly unredeemable and ceased to write in it or to speak in its cadences. Like Celan, Jean Améry romanized his Germanic name (Meyer) with a near anagram; for Améry, this divestiture marked the end of all Teutonic associations. After the war, he recalls, "I avoided speaking it, my language, and chose a pseudonym with a Romance ring" (65). Améry's estrangement from his native tongue had begun years earlier; racial laws enacted in the German tongue against Jews irredeemably tainted the language. He recollects, "since the day when an official decree forbade me to wear the folk costume that I had worn almost exclusively from early childhood on, I no longer permitted myself the dialect" (43). Similarly, Jakov Lind, also a Jewish Austrian survivor of the concentrationary universe, after initially publishing several fictional works in German, wrote a sequence of memoirs and essays in English rather than in his native tongue. "English, after May 1940, was simply the sound of defiance, the language of reason," Lind explains. For Lind, the Nazi genocide has forged an intimate association of German with atrocity, of French with collaboration ("John Brown" 589). Lind's love for the German language, "was destroyed forever by the millions of people who later drowned in a Teutonic abyss of *Achtungs* and *wird erschossens*, which followed the *Judenraus* and the *Judasverecke* language" (*Numbers* 75). By abrogating their civil rights and ultimately their right to exist, German racial laws deprived Jews of legal voice, ultimately imposing the radical muteness of death. Like many other Jews who survived the Nazi genocide, Lind and Améry respond with a willful muteness in the German tongue after the war.

Whether something inherent to German language or culture lent itself easily to the Nazi purpose, or whether a particular constellation of historical events placed the language of Goethe and Rilke in the mouths of Hitler and Goebbels, the language and the phenomenon remain inextricably yoked in subsequent considerations of the era. Much of the force of Charles Chaplin's parody of Adolf Hitler in his 1940 film *The Great Dictator* stems from Führer Adenoid Hynkel's guttural sputter in an incomprehensible babble. In approximating and also caricaturizing German, Chaplin mocks Hitler's emotionally charged but intellectually bankrupt harangues in meaningless throat explosions. In truth, however, few laughed at Hitler's speeches. Most listeners found Hitler's (and Goebbels's) voice mesmerizing and compelling. On radio, at rallies, in newsreels, the voice of Hitler stood for Hitler and also for Germany, and came to be identified as the essence of Hitler and of Germany. That voice acquired the power to set off wave upon wave of destruction.

George Steiner's novella *The Portage to San Cristobal of A.H.* imagines a fugitive Hitler who survives the war. In the novella, Hitler's voice poses a threat to the men who track him down in South America and bring him to justice. Their journey through deep jungle to a small airstrip in San Cristobal is the "portage" of the title. The isolation of the jungle cuts off the group from civilization, except for a faint and intermittent radio link with their headquarters. The radio, once the vehicle for Hitler's racial ideology and the instrument of his power, symbolizes in Steiner's narrative the struggle to control speech, to be the sole voice that is heard. Over the airwaves, the leader of the operation cautions his men not to mistake the Führer's apparent enfeebled agedness for impotence. Hitler's power resides in his tongue and should not be underestimated.

> You must not let him speak, or only few words. To say his needs, to say that which will keep him alive. But no more. Gag him if necessary, or stop your ears as did the sailor. If he is allowed speech he will trick you and escape. . . . His tongue is like no other. (27)

Even the Nazi-hunters should not trust their own resolve to remain untouched by Hitler's skillful manipulation of language; the man who bent a nation to his malignant will may bend theirs too.

Hitler's words take on a metaphysical dimension in Steiner's novella. They represent the antipodal force to the creative power of the God of Genesis whose utterances bring the world into being. The radio transmission quotes to them from a sacred text:

> . . . there shall come upon the earth in the time of night a man surpassing eloquent. All that is God's, hallowed be his

name, must have its counterpart, its backside of evil and
negation. So it is with the Word, with the gift of speech that
is the glory of man and distinguishes him everlastingly from
the silence of animal noises of creation. When He made the
Word, God made possible also its contrary. Silence is not the
contrary of the Word but its guardian. No, He created on
the night-side of language a speech for hell. Whose words
mean hatred and vomit of life. Few men can learn that
speech or speak it for long. . . . But there shall come a man
whose mouth shall be as a furnace and whose tongue as a
sword laying waste. He will know the grammar of hell and
teach it to others. He will know sounds of madness and
loathing and make them seem music. Where God said, let
there be, he will unsay. (27)

Perhaps, warns the transmission, Hitler embodies the fulfillment of
that dire prophecy, the archvillain who will utter the "*one* word . . .
which if spoken in hatred, may end creation, as there was one that
brought creation into being" (27). The transmission concludes with a
lengthy incantatorial recitation of Nazi cruelties, linking the apocalyptic vision with the massive destruction that has already occurred.
The recitation, several pages of sentence fragments, evokes a Bosch-like
canvas of the sufferings of hell, with multiple scenes of human misery
occurring simultaneously. Indeed, reminds the radio voice, Hitler's
"words tore up our lives by the root" (82). As such, they herald the
apocalypse and precipitate the end of days.

In *Reflections of Nazism*, historian Saul Friedländer criticizes
what he views as the demonification of Hitler in Steiner's novella.
Friedländer's book discerns a "new discourse [on Nazism] . . . this transformation, this reelaboration, [of the past]" (12) which emerges more
than three decades after the collapse of the Third Reich. Friedländer's
critique focuses on fictional representations of the era—both in literature and in film—because, produced in increasing numbers, these imaginative representations command a growing audience, influencing the
way our culture(s) comes to know and understand the Nazi era. Moreover, in imaginative works "themes and aesthetics . . . allow us to perceive something of the psychological hold [of] Nazism" (18). Steiner's
portrayal of Hitler as "a demigod who, by the word, can invert the order
of things" disturbs Friedländer; the "quasi-metaphysical" aspect of
Steiner's version of Hitler's speech shifts focus from the human sphere
to the divine, thereby evading the issues of human responsibility and
historical accountability. In Friedländer's view, by linking Hitler with

supernatural forces of evil, Steiner removes not only Hitler but all Nazis from human judgment.[9] In actuality, Steiner's novella does not turn on an affirmation of Hitler's apocalyptic status. Rather than defining his moral and metaphysical stature, the power attributed to Hitler's speech by the (presumably Jewish) counter-voice on the radio expresses in surprisingly concrete terms the historical upheaval engendered by Hitler's words. By means of his diabolical metaphor, Steiner poses a seminal question: how was it possible that Hitler's words launched a reign of terror, which surpasses in cruelty what had heretofore been reserved in the human imagination for visions of hell and the end of days?

As in other writing about the Shoah, what at first appears to be metaphor and imaginative invention turns out to be a close approximation of actual events. Isser Harel, chief of the Israel task force that captured Eichmann, recollects the regulations that governed the operation:

> The guards were under strict instructions never to talk to Eichmann except with regard to personal requirements, such as eating and bathing. Gabi insisted that this was an indispensable security measure and must be meticulously observed, for he was sure that Eichmann, who had held such a crucial position in Hitler's Germany, must be a man of unusual craftiness, capable of taking us by surprise with some unexpected stratagems or cunning move. (201)

Harel remembers that "The men believed they had to contend with a satanic brain, a brain capable of springing a daring surprise on them" (202).[10] In Steiner's imagined and in Harel's factual account, the only antidote to the destructive capacity of Nazi speech is to impose muteness.

The morally confusing glibness traditionally ascribed to satanic forces underlies Steiner's metaphoric reflection on a regime whose rhetoric camouflaged terror with legalism and legitimacy. In an essay exploring the link between terror and the sublime, Saul Touster insists upon distinguishing the "innocent sublime," representing "divine sanction" and "justice," from the "demonic sublime," representing only destructive terror (149). Far from mystifying the Nazi movement and placing it beyond accountability, the demonic tropes in Steiner's and other writers' works expose Hitler's own Manichaean vision of the Germans as divine agents and the Jews as Satan incarnate.[11] These tropes also help to explain what enables ordinary men to commit demonically evil acts.

Like Steiner's novella, Touster's analysis focuses on the relationship between the innocent and the demonic because "when the destructive powers of the world wrap themselves in the cloak of legitimacy, as the Nazis did . . . the need to distinguish becomes more pressing, if more difficult" (149). The millennial terminology in which Hitler couched his new order made such distinctions difficult. The seductiveness of the Nazi apocalyptic vision provides the starting point for reading works such as Steiner's. Friedländer attributes to Steiner a perverse fascination with the Hitlerian mystique, grouping the novella with works such as Albert Speer's memoirs. Nonetheless, in his assessment of the power of "le verbe hitlérien" (*Reflets* 82) Friedländer himself reiterates the configuration of Harel's recollection of Eichmann's capture and of the cautionary radio transmission in Steiner's novella. Friedländer insists that any attempt to comprehend the events of the Third Reich must consider "the function of language . . . for language was always the decisive component of Hitler's influence" (79). According to the historian,

> Through his words, Hitler holds crowds under his spell, hypnotizes his entourage, paralyzes his domestic enemies, subjugates his foreign opponents; through his words, he establishes his power and provokes destruction. (79)

Steiner's focus on the power of Hitler's speech paradoxically deflects the reader's attention from Hitler as individual to the function of language in the Third Reich. Initially the target of Steiner's narrative appears to be the German language, which stands accused in several of Steiner's essays and which the novella identifies with the person of Hitler. Hitler's first spoken communication in the narrative—indeed, his only utterance for many chapters—is the novella's sole German word in the text, "Ich." Hitler is the German language, German utterance. Steiner's focus broadens, however, to examine a type of discourse—not *a* language, but language, not *a* speech, but speech. The counter-voice transmitted by shortwave radio fears the effect that the captive Hitler's words may exert upon the uninitiated—upon, for example, the young Israeli Nazi-hunter who "knows but does not remember" (28). This fear reflects the ability of language to obscure and even displace historical reality, to dislodge the listener from what he "knows" to be true. Thus, to escape the corrupting power of speech, the Israeli guardians must keep their captive mute.

Friedländer, too, urges a critical study of "not what Hitler said, but the way in which he said it" (79). For Friedländer the key to the overwhelming power of Hitlerian speech resides in "Hitler's other face, the face of silence" (80). The machinery of atrocity was set into motion secretly and in silence, left unarticulated although encoded in a Nazi rhetoric of hate.

> When we approach the final, irrevocable dividing line, the point of total rupture and no return—the decision to exterminate the Jews of Europe down to the last one—we are confronted only by silence. . . . Then comes the decision, in silence; the setting in motion of the machine of destruction, in silence; the end, in silence. (80)

The policy of *Nacht und Nebel* (night and fog) used not only words but also silence to enact the Nazi purpose. As configured in Steiner's novella, speech emerges as malignant, silence benign. Friedländer also makes more complicated difficult distinctions—between speech and speech, between silence and silence.

More importantly, Steiner's novella and Friedländer's critique point to an erosion of trust in the literary enterprise. The writer shares an unsettling kinship with the propagandist; the manipulation of words, symbols, and tropes becomes associated with the enactment of atrocity. Thus, Steiner suggests, after the Holocaust, the writer plies his craft with reluctance; Steiner's novella distrusts not only Hitler's but all forms of eloquence, whether spoken or written. Elsewhere Steiner elaborates, "Eloquence is suspect, formal speech is palsied with the lies, political, theological, moral, which it articulated and adorned. The honest man sings or mumbles" (*On Difficulty* 10). Hence, for example, the linguistic obscurity of Celan's poetry and Lind's fiction. The impenetrability of their works approximates muteness within articulation and implies that readers ought to approach all texts with suspicion. The antidote to facile credulity resides in language that yields up its meaning only with considerable effort.

In essence, these works suspect themselves, the medium that allows them to be written and read, and the eloquence that quickens them. In "A Conversation Piece," Steiner's extended Midrash on the *Akedah* (the biblical binding of Isaac, recounted in Genesis 22), Jews in the gas chamber wonder whether, in agreeing to sacrifice his son, "Abraham might have taken for the voice of God that of a demon" (106). Moments before dying, one of the Jews cautions the others "that these two voice, that of God whom we must not name and that of un-nameable evil, are so utterly alike. That the difference between them is only that of the sound of a rain-drop in the sea" (106). Awaiting the radical silencing of their life narratives, the Jews debate the wisdom and ethics of Abraham's unprotesting acquiescence to God's command, the bravery or cowardice of Isaac's silent acceptance, the implication of Sarah's silence, and the silence of God in their own time. While some of them suggest that Abraham's act may have been misguided, it is not these descendants of Abraham but their murderers who have inverted the voices of God and demon, good and evil, life and death. In this short fiction, which Steiner terms a parable, only the silencing of the voice that overwhelms by power and eloquence would allow other voices to continue speaking.

As figured in fictional responses to the Shoah, Nazi-Deutsch is an encoded language system constructed to veil the intent of its speaker while actualizing it. Like the historical Eichmann, the fictional Wohlbrecht and Mückenpelz, the historical Hitler and the fictional AH, the speaker of Nazi Deutsch utilizes a powerful rhetoric of persuasion and evasion to enact atrocity. Embedded in the eloquence of Nazi jargon is a muteness about concrete events, a muteness that masks the true purpose of the Nazi speech act. So long as one remains within that language system, one acquiesces to the atrocity built into the discourse. And yet, these works suggest, one need not remain stuck irrevocably in Nazi-Deutsch, victimized and made victimizer by language. However imperfectly, one has the choice to step outside that language, to make its mutenesses speak, however imperfectly.

8

Refused Memory

In the beginning was the Word: the Word was with
God and the Word was God. . . .
The Word was the true light that enlightens all men;
and he was coming into the world. . . .
The Word was made flesh, he lived among us, and we
saw his glory. . . .
                                              —John (1:1, 9, 14)

We had the chance to observe how the word became
flesh and how this incarnated word finally led to
heaps of cadavers.
                            —Jean Améry, *At the Mind's Limits*

Sounding a counter-note to the mute figures of Shoah literature, primarily victims, novels about collaboration often feature spectacularly articulate and loquacious characters. Rather than relying on the conventions and encoded references of Nazi-Deutsch to selectively exclude from language certain unsavory facts, these consummate talkers develop a private lexicon and highly complex symbolic system that substitute for concrete events. The presence of these hyperfluent characters opens up a means of exploring the seductions of Nazism.

Hyperfluent characters dazzle the reader with displays of linguistic cleverness and verbal expertise. Their oral masterliness creates the linguistic texture of the novels they inhabit—novels such as Michel Tournier's *The Ogre* and Günter Grass's *The Tin Drum*. As these novels make clear, excessive talking represents not the antipode of muteness but its other face. The preternatural eloquence of hyperfluent characters distracts the reader from what remains excluded from their engaging recitations: the murderous practices of the Third Reich.[1] Their hypnotic words and loaded silences associate them with Hitler whom they come to represent, to critique and to parody.[2] The narratives further connect hyperfluency and muteness with tropes of decay, excrement, and cannibalism, evolving in this a critique of certain language practices.

The hyperfluent character benefits from an unacknowledged association with Nazism by constructing elaborate and complicated symbolic networks, through whose grid atrocity simply disappears. The narrative's engagement with the character's creative brilliance opens up a means of critiquing genius, of making art and the artist available for ethical and not merely aesthetic judgment. The presence of the genius-speaker serves as a touchstone to the crisis of art set off by the Shoah. In narratives about victimization and survival, the figure of the mute witness triggers the question of art's adequacy to "represent" the Holocaust, to speak out of and for the events of history. However, in narratives about collaboration, the hyperfluent character implicates art—the symbolic and artistic imagination—in the construction of Nazi genocidal ideology and practice. In so doing, it dislodges "art" from its place of privilege. Art, in this light, is treated neither as a neutral site unaffected by ideology and politics (as the glib actor featured in Klaus Mann's *Mephisto* asserts) nor a site of moral privilege where moral questions are seen as inappropriate. Rather than isolating art, separating it out of the spheres of law, philosophy, ideology, and behavior, the figure of the hyperfluent genius suggests a radical interrogation of the artistic imagination and its complicitousness in the construction of atrocity.

This is superlatively illustrated in Michel Tournier's *The Ogre*, a novel about the life and secret writings of quirky and brilliant Abel Tiffauges during the war years. The novel traces the checkered life of Tiffauges, a self-proclaimed gentle ogre who inhabits simultaneously the seemingly incompatible realms of myth and history. Tiffauges has evolved an eccentric ideology to explain events in his personal life which he believes is bound up in some mysterious fashion with the events of history. He presumes that the external world configures itself to reveal and accord with his inner reality. In childhood, his boarding school burns down the very day he faces severe punishment for a prank gone awry; later, the French entry into the Second World War saves him from a lengthy prison sentence for the rape of a young girl. Both crimes were falsely attributed to him. A social misfit in his native France, Tiffauges thrives in exile. As a French prisoner of war in Nazi Germany, he gradually penetrates the Nazi power circle. After his capture by the Germans, Tiffauges manages, through a happy concatenation of events, to serve in succession as a forester's assistant, then as forester in Göring's private hunting estate, and, finally, as talent scout—that is, kidnapper—for a Napola (Nationalpolitische Erziehungsanstalten), an elite paramilitary training school for young exemplars of the Nazi racial ideal, destined for the SS.

The novel interweaves Tiffauges's private meditations as set down in his "sinister writings" (*écrits sinistres*)—literally, a journal he writes with his left hand—with conventional third person narrative. In both narratives Tiffauges explores the manifold signs by which the world of appearances indicates essential reality. Tiffauges elaborates an intricate symbolic network that radiates out from the key act of "phoria" (*la phorie*)—carrying—through benign and malign inversions. Symbolic meanings dictate Tiffauges's life choices; ultimately they lead him to become an unwitting participant in the concentrationary universe, whose symbolic order, he discovers late in the narrative, corresponds perversely to his own. What Tournier elsewhere terms the "hyperrealism, hyperrationalism" of his narrative (*Wind* 93), a surfeit of facts and scholarship, paradoxically unloose the novel from its specific historical underpinnings. Tiffauges wishes to commit the ultimate act of "phoria": carrying a child to safety as St. Christopher bore Christ across the water. Phoria promises "euphoria" whose joys exceed sexual ecstacy. His obsession meshes with the needs of the Third Reich. In this novel Tournier utilizes Tiffauges to examine the stance of the collaborator or the bystander who remains willfully unaware of the nature of his ally yet continues to benefit from the alliance.[3]

Tournier writes out of a strong but ambivalent connection to the German *Geist*. Raised in a family of Germanophiles—both his parents completed advanced degrees in Germanic studies at the Sorbonne— he grew up steeped in German culture. In his intellectual memoir, *The Wind Spirit*, Tournier explains that these intimate ties with Germany left him impervious to the seduction of Nazism but, at the same time, profoundly jarred by its essential connection with German culture. He contrasts himself with most of his French contemporaries who, he believes, "had only the most abstract idea" of Germany, seen through the "smoked lenses provided by France's inept and ignorant propaganda machine." By contrast, he explains, his family "knew it better. Having witnessed the birth of Nazism, we had been vaccinated against its blandishments. We knew what it whispered in private and mistrusted its intentions" (58). Tournier's fascination with German philosophy, with Fichte, Schelling, Hegel, Husserl, and Heidegger, brought him to the University of Tübingen shortly after the war, where he remained for several years. Despite Germany's apparent rapid economic recovery after the war, Tournier believed that German culture had been radically and profoundly impoverished by its anti-Semitic madness.

> the German Jew . . . those two elements combined to form such a happy marriage, yielding among other things the three pillars of modern Western civilization: Marx, Freud, and Einstein. . . . Consummated by a murderous wave of anti-Semitism, that divorce was the beginning of the end for Germany. . . . For Germans the loss was incalculable. (142–43)[4]

Had it not been for Hitler and the Nazis, Tournier feels that the German world "would have formed an economic and cultural unit comparable in power and influence to France in the seventeenth or England in the nineteenth century. . . . the world would have continued to be European, and it would have been German" (121) In *The Ogre* Tournier symbolically thinks through his ambivalent feelings about German culture and his dismay that this genius-producing culture produced an unprecedented machinery of atrocity.

In *The Ogre*, Tiffauges's appeal as a character lies in his virtuosic skill with the written word and in the eloquence and wit of his interior monologues. His discomfort with the spoken word stands out in curious contradiction. For Tiffauges, language is not social interaction but an internal event, one that eventually comes to be represented symbolically by the act of defecation.

Expansive in the privacy of his mind or his journal, he values texts but prefers to remain silent in public. A childish shyness evolves into stubborn reticence as an adult. Later, in the French army and in a German prisoner-of-war camp, he does not speak for long periods of time. Eventually, he entirely abandons speaking French, preferring the language of exile, German. From the beginning of the narrative, Tiffauges shows a marked distaste for conversation. With a cryptic silence, he cuts short a heated conversation with his lover, reasoning that since "for her, speech is always either caress or aggression, never a mirror of truth" (15), he needn't bother expressing his thoughts. In fact, her words prove more precise that his, her metaphors more apt and illuminating. When she calls him an "ogre" (22) or "a canary" he immediately understands her and concurs. Yet when he attempts to explain how he views her, he speaks in such generalities, constructing abstract categories of womanhood and sexuality, that she cannot understand him. In truth, he does not wish her to hold him accountable for his words and so withholds them. Only in his journal does he fully express himself, subject solely to his own indulgent scrutiny.

Even as a schoolboy, Tiffauges finds speech disappointing, almost useless. At his boarding school, students read aloud from the lives of saints during lunch. Because of the din, the reader must "bawl out the words *recto tono*, i.e., on a single note, without any intonation . . . a strange drone that pitilessly ironed out every shade of expression, whether interrogative, ironic, threatening, or amused, and made every sentence equally pathetic, plaintive, aggressive and vehement" (38). Thus, for Tiffauges, oral communication seems doomed to failure; only written texts carry meaning.

However, Tiffauges's journal—and the novel as a whole—ironically undermines the faith in texts that Tiffauges propounds. In one protracted scene, Tiffauges's childhood mentor, Nestor, rummages painstakingly through the teacher's trash basket for what will serve as toilet paper. When he finally leaves the classroom with a suitable fragment of paper, Tiffauges learns that Nestor's criteria center not on physical enhancements (softness, size, cleanliness) but on content— the text written on the paper. At a clandestine, nocturnal meeting in the stalls of the dormitory lavatory, Nestor squats over a toilet and relieves himself slowly and with intense concentration and visible satisfaction, expounding now upon his cosmological theories, now upon the deep meaning of feces, now upon the juncture of the two, finally extracting from his pocket "a rare kind of paper covered with the signs of a superior mind . . . [reserved for an exceptional occasion]" (57). For Nestor, excretion represents more than a necessary bodily function; it constitutes the supreme spiritual and intellectual act, the ultimate stage of a tripartite dynamic process: "His life's rhythm was the trilogy ingestion-digestion-defecation, and these three operations were surrounded by general respect" (20). The link between text and excrement comments derogatorily upon text.

This entire three-part process assumes a ritual aspect with Nestor and later with Tiffauges himself. The process serves as a metaphoric replacement for speech. Embedded in the extended metaphor are implications regarding the way one views and speaks of the self and the other. For Nestor and Tiffauges, matter signifies only the use one makes of it—nourishment, cleansing, omens—but never something in and of itself. In the same way, language, for Tiffauges, is always only reflexive; he speaks exclusively of and to the self. As Tiffauges interprets them, words and symbols never gesture toward any event or being outside of himself. Like his food system, Tiffauges's symbolic

order exemplifies the refusal, inherent in Nazi ideology, to see the other
as an other. The intimation of cannibalism, always present in
Tiffauges's ritualized meditations on eating, reinforce the disappearance of the other. Cannibalism destroys the other by absorbing the
other into the self for the good of the self.

In Tiffauges's system, the acts of ingestion and communion coalesce. Because eating functions as a metaphoric replacement for speech,
Tiffauges almost always eat silently. His lover accuses him, "You reduce
me to the level of a steak" (9); the novel opens with her complaint,
cited in Tiffauges's sinister writings: "You're an ogre" (3). This suggestion of cannibalism delights Tiffauges. The conjunction of eating and
loving imbue both with spiritual significance: "there's nothing degrad-
ing about likening love to eating. Many religions make a similar comparison—first and foremost Christianity, with the Eucharist" (9).
Tiffauges literalizes Rachel's metaphor after his induction into the
army. Instead of figuratively "devouring" his lover as though she were
"raw flesh" (8), he develops a love for horses, consumes massive quan-
tities of raw horsemeat, and views it as a love act.[5]

> When I say I love meat and blood and flesh the only thing
> that matters is the word "love." I am all love. I love eating
> meat because I love animals. I think I could even slaughter
> with my own hands an animal I'd raised as a pet, and eat
> with affectionate appetite. (67)

As Freud points out in *Totem and Taboo*, the cannibal wishes to absorb
by magic some essence of another being by consuming a portion of that
other. In that context, cannibalism, like speech, represents an oral
exchange—but one predicated upon the destruction of the other.
Tiffauges's obsession with "phoria" makes of the horse a totem. After
partaking of horsemeat, he grows horselike, all his muscles and bulk
concentrated in his back and hind quarters. Tiffauges's movement from
appreciation of horsemeat to appreciation of horse prepares him for
more drastic forms of cannibalism.

Although in the army Tiffauges simply cannot master Morse
code—a contrived set of arbitrary audible signs to transmit human
meaning over long distances—he shows natural talent for handling
homing pigeons, "living, throbbing sign-bearers" (150). He takes their
speechlessness as an analogue to his own, absorbing their being into his
own identity. During an attack, starving soldiers skewer and roast
three of Tiffauges's favorite pigeons. Initially disgusted by the suggestion that he, too, partake of their corpses, he resolves to starve rather
than eat his beloved companions. But hunger impels him to reconsider.
"Wasn't he in fact the only one who *ought* to eat the little murdered

corpses?" (150). Again conjoining love, eating, and spirituality in mute communion, Tiffauges muses that "the silent, devout ingestion of the three little murdered warriors would be something almost religious, the best homage that could be paid them" (150). Tiffauges denies his bereavement, displacing it through quasi-religious discourse. He disregards his sense of loss, his chagrin at failing to protect the birds, his guilt at partaking of their flesh. Instead, he explains that he eats not to sate his hunger, but to "feed his soul through intimate communion with the only creatures he'd loved for six months" (154).

In *The Painted Bird*, when the boy must participate in killing an animal he has befriended, or use its body for profit, he does so reluctantly and with horror. In a particularly grotesque and gory scene, the boy attempts to skin one of the rabbits he has tended—one whose cage he sleeps in—not realizing his blows have only stunned, but not killed, the animal. The half-skinned rabbit whose bloody pelt hangs in strips from his body as it hops madly about, and the boy's forced complicity in cruelty, are emblematic of the extreme cruelty of the Nazi era. The boy empathizes with the animal, witnessing its suffering. On the other hand, in *The Ogre*, Tiffauges shows no empathetic sense of the birds' suffering. He dispels his grief at their death by constructing a conceptual framework in which those deaths become bearable, even desirable. Significantly, he does so not by honestly assessing the pressing needs of the moment (his hunger, the lack of food, the birds' availability) that shape his desire, but by establishing an abstract system that redefines his deed. To construct this system, arbitrarily imposed on his material situation, he usurps a religious terminology of transcendence, suggesting a parallel with Nazi rhetoric, which the novel develops further.

The narrative seizes upon the ogrish aspect of Nazi Germany, portraying the regime as a monster that cannibalizes its own youth. Tiffauges links the mythological flesh-eating giant (such as the one who menaces Jack atop the beanstalk) with Göring, "the ogre of Rominten" (Göring's hunting lodge), and Hitler, "the ogre of Rastenburg" (Hitler's country retreat). The annual induction of ten-year-old boys and girls into Hitler Youth on Hitler's birthday suggests a primordial sacrifice of virgins to propitiate an insatiable and all-powerful man-eating beast:[6] "the ogre of Rastenburg . . . demanded of his subjects the exhaustive birthday gift of five hundred thousand little girls and five hundred thousand little boys, ten years old, dressed for the sacrifice, or in other words naked, out of whose flesh he kneaded his cannon fodder" (236). Repeatedly satisfying Hitler's carnivorous demands transforms Germany into a self-consuming monster, a cannibal who ultimately eats his own flesh.

The ogrish link between Tiffauges and Hitler gives the cannibal motif its specific resonance. Dubbed "the ogre of Kaltenborn" (the estate appropriated for the Napola) by fearful parents, Tiffauges roams the countryside kidnapping prepubescent Aryans, literally sniffing them out, ogrelike.[7] In an obvious parallel to his work with pigeons, Tiffauges collects and cares for scores of young boys at the Napola. Tiffauges forms a special attachment to four of the boys, whose hair color corresponds to the plumage of his favorite birds. When Russian forces bombard the Napola, Tiffauges finds three of his favorites impaled upon heraldic spears, imagistically recapitulating the three roasted pigeons. While Tiffauges does not actually devour the boys, the pattern of repetition maintains the ogrish motif and the suggestion of cannibalism.

The repetitive pattern of love-ingathering-destruction underscores Tiffauges's role in the violent death of all the Napola boys. The Russian attack on the Napola shifts the Tiffauges/Hitler/ogre convergence out of myth and into history. The carnage Tiffauges witnesses underscores the complicitousness inherent to his willful unknowingness. The figure of the ogre then becomes the emblem not of a demonized Führer but of Germany itself, complicitous in its own destruction.[8]

One result of cannibalism is that whatever one perceives as other, as external to oneself, becomes incorporated into and identified with oneself. Thus, the impulse toward empathy with the other becomes only pity for oneself. Tiffauges's initial love/grief for his slaughtered pigeons—pity for the other perceived as other—is immediately displaced (through the act of eating) by love/pity for himself. Later, Tiffauges kidnaps young German boys from their home to place them in his abstract, symbolic order, which is also the brutally physical order of Nazism. Because Tiffauges narcissistically blurs the distinction between self and other, consuming the other into the self, he believes he is taking them home. Tiffauges remains oblivious to the boys' anguish at being torn from home and family, convinced he is reconstituting a pure and organic society. Tournier's superimposition of the image of the skewered birds and the skewered boys underscores the essential cannibalistic narcissism of Tiffauges's role as collector. Rather than becoming an empathetic witness to the suffering of loved ones, Tiffauges enfolds the reality of death—of the pigeons, of the boys—into a symbolic operation.

The elaborate symbolic order Tiffauges constructs is crucial to maintaining a willful ignorance of Nazi destructiveness. While evidence of Nazi violence abounds, Tiffauges translates his observations into abstract terminology laden with symbolic (but not literal) meaning.

Tiffauges keeps out of language any concrete acknowledgement of actual events in Germany, of the destiny of the boys he collects. This selective muteness about certain historical events finds symbolic expression in the two functions, cannibalism and defecation, both inversions of intelligible utterance whereby the speaker orally imparts some meaningful part of his thoughts and feelings to another, the listener. Just as ingestion substitutes for communion, for the worded and wordless exchanges between intimates, so defecation displaces speech.

As communion, eating is a form of remembering. In partaking of the Eucharist, for example, the eater corporeally becomes one with memory, and memory becomes part of the self. Defecation, then, is way of forgetting, of making external to the self what was previously taken in. What had been eaten earlier and become part of the self as memory is impelled out of the body, turned into a disconnected object that is no longer one's memory and may be disposed. As an act of refusing memory—that is, both denying it and turning it into refuse (waste)—Tournier's novel inverts the significance of the excremental vision that predominates in the reflections of Nazi victims. In Kosinski's *The Painted Bird*, for example, the protagonist's muteness is associated with his forced immersion in a pool of excrement; in Lena Wertmüller's *Seven Beauties*, the anarchist ironically escapes the moral complicitousness inherent to his survival by plunging into a latrine whose filth engulfs him. In Kitty Hart's and Charlotte Delbo's remembrances, being soiled with one's own waste becomes an emblem for the dehumanizing atrocity they endured. In these works and others, the pervasive sight and stench of excrement comes to represent the concentrationary universe, a concrete manifestation of what the Nazis termed *anus mundi*. Shaped by disease and a deliberate policy of humiliation, the cloacal world of the ghettos and camps reminded their victims in inescapable physical terms of their utter helplessness to control even their own bodily functions.

By contrast, Tournier's protagonist takes pleasure in an excessively detailed concern for his excreta. He regards defecation as a means of creative expression, which is also a withdrawal from human discourse and historical memory. Even before he reaches Germany, Tiffauges develops a ritual to mitigate despair: *le brame*—a staglike bellowing. This roar represents "at one and the same time a mime of despair and a kind of rite to overcome it" (42). For Tiffauges, the *brame* wordlessly expresses anguish while cathartically cleansing and calming him. In enacting this inhuman roar, Tiffauges does more than exchange animal for human discourse. He shifts the very medium from linguistic to digestive, from symbolic to physiological. Tiffauges describes the *brame* as "a sort of deep long-drawn-out belch which seems to rise from my innards and makes my neck vibrate. It exhales all the sorrow of living and all the anguish of dying" (42). Tiffauges's despair is vocalized in a long belch, a case of cosmic indigestion that evolves finally into a ritual he calls "the john shampoo or the caca-shampoo" (42). To enact this, he plunges his face into the toilet bowl and flushes. Unlike Kosinski's protagonist who is sickened and horrified by his fetid plunge, Tiffauges feels exhilarated by his excremental encounter. The boy emerges from the cesspool in despair, convinced that evil forces rule the world. Tiffauges emerges from his "caca-shampoo" soothed.

The more Tiffauges withdraws from speech, the more he feels drawn toward excrement. He withholds words as a child might withhold feces. The dynamics suggests an interrelation, developed in another context by Terry Eagleton, between Freud's theory of anal eroticism and literary discourse. According to Eagleton,

> Through an erotic fissure in the replete body, products may emerge to dominate or cajole those around us, gifts which are also weapons, artfully wrought communications than which nothing, after all, could be more nature. The pleasure of creating for its own sake, with no particular end in mind, mingles with the most calculatedly instrumental of emissions— just as the destructive thrill of self-undoing is overshadowed by the anxiety of loss.[9]

Tiffauges's undersized genitalia underscore the infantile aspect of his arrested anal development. Although for Tiffauges "Constipation is a major source of moroseness," ease in defecation compensates for difficulty in communication. When the wordless *brame* fails to soothe Tiffauges, he seeks consolation in feces.

> A big roar. Two big roars. No relief. The morning's only consolation was of a fecal nature. Unexpectedly and impeccably I produced a magnificent turd, so long it had to curve at the ends to fit into the bowl. . . . I contemplated fondly the fine chubby little babe of living clay I'd just brought forth, and my zest for life returned. (88)

Seen as a birthing, a creative act performed in private, defecation connotes the aspects of Tiffauges's personality that his society condemns. The *brame* imagery connects thus with Tiffauges's desire for prepubescent boys. It also actualizes his wish for an asexual (and womanless) form of reproduction, which would fulfill his drive for "phoria," the "bearing" of a child by a man.

The narrator symbolically links Tiffauges's excreta to his sinister writing, the left-handed journal that comprises the novel's alternate narrative. Produced in secret, the journal similarly expresses his deviant self, both by its content and its "left-handedness" (*gaucherie*). Because society forces right-handedness on children irrespective of natural inclination, left-handedness becomes for Tiffauges a Nieztchean act.

> I thus have two sets of writing: one that is "adroit," pleasant, social, commercial, reflecting the masked character I pretend to be in the eyes of society; and one that is "sinister," distorted by all the "gauchenesses" of genius, full of flashes and cries—in short, inhabited by the spirit of Nestor. (30)

Like his "obstinate muteness" in the company of others, the journal pulls him away from others; in this paradoxical sense, it constitutes a language outside of language. The constellation of left-handedness, asociability, and excrement frame the narrative's critique of Tiffauges's behavior. "[G]auche and taciturn," he marks the boundary between himself and others; he relieves himself alone in the woods rather than share latrines used by others.

Even in his most private of journals, Tiffauges does not write ingenuously; like the feces Eagleton discusses, these *écrits* are "artfully wrought communications . . . the most calculatedly instrumental of emissions." Superficially, the flow of words in Tiffauges's journals appears antipodal to his stopped-up speech. However, a closer inspection exposes this seemingly spontaneous outburst as a highly controlled manipulation of language, a self-conscious creation based upon the withholding and confiding of information. Thus Tiffauges not only emulates Nestor's obsession with defecation but reinforces the pejorative link between text and excrement.

The harsh conditions in the German prisoner-of-war camp enhance Tiffauges's excretory abilities. Faced with the reality of history, with something to remember, he acquires "great fecal felicity" (168). While ingestion constitutes for Tiffauges an intimate if destructive bonding with other beings, defecation consummates "his secret and fruitful union with the Prussian soil" (169). Feces is imagistically conflated with semen as Tiffauges and Prussia become impregnated with a mutual destiny. According to Tiffauges, the German military success vindicates the asocial behavior for which he was persecuted in France.

> Out of his downtrodden childhood, his rebellious adolescence, and . . . ardent youth . . . there had arisen like a cry, a con-

demnation of an order that was criminal and unjust. And heaven had answered. The society under which Tiffauges had suffered had been swept away, with its judges, its generals and its prelates, its codes, its laws and its decrees. (159)

Exile and prison bring Tiffauges "a feeling of freedom such as he had never known before" (162). Germany liberates Tiffauges's hidden self, the self explored in his sinister writing—a liberation symbolized by the ease of defecation "performed generously and without excessive effort, by a regular descent of the turd into the lubricated sheath of the mucous membranes" (168).

Tiffauges's "fecal felicity" and its homoerotic undertones suggest the liberation of a deviance kept in check under the social restraints of France. Indeed, Tiffauges describes the French prisoners of war who thrive in Germany as sociopaths. Victor the Madman, for example, joined the army to commute a prison sentence, flourishes in the chaos of war, and eventually achieves prestige and power in the German civil administration under the Third Reich. Similarly, Tiffauges finds that Nazi Germany gives him a mandate to fulfill his particular pederasty. Defecation, an infantile source of presexual eroticism, consummates his intimate bond with Germany. Tiffauges fetishizes feces, reading into it meaning and memory (rather than the voiding of meaning and memory), finally regarding it as an objective referent for the self.

Excrement links Tiffauges's private, asocial deviance with the breakdown of restraints in Nazi Germany. One of Tiffauges's many narrative doubles, Göring (the "ogre of Rominten") also fetishizes excrement. Göring exhibits an expertise in "the interpretation of the droppings of game . . . deciphering all the messages written in the dejecta of the animals. . . ." (212). No less than two pages of detailed descriptions of game droppings amply evidence Göring's "coprological vocation" (332–33). In addition, Göring interprets the correspondence between the stag antlers and genitalia. After hunting, he ritually castrates downed Phallus-phoric (or phallus-bearing) Angels (Tiffauges's term for stags). Tiffauges admires Göring, grateful to be "servant and secret pupil of the second most important person in the German Reich, an expert in Phallology and coprology" (213). Tournier portrays Göring like Tiffauges, as playing with feces and never maturing sexually. The narrative's grotesque parody of the historical Göring suggests that under Nazi leadership, fantasies normally kept in check—fantasies of brutality, crime, cruelty—suddenly acquire legitimization.[10] Moreover, the coprological projections of Nazi discourse, scatological and pornographic anti-Semitic propaganda, depict the Jew as foul, filthy, deviant, perverse.[11] Tournier literalizes Nazi rhetoric; Göring handles not *Scheissejuden* but *Scheisse*.

Defecation undoes the memory of eating by externalizing and (r)ejecting it from the body. Briefly objectified and available for contemplation in a way that ingested matter (which has become part of the self) is not, excreta masquerades as memory. Inevitably abandoned to certain and rapid deterioration, however, feces represents oblivion, or the absence of memory. In falsifying the memory inherent to the communion of eating and in reifying excreta, Tiffauges inverts the two acts, masking the refusal of memory with the false memory of refuse.

Martin Amis's novel *Time's Arrow*, also about a Nazi proactivist, reverses even more concretely the symbolic progress of eating/digestion/defecation. Amis's novel is built upon the premise that at the instant of death, a new soul enters the body of a former Nazi doctor. This second soul relives the man's life backwards, from the moment of death to the moment of conception—from oblivion to oblivion. This second, observer soul feels the body's sensory experiences and the psyche's emotions. But, living the doctor's life backwards, it shares none of his consciousness. The soul, in other words, possesses nothing of the doctor's memory.

In a sense, Amis's device gives symbiotic existence to Robert J. Lifton's idea of the Nazi doctor's second self. In his psychological exploration of Nazi physicians who facilitated death and atrocity in concentration camps, Lifton posits a splitting of the Nazi perpetrator into two distinct selves—what he refers to as the normal and the Auschwitz self.[12]

As Amis's observer soul understands it, his host body absorbs nutrients by incorporating feces from the toilet, often a painful procedure. After a while, the doctor secretes and ejects chewed matter from his mouth, forming it into whole food products, which he wraps and exchanges at the market for money. Thus feces (the absence of memory) is absorbed into the self and food (memory) is externalized, commodified, and disposed. The observer soul moves into the unremembered past, which constitutes the memory of the Nazi doctor. He transverses the deathcamps, the refused memory of the narrative. "The Auschwitz universe . . . was fiercely coprocentric. It was *made* of shit" (123), the soul observes. For the soul, however, this marks the redemptive character of the concentrationary universe; as life passes in reverse, feces is the staff of life. "[W]e sometimes refer to Auschwitz as Anus Mundi. And I can think of no finer tribute than that" (124).

The soul passes through the exuberant moment when hundreds of Jewish corpses spring to life. Exhumed from mass graves in a temporal reversal of historical events, they revivify noisily in gas vans. "[T]he Jews are my children and I love them . . . and only wish them to exist, and to flourish, and to have their right to life and love" (152), the soul reflects. The observer soul in Amis's novel fulfills the redemptive desire inherent in Walter Benjamin's angel of history, similarly figured with his face "turned toward the past."[13] Although forcibly moved into the future, the angel of history feels the past as always present. Resisting the pull of causality, the angel of history insists on an all-encompassing and ever-present memory. "Where we perceive a chain of events, he sees one single catastrophe which keeps piling wreckage upon wreckage and hurls it in front of his feet." Like Amis's observer soul, Benjamin's angel of history aspires to reverse temporal movement, to undo history, and to reconstitute the wreckage into its original wholeness. "The angel would like to stay, awaken the dead, and make whole what has been smashed" (259). But to do so, the angel needs—impossibly—to leave the confines of history and temporality. Unlike the second soul of Amis's novel, who restores and resurrects— and thus redeems history—Benjamin's angel is "irresistibly propel[led] . . . into the future" (260) against his will, unable to undo the catastrophe he continues to watch.

Fixing his gaze on "the pile of debris" while continuing to progress in time, the angel of history brings the past into the present. Amis's observer soul reverses the flow of historical time, but only provisionally: as he moves backwards, the Nazi physician whose body he cohabits continues to move forward. Thus, just as the soul restores the damage caused by the body, the soul's acts of resurrection are perpetually undone by the doctor's acts of killing. The past is never wholly past but also never present. From their differing orientations, neither the soul nor the physician see the mounting "piles of debris"—in this case piles of corpses. Out of their symbiosis, no history—no accountability—is possible. The soul "remember[s] names and faces" seen at extermination sights but has no recollection of killing. The doctor flees from memory, from association with the past. The observer soul's redeptive capacities prove illusory, because it cannot account for history, as Benjamin's angel does. Finally, the second soul cannot even redeem the doctor whose body he inhabits and who continues to commit the atrocities that un-happen in the soul's consciousness.

The narrative structure and symbolic order of *The Ogre* make clear that one cannot undo history. If at all possible, redeption entails accountability. Early on the novel structurally and symbolically links Tiffauges's all-consuming desires with Nazism. The protagonist, however, acknowledges the implications of his cloacal bond with Göring only when, late in the narrative, he meets Ephraim, a young death-camp refugee. By elaborating his origins, "the Anus Mundi, the great metropolis of degradation, suffering and death" (353), Ephraim unmasks the falseness of Tiffauges's fecal memories. A child of Oswiecim (Auschwitz) without recollection of other parentage, "Ephraim had been so young when he went there it seemed to him he'd been born there" (353). Tiffauges finds him encrusted with filth, like a desiccated amnion. The sheer physicality of Ephraim's excrementally ridden suffering pre-vents Tiffauges from assimilating the boy's damning evidence into the established symbolic order. Despite having successfully integrated into his meta-philosophy the suffering or death of his lover, his pigeons, and the Napola boys, after encountering Ephraim, Tiffauges's obsession with the metaphysics of feces gives way to physiological concern, and he nurses the emaciated child through a bout of dysentery. Ephraim's "whitish, blood-streaked stools" (352) appear to Tiffauges for what they are: not ciphers of a meta-reality but symptoms of dying. Ephraim's life-threatening struggle with the process of ingestion-digestion-defe-cation undermines the symbolic construct of the narrative, which hid the implications of Tiffauges's behavior (and, by extension, the behavior of all collaborators) behind a lofty and seamless ideological rhetoric. Ephraim comes to represent Shoah victims; the inmates of the concen-trationary universe, *anus mundi*, literally wallowed in excremental filth. Unlike the protagonist's childhood friend Nestor, who relieved himself on "his throne," and unlike Tiffauges who would "sacrifice on the defecatory altar . . . in dreamy meditation" (172), the inmates of what has been referred to as the "Jewish kakatopia" (Bosmajian, 12) were wracked with dysentery. Forbidden to use the latrines according to need, they would soil themselves, their clothing, the planks that served as their beds.[14] Sometimes they ate from the same bowl they utilized as chamberpot (*Kitty*), and sometimes they were forced by guards to eat their own feces (Krystal, 18).

Tiffauges withdrawal from speech, which begins in France and intensifies through his army service and subsequent internment as prisoner-of-war, culminates not in muteness but in an abandonment of the native tongue in favor of the language of Nazism. Although he con-tinues to write in French, in speaking he shifts to German. Tiffauges's preference for his exilic tongue underscores his ironic sense of freedom in captivity. Initially, Tiffauges finds the German language liberating because of his own lack of fluency. The sense of linguistic strangeness affords him a measure of unaccountability impossible in French. During Tiffauges's first encounter with Göring, the Frenchman finds that

the German language . . . interposed between him and the
rest a sort of translucid but not transparent screen, which
took the edge off their grossness and enabled him to address
the second most important person in the Reich in terms and
in a tone that would never have been tolerated on the part of
a German. (203)

However, as his facility in German increases and his sense of strangeness
with the language diminishes, Tiffauges continues to prefer its cadences.
He finds he can be more direct in that language, more brutal, more raw.
"There are things I could never manage to say in French—harsh things,
confessions—which escape my lips quite easily disguised in hard German
speech" (272).

In the residual foreignness of an acquired tongue, Tiffauges
locates a "slight opacity of language" that leaves a "gap between my
thoughts and my words" (271). While Tiffauges describes a relationship
typical of non-native speakers, he has also discovered the condition of
all language: the gap between word and thing, word and idea, word
and self, the inadequacy of language, the impossibility of "pure" representation. Freed thus from the imperative toward a literal accountability, Tiffauges invents a system of reading the world, whose signs
merge with Tiffauges's desires. This discovery and invention makes it
possible for Tiffauges to not "see"—and thus not speak of—the atrocity
taking place around him and with his collusion, the atrocity that his
highly intellectualized acts of symbol-making and sign-interpretation
facilitate.

As obscurant as Nazi jargon, the "winged words" of Himmler that
so awed Eichmann, Tiffauges's language "makes a sort of wall" (271)
between himself and others, between himself and the world of phenomenon. He speaks of "the Spirit of Defecation, the Anal Angel,
and . . . Omega the key of its essence" (his horse) (226), and "the persecution of the Phallophoric Angel by the Anal Angel, the pursuit and
putting to death of Alpha by Omega" (hunting) (226). Most notable in
Tiffaugean theory is the absence of human agency, of personal responsibility. The very cleverness of Tiffauges's circumlocutions adds to their
seductiveness. Caught by the labyrinthine sign-reading of Tiffauges's
sinister journal, which intrudes irregularly on the straightforward
chronicle of the third-person narrative, the reader is pulled by the
novel's structure and internal symbolic order to a momentary forgetting
of history. Tiffauges's fearful awakening from his unowned complicitousness and into history is also the reader's return from a kind of literary oblivion.[15]

An association with animals, and a preference for animal over human discourse, accompany Tiffauges's retreat from the spoken word. Even before devising the cathartic *brame*, Tiffauges describes himself by means of animal imagery. He compares himself to a little goat (8), a wolf, a bear (178). For Tiffauges, figuring himself as an animal is more than a metaphoric device. In fact, he prefers animal to human company. He stereotypes women, Frenchmen, soldiers, but sees in each of his homing pigeons "its own irreplaceable personality" (145). Like the boy in *The Painted Bird*, Tiffauges identifies with animals, unconsciously at first, and then consciously and deliberately. In part, Tiffauges flees human interaction to escape the inevitable corruption of language, which comes already laden with an ideology not of his own making. By contrast, the pigeons suggest other possibilities. He shuns army conversation for the "downy, cooing quiet" (145) of the coop.

In identifying with animals, Tiffauges consistently figures himself as victim. He compares himself, for example, to "Monsieur Seguin's little goat, who made it a point of honor to fight the wolf all night and not let herself be eaten up till the first ray of sunlight" (8). "[C]overed with droppings and feathers" (145), he identifies with sickly pigeons in whose eyes he sees "a mind deepened and disillusioned by premature experience of loneliness and sorrow" (146). Even figuring himself as a deadly beast, Tiffauges casts himself in the role of victim. Invited for the first time into a German home, he feels awkward and ill at ease: "A wolf or bear straying into a bedroom would probably have felt the same kind of panic" (178). This insistence on his own vulnerability (and the vulnerability of his animal surrogates) in all situations mimics the contradictory but seductive way in which Nazi discourse figured Germany as both unconquerably powerful on the battlefield and fatally vulnerable to the threat of racial impurity. In the extended lupine/orsine analogy, the larger threat that the straying animals pose to the bedroom's rightful human inhabitants is lost in Tiffauges's contemplation of the animals' (that is, his own) awkward panic. That Tiffauges eventually intrudes into German homes to kidnap their young boys to serve (and finally to die for) Hitler makes his identification with the errant wolf or bear more telling. Tiffauges's rhetorical and symbolic processes conceal the threat he himself actualizes against others. In that sense, Tiffauges represents the "Nazi beast," which insists on its own vulnerability while lethally preying on helpless and harmless victims.

Like Tiffauges's insistence on an animal vulnerability, his animal-muteness stems not from a mounting sense of horror at historical events (as in Kosinski's novel) nor from a frustration with the inadequacy of language to convey an unprecedented and unspeakable experience (as in

Wiesel's novels). Rather, Tiffauges's muteness is an evasive practice, a refusal to know too much, to communicate too accurately. Through this equivocal silence he identifies simultaneously with the victimized and the victimizer. Tiffauges's animal alter egos underscore the protagonist's oscillation between language and muteness. For example, while a prisoner-of-war Tiffauges befriends a giant blind elk in whom he sees his own myopia and bulk. Although not deliberately malicious, the huge, sightless animal blunders destructively. Local foresters refer to it as "l'Unhold"—the monster, the fiend. This strange creature, described as part horse, part buffalo, part stag, becomes another surrogate for Tiffauges, who sees himself as freakishly monstrous (14). For Tiffauges, the elk's mythological appearance—"a half-fabulous beast that seemed to emerge from the great Hercynian forests of prehistory" (176)—reinforces his sense of being himself a quasi-mythological figure, "a fabulous monster emerging from mists of time" (3). More importantly, Tiffauges's consideration places both the elk and the man outside the bounds of historical time, outside of historical accountability.

The two like beings communicate in a language outside of language. Tiffauges speaks through his *brame*; the Monster, through ingestion and silence. The blind elk must sniff out its food, setting its nostrils and upper lip quivering. Tiffauges finds this alimentary "plea of that upper lip . . . so eloquent" (176), and close to his own displaced mode of expression. Once Tiffauges feeds the animal, the two converse:

> Then they talked to each other. Tiffauges drew his finger-nails up and down between the two long, amazingly sensitive and expressive ears, telling the Monster he was beautiful and gentle, strong and without malice, and that the world was wicked and treacherous. The Monster answered with a modulated roar, so deep it sounded like the laugh of a giant ventriloquist. . . . (182–83)

The elk is one of a series of doubles that Tiffauges encounters—among them also a murderer (on the day of execution) and Adolf Hitler. This unnatural Monster, paradoxically, is benign.

As in the case of Kosinski's boy, the close association of the protagonist with an especially vulnerable animal underscores the human sense of vulnerability and the danger that the protagonist fears from an indifferent or malign universe and from other men. The Monster's extreme myopia feminizes him: "a blind elk who's probably afraid to stay with the others because the males would stab him with their antler" (182). The blind elk's antlers, the mark of his maleness, are useless as weapons either of aggression or protection. However, they cause random damage as he blunders into things. Tiffauges, too, deviates from "normative" male sexuality. His voyeuristic compulsion to photograph children earns him a wrongful conviction for rape. Later, Tiffauges lovingly and dotingly collects young boys for the Napola, unwittingly leading them to destruction. Thus, Tiffauges's kinship with the beast brings to the surface not only his vulnerability but the essential dualism of his character—at once Nazi victim and Nazi, imprisoned and imprisoner, exiled and exiler.

If the Monster inflicts harm through his sightless foraging, he does so unawares, blindly bumping into objects. Tiffauges, however, actively refuses any knowledge of the Nazi purpose in order to better serve his own avaricious needs:

> It was true that the SS filled him with the most acute repugnance. But the Napola, whose discipline, uniforms and crazy songs went against all his inclinations and anarchist beliefs, forces him to make every possible allowance because it was so obviously a machine for both subjecting and exalting fresh and innocent flesh. (252–53)

The Monster looks more menacing than he turns out to be. The forester deflates the Monster's supernatural and threatening aura by explaining the physiological cause for the elk's eerie appearance: "*Monster* [Unhold]. You understand? That means brute, ungracious, but also sorcerer, devil. It's that he frightens people with his white eyes. . . ." Tiffauges, however, turns out to be far more diabolical than his double.

The connection between Tiffauges and the Monster hinges on the extreme myopia of both sufferers. Sight, with its metaphoric connotations of insight and inner vision, connects closely with the narrative's exploration of language and rhetoric as a means of owning or disowning knowledge. Behind the thick lenses of his eyeglasses, Tiffauges boasts a compensatory "prophetic eye" (178). With this keen inner eye sharply focused on the mysterious workings of fate, Tiffauges finds his severe nearsightedness amply recompensed by "the long-distance, detached, speculative vision . . . the vision best suited to reading the lines of fate" (178). If he sees more poorly than others, he claims to see also more deeply. Tiffauges asserts, "All is sign. But only a piercing light or shriek will penetrate our blunted sight and hearing" (5). An obsessive reader of "signs," Tiffauges believes that, like Oedipus's blind seer Teiresias, his dim vision shields him from the mundane distractions of the world of appearances in order to stare full-faced at truth.

Like his muteness, Tiffauges's blindness operates only partially and selectively. While Tiffauges links his myopia with wisdom and inner vision, Tiffauges's "ogrish vocation" evokes the man-eating Cyclops as well as the fabled blind giant who sniffs out young boys for his dinner. These associations reinforce the suggestion of cannibalism that the narrative repeatedly raises. Tiffauges near-blindness is thus linked with predacity and with forgetting. Eyeglasses, however, are a double sign in Tournier's narrative. In Nazi imagery they symbolize intellectuality and Jewishness: "intelligence, study and speculation. In short, the Jew" (203), the locus of memory and victimization. Once again the narrative figures Tiffauges ambivalently—the eater and the eaten, the forgetter and the rememberer.

In Kosinski's novel, the protagonist's unusual eyes underscore his function as witness. He sees, absorbs, and stores information that he cannot speak, muteness somehow honing his powers of observation and memory. For Tiffauges, the contrast between physical blindness and metaphysical insight parallels the discrepancy between oral laconism and written verbiage. Quite literally, Tiffauges does not see the world as others do; he scarcely sees at all. In the privacy of his journal, he freely expatiates his private vision. Unable to view reality without the mediation of his corrective lenses, which distort light to suit his limitations, he can act upon reality only through the mediation of his written text, which contorts events to suit his desires. A German racial scientist's play of words on the name *Tiffauges* underscores the link between vision, language, and reality. The scientist offers two etymological variations for the name. First:

> Tiffauges is a modified form of Tiefauge, and conceals a distant Teutonic . . . origin.
> ". . . Tiefauge means deep eye, an eye set deep in its socket. And the meaning of the name is so plain just to look at you, Herr von Tiefauge, one might almost wonder if it isn't a nickname!" (260)

Later disturbed at Tiffauges's sloppy performance in the laboratory, the racial scientist offers an alternative derivation:

> "Watch what you're doing, Herr Triefauge," he said.
> I know enough German to know that *triefauge* means sick, tearful, or, to be precise, rheumy eye! My terrible myopia and the thick glasses without which I can't see anything make me liable to this sort of insult. (262)

The addition of one letter changes *Tiefauge* (deep eye) to *triefauge* (rheumy eye), raising the possibility that what passes as "prophetic" may be merely "sick."

Tiffauges's consternation over what amounts to a textual emendation suggests that Tiffauges views himself as a written text and that words determine or construct reality. The scientist's dubbing him *Tiefauge*—"the deep eye"—makes him so, and thus he defends this flattering derivation against its less complimentary variant.

The attention toward vision and blindness underscores the discrepancy between events as Tiffauges sees them, and events as they are.[16] Only when Ephraim knocks off Tiffauges's thick eyeglasses does the latter acknowledge Nazi atrocity. And yet, the evidence has been available to Tiffauges all along; most people seem to know in great detail about the Nazi war against the Jews. For example, when Tiffauges brings sacks of Napola boys' hair to a local woman so she can weave it into a fabric for him, she recoils. Tiffauges describes her reaction as "violent and incomprehensible. She suddenly started to tremble and shrank away, repeating, 'No, no, no,' . . . . I wonder what frightened her so much about my sack of hair?" (325). Much later on, Tiffauges learns from Ephraim the reason for the woman's fright—the harvesting and utilization of body parts from deathcamp victims. Tiffauges realizes what the reader has known all along: the woman "must have heard about the hair at Auschwitz and thought she was being asked to take part in that vast and macabre manufacture" (355). Belatedly Tiffauges acknowledges that she has horrifyingly mistaken his innocent intention. In implying a contrast between his intention and her misapprehension, Tiffauges asserts his innocence. However, by kidnapping boys who are to be trained as murderers, and who end up dying horrifyingly, Tiffauges, too, participates in the "vast and macabre" machinery of Auschwitz.

Tiffauges utilizes his special vision, special language, and sign reading ability to perpetuate his unknowing. Although he attends SS training classes, lectures on racial purity, and intimate talks with Nazi leaders, Tiffauges refuses to "know" of the concentrationary universe. Yet the camps were neither hidden away nor few in number. As Ephraim explains to him:

> Over all Wehrmacht-occupied Europe, but chiefly in Germany, Austria and Poland, nearly a thousand villages and hamlets made up an infernal map of its ordinary country. . . . Schirmeck, Natzviller, Dachau, Neuengamme, Bergen-Belsen, Buchenwald, Oranienburg, Theresienstadt, Mauthausen, Stutthof, Lodz, Ravensbruck. . . . (353)

Tiffauges remains blind to this aspect of Germany, seeing not with a "deep eye" but with a "sick eye" because his career flourishes in tandem with his desires. He represents the filmmaker, journalist, philosopher, or writer who neither kills nor advocates killing but who thrives by placing his intellectual gifts in service of a regime that does. While Wiesel, Delbo, Kosinski, and others insist on the inadequacy of language to render the horror of the concentrationary universe, Tournier exposes the ability of language to veil reality and thereby sidestep moral responsibility.

Tiffauges construes his greatest outpouring of language, the sinister journal, as a quest for spiritual meaning, a kind of deep remembering. In actuality, Tiffauges's linguistic genius fuels his quest for oblivion. Tiffauges can profit from Nazism by ordering and interpreting facts to keep hidden what he wishes hidden, remaining free to protest his ignorance later. With the exception of Ephraim, the victims who intrude infrequently on the narrative remain mute, neither challenging nor refuting the Tiffaugean construct. Caught under the seductive spell of Tiffauges's linguistic cleverness, the reader cannot help but be drawn into the web of signs, myths, and symbols that he weaves, cannot help but accept, albeit tentatively and temporarily, the meanings he assigns.

Many readers have criticized Tournier's novel for mirroring and excusing the appeal of the Nazism in an aesthetically mesmerizing narrative. Jean Améry was disturbed by the novel's aestheticization of Nazi atrocity.[17] Saul Friedlander worries that Tournier's novel mystifies and mythicizes Nazism, resulting in what he terms "the kitsch of death." According to Friedlander, the profusion of mysterious symbols and the affable but demonic protagonist prevent any meaningful grappling with the central moral issue raised by the Holocaust, that of human responsibility.

> . . . as Michel Tournier explains it, the entire chain of Nazi crimes is only the manifest expression of hidden forces, and the book proposes to decipher the signs that would indicate something about these mysterious impulses—something that directly puts the crime outside the human condition. And when we are presented with a clearly criminal personality, he becomes isolated by an emphasis on his special characteristics, which puts him more in the demonic category than the human. (102)

I would like to argue here instead that by positing the eccentric Tiffauges in this pernicious milieu, Tournier mounts a critique of collaboration, particularly on the part of French and German intellectuals. Tournier's novel deliberately calls attention to the damning kinship between Tiffauges's masterly misuse of language and myth to put forth an all-encompassing symbolic system and the totalizing rhetoric of Nazi ideology. At the same time, by a strategic practice of misreading, Tiffauges radically subverts the literary enterprise and its symbolic and mythic modes. Tiffauges treats life as a fictional text whose aesthetic patterns can be ordered and reordered to produce coherent meaning.[18] He sees Germany as "a white page covered with black signs" (167), a page on which he may both read and inscribe the "hieroglyphics" of his own destiny. In addition, Tiffauges presents himself as both literary artist and literary text, writing himself into existence, as it were, through his *écrits sinistres*. As such, he both embodies and parodies the Romantic/symbolist poet/hero, who also inhabits his own literary creation. Tiffauges mirrors the psycho-social elements exemplified by romanticism—restless individualism, passionate emotions, frustration with petty convention, yearning for exotic locale. Obsessively introspective, self-consciously grandiose, Tiffauges suffers from an isolation that he accepts as both mark and burden of his superior sensibility; he describes himself as "the better man, the strongest, the only one elect and innocent" (150). His preoccupation with *phoria* corresponds to the exalted passions and the quest for the perfect but elusive love that characterize the Romantic sensibility.

Tiffauges's flight from France represents flight from bourgeois conventionality. His photographs of young children and his clandestine recordings of their laughter are misconstrued as criminal rather than creatively passionate tendencies; he is wrongly accused of child molesting. Tiffauges's incongruous sense of liberation as a German prisoner-of-war figures the exotic and remote Prussian terrain as a sublime landscape: "Germany was revealing itself as a promised land, the land of pure essences" (180). The romantic vision common to both Tiffauges and Nazism is expressed through nostalgia for a distant, mythic past and a dream of a distant, glorious future. Tiffauges's obsession with "pure essences" suggests, of course, the Nazi investment in "racial purity."

Tiffauges's concern with discerning these pure essences links him most closely with the nineteenth-century symbolist poet Charles Baudelaire. Common to both are a boarding school background and expulsion for unruly behavior. "All is sign," Tiffauges announces early and repeatedly in his sinister journal, as he charts the sharpening of his sign-deciphering skills. For Tiffauges, concrete phenomena and historical events merely reflect the essence of reality—an essence not physical but metaphysical. Recollecting his first glimmering of this metareality, Tiffauges gestures clearly to Baudelaire. Tiffauges explains, "I've always been aware of hieroglyphs written across my path and a con-

fused murmur of words [des paroles confuses] in my ear. . . ." (5). His
phrase, "des paroles confuses," calls up an association with the Baudelaire poem "Correspondances," where an almost identical phrase
appears in the first stanza:

> La Nature est un temple où de vivants piliers
> Laissent parfois sortir de confuses paroles;
> L'homme y passe à travers des forêts de symboles
> Qui l'observent avec des regards familiers.
>
> [Nature is a temple where living columns
> Sometimes let fall confused words.
> Man passes through the forest of symbols
> That watch him with a familiar gaze.]

Baudelaire's poem suggests a spiritual reality inherent in nature, for
which everything in nature serves as symbol. The *"confuses paroles"*
point toward a hidden meaning, grasped intuitively rather than ratio-
nally. This meaning underlies and links synaesthetically all that the
senses may apprehend. Like Baudelaire, Tiffauges listens for the resonances of spiritual meaning that underlie the world of external appearance; he, too, searches for *correspondences*.

Unlike Baudelaire, whose expansive and precise symbolic language suggests intuitions, illusive feelings, and deep memories he can
neither contain nor define in logical terms or representational writing,
Tiffauges uses symbolist language to deflect memory and analysis. Inter-
spersed with what Tournier terms the language of hyper-realism—the
minutia of scientific and historical detail—Tiffauges's symbolic network
obscures rather than expands his vision. Tournier constructs Tiffauges
as a parody of the Baudelairean poet, lost in the Reich's symbolic forest.
As such, the parodic link implicates the literary imagination in the creation of the concentrationary universe. The juxtaposition of the symbolist poet with the Romantic ideation of the Third Reich critiques the
Romantic roots of Nazi discourse.

Tiffauges continually acts upon the external world based upon a
symbolic system of symbols he sets up as a correlative of his inner life.
He relegates actual events to an inferior reality, which fades away in
Tiffauges's perceptions of life and history. For example, rather than
frightening him, the sound of German bomber planes over France
strikes Tiffauges as "nothing but a confrontation of ciphers and sign, a
purely audio-visual tussle where the only possible risk was obscurity or
misinterpretation" (136). Tiffauges observes patterns that signal a
meaning beyond the real, while ignoring the real. In an act of intellec-

tual legerdemain, Tiffauges remolds evidence that threatens to controvert his intricate system. This act he terms "malign-benign inversion," a curious "change of sign: plus has become minus, and vice versa" (81).

Tiffauges's initial discovery of the process of malign-benign inversion constitutes a promethean act of rebellion, a willingness to call society's good his evil, and its evil, his good. Elsewhere, Tournier explains the Tiffaugean process of inversion more fully, as "a mysterious operation which, without causing any apparent change in the nature of a person or a thing, alters its *value*, putting less where there was more and more where there was less" (*Wind* 102). In other words, these inversions comprise a Nietzschean transvaluation, an overturning of traditionally held values. For example, Tiffauges condemns the legalized murder that governments enact through war and capital punishment. Instead, he seeks "Parliamentary immunity . . . *benign inversion* to give every citizen the right to shoot at sight and without license any politician who comes within range" (73). Tiffauges proposes "benign inversion" as a corrective measure to society's "malign inversion" of the natural order. Tiffauges understands this malign inversion as a linguistic reversal, a rhetorical construct that both strengthens and obscures the malevolent and repressive acts of government and of bourgeois society. The concept of malign inversion allows Tiffauges to read Nazi discourse critically, to undermine its rhetorical power. Tiffauges critiques the German wartime slogan, "Guns before butter," as "the lowest form of the great *malign inversion* at work everywhere. . . . death before life, hate before love!" (63).

Tiffauges explains the Nazi obsession with racial purity as "the malign inversion of innocence" (75). He explains:

> Innocence is love of being, smiling acceptance of both celestial and earthly sustenance, ignorance of the infernal antithesis between purity and impurity. Satan has turned this spontaneous and as it were native saintliness into a caricature that resembles him and is the converse of its original. Purity is horror of life, hatred of man, morbid passion for the void. (75)

Linked with hatred and death, malign inversion sours natural pleasures. Its linguistic enactment erects a satanic looking glass in whose crisp but false reflection "right becomes left, left becomes right, good is called evil and evil is called good" (74). To reverse that, Tiffauges invokes benign inversion, a corresponding but opposing linguistic operation that restores the world to its natural order.

Tiffauges's understanding of benign-malign inversion as a purely linguistic operation, however, results in the equalization of all political and historical positions.

War, as absolute evil, is inevitably the object of a satanic cult. It is a black mass celebrated in broad daylight by Mammon, and the blood-boltered idols before which the duped masses are made to kneel are called Country, Sacrifice, Heroism, and Honor. (74)

Although France fights a defensive war against an invading, genocidal empire, Tiffauges places the struggle outside of history. Couched as an antibourgeois invective, Tiffauges's assessment of war equalizes all participants, making the victims of Nazi brutality invisible. His linguistic/symbolic system disables him from discerning the activities of the Reich. Tiffauges decries the French government as "murderers" (122), for example, but regards Göring with amusement, Hitler with fascination. He evolves then from a rebel against bourgeois conformity to a participant in a fascistic regime of racist hatred, seduced by the totalizing vision of "a *significant reality* which is almost always clear and distinct" (260). Initially Tiffauges's understanding of the linguistic operation of malign-benign inversion enables him to deconstruct totalizing rhetoric and thus resist the pressures of conformity; eventually, however, the seductions of Nazism induce him to construct an infinite series of self-reflecting images whose inversions occlude and finally displace reality. Under the endless shifting of valences—plus to minus to plus to minus—memory and accountability become impossible. Lost in a "forest of symbols" where the signified eclipses the signifier, Tiffauges's increasingly hermetic vision finally refers only to itself. The Romantic rebel comes full circle, ultimately espousing the self-serving values and totalizing vision he criticized in bourgeois society.

Goethe's poem "Der Erl König" gives the novel its title in the French original—*Le Roi des Aulnes.* The poem's importance illustrates the elusiveness of symbolic correspondences and the narrative link between German Romanticism and Nazi atrocity. Tiffauges repeatedly identifies (and is identified by others) with the mysterious and menacing Elder or Erl King. The violent death of a Napola boy in a landmine explosion underscores Tiffauges's association with Goethe's menacing figure. Like the dreadful Elder King, Tiffauges kidnaps young boys, wresting them from the arms of helpless parents.[19] The ogre and the Elder King meld into a teutonic archetype that murders children.

But the identification of Tiffauges with the figure of the Erl King comprises only one aspect of his fourfold connection with the characters in the poem, ogre, father, child, and horse. Tiffauges not only threatens but also safeguards the Napola boys' welfare. In addition to his predatory role, he sees in himself the *"pater nuritor* . . . a piquant inversion of his ogrish vocation" (244), gathering food for his charges amid the scarcity of wartime provisions. Like the helpless father of Goethe's ballad, he, too, proves powerless to save his children from annihilation. Tiffauges brings destruction upon the children he loves, while murmuring to himself words of false comfort. Like the father in Goethe's poem who speeds home only to find himself cradling a dead child in his arms, Tiffauges perceives danger only when he can no longer save the boys.

Tiffauges's vulnerability to the real but unseen menace of the Reich culminates in his own destruction. Like the child in Goethe's poem, carried off by the Elder King, Tiffauges sinks into the marsh from which the bog corpse, dubbed the *Elder King* (Roi des Aulnes) emerged. Finally, Tiffauges's "phoric" ambitions link him also to the horse that carries the father and son in Goethe's poem. Tiffauges thinks of himself as horselike, blurring boundaries between rider and horse. Once, while his horse urinates, Tiffauges is gripped by "the intoxicating feeling that it was he, Tiffauges, proudly relieving himself" (228). This fourfold identification with the figures in Goethe's poem echoes the elusiveness of the symbolic equivalences that Tiffauges attempts to pin down in the narrative. As one signification displaces another, Tournier deconstructs the Tiffaugean and the Nazi claims to a totalizing system of meaning.[20] Additionally, in conflating the ogre, protector, victim, and vehicle, the novel posits Nazi Germany as a self-consuming cannibal, destroying itself and its memory.

In *The Origins of Totalitarianism*, Hannah Arendt links the development of German racism with the preponderance of "political romanticism" (167), a connection that sheds light on Tiffauges's development as a Romantic figure. Arendt points out the dangers in Romanticism's cult of the individual, the genius whose "entirely arbitrary game of . . . 'ideas,' could be made the center of a whole outlook on life" (168). In Tournier's novel, Tiffauges's Romantic individualism fuses with his identification with the figure of Hitler, whom he regards aesthetically rather than historically. The link between Tiffauges's elaborate intellectual systematizing and Hitler's mythic vision implicates the philosophers, artists, and critics whose works were consonant with the enactments of Nazism. As Arendt scathingly observes, the intellectual community has "proved more than once that hardly an ideology can be found to which they would not willingly submit if the only reality—which even a romantic can hardly afford to overlook—is at stake, the reality of their position" (168). Intellectually opportunistic, Tiffauges belatedly acknowledges a "*contre-semblance*" (558) between his private order and Nazi ideology and practice. Horrified by the parallels, he faults language and symbolic expression rather than his own ambition and desire.

Tiffauges neatly subsumes all manifestations of concrete reality under the rubric of certain abstract categories—"phoria" and "inversion," for example—for which they serve as objective referents. For instance, Tiffauges rejects his physician's dismissal of a causal connection between Tiffauges's chronic respiratory ailment and his sternal funnel. The physician's diagnosis makes sense physiologically, but Tiffauges is more interested in the "relationship of symbol and symbolized" (69). Unlike the man who transverses the Baudelairean forest of symbols, Tiffauges does not limit himself to simply observing, or even interpreting, signs. Rather, he reshapes the external world—the world of history—so that it reflects his symbolic valuations. Tiffauges's clever and engaging meditations on symbolic representation allow him to deny causality in any real sense. Tiffauges revels in "phoria" as he lovingly abducts Aryan boys for the Napola. Because phoria contains the key to existence and all possibilities of passion, redemption, and meaning, Tiffauges ignores the abhorrent ideology and physical danger of the SS training. Arendt's remarks on ideological thinking comment on Tiffauges's proclivity for symbol-making and its resemblance to Nazi ideology. Arendt's observes:

> Ideologists who pretend to possess the key to reality are forced to change and twist their opinions about single cases according to the latest events, and can never afford to come into conflict with their ever-changing deity, reality. It would be absurd to ask people to be reliable who by their very convictions must justify any given situation. (174)

Arendt describes a process that Sander Gilman develops in *Difference and Pathology*. Pathological stereotyping, according to Gilman, is a way of knowing or interpreting which remains unshaken by contradictory evidence. Tournier constructs Tiffauges as a representation of a charming but dangerous ideologue who refuses evidence that controverts his already formed assumptions.

Through a displaced French protagonist who speaks in German but writes in French, Tournier attacks the roots of German racial thinking and their integral absorption into French thinking and culture. Racial doctrines surfaced in France during the eighteenth century, simultaneous with the Enlightenment. Early French racial ideas, promulgated to buttress aristocratic privilege at the moment of its erosion, posited an historical link between Germanic and Frank tribes, the purported ancestry of the German and French nobility. Racial theory argued the superiority of those tribes over the Gauls, seen as the ancestors of the French lower classes. These racial theories offered a "natural" justification for the social order. Arendt observes that "all French racial theories have supported the Germanism or at least the superiority of the Nordic people against their own country" (*Origins* 164). For Tiffauges, the contrasting landscapes of the two countries metaphorically represent the enduring idea of Germanic racial purity and the danger of racial dilution with inferior French races.

> Unlike the oceanic land of France, shrouded in mists, its lines blurred by receding shades, continental Germany, more harsh and rudimentary, was the country of strong, simplified, stylized drawing, easily read and remembered. . . . the French propensity led to the weakness of faded colors, spinelessness, dangerous laxities like promiscuity, dirt and cowardice. . . . Germany was revealing itself as . . . the land of pure essences. (179–80)

The strong, simple lines of the German landscape signify resistance to profligacy (promiscuity, filth, wantonness), the cause and effect of a diluted bloodline, and to the bold and clear lines ("easily read") of racial hierarchy.

Tiffauges's Germanophilia, his scorn for the French language and its speakers, his ease in the German tongue and his fascination with its culture, all emanate from his own refutation of inferiority. He describes his natural (if hidden) superiority in terms of popular nineteenth-century racial theories, notably those of Count Arthur de Gobineau. Gobineau maintained that despite the deterioration of the elite classes brought about through racial mixing, the true nobility—the "fils des rois" (sons of king)—could sense within themselves evidence of their superior bloodline and aristocratic origins. Arendt links Gobineau's "fils des rois" and other racialist paradigms with nineteenth-century Romanticism.

> the romantic heroes, saints, geniuses and supermen of the late nineteenth century . . . can hardly hide their Germanic romantic origin. The inherent irresponsibility of romantic opinions received a new stimulant from Gobineau's mixture of races, because this mixture showed a historical event of the past which could be traced in the depths of one's own self. This meant that inner experiences could be given historical significance, that one's own self had become the battle field of history. (*Origins* 175)

Tiffauges's sense of history's "complicity with my own personal history—in short, that something of Tiffauges might enter into the course of events in general" (27) confirms his belief in his own genius. The correspondence of his inner landscape to cosmic purpose justifies his actions, even when others suffer. In *The Wind Spirit* Tournier makes explicit the relationship between Nazism and early racialist thinking, which stresses the natural superiority of the ruling class and its inevitable racial deterioration. Tournier sees in the racialist an "overestimation of the importance of heredity . . . an uncompromising pessimism quite typical of right-wing ideology . . . carried to an extreme that led logically to the extermination camps and crematories" (202). In Tournier's intricately constructed narrative, Tiffauges incarnates a blend of racism and romanticism that predates the Third Reich but that resurfaces in more pernicious form.

In the meditations of his sinister journal, Tiffauges explores the way cultures appropriate myth and literature, coopting meaning to promote their own vision.[21] Tiffauges reflects on the evolution of the Atlas myth:

> Atlas carried on his shoulders . . . not earth, as is usually depicted, but the sky. . . . But that all had to be changed. Instead of the blue and gold infinity which both crowned and blessed him, he was burdened with the terrestrial globe, a lump of murky mud which bent his neck and blocked his view. And so the hero is debased and fallen. (82)

For Tiffauges, shifting the representation from sky-bearer to earth-bearer degrades and constrains Atlas. In transmitting the myth, subsequent cultures have weighed down the *astrophore*. As with Tiffauges and other men of genius, society forcibly replaces etherial aspirations with mundane concerns. At issue here is the rereading and misreading of cultural, literary, and historical artifacts to suit present exigencies. Western culture gradually reinterprets the Atlas myth; Tiffauges in turn interprets that reinterpretation. While Tiffauges bemoans the degradation of transmitted archetypes, he, too, refashions mythic figures (for example, Don Juan, St. Christopher, Abel) so that they reflect and affirm his own ideology. While he criticizes such (mis)appropriation when others enact them, he does not acknowledge his own misappropriations. That he also ignores Nazi misappropriation of German myth, literature and culture is a measure of his co-optation.

Tournier makes explicit the Nazi (mis)appropriation of cultural artifacts when a strangely preserved cadaver emerges from a German bog. A German anthropologist examines the bog corpse. In identifying it, he projects his own Nazi values onto history and artifact, seeing in the corpse a correlative of Third Reich mythos. His reading ignores the corpse's most significant accouterment: "a six-pointed star of gilded metal" fastened to a cloth band encircling its skull and eyes. In a regime marking all Jews for death with the mandatory yellow six-pointed star, the professor's failure to make the obvious association appears remarkable. The anthropologist's misreading is underscored by the narrative's second iteration of a bog corpse. The second corpse, much fresher, bears "a number tattooed on the left wrist and yellow J on a red star of David sewn on the left front the clothing" (351). The anthropologist dubs the first bog corpse *The Erl-King* (*Le Roi des Aulnes*—the book's title in the original French) after Goethe's poem, "Der Erl König," described as "the true quintessence of the German soul" (189). Tournier elsewhere recollects that for Frenchmen, Goethe's ballad represents "*the* German poem par excellence . . . a symbol of Germany herself" (*Wind* 97). Its use here as a projection of Nazi values implicates German culture, philosophy, literature, and its Romantic *Geist* in the creation of Nazi ideology.[22]

A line from a Napola ceremonial recitation following the screening of the SS propaganda film, *Hitlerjunge Quex*—based on the "martyrology" of young Herbert Norkus—exemplifies the utilitarian appropriation of culture: "His lips are silent, but his example lives!" (267). Norkus's story opens up to interpretation as it transmutes from actual event into aesthetic object (film) precisely because of the muteness that death imposes. Significantly, Tiffauges describes not only the film but also the ceremony that follows it and refracts its meaning. The filmmaker does not have the last word on the meaning of his film any more than Norkus does on his life. Like the murdered Norkus, art may be construed as mute; just as the filmmaker and then the viewer interprets Norkus's silence, the viewer/reader may impose a multiplicity of meanings on any work of art. While neither art nor the murdered Norkus begins in muteness, neither can successfully defend against misappropriation.

This provides a means of understanding the incompatible conjunction of high culture with atrocity in the Third Reich. In *Language and Silence*, George Steiner wonders how "a man can read Goethe or Rilke in the evening, that he can play Bach and Schubert, and go to his day's work at Auschwitz in the morning" (15). Steiner's phrasing suggests a neat compartmentalization—"Rilke in the evening . . . Auschwitz in the morning"—which neutralizes art, separating it from life and from history. Atrocity thus remains impervious to whatever humanizing effect Steiner ascribes to high culture. Steiner alludes to a more intimate link, "as yet scarcely understood, between mental, psychological habits of high literacy and the temptations of the inhuman . . . preparing it for the release of barbarism" (16).[23] In a later work, he asks:

> Why did humanistic traditions and models of conduct prove so fragile a barrier against political bestiality? In fact, were they a barrier, or is it more realistic to perceive in humanistic culture express solicitations of authoritarian rule and creativity? (*Bluebeard* 30)

Tournier's novel suggest another possibility—that the ambiguity and expansiveness inherent to a literary work interpretation allow for the (mis)appropriation of its rhetorical and symbolic power. If so, what distinguishes "good" from "bad" interpretations at a given moment is the political clout to enforce one's reading.[24]

The tattooing incident at Tiffauges's childhood boarding school illustrates the availability of texts for multiple and purposive interpretations. Young Tiffauges harbors a secret crush on an older schoolboy whom he persuades to participate in the children's "tatoo" craze. Tiffauges proposes tattooing on the other boy a heart pierced by an arrow, encircled with the phrase "*A toi pour la vie*" (*Roi des Aulnes* 26) [lit: yours for life]. However, when the older boy allows Tiffauges to draw the design on his skin, Tiffauges makes a slight change in the text, writing "*A T pour la vie*" [A T for life]. Tiffauges insists that foreign legionnaires abbreviate *A toi* with the letters *A T* to signify also "Athée" [atheist], pronounced in French like the letters "A T." In explaining that A T can represent *A toi* and *Athée* at the same time, he reveals to the other boy the ambiguity of literary symbols. ". . . soit pour *A toi*, soit pour manifester leur révolte contre Dieu (Athée pour la vie), soit de façon équivoque pour signifier l'un et l'autre à la fois" (27) [whether it stands for *Always Thine*, whether it shows their revolt against God (Atheist for life), whether it signifies equivocally one and the other simultaneously].[25] However, the older boy soon realizes the motivation behind Tiffauges's textual alteration, and the singular meaning that Abel really intends: "A T. . . . "They're your initials. Abel Tiffauges" (27). For Tiffauges, meaning is malleable and expedient; interpretation fulfills the unspoken desire of the interpreter.

Although in his sinister journal Tiffauges claims to write "with the sole purpose of unburdening myself and proclaiming the truth" (6), he writes to mislead and to distract from the truth. Like the German anthropologist who misappropriates Goethe's poem to his own political beliefs, Tiffauges uses the literary imagination for his own purposes.

Like the musical abilities of SS officers who play Bach or Schubert, Tiffauges's extraordinary literary talents coexist with atrocity. The ease with which cultural artifacts lend themselves to such appropriations underlies the novel's critique of intellectual work and high culture. One wonders, along with George Steiner, whether high culture's "deep-set ambiguities . . . solicited barbarism" (*Bluebeard* 85).

Tournier's parodic, self-deflating novel mounts an attack on literary discourse for two reasons: first, because the rhetoric of Nazism resembles the language of literary discourse, and second, because Nazism incorporated and misused the symbolic imagination. The novel sets up an equivalence between Tiffauges's private symbolic order and the rhetoricity of Nazi racism, myth, and romantic nationalism. As the narrative deconstructs Tiffauges's arcane and inflated rhetoric, it reveals the underbelly of atrocity, hidden by language and interpretative practices. Ultimately Tiffauges recognizes in Auschwitz "an infernal city . . . which corresponded stone by stone to the phoric city he himself had dreamed of. . . . inverted and raised to hellish incandescence" (357). Only when Ephraim's presence deconstructs Tiffauges's symbolic interpolation does Tiffauges acknowledge the "monstrous analogy" and become accountable for his own complicity.[26]

In the novel's critique of the language of collaboration, both Tiffaugean and Nazi rhetoric posit a symbolic interpretation of reality that precludes consciousness and conscience. Substituting symbol for reality, both posit an exclusive and singular totalizing interpretive system. An anti-Nazi Commander later silenced by the Gestapo observes to Tiffauges that "ever since it began the Third Reich has been the product of symbols, which have taken over control" (304). The Commander envisions "a terrifying moment when the sign no longer accepts being carried by a creature as a banner is carried by a soldier. It acquires autonomy, it escapes the thing symbolized . . . it takes over that thing" (302–23). The "phoric" reversal of sign and sign-bearer reverberates with a physical exchange involving children and deadly weapons. When warfare training begins at the Napola, Tiffauges notes:

> The toy is no longer carried by the child—drawn, pushed, tilted, rolled, as an imaginative object in destructive little hands. Now it is the child who is carried by the toy—swallowed up in a tank, shut in the cockpit of a plane, imprisoned in the swiveling turret of a machine gun. (292)

What Tiffauges terms *"the overturning of phoria by malign inversion"* (292) underscores the causal progression from Nazi symbolic construct to the violent deaths of the weapon-borne children. Tiffauges insists

that the reading of symbols connects him to a higher reality and on
that basis asserts his innocence. The relationship between abstract
construct and real violence impugns the symbolic imagination and
implicates the "reader of signs" (302) in atrocity.

Governed by "his instinct for power, sometimes with farfetched
subtleties as shown in his 'Sinister Writings'" (317), Tiffauges develops
a brilliant theory of signs that enables him to exploit those around him
without accountability. When his three favorite boys are impaled upon
heraldic swords during a Russian advance, Tiffauges sees the culmi-
nation of his symbol-making and symbol-reading: "the union of sign
with flesh, which for him was the final end of everything, and particularly of the war" (136). As Jean Améry notes in his memoirs and reflections on the Nazi era, "We had the chance to observe how the word
became flesh and how this incarnated word finally led to heaps of
cadavers" (x). The grotesque impalement of the kidnapped youths thus
implicates Tiffauges, the Reich, and the symbolic imagination.

Having exploited to exhaustion the language of literature, myth,
and symbol in a pseudo-apocalyptic vision, Tournier's novel exposes
the empty *form* of apocalypse. Tiffauges first assumes and then deflates
the pseudosignification of Nazi rhetoric. In *The Wind Spirit*, Tournier
discusses the narrative strategy of *The Ogre*: "to portray systematic,
logical madness . . . allow one's characters to speak for themselves. . . .
while the self-effacing author remains hidden, a voyeur enjoying the
confrontation" (94). The narrative lapses repeatedly into myths of
denial, then debunks these myths as elaborate psychological maneuvers, transparent fictions, created by characters to avoid facing self,
atrocity, memory. The repetition and elaboration of symbolic patterns
and mythic associations build up expectations for an aesthetically neat
resolution—expectations that the novel meets but deconstructs.

Tournier's strategy encourages the reader's absorption into
Tiffauges's network of symbols and signs only to discredit Tiffauges's
interpretation of historical reality. Episodes such as the tattooing incident shed doubt upon both Tiffauges's written and spoken word, a
doubt reinforced by his coprological obsession and its link with text. As
George Steiner says of Céline, "words had become a substitute for reality. Logorrhea is the very condition of [his] achievement and limita-
tion. . . . He was a master of words but was also mastered by them"
(*Extraterritorial* 43). As Tiffauges uses fiction to double himself—that is
to maintain innocence while acting sadistically—so the reader doubles
in the act of reading, simultaneously attracted to and repulsed by the
shifting terms of reality. As we read Tiffauges's journal, we, too, sub-

stitute aesthetic structure, signs, and tropes for reality. The novel's transparency, its awareness of itself as artifice, ironically confronts our myth-making proclivity, examining the interplay between imagination and reality, myth and deed.

The Ogre presents a cleverly and intricately constructed narrative, which absorbs the reader into its pattern of symbols and interpretations. Not only Tiffauges's journal but also the third-person narrator affirms the aesthetic tightness that substitutes for historicity and causality. *The Ogre* draws the reader into its complicated web of mythic and literary associations, its astonishing aesthetic coherence that mimics the totalizing interpretive systems. Except for the rare reader who cannot forget, even momentarily, that the "'hero' is indirectly responsible for the deaths of hundreds of adolescents" (Cloonan, 37),[27] one experiences pleasure at one's own cleverness in following Tiffauges's symbolic meditations and in recognizing the narrative's imagistic patterns. To the extent that one enters into the pleasures of this text, one momentarily forgets the real history that comprises its milieu. Like Tiffauges, the reader focuses on an aesthetic or philosophical system instead of seeing the carnage. Seduced, if only momentarily, the reader enacts Tiffauges's refusal of memory; reawakened into history, one must consider the possibility of one's own complicity, one's own forgetfulness.

In many fictional responses to the Holocaust, aesthetic pleasure collides with the remembrance of atrocity. The connection between Nazi rhetoric and literary discourse engenders conflicted feelings toward the act of writing itself, whose tenuous resolution results in a consistent movement of displacement on several levels. Some writers consign themselves to muteness in the language in which they experienced atrocity and choose to write only in an exilic tongue. The language choice mimics the personal and collective narrative of displacement. Elie Wiesel, for example, writes in French rather than Hungarian (or Yiddish); Jacov Lind gives up German for English. For many writers not only a particular language but broad patterns of rhetoric and literary structures become tainted. This degenerative distrust of rhetoric, as implicated itself in the catastrophe, deepens until language, in its encounter with violence, is displaced toward radical self-repudiation. In Tournier's novel, totalizing symbolic systems ultimately collapse as the narrative exposes not just the limitations of the literary imagination, but also its pernicious possibilities.[28] The novel explores the intimate links between abstract construct and real violence. Thus, an ironic tension emerges, in response to the writer's acknowledgment of the dangers inherent to literary discourse. The internal undercutting of the power generated by the writer's own work constitutes a paradoxical wedding of silence and language, muteness and speech, memory and forgetting. As Celan observes,

> Welches der Worte du sprichst
> du dankst
> dem Verderben.

> [Whichever word you speak
> you thank
> destruction]

> (*Gedichte I* 129)

9

The Chain
of Testimony

do not destroy the cosmos of words,
do not dissect with blades of hate
the sound, born in concert with
the breath.
       —Nelly Sachs

After a long hiatus, the narrator of Ida Fink's short fiction "A Scrap of Time" reaches into "the ruins of memory" to narrate the story of her city's "first action"—that is, the first roundup of Jews for mass slaughter. A Jewish woman who survived the Holocaust as a child in Poland (we never learn how), she offers as testimony her recollection of what happened to her and to others on that day. She introduces her narrative with the following:

> I want to talk about a certain time not measured in months and years. For so long I have wanted to talk about this time, and not in the way I will talk about it now, not about this one scrap of time. I wanted to, but I couldn't, I didn't know how. I was afraid, too, that this second time, which is measured in months and years, had buried the other time under a layer of years, that this second time had crushed the first and destroyed it within me. But no. Today, digging around in the ruins of memory, I found it fresh and untouched by forgetfulness. (3)

Although the woman finds her memory of that morning "still fresh; its colors and aromas have not faded" (5), although she (re)affirms both the validity of that memory and her eagerness to share it with her listeners, she has difficulty telling it in a straightforward manner. The story opens with a series of affirmations and denials, of sayings and unsay-ings, which seemingly run counter to her simple desire to bear wit-ness. She "want[s] to talk," but not in this way and not of this "scrap of time." On the next page, she contradicts herself, calling her story "the scrap of time I want to talk about" (4). She fears the destruction of memory, but finds hers "fresh and untouched by forgetfulness."

That she should check memory's inventory and evaluate its con-tents before beginning her tale should not surprise us. In *The Drowned and the Saved*, Primo Levi notes among Holocaust survivors, many years after the event, "a drifting of memory" (32) that works counter to the testimonial impulse. He, too, he tells us, scrutinizes his store of anec-dotes, pronouncing them "unaffected by the drifting I have described" before enclosing them in written text. But while Levi recounts with con-fidence remembered episodes and snatches of conversation (even in languages he cannot understand), the narrator of Fink's story lingers at the edge of narrative. Rather than plunge from contemplation of mem-ory directly into remembered event (now affirmed as "untouched by forgetfulness"), the narrator moves into an extended consideration of etymologic distinctions—of "action" and "round-up." The shifting lin-guistic values convey meaning through indirection: "I don't know who created this technical term [action], who substituted it for the first term, 'round-up'. . . . Round-ups were for forced labor" (4). And "actions?" The narrator does not specify, but the initiated already understand the term, defined through omission, then negation. "We called that first action . . . a round-up although no one was rounding anyone up" (4). The linguistic indirection, contradiction, and circularity mirror the beginning of the narrative and anticipate the disclosure of memory. The missing definition corresponds to the missing "scrap of time," the as yet undisclosed memory. The parallel suggests that both word and memory hover slightly beyond our focus out of neither igno-rance nor forgetfulness, but out of consideration for both speaker and listener. Both word and memory enclose horror—the same horror, mass slaughter. At the same time, our grasp of the import of the undefined word implies the paradoxical unfolding of memory also through ellipse.

The postponed disclosure, when it finally begins, immediately thwarts our expectations. Although the narrator opens with a promise of a "fresh and untouched" story rooted out from the "ruins of mem-ory"—her memory—we quickly realize she does not intend to tell us *her* story at all, but someone else's.

> In the middle of the marketplace . . . we were ordered to
> form ranks.
> I should not have written "we," for I was not standing
> in the ranks. . . . (4)

Her "I" becomes a "we" that in turn becomes "not . . . we." Misled initially, we may wonder fleetingly whether this narrator, like Levi, can
truly claim to have "diligently examined" her story and found it "in
good consonance" (Levi, *Drowned* 34). She subsequently clarifies the
discrepancy. From an unobserved vantage point, she sees the action on
the marketplace, yet remains unseen. Thus, we learn, an eyewitness
(but not a participant) to the round-up (which was not a round-up) at
the marketplace recounts to us the story. And since—we later learn—
the massing on the marketplace serves as a prelude to mass murder,
only because she was not a participant could she become an eyewitness
(that is, a survivor). Precisely this exclusion from action—the "not-
we"—permits the inclusion of memory in narration.

The exclusion that permits disclosure leaves the narrator at one
remove from the event she narrates. Of necessity, because the dead
cannot relate their own story, her narration shifts into what Levi terms
"a discourse 'on behalf of third parties,' the story of things seen at close
hand, not experienced personally" (84). However, despite her repeated
assurances that the memory remains "fresh" and "unfaded," Fink's
eyewitness offers us a testimony remarkably spare in detail.

> There was the square, thick with people as on a market day,
> only different, because a market-day crowd is colorful and
> loud, with chickens clucking, geese honking, and people talk-
> ing and bargaining. This crowd was silent. In a way it resem-
> bled a rally—but it was different from that, too. I don't know
> what it was exactly. (6)

She cannot quite tell what she saw there or exactly why it frightened
her. Instead, she describes the scene that morning in terms of what it
was not, just as earlier she defines "action" by what it was not. She sets
the new word, "action," against the old, the known, "round-up," elabo-
rately explaining the latter, leaving the former to the imagination of the
listener. Here, too, she details the familiar—the square on a market
day, a rally—and defines by absence what she saw. Like the "action"
she cannot define and the "scrap of memory" she cannot tell, the scene
on the square eludes description.

If at all we can consider this narrator an eyewitness, narrating
from a "privileged observatory" (Levi's term, *Drowned* 18), it is only

momentarily. The girl quickly flees in fright from the growing crowd on the square, distancing herself still further from the event she narrates. She hides out among the bushes on a hillside, from where she sees not the marketplace, but her own house, her garden, her neighbor's house and hears not the sounds of selection but the neighbor beating carpets. Only when she returns home does she actually learn what was taking place at the square—only then do we learn the subject of her narrative, the meaning of "action." Specifically, she learns—and now wishes to rescue from oblivion by telling—the fate of her cousin David who, unlike herself, moved from *not-we* to *we*—joined the crowd rather than save himself in isolation. Thus, we realize, finally, it is David's story, and not her own, that she unearths from the "ruins of memory"—a story she neither saw nor experienced.

Here her role as survivor/witness, or even "privileged" eyewitness, breaks down. If she is at one level removed from the morning's event at the marketplace, which she glimpses, absorbs, and escapes, she is at many levels removed from David's story, which comes to her in bits and pieces through an already unreliable chain of transmission. By the time she returns home, David has already disappeared, together with the other men who gathered at the marketplace. According to unnamed "people" present in the square that morning, and through whom David has transmitted word to his family, the narrator learns that, like herself, he observed the action on the marketplace, alone and unseen, also a *not we*. Unlike the narrator, he chooses to join the crowd, to include himself in the *we* rather than escape in isolation. He steps into the collective narrative of which the narrator has caught a glimpse. He transmits an oral message for his mother and later writes her a note, adding his personal narrative to the collective one. Based on the received transmissions, Fink's narrator attempts to tell David's story. However, the line of transmission is indirect, yielding incomplete and sometimes contradictory information—scraps of knowledge, corresponding to the scraps of time with which Fink begins the fiction.

David's story (personal and collective) reaches the narrator through five sources: (1) the people who spoke to him at the square, (2) the note, (3) the peasant who delivers the note, (4) postcards from deportees, (5) anonymous rumors. The amassing of information takes place over time, beginning the afternoon of the action and ending after the war. The narrator returns home to learn what happened in the square during her absence ("the women had been told to go home . . . that only the men were ordered to remain standing there" [7]) and what message David sent to his mother ("he did violence to his own fate"—moving out of hiding and into the crowd). That evening, an unnamed peasant delivers the note, tossed from a truck packed with human cargo. While the peasant delivers that missive intact, he does not share all he knows with David's family. "The peasant who delivered the note did not dare to tell us what he saw" (7). Like the people in the square, the peasant does not reveal what occurs upon leaving the marketplace.

> The peasant that evening brought the note that said, "I myself am to blame, forgive me," was somber and didn't look us in the eye. He said he had found the note on the road to Lubianki and that he didn't know anything else about it; we knew that he knew, but we did not want to admit it. (9)

David's messages indicate his emotional state but offer no further illumination about what transpires. Their transmission, while complete, conveys incomplete information. The peasant's truncated testimony, on the other hand, deliberately withholds more complete knowledge. The narrative repeatedly promises (dis)closure through prolepsis—"He [the peasant] left, but he came back after the war to tell us what he has seen" (9); "Only the end of the war brought us the truth about his [David's] last hours" (7)—simultaneously heightening our awareness of the absence of narrative disclosure.

Subsequent transmissions tentatively fill in the missing information. Postcards arrive from several of the deportees—the rabbi, an accountant, an unnamed writer of an "almost indecipherable" script—which tell of a labor camp somewhere in the Reich. The cards shore up hope that the missing men live and thrive. In Claude Lanzmann's film, *Shoah*, Raoul Hilberg explains the importance to a historian of documentary evidence.

> . . . when I hold a document in my hand, particularly if it's an original document, then I hold something which is actually something that the original bureaucrat held in his hand. It's an artifact. It's a leftover. It's the only leftover there is. The dead are not around. (142–43)

The document that Hilberg holds (in this case, a train schedule indicating routes to deathcamps) functions as a trace—a corroborative remnant—of an event whose vestiges were all but erased by the perpetrators. Like the memories of survivors, the traces of catastrophe (the bones Kitty digs up, for example, the ruined deathcamps, the train schedules) help us know what occurred. In Fink's narrative, however, the seemingly concrete, documentary evidence of the deportees' fate is at odds with unsubstantiated rumors of artifacts of a different sort.

> But rumors told a different story altogether—of soggy earth
> in the woods by the village of Lubianki, and of a bloodstained
> handkerchief that had been found. These rumors came from
> nowhere; no eyewitnesses stepped forward. (10)

The two competing sets of evidence vie for primacy in the construction
of the authoritative narrative. The contradictory physical traces (postcards, handkerchief) and language traces (postcard message, rumors)
alternately displace one another in the minds of those who remain at
home, waiting.

Which set of artifacts tell the true tale—or, perhaps more correctly, how one properly interprets artifacts—becomes clear only after
the war, with the completion of the peasant's truncated narrative.

> The peasant who had not dared to speak at the time came
> back after the war and told us everything. It happened just
> as rumor had it, in a dense, overgrown forest, eight kilome-
> ters outside of town, one hour after the trucks left the mar-
> ketplace. The execution itself did not take long, more time
> was spent on the preparatory digging of the grave. (10)

With the peasant's disclosure to the narrator's family comes also the
disclosure to the reader of the narrator's memory, the "scrap of time"
present yet missing since the beginning of the narrative—David's
death, and the deaths of the other deportees. However, while the peasant tells the narrator and her family "everything," the narrative that
we read, by contrast, remains truncated. We learn only that the story
exists; we do not read it to completion. The brief narration of the circumstances surrounding David's death serve also as metaphor for the
narrative itself. Like the execution that "itself did not take long," the
actual telling of the story takes far less time than the "preparatory
digging"—in earth and in memory.

Once again—as with "action," the marketplace, the "scrap of
time"—we learn through omission. The missing details, the missing
definition, connote death which remains (always) unarticulated, outside
of narrative. This explains, finally, the elliptical nature of Fink's story,
the non-narrated narration that discloses through withholding. The
narrative gaps function not only as absence but also—as Pierre Van der
Heuvel states in his discussion of Camus—as "l'acte de la *non-parole* ou
du *non-mot*. . . . Ce silence, ce vide textuel, est évidemment *signe* au
meme titre que la parole. . . ." (57) [an act of *non-utterance* or of *non-
word*. . . . This silence, this textual emptiness, is evidently *sign* for the
same reason as utterance . . .]. The ellipse enables the narrator to tell a

story not only of survival but of what Lawrence Langer calls "surmortal"[1]—a narrative of both living through and dying through the Holocaust. The narrator tells the story of David because he cannot tell it himself. In order to do so, she must leave the confines of memory and witnessing for the realms of imagination and hearsay. Using bits of memory, fragments of narrative, "scraps of time," she traces in her mind the route by which David reaches the square, his solitary considerations while in hiding, his intuition of his impending death. To do this, the narrator must temporarily place herself alongside David, become the *we*, and live out—in her imagination and in this narrative—an alternative different from the one she herself lived out the day of the first action. She must imagine what she can never know—David's last moments, last feelings, last posture, before he falls victim to mass slaughter.

In contrast to the narrator of Jorge Semprun's *The Long Voyage*—who can speak to the dead (with a "pure, fraternal look") but not of them—and unlike Kitty (in Morely's film) who anchors her memories in the deathcamp that both prompts and validates them, Fink's narrator sees herself as distanced experientially (although not emotionally) from David and those who died with him. Her problematic role as eyewitness who did not see what she relates, nonetheless exemplifies the status of the survivor who—spared the worst—cannot speak entirely from personal experience. In *The Drowned and the Saved*, Levi observes:

> . . . the history of the Lagers has been written almost exclusively by those who, like myself, never fathomed them to the bottom. Those who did so did not return, or their capacity for observation was paralyzed by suffering and incomprehension. (17)

For this reason, explains Levi, "We speak in their stead, by proxy" (84)—as Fink's narrator does on her cousin's behalf. The ellipse, the omission, signals the unknowable and inarticulate death. Maurice Blanchot touches on the connections between death, survival, memory, and testimony in *The Writing of the Disaster*: "It is not you who will speak; let the disaster speak in you, even if it be by your forgetfulness or silence" (8). As Fink's narrator transforms her subject from *I* to *we* to *not we* to *he* then finally back to an *I* that contains *I* and *we* and *not we* and *he*, the chain of testimony moves—however imperfectly—to and through the narrator and the narrative. Willingness to hear, remember, imagine, and tell compensates for absence of experience, and the narrator produces a good enough testimony—one that rescues David and his fraternal dead from oblivion.

And what of the reader in this chain of testimony? What will constitute our link, we, who at still greater remove from the narrator manage
to extract from her ellipses the undisclosed story? Like Fink's narrator, we
garner fragments of memories and bits of stories—other people's memories, other people's stories—which cohere though empathic imagination
and willingness to bear witness. The act of reading places us in equiva-
lency to the narrator. As she is to David, so we are to her: distanced experientially from what we attempt to understand, but willing to engage
wholly—intellectually, emotionally, imaginatively—with that which we
seek to recover. Particularly for those of us who come after, or who were
not present, such an engagement constitutes our only means to recover
lost memories, to uncover hidden facts, to discover new knowledge. Like
Fink's narrator, we find individual artifacts suggestive, but not defini-
tive. In *Shoah*, Hilberg observes,

> One cannot even read Göring's famous letter to Heydrich at
> the end of July 1941 charging him in two paragraphs to pro-
> ceed with the "final solution," and examining that document,
> consider that everything is clarified. Far from it. It was an
> authorization to invent. It was an authorization to begin
> something that was not as yet capable of being put into
> words. I think of it in that way. (72–73)

In his capacity as a historian, Hilberg tracks down, unearths, amasses
letters, train schedules, documents—pieces of the concentrationary
universe "that the original bureaucrat held in his hands." While these—
like the bone fragments Kitty unearths at Auschwitz—constitute the
traces of catastrophe, Hilberg's piecing them together and interpreting
their significance—like Kitty's narrative, and that of Fink's narrator—
enable them to disclose their evidence. Like Fink's narrator, we, too,
can transmit the testimony that results from the piling up, examining, and absorbing a panoply of detail. As the "scraps of time" recede
and survivors become fewer, the act of reading, too, becomes an act of
testimony, a staving off of forgetfulness.

But reading the Holocaust—what can that mean? The survivor's
difficulty bearing testimony mirrors itself in our difficulty receiving it.
How are we to sift through, interpret, evaluate, absorb, and teach the
scraps, which are all that remain of the Holocaust? The fragmentary
nature of these traces of catastrophe complicates their import for us.
We view photographs and film footage that require a survivor's narrative for meaning; we hear survivor's testimony that requires documents
and photographs for corroboration. In a vignette titled "Traces," Ida
Fink measures a photograph of a ghetto street scene against the mem-

ory of a survivor of that ghetto. Presented as a fictional fragment of an interview with a ghetto survivor, "Traces" explores the nature of testimony and evidence. As a historical document, the photograph rings true but incomplete. It depicts snowdrifts on a market street—and "In the foreground are traces of footprints" (135). The photo prompts the pouring forth of narrative and tears, both of which the survivor had previously suppressed, both of which the survivor now grudgingly releases. The narrative reveals the tertiary nature of the "Traces" of the title: a photograph of "traces of footprints"—traces three times removed from the children who looked like "little gray mice" (137), on the way to their death. Provoked by the photograph, the survivor's testimony displaces the photograph in the vignette and in the title: "A trace of those children. And only she can leave that trace, because she alone survived" (137).

In "Traces," Fink privileges the narrative of memory and survival over the concrete documentation of a photograph. In "The Table," she raises questions about the reliability of survivor memory and about the rigorous demands of the historian. A short play in which four survivors testify in court about an "action" that they witnessed or escaped, "The Table" brings together four testimonial narratives that—while they may agree in essence (there *was* an "action")—disagree on details. Was there a table in the marketplace? How large was it? When and where was it placed in the marketplace? Was there a chair? How many people sat at the table? The prosecutor explains that he "torments" the survivors with his questions because he requires "something concrete." He looks for an agreement on details so that the separate narratives may corroborate one another. The four witnesses cannot agree on the specifics of the table. They all testify that the snow in the marketplace was drenched with blood, but—as the prosecutor tells them—"snow doesn't constitute proof for judges, especially snow that melted twenty-five years ago" (156). Fink's play raises the issue of "tainted memory"— a term Lawrence Langer uses to describe the unfolding of videotaped survivor testimony. Survivor narrative is pulled into (and out of) shape by the survivor's sense of the demands of convention, the expectations of the listener (or interviewer or reader), and the massive trauma of the event itself. In judging survivor testimonies that may be at odds with one another (or with a piece of documentary evidence), do we decide to silence some? In "The Table," the prosecutor may decide to privilege one voice over the other three, or he may discredit all four. Who is on trial in Fink's play?

The Drowned and the Saved attests to Primo Levi's despair that the chain of testimony has already shattered, that the knowledge and memories "that we survivors of the Nazi Lagers carry within us are extraneous to the new Western generation and become ever more extraneous as the years pass" (198). While the narrator of "A Scrap of Time" does not doubt her listeners' interest, characters in other stories in Fink's collection do. The youthful protagonist of "Splinter," for example, finds that his girlfriend has fallen asleep as he narrates his mother's violent and heroic death. In "Night of Surrender," an American soldier tells the pretty Jewish survivor whom he wishes to marry to forget her past, her family, even her name. "'Klara,' he repeated. 'Clear one . . . but you'll always be Ann to me" (101). These narrators, like Levi and others, struggle not only with memory but against reluctant listeners who see the Holocaust as "distant, blurred, 'historical'" (*Drowned* 198). The chain of testimony, thus, has two senses: the successive tellings and retellings (links), the binding obligation to testify (fetters). Levi observes:

> For us to speak with the young becomes ever more difficult. We see it as a duty and, at the same time, as a risk: the risk of appearing anachronistic, of not being listened to. We must be listened to:. . . . It happened, therefore it can happen again: this is the core of what we have to say. (199)

For the weak links in the chain, the survivor/witness blames both the listener, reluctant to face harsh realities, and the intractability of memory, "a marvelous but fallacious instrument" (*Drowned* 23). More fundamentally, Blanchot wonders, "*How can thought be made the keeper of the holocaust where all was lost, including guardian thought?*" (47).

If the articulate survivor/witnesses despair of adequately describing what they have seen and experienced, we must despair of adequately knowing; if they refuse to forget, so should we. The Holocaust also is our burden—and we live under its shadow. For the sake of our own future as much as any moral imperative to commemorate the victims, we struggle to absorb it, to understand it, to learn from it. As the works treated here suggest, we must do so with language, against language, and beyond language.

Notes

1. INTRODUCTION

1. Quo. in Claudia Dreifus, "Art Spiegelman," *The Progressive* 53 (1989), 34.

2. "Art Spiegelman: The Road to Maus," exhibit, Museum of Art, Fort Lauderdale, February-April 1993. The museum brochure distributed at the exhibit explicitly echoes Spiegelman's insistence that the *Maus* sequence is not "in any sense a fictionalized account, despite the artistic liberties taken with both text and illustrations. . . ."

3. For a discussion of the role of the listener in Holocaust survivor testimony, see Dori Laub, "Bearing Witness, or the Vicissitudes of Listening," *Testimony*, pp. 57–74.

4. While accepting Lanzmann's assertion that the "truth kills the possibility of fiction," in her discussion of *Shoah* Shoshana Felman explains that "the truth does not kill the possibility of art" (206).

5. According to Lanzmann, "The length of the film is the length of the pensée, of the thinking" (quo. in Gussow C15).

6. "Resurrecting Horror: The Man behind *Shoah*," Interview with Deborah Jerome *The Record* 25 October 1985.

7. David Hirsch ably articulates the dangerous potential of certain trends in postmodernism in *The Deconstruction of Literature: Criticism after Auschwitz*. See also Friedlander's *Probing the Limits of Representation*.

8. It is interesting to note that Thomas Keneally similarly protested the categorization of his novel, *Schindler's List*, as fiction. Simon & Schuster categorizes Keneally's book as fiction, describing it as "a factual account done with fictional techniques" or a "non-fiction novel," according to Sarah Lyall, "Book Notes," *New York Times* 9 March 1994; thus the novel remained on the *Times* fiction list.

9. The controversy regarding the autobiographical claims of Kosinski's novel reopened discussion of the novel's aesthetic merits, its ethical import, and its legitimacy as Holocaust representation. For an overview on this controversy, see James Park Sloan, "Kosinski's War."

10. Personal interview.

11. For discussion of the role of the lost childhood in *Wartime Lies*, see Naomi Sokoloff's excellent treatment.

12. Craig Barclay notes,that the ego's self-schema "functions to provide consistency between one's life as lived and the abbreviated story told at any time" (83). See also William F. Brewer, "What is autobiographical memory?"

13. Dennis B. Klein, "History versus Fiction," *Dimensions: A Journal of Holocaust Studies* 8 (1994)1:2.

14. The phrase is Yeats's, used in this context by Terrence Des Pres ("The Dreaming Back").

15. "For Some Measure of Humility," *Shma* 5/100 (1975) 314.

16. See, for example, Saul Friedlander, *Probing the Limits of Representation: Nazism and the "Final Solution"* (Cambridge, MA: Harvard University Press, 1992).

17. *The Exile of the Word*, published originally as *L'Exil de la parole*.

18. For discussion of Nazi-Deutsch, see also Nachman Blumenthal, "On the Nazi Vocabulary"; Lucy Davidowicz, *The War Against the Jews 1933–45*; and Shaul Esh, "Words and their Meanings: Twenty-five Examples of Nazi Idiom."

19. Ann Mason has explored this "problem of symbolism"—that is, "the way in which Nazism misused the symbolic mode" (69).

20. See, for example, Louis O. Mink, "Narrative Form as a Cognitive Instrument," and Hayden White, *The Content of the Form*, 1–57. Alvin Rosenfeld's analysis of Hugh Trevor-Roper's reconstruction of Hitler's last days—a reconstruction that, while aiming at *factuality* and *objectivity*, would "both dampen and excite a new Hitler myth" (*Imagining Hitler* 20)—provides a good case in point. Rosenfeld teases out the mythopoeiaic, religious, figurative language embedded in Trevor-Roper's and seized upon by Trevor-Roper's successors.

21. See also Eric Satner, *Stranded Objects: Mourning, Memory, and Film in Postwar Germany*, especially his discussion of Paul de Man, pp.13–30.

22. For a cogent critique of the tendency to "define[] science as the adversary or antithesis of rhetoric . . . conjoined with a defense of a 'plain style' that attempts or pretends to be entirely transparent to its object," see Dominick LaCapra, *History and Criticism*, pp.15–44.

23. Vidal Naquet makes a similar point in *Assassins of Memory*:

"Between memory and history, there can be tension and even opposition. But a history of the Nazi crimes which did not integrate memory—or rather, diverse memories—and which failed to account for the transformation of memories would be a poor history, indeed" (xviii).

24. For a discussion of midrash, see David Stern, *Parable in Midrash: Narrative and Exegesis in Rabbinic Literature*, and Daniel Boyarin, *Intertextuality and the Reading of Midrash*.

25. For further discussion of the political and ideological aspects of midrash, see David Stern, *The Parable in Midrash*.

26. For discussion of the Haggadah as paradigm for the representation of the Shoah in popular culture, see Eric Goldman, "Film as Haggadah for the Holocaust," *Shoah* 4, no.1–2 (fall/winter 1983–84):4.

27. For a discussion about how different listeners impede or encourage the flow of testimony, see Lawrence Langer *Holocaust Memories*, and Dori Laub, "Bearing Witness, or the Vicissitudes of Listening" in *Testimony: Crises of Witnessing in Literature, Psychoanalysis, and History* by Shoshana Felman and Dori Laub.

28. George Steiner calls history "the *kaddish* against lies, and that greatest lie is forgetting" ("Long Life" 58). However, he finds its facticity incomplete; historical accounts, he asserts "have not . . . illuminated the deeper-lying roots of the inhuman" (58).

29. In a discussion of the conjunction of history and fictional texts in *History and Criticism*, Dominick LaCapra observes that literature becomes "paradoxically most superfluous" when it cleaves most closely to documentary sources (126). LaCapra suggests a move toward reading texts in "ways that engage the interpreter as historian *and* critic in an exchange with the past" (127).

30. James Young has examined the hermeneutic distinctions between historical and fictional discourses in his highly original *Writing and Rewriting the Holocaust*.

31. Similarly, for David Roskies, the "scribes of the ghetto"—the diarists who recorded their ongoing experiences at great peril—produced a vital and invaluable record of the events. See both *Against the Apocalypse: Responses to Catastrophe in Modern Jewish Culture* and *The Literature of Destruction*.

32. The strength of the "pseudofactual novel," Foley insists, derives from the fact that "the object of representation is not an imagined configuration of characters and events, but a putative historical document that records such a configuration" (351).

33. The documentary mode, explains Bosmajian, "permits the viewer to secretly thrill over the unanimous crowds and the horror of destruction while leaving him secure in his moral rightness" (11).

34. A striking example is *Zlata's Diary*, begun in 1991 by thirteen-year-old Zlata Filipovic. As she narrates the ongoing siege of Sarajevo, Filipovic consciously invokes *The Diary of Anne Frank*: "Hey Diary! You know what I think? Since Anne Frank called her diary Kitty, maybe I could give you a name too" (29).

35. See, for example, James Young, *The Texture of Memory: Holocaust Memorials and Meaning*, Yael Feldman, "Whose Story Is It, Anyway? Ideology and Psychology in the Representation of the Shoah in Israeli Literature," Alvin Rosenfeld, "Popularization and Memory: The Case of Anne Frank," and Jonathan Boyarin, *Storm from Paradise: the Politics of Jewish Memory*.

36. See, for example, Shoshana Felman, "Education and Crisis, or the Vicissitudes of Teaching," and Dori Laub, "Bearing Witness, or the Vicissitudes of Teaching," *Testimony: Crises of Witnessing, Literature, Psychoanalysis, and History* by Felman and Laub, pp. 1–56 and 57–74.

37. For example, Lawrence Langer's *Holocaust Testimonies: The Ruins of Memory*, James Young, *The Texture of Memory*, Geoffrey Hartman, ed., *The Shapes of Memory*, and Peter Hayes, ed., *Lessons and Legacies: The Meaning of the Holocaust in a Changing World*.

38. See, for example, Andreas Huyssen, *Twilight of Memories: Marking Time in a Culture of Amnesia*. He notes, "the old dichotomy between history and fiction no longer holds. Not in the sense that there is no difference, but on the contrary in the sense that historical fiction can give us a hold on the world, on the real, however fictional that hold may turn out to be" (101).

39. Some critics have also, of course, continued to write insightfully and illuminatingly about imaginative literature and the Shoah; see, for example, John Felstiner, "Translating Paul Celan's 'Todesfuge': Rhythm and Repetition as Metaphor," *Probing the Limits of Representation*, ed. Saul Friedlander, pp.240–58.

3. VOICES FROM THE KILLING GROUND

1. An earlier version of this chapter appeared in *Holocaust Remembrance: The Shapes of Memory*, ed. Geoffrey Hartman (Cambridge, MA: Basil Blackwell, 1994), pp. 42–58.

2. The phrase occurs recurrently in her essays in *Testimony*.

3. See her introductory essays to the two special issues of *American Imago* edited by Cathy Caruth on *Psychoanalysis, Culture, and Trauma* (Spring and Winter 1991), and her "Unclaimed Experience: Trauma and the Possibility of History." Page references in this chapter are from "Introduction" (Spring 1991).

4. Robert J. Lifton develops the idea of psychic numbing as a response to massive psychic trauma in work on survivors of Hiroshima, the Holocaust, and the battlefield. See, for example, *Death in Life* and "Interview."

5. Henry Krystal's complex understanding of the effect of massive trauma on survivors has enriched our understanding of this difficult subject. See, for example, his early *Massive Psychic Trauma* and the more recent "Integration and Self-Healing in Post-Traumatic States: A Ten Year Retrospective." Page references in this chapter are from "Integration and Self-Healing."

6. Dori Laub's ongoing work with the Fortunoff Archives for Holocaust Testimonies at Yale University, his therapeutic interactions with survivors, and his own experiences as a child survivor have yielded the insights of his highly compassionate work on trauma and testimony. All page references in this chapter are from his essays in *Testimony*, edited with Shoshana Felman.

7. For discussion of primary repression and the return of the repressed in the context of Holocaust survivors, see Cathy Carruth, "Unclaimed Experience: Trauma and the Possibility of History"; Dori Laub, "An Event Without a Witness: Truth Testimony and Survival," *Testimony*, pp. 75–92; and Henry Krystal, "Integration and Self-Healing in Post-Traumatic States: A Ten Year Retrospective." Dominick LaCapra discusses primary repression and the writing of history in *History and Criticism*.

8. In framing the concept of "the crisis of witnessing" central to their coauthored *Testimony*, Shoshana Felman and Dori Laub refer repeatedly to the Nazi genocide as "an event without witness," an overstatement of the complexities of survivor testimony that threatens to efface actual testimonies. For further discussion of this point, see my "Rethinking Holocaust Testimony: The Making and Unmaking of the Witness."

9. Among the documented cases of partial or total Holocaust amnesia, the most radical are by former child victims, where the experience and inscription of psychic trauma is complicated by the discrepancy between the observing, experiencing child (present at the moments of trauma) and the narrating adult (who possesses or is possessed by the memory of trauma). In "After the Holocaust," Aharon Appelfeld observes, "Ultimately the children did not absorb the full horror, only that portion of it which children could take in" (90).

10. In *Act and Idea in Nazi Genocide*, Berel Lang evokes the Passover Haggadah and its ritualized storytelling differently—as an enactment of history that becomes a means of re-vision.

4. THE MUTE LANGUAGE OF BRUTALITY

1. Gail Mortimer terms the boy's speech, suddenly and inexplicably restored on the last page of the novel, the "'word salad' of the totally disintegrated personality" (325); Krystyna Preudowska views it as evidence of his "having become mentally and physically strengthened by evil" (6); Stanley Corngold sees in it the triumph of the "boy poet" over the "boy wanderer," and the "exultant abstraction of language from a world of ends" (162); while R. J. Spendal regards it as a healthy sign of an identity regained. The implications of the boy's recovered faculty, however, cannot be fully appreciated without an exploration of the specific role muteness plays in Kosinski's novel, with an eye toward its function as leitmotif in Holocaust literature in general.

2. In "As I Ebbed with the Ocean of Life."

3. According to its mother, a Hiroshima infant did not utter a sound for a full year following the explosion (Lifton, *Death in Life* 65).

4. Examples of this abound both in fiction and in memoirs. Hebrew novelist Aharon Appelfeld, a Holocaust survivor, reveals, "For two years, from the ages of eight to ten, I wandered about from place to place as a shepherd boy, afraid to speak to anyone" (quoted in Freema Gottlieb, "A Talk with Aharon Appelfeld" 41). It is interesting to note that in Isaac Bashevis Singer's novel, *The Slave*, Sarah—a seventeenth-century convert to Judaism—feigns muteness although she has mastered Yiddish so that her accent will not reveal her gentile origins to the Jews of her shtetl. Here, too, language and linguistic difference functions as an emblem of otherness.

5. Memoirs, fiction, and documentation all point up the alluring lies used to coax victims to meet their death with little resistance— lies couched in euphemistic terms such as "resettlement" and "transports" to deathcamps.

6. Both historical and fictional narrative of the Holocaust offers many instances of such tragic incidents—for example, mothers who deny their small children in order to be spared immediate death.

7. For summary of use of insect terminology in the concentrationary universe, see George Steiner, *Language and Silence*. According to Richard L. Rubenstein in *After Auschwitz: Radical Theology and Contemporary Judaism* (33), Zyclon B, the lethal gas used in Nazi gas chambers was a derivative of Zyclon A, a common insecticide composed of cyanide, chloride, and nitrogen.

8. Corngold views the boy's association with the painted bird image ambivalently, as one of strength as well as of destruction: self-definition along with otherness. According to Corngold, "all self-consciousness is a

force. These are the colors which the boy paints himself and his world; they emblemize the power of the imagination. . . . The colors of the bird make the inception of its wound—and of its free flight" (165). The text, however, does not support so felicitous an interpretation.

9. For a psychoanalytic modeling of the mechanisms of stereotyping and the relationship between the normative group and the outsider, see Sander L. Gilman, *Difference and Pathology*.

10. See Rubenstein, chapter 1.

11. In Claude Lanzmann's film, *Shoah*, he interviews several residents of Grabow, Poland—a waystation for transports of Jews en route to the deathcamp Chelmno. The people shared with Lanzmann their recollections of those transports and of the disappearance of their own Jewish neighbors. Even four decades after the liberation of the camps— and after full disclosure of what transpired there—these people echoed the sentiments expressed by the peasants of Kosinski's novel. One man recounted a story told to him by a friend: a rabbi comforted his doomed congregation, locked inside a church and about to be burned alive, by explaining to them the justice of their death. ". . . il y a très, très longtemps de ça, à peu près deux mille ans, les Juifs ont condamné à mort Christ qui était tout à fait innocent" (112). [". . . around two thousand years ago the Jews condemned the innocent Christ to death" (100)].

12. See his *Holocaust and the Literary Imagination*, p. 188.

13. For exploration of the death/rebirth motif in *The Painted Bird*, see Mortimer.

14. See, for example, André Neher, *L'Exil de la parole: Du Silence biblique au silence d'Auschwitz* and Theodor Reik, "Die psychoigische Bedeutung des Schweigens" in *Wie Man Psychologe Wird*.

15. (Boston: Houghton Mifflin, 1965).

5. THE RELUCTANT WITNESS

1. Quoted in Insdorf, p. 194.

2. Quoted in Ramon Guthrie, "Introduction" to *The Other Kingdom* by David Rousset.

3. For a discussion of self-schema in autobiographical memory, see William F. Brewer, "What is autobiographical memory" and Craig R. Barclay, "Schematization of autobiographical memory" in *Autobiographical Memory*, ed. David C. Rubin (25–49 and 82–99). Lawrence Langer discusses the playing out of two different memory tracks in videotaped survivor testimony in his *Holocaust Testimonies*.

4. An earlier version of the above discussion of the Holocaust as "an event without witness" appears in my "Rethinking Holocaust Tes-

timony: *The Making and Unmaking of the Witness.*"

5. For discussion of this topic, see, for example, Bruno Bettel-heim, *Surviving and Other Essays*, and Henry Krystal, ed., *Massive Psychic Trauma*.

6. I do not wish to imply that the catastrophes at Hiroshima and the concentration camps were identical; they were not. The American bombing of Hiroshima was a declared act of war, utilizing a new and devastatingly powerful weapon aimed at a belligerent nation. The Nazi machinery of atrocity, aimed at a passive internal population, included many years of planned, systematic persecutions, humiliation, sadism. However, for certain specific purposes, a comparison between the two events is illuminating. They both involve a tragedy of proportions previously unforeseen and unimaginable. They affected civilian populations and led to widespread suffering, the breakdown of normal familial relations and of systems of belief. Finally, the survivors of both catastrophes suffer long-lasting effects from their traumatic experience.

7. Quoted in Emil L. Fackenheim, *From Bergen-Belsen to Jerusalem: Contemporary Implications of the Holocaust*.

8. Roskies, "Holocaust" 210.

6. MUTED CHORDS

1. Roskies develops this critique in "The Holocaust According to the Literary Critics." Ian Frazier's mounts a similar critique in his satirical fiction, "The Stuttgart Folders," in which Hitler attends a staff conference completely nude. He remonstrates a shocked Himmler, "'Do we care whether the Reich lasts a thousand years or twenty minutes? . . . Do we care in the slightest about this red herring of a war which we have thrown across the path of the non-Aryan world?' . . . 'Our dream is that the Third Reich, in the person of its Führer, Adolf Hitler, shall become the greatest plot device the world has ever known,' Himmler said, in the singsong tone of one repeating an oft-recited maxim" (26–27).

2. This accounts, in part, for what is termed "survivor guilt," a phenomenon discussed at length in, for example, *Massive Psychic Trauma*; Bettelheim, *Surviving and Other Essays*; Lifton, *Death in Life: Survivors of Hiroshima*; and Wiesel, "Eichmann's Victims and the Unheard Testimony."

3. In this context, it is interesting to note that many European writers grappling with the events of the mid-century claim Hemingway as a major influence—writers as diverse as Albert Camus in French and Tadeusz Borowski in Polish.

4. This dichotomy had always existed, of course. Alan Mintz notes, in "The Rhetoric of Lamentations and Representations of Catastrophe," that "this same sense of impossibility is the experience and lot of writers in every age, whether the Sumerian poet two millennia before the Common Era who cried 'There are no words' or . . . the poets of Lamentations, fifteen hundred years later, who stood before an unprecedented event equipped and burdened by long-used traditions of communal laments and funeral songs. Ancient writers, no more than their successors, were denied the possibility of transcribing directly and unaffectedly the authentic cry of human pain in the purity of its original expression" (1).

5. As Adams observes, "From Julien Sorel to Des Esseints, from Keats to Mallarme, from Novalis to Ibsen, they all testify that anticipation, imagination, and memory . . . are richer experiences than experience itself" (132). Baudelaire, for example, pursues the void "because it frees us from the sounding box of a finite universe and from all the reverberations of our sad selves" (116).

6. Adams explains that Mallarme's desire for the void grew out of a basic, inalterable disgust for material existence. Mallarme simply felt that his basic self was conditioned to another sphere; he was, in this life, like a watchmaker with incurable elephantiasis" (172–73).

7. In "The Embourgeoisement of the Holocaust," George L. Mosse terms the Holocaust "a middle-class event" supported by and reflecting bourgeois attitudes and values.

8. Wiesel indicates the influence of Jewish mystical thought on his word in "Why I Write," in Rosenfeld and Greenberg, eds., *Confronting the Holocaust*: "'When Israel is in exile, so is the word,' says the Zohar. The word has deserted the meaning it was intended to convey—impossible to make them coincide" (201). See also Harry James Cargas, *In Conversation with Elie Wiesel* (45–59); Mary Jean Green, "Witness to the Absurd: Elie Wiesel and the French Existentialists" (170–84); Friedman, *To Deny Our Nothingness* (335–54), for the influence of Camus.

9. David Kraemer, *Responses to Suffering in Classical Rabbinic Literature*, p. 190. All quotations are from this volume. I am grateful to David Kraemer for bringing this passage in Berachot to my attention.

10. The Talmudic discussion seemingly anticipates contemporary theological reflections about the possibility of a discourse that would include both God and the Shoah. In "The Long Life of Metaphor," for example, George Steiner wonders, "in what conceivable language can a Jew speak *to* God after Auschwitz, in what conceivable language can he speak *about* God?" (55).

11. David Kraemer's analysis of this passage indicates that

although one of the discussants asserts that "even children in school" know that Torah study protects the individual from suffering, the Talmudic ensuing discussion interrogates this assumption.

12. In the account of Aqiba's recorded in Berachot, Aqiba tells his disciples, "All of my days I was troubled by this verse, 'with all of your soul' (Deut. 6:5), [meaning] even if [God] takes your soul. I said, 'When will this [obligation] come to my hands, that I may fulfill it? And now that it has come to me, shall I not fulfill it?!'"

13. In a variant of this story, Moses challenges God with these same words, having witnessed Aqiba's torture and death (Menachot 29b). I am indebted to David Kraemer for his analysis of the account of Aqiba's death in a discussion of classic rabbinic attitudes toward protest of suffering.

14. In *A Beggar in Jerusalem*, the rabbi evokes the silencing of the ministering angels, this time as testimony to Jewish suffering. Awaiting the brutal massacre of his Eastern European village, he assures his disciples that, like them, God shall be condemned to an eternal realm of deathlike silence: "I promise you that the angels, in shame, will bow their heads, and will no longer praise the creator of the universe—never again!" (79).

15. In the original French edition, Gregor reflects, "Time began again to exist" (16).

16. George Steiner notes, in *Bluebeard's Castle*, "If only because of its highly ambiguous implication in the holocaust, Christianity cannot serve as the focus of a redefinition of culture" (88). In *A Distant Mirror*, Barbara Tuchman observes, "That the Jews were unholy was a belief so ingrained by the Church that the most devout persons were the harshest in their antipathy. . . . If the Jews were unholy, then killing and looting them was holy work" (41). See also Richard L. Rubenstein, *After Auschwitz*; Irving Greenberg, "Cloud of Smoke, Pillar of Fire: Judaism, Christianity and Modernity After the Holocaust."

17. These disputations, which flourished during the Middle Ages but occurred throughout the ages, even in Talmudic times, find expression in Jewish folklore, as well. Although in actuality, these disputations were serious events that generated much scholarship and subsequent publications, in folklore there exists the tradition of the simpleton who, without realizing the import of his words, saves the day while wiser men are stumped.

18. For discussion of this notion, see Alter's *Defenses of the Imagination* and Maurice Samuels's *In Praise of Yiddish*.

19. In an interview recorded in Gene Koppel's *Elie Wiesel: A Small Measure of Victory*, Wiesel lists the following as major influences on his

writing: the Talmud, Hasidic lore, Dostoyevsky, Kafka, Camus, Mauriac, and Malraux. Critical treatment tends to focus on only on one aspect of Wiesel—the absurd (e.g., Friedman, *To Deny Our Nothingness*) or the Jewish tradition (e.g., Byron L. Sherwin, "Elie Wiesel on Madness"). Josephine Knopp brings the two together in "Wiesel and the Absurd" although she does not treat *A Beggar in Jerusalem.*

20. In *The Theater of the Absurd,* Martin Esslin points to the events of World War II as major precipitants for the absurd as movement and as revelation (or antirevelation). Esslin observes the "sense that the certitudes and unshakable basic assumptions of former ages have been swept away, that they have been tested and found wanting, that they have been discredited as cheap and somewhat childish illusions" (xvii).

21. According to Green in "Witness to the Absurd," Wiesel is hostile to Sartre's influence. "While Wiesel has been willing to enter into dialogue with those atheists who have wrestled with the question of God, he seems to recognize that Sartre has never really taken the existence of God seriously" (181).

22. For example, *The Plague* is often regarded as an allegorical treatment of the Nazi occupation of France; *The Fall* is set in the Jewish quarter of Amsterdam, "sur les lieux d'un des plus grands crimes de l'histoire" (15). In *Carnets, janvier 1942—mars 1951,* Camus comments upon the works of David Rousset and other accounts of the concentrationary universe.

23. Other Holocaust writers, attempting to convey the horror and fragmentation under Nazi rule, also feel drawn to absurdist fiction, theater of the absurd, and its precursors. Rousset uses Jarry's Ubu plays to depict a fascistic reign of terror and a loss of moral center.

24. Melville's Ishmael expresses his sense of this painful yet laughable incongruity between expectations and reality: "There are certain queer times and occasions in this strange mixed affair we call life when a man takes this whole universe for a vast practical joke, though the wit thereof he but dimly discerns, and more than suspects that the joke is at nobody's expense but his own" (225).

25. For exploration of the effect on the human sensibility of the changing nature of death in our century, see Langer, *The Age of Atrocity.*

26. For discussion of the motif of laughter in absurdist literature, see Zipporah Porat, "Ha-Tzavu'ah ha-Tzo-hek." Porat links laughter with creativity, the artistic endeavor in face of the meaninglessness of the absurd.

27. For further discussion of the life, thought, and stories of Rabbi Nachman, see Arnold Band, ed., *Nahum of Bratslav: The Tales*; Arthur

Green, *The Tormented Master*; Adin Steinsalz, *Beggars and Prayers*; Moshe Hallemish, "Nahman (ben Simhah) of Bratzlav"; and James F. Watts, Jr., "Nahman (ben Simhah) of Bratzlav."

28. See Steinsalz, 174.

29. See Steinsalz and Band.

30. According to Rabbinic tradition, the archangel Gabriel represents manifestations of God's glory in the physical universe and man's intellectual/spiritual limitations.

31. The standard modern Hebrew dictionary, Abraham Even-Shoshan, *Milon Hadash*, defines *maggid* as: (1) storyteller, (2) synagogue commentator who interprets religious and ethical matters, (3) in Rabbinic literature, an angel who reveals himself to man and tells him mystical secrets. In Wiesel's work, the term implies a blending of all three of these.

32. Wiesel explores this theme in *Le Jour*. Also Krystal discusses the difficulty which survivors experience in establishing and maintaining love relations. Delbo's trilogy traces the lives of different survivors, and the distancing effect their experience has on subsequent relationships.

33. In writing this description of ritual practice, I hesitated over the word "Jew," and considered substituting "Jewish men." In traditional Jewish practice, only men are ritually obligated to wear *tefillin*; by using the term "Jew," however, I do not mean to imply that it excludes Jewish women. Rabbinic sources argue whether women are permitted to wear them and cite cases of exceptional women who do so. In contemporary Jewish practice, some Jewish women also wear *tefillin*; thus, I have employed gender-neutral language throughout this description.

34. One wraps the phylacteries around the nondominant arm; thus, left-handed wearers wrap it around the right arm.

7. THE NIGHT SIDE OF SPEECH

1. Quoted in Leiser, 12.

2. See Michel Foucault, *Discipline and Punish* (3–31).

3. See, for example, his novel *Landscape in Concrete*.

4. As an interesting sidenote, Lind's autobiographical *The Trip to Jerusalem* describes an encounter with a camp survivor years after the war. The survivor recalls a banquet given by the SS for Jewish concentrationees just prior to the Allies's liberation of the camp. The SS officers wanted the Jews to sign certificates of good behavior on their behalf, in order to exonerate them from charges of war crimes.

5. Schwarz-Bart has taken some liberties with the myth of the *lamed-vov*—notably making it dynastic and public.

6. For a detailed reading of this poem, see John Felstiner's excellent essay, "Translating Celan's 'Du sei wie du.'" See also his "Translating Celan's Last Poem": "Each line struggles not just with but against the language itself" (22); "Celan in his last decade liked to close off a stanza or poem with some Hebrew term which, set off in italics, doubtless looked strange to his German readers" (24); "My guess is that Celan liked archaisms because they reverted to pre-Holocaust, before 'Nazi-Deutsch' set in" (25). For a general discussion of Celan's work, see Jerry Glenn, *Paul Celan*.

7. "Sie, die Sprache, blieb unverloren, ja trotz allem. Aber sie musste nun hindurchgehen durch ihre eigenen Antwortlosigkeiten, hindurchgehen die tausend Finsternisse todbringender Rede. Sie ging hindurch und gab keine Worte her für das, was geschah; aber sie ging durch dieses Geschehen. Ging hindurch und durfte wieder zutage treten, 'angereichert' von all dem" (*Ausgewälte Gedichte* 128).

8. Celan drowned in the Seine River in April 1970 in an apparent suicide. Tadeusz Borowski committed suicide in 1951, Primo Levi in 1987.

9. See also Lawrence L. Langer's criticism of Steiner, in passing, in *Versions of Survival* (11, 64, 92).

10. *The House on Garibaldi Street*.

11. For treatment of this aspect of Hitler's vision, see the first chapter in Lucy S. Dawidowicz, *The War Against the Jews*.

8. REFUSED MEMORY

1. For a discussion of hyperfluency in Günter Grass's writing, see Ann L. Mason's two essays, "Günter Grass and the Artist in History," and "Nazism and Postwar German Literary Style." Mason sees in Grass a comment not only upon those genuinely seduced by Nazi rhetoric but also upon the silent intellectuals of the time who avoided self-judgment and evaded political oppression by "acting the part of the old picaros. . . . When Oskar, adopting the child's perspective, records with false naïveté the violence going on around him, the grotesqueness of historical fact is heightened by the grotesqueness of the conscious naïveté with which it is recorded" ("Nazism" 64–65).

2. Precisely this similarity between literary creation and historical phenomenon leaves Friedländer feeling "that malaise so often difficult to grasp" after reading the Tournier novel, because "what is said about the reflections of Nazism seems to me true for Nazism itself" (*Reflections* 78).

3. Many readers are troubled by the ethical implications of Tournier's treatment of Nazism. Friedländer sees in Tournier's novel the same occultization of Nazism that he sees in Steiner's work: "the ogre . . . and all that surrounds him, e.g., Hitler as the false Messiah predicted by the wise men, are only toys of occult forces that relieve man of all responsibility" (100). This, together with the "pseudospirituality" (44) of the novel, Friedländer contends, deflects the focus of the reader from the moral dimension of the Third Reich. Similarly, Karl Miller deems unsatisfactory the "dubious" malignity of Tournier's Nazis in a Germany "presented as a country of the mind, a country without politics, tenanted by evil magicians poring over pints of blood and suint and measuring skulls and noses in the interest of purity. . . . Tournier documents the behavior of his cranks and pedants with reference to the evidence obtained for the Nuremberg Trials; but the evidence submitted there hardly tends to show that the behavior of these cranks was central to the history of the Reich. But it would appear that he has misrepresented that history while using it as a setting for an account of a fairly exotic psychological state" (42–43). Pearl K. Bell observes in "Sterile Diversion" that Tournier, "with oddly Teutonic ardor for a Frenchman, is fascinated by the abstractly intellectual and formal ingenuity of his fictional house of mirrors than his is by the human implications of the characters and events so cleverly reflected here. . . . Tournier deals with it and his victims as operatic metaphors only, not as the actualities of evil and slaughter that we know them to be." For this reason, Bell judges the novel "a profoundly unforgivable work" (77).

4. For the purposes of the present discussion, I am not pausing to reflect on Tournier's "divorce" analogy. By comparing the relationship of Germany to its Jews, Tournier's analogy suggests a mutuality of disaffection and behavior, effacing German brutality and Jewish victimization.

5. For discussion of the movement from metaphor to myth in *Le Roi des Aulnes*, see Michael J. Worton, "Myth-Reference in *Le Roi des Aulnes*.

6. In *The Wind Spirit*, Tournier makes the connection more specific: "As my research progressed, I gathered abundant proof of the Nazi regime's ogrish nature. . . . The Führer . . . assumed the aspect of the Great Ogre, the Minotaur to which an entire generation of children was sacrificed as a birthday offering" (86).

7. Tournier notes, "The ogre has a keen nose. . . . And we know from biology that the sense of sight in animals is frequently inversely proportional to the sense of smell" (*Wind* 95–96).

8. The cannibal motif recurs in literature of the Holocaust: for example, in Jakov Lind's, "Journey Through the Night" in *Soul of Wood*

and Tadeusz Borowski, "The Supper" in *This Way for the Gas, Ladies and Gentlemen*. In Kosinski's *The Painted Bird*, the protagonist reflects, "Didn't they say in the villages that no one could resist the power of the German because he gobbled up the brains of the Poles, Russians, Gypsies, and Jews?" (93). In his psychoanalytic work on Holocaust survivors, Henry Krystal notes that cannibalism sometimes enabled people to survive in the camps (18). Stephen Karpowitz points out, "Cannibals are without conscience. They believe in the mechanical power of magic—in the might of their wishes, spelled out in words and enacted in rites, to change the world." Richard Rubenstein observes, "There is a psychologically cannibalistic element in regarding eliminating the other as the only possible mode of dealing with him" (*After Auschwitz* 37).

    9. *The Rape of Clarissa*, 55.

    10. Other readers have seen in Tournier's portrayal of Göring a trivialization of the Holocaust and the true role of Nazi leadership, with Göring seen as no more than a comic "crank"—albeit "the wrong sort of crank" (Miller, 43)—unconnected to the historical Göring's centrality to the furthering of Nazi atrocity.

    11. See Blumenthal (5–8); see also Louis-Ferdinand Céline, *Bagatelles pour un massacre*, where he describes the Jews as "ordure."

    12. *Nazi Doctors*.

    13. See "Theses on the Philosophy of History," esp. IX, in *Illuminations*.

    14. See Delbo, *Auschwitz et Après* and Levi, *Survival in Auschwitz*. According to Fackenheim, "The SS logic of destruction aimed at their victims' *self*-destruction as well. This found no clearer or more systematic expression than what is called—this too rightly—'excremental assault.' . . . Clearly, excremental assault was *designed* to produce in the victim a 'self-disgust' to the point of wanting death or even committing suicide" ("Spectrum of Resistance" 119).

    15. Tiffauges's narrative criticizes France, as well. Innocent of the charges brought against him, he proves an easy scapegoat because he is a nonconformist with few friends. As Richard Weisberg notes in "Avoiding Central Realities: Narrative Terror and the Failure of French Culture Under the Occupation," "Accounts of the Vichy years reveal that the French language, too, was capable of sowing atrocity as it thought itself merely tending its own garden" (152).

    16. In the novel, Tournier alludes to the Nordic fairy tale, "The Snow Queen" (123), and its connection with sight and insight. In *The Wind Spirit*, Tournier recollects the tale: "The devil has made a mirror—a distorting mirror, naturally. Even worse: an inverting mirror.

Whatever beauty is reflected in it becomes hideous. Anything wicked seen in it becomes irresistibly attractive." Satan attempts to place this mirror before God; however, "the closer he comes to the Supreme Being, the more the mirror writhes, bends, and twists, until finally it breaks, shattering into thousands upon thousands of pieces. This accident is a terrible misfortune for mankind, for the entire earth is spangled with glass shards, pellets, and particles which distort the appearance of every object and living thing. Some pieces . . . are big enough to be made into eyeglasses—but woe unto those who wear such glasses" (36). Tournier's retelling of the myth resonates inversely with the kabbalistic creation account of the shattering of the vessels and the concept of *tikkun olam*.

17. See "Asthetizismus der Barbarei: Über Michel Tourniers Roman 'Der Erlkönig.'"

18. See Cloonan's discussion of the aspect of fictionality in the novel.

19. The figure of the Elder King has become a metaphor for the threat of nuclear destruction, because it exposes the helplessness of the parent to protect the child from a powerful but invisible menace. See, for example, Russell Hoban's novel *Riddley Walker*, set hundreds of years after a nuclear catastrophe has devastated the planet, setting back technology to the iron age. "They ben the old 1s or you myt say the *auld* 1s and be come chard coal. Thats why theywl tel you the aulder tree is bes for charring coal. Some times youwl hear of a aulder Kincher he carrys of childer" (4).

20. Erik H. Ericson's discussion of "wholeness" versus "totality" in individual personality—and its relationship to the concept of totalitarianism—helps shed light on the relationship between Tiffauges's rigid system of symbols and the Nazi appropriation of the role of symbolmaker and interpreter: "Wholeness seems to connote an assembly of parts, even quite diversified parts, that enter into fruitful association and organization. . . . As a Gestalt, then, which emphasizes a sound organic, progressive mutuality between diversified functions and parts within an entirety, the boundaries of which are open and fluid. Totality, on the contrary, evokes a Gestalt in which an absolute boundary is emphasized: given a certain arbitrary delineation, nothing that belongs inside must be left outside, nothing that must be outside can be tolerated inside. A totality is as absolutely inclusive as it is utterly exclusive—whether or not the category-to-be-made-absolute is a logical one, and whether or not the constituent parts really have an affinity for one another" (80–81).

21. For an exploration of the function of myth in the novel, see Worton.

22. Susan Sontag notes that "Hitler has contaminated Romanticism and Wagner, that much of nineteenth-century German culture is, retroactively, haunted by Hitler" ("Syberberg's Hitler," 151).

23. In "Syberberg's Hitler," Susan Sontag notes that "Hitler has contaminated Romanticism and Wagner, that much of nineteenth-century German culture is, retroactively, haunted by Hitler" (151).

24. Ada Louise Huxtable makes a similar a similar point about Nazi architecture. "In sum, forms in themselves are innocent. But that they can be used to seduce the spirit has been understood by every age of builders. The benign expression of this truth is part of any great structure that moves us through its art. The point is that architecture has this power to an extraordinary degree, and it is therefore one of the most effective and dangerous of totalitarian tools, which is why dictators have always used it so extravagantly. That is the lesson to be learned and that is the knowledge to be carried in the conscience of the architect" ("Totalitarian Tools of Seduction" 31).

25. This symbolic exchange is buried in the English translation, *The Ogre*; for this reason, I have reproduced and translated the language of the original.

26. A significant aspect of *phoria* is the link between Tiffauges's pedophilia and the glorification of youth characteristic of fascism. In *The Wind Spirit*, Tournier observes that "Adding racism to this 'juvenophilia' introduced some maniacal aspects. For the Nazis were interested in children from birth, and not merely as soldiers but as the biological substance of the German people; hence juvenophilia turned to pedophilia" (86). See also Mosse, *Nazi Culture*: "Fascism in all countries made a fetish of youthfulness" (xxxiii).

27. This is Cloonan's description of Friedländer's reading of *The Ogre*.

28. Similarly, see Ann L. Mason's "Nazism" for treatment of the response of German writers: "One way, then, in which postwar writers cope with the dilemma of finding symbols that express Nazism—at the same time that they reveal not only their inadequacy as representatives of historical fact but also the danger latent in the kind of imagination that creates symbols—is to suggest something as a symbol and then at some point in the work, reveal its limitations" (71).

9. THE CHAIN OF TESTIMONY

1. See *Holocaust Testimonies*.

Bibliography

IMAGINATIVE LITERATURE

Aichinger, Ilse. *Herod's Children*. Trans. Cornelia Schaeffer. New York: Atheneum, 1963.

———. "My Language and I." Trans. Richard Mills. *Dimension: A Reader of German Literature Since 1968*. New York: Continuum, 1981.

Amichai, Yehuda. *Not of This Time, Not of This Place*. Trans. Shlomo Katz. New York: Harper, 1963.

Amis, Martin. *Time's Arrow*. New York: Harmony Books, 1991.

Appelfeld, Aharon. *Ashan*. [Smoke]. Jerusalem: Ahshav, 1962.

———. *Badenheim 1939*. New York: Washington Square-Simon, 1980.

———. *Tzili: The Story of a Life*. Trans. Dalya Bilu. New York: Dutton, 1983.

———. *The Immortal Bartfuss*. Trans. Jeffrey Green. New York: Weidenfeld & Nicolson, 1988.

———. *The Retreat*. New York: Penguin, 1984.

———. *To the Land of the Cattails*. Trans. Jeffrey M. Green. New York: Weidenfeld, 1986.

Baudelaire, Charles. *Les Fleurs du mal et autre poemes*. Paris: Garnier-Flammarion, 1964.

Becker, Jurek. *Jacob the Liar*. Trans. Melvin Kornfeld. New York: Harcourt, 1975.

Beckett, Samuel. *En Attendant Godot*. Paris: 1952.

———. *Act Without Words. Endgame*. London: Faber, 1958.

———. *Happy Days*. London: Faber, 1962.

Begley, Louis. *Wartime Lies*. New York: Knopf, 1991.

———. *The Man Who Was Late*. New York: Knopf, 1992.

Bellow, Saul. *Mr. Sammler's Planet*. New York: Viking, 1970.

Borchert, Wolfgang. *The Man Outside*. Trans. David Porter. New York: New Directions, 1971.

Borges, Jorge Luis. "Deutches Requiem." *Labyrinths: Selected Stories and other writings*. New York: New Directions, 1962, 141–47.

———. "The Secret Miracle." *Labyrinths: Selected Stories and other writings*. New York: New Directions, 1962, 88–94.

Borowski, Tadeusz. *This Way for the Gas, Ladies and Gentlemen*. Trans. Barbara Vedder. Harmondworth: Penguin, 1967.

Brecht, Bertolt. *Selected Poems*. Trans. H. R. Hays. New York: Reynal and Hitchcock, 1947.

Camus, Albert. *La Peste*. Paris: Gallimard, 1947.

———. *La Chute*. Paris: Gallimard, 1956.

Celan, Paul. "Ansprache anlässliche der Entgegennahme des Literaturpreisesder Freien Hansestadt Bremen." *Ausgewählte Gedichte*. Frankfurt: Suhrkamp, 1970.

———. *Gedichte I*. Frankfurt: Suhrkamp, 1978.

Delbo, Charlotte. *Une Connaissance inutile*. Paris: Editions de Minuit, 1970.

———. *Aucun de nous ne reviendra*. Paris: Editions de Minuit, 1970.

———. *Mesure de nos jours*. Paris: Editions de Minuit, 1971.

———. *Auschwitz and After*. Trans. Rosette C. Lamont. New Haven: Yale University Press, 1995.

Dickinson, Emily. *Final Harvest: Emily Dickenson's Poems*. Ed. T. Johnson. Boston: Little, 1961.

Epstein, Leslie. *King of the Jews*. New York: Coward, 1979.

Fink, Ida. *A Scrap of Time: Stories*. Trans. Madeline Levine and Francine Prose. New York: Random House, 1987.

———. *The Journey*. Trans. Joanna Weschler and Francine Prose. New York: Farrar, Straus & Giroux, 1992.

Frazier, Ian. "The Stuttgart Folders." *New Yorker* January 1982:26–27.

Fuks, Ladislav. *Mr. Theodore Mudstock*. Trans. Iris Urwin. London: Jonathan Cape, 1969.

Gascar, Pierre. *Les Bêtes*. Paris: Gallimard, 1953.

Glatstein, Jacob. *The Selected Poems of Jacob Glatstein*. Trans. Ruth Whitman. New York: October, 1972.

Gouri, Haim. *The Chocolate Deal*. Trans. Seymour Simckes. New York: Holt, 1968.

Grade, Chaim. "My Quarrel with Hersh Raseyner." *Seven Little Lanes*. Trans. Curt Leviant. New York: Bergen Belsen Memorial, 1972.

Grass, Günter. *Die Blechtrommel*. Berlin: Hermann Luchterhand, 1959.

Greenberg, Uri Zvi. *Rehovot ha-Nahar*. [Streets of the River]. Jerusalem: Schocken, 1954.

Grossman, David. *See Under Love.* Trans. Betsy Rosenberg. New York: Farrar, Straus & Giroux, 1989.

Hecht, Anthony. *The Hard Hours.* New York: Atheneum, 1967.

Hemingway, Ernest. *A Farewell to Arms.* London: Penguin, 1929.

——. *A Moveable Feast.* New York: Bantam, 1964.

Hoban, Russell. *Riddley Walker.* New York: Summit, 1980.

Karmel, Ilona. *An Estate of Memory.* Boston: Houghton, 1969, rpt. New York: Feminist Press, 1986.

Kosinski, Jerzy. *The Painted Bird.* Boston: Houghton, 1976.

Kuznetsov, Anatoli. *Babi Yar.* Trans. David Floyd. Rev. ed. London: Jonathan Cape, 1970.

Langfus, Anna. *Le Sel et le soufre.* Paris: Gallimard, 1960.

——. *Saute Barbara.* Paris: Gallimard, 1965.

Levi, Primo. *If Not Now, WHEN?* trans. William Weaver [*Se Non Ora, Quando?* Torino: Giulio Einaudi Editore, 1982]. New York: Simon & Schuster, 1985.

Lind, Jakov. *Soul of Wood and Other Stories.* Trans. Ralph Manheim. New York: Grove, 1964. [*Eine Seele aus Holz: Erzählungen.* Berlin: Luchterhand, 1962.]

——. *Landscape in Concrete.* Trans. Ralph Manheim. New York: Grove, 1966.

Lustig, Arnost. *A Prayer for Katerina Horovitzova.* Trans. Jeanne Nemcova. New York: Harper, 1973.

Mann, Klaus. *Mephisto.* Munish, Nymphenburger, 1971.

Modiano, Patrick. *La Place de l'étoile.* Paris: Gallimard, 1968.

Penguin Book of Hebrew Verse. Ed. and trans. T. Carmi. Harmondsworth: Penguin, 1981.

Rawicz, Piotr. *Blood From the Sky.* Trans. Peter Wiles. New York: Harcourt, Brace and World, 1964. [*Le Sang du ciel.* Paris: Gallimard, 1961.]

Reich, Tova. "Mengele in Jerusalem. *Harper's* June 1985: 64–68.

Rozewicz, Tadeusz. *The Survivor and other poems.* Trans. Magnus J. Krynski and Robert A. Maguire. Princeton, NJ: Princeton University Press, 1976.

Sachs, Nelly. *The Seeker and Other Poems.* Trans. Michael Hamburger. New York: Farrar, 1970.

Schwarz-Bart, André. *Le Dernier des Justes.* Paris: Editions du Seuil, 1959.

Semprun, Jorge. *The Long Voyage.* Trans. Richard Seaver. New York: Grove, 1964. [*Le Grand Voyage.* Paris: Gallimard, 1963.]

Shakespeare, William. *King Lear.* Signet Edition. New York: NAL, 1963.

Sophocles. *Oedipus the King. Sophocles I: Three Tragedies.* Trans. David Green. Chicago: University of Chicago Press, 1942.

Spiegelman, Art. *Maus I: A Survivor's Tale: My Father Bleeds History.* New York: Pantheon, 1986.

——. *Maus II: A Survivor's Tale: And Here My Troubles Began.* New York: Pantheon, 1991.

Sperber, Manès. . . . *than a tear in the sea.* Trans. Constantine Fitzgibbon. New York: Bergen Belsen Memorial, 1967.

Thomas, D. M. *The White Hotel.* London: Faber, 1981.

Tournier, Michel. *The Ogre.* Trans. Barbara Bray. New York: Doubleday, 1972. [*Le Roi des Aulnes.* Paris: Gallimard, 1970.]

Twain, Mark. *The Adventures of Huckleberry Finn.* New York: Collier, 1962.

Voices Within the Ark: The Modern Jewish Poets. Eds. Howard Schwartz and Anthony Rudolf. New York: Avon, 1980.

Wallant, Edward L. *The Pawnbroker.* New York: MacFadden, 1964.

Wertmüller, Lena. *The Screenplays of Lena Wertmüller.* Trans. Steven Wagner. New York: Quadrangle, 1977.

Wiesel, Elie. *Night.* Trans. Stella Rodway. New York: Hill and Wang, 1960.

——. *The Accident.* trans. Anne Borchardt. New York: Avon, 1962.

——. *The Town Beyond the Wall.* Trans. Stephen Becker. New York: Avon, 1964.

——. *The Gates of the Forest.* Trans. Frances Frenaye. New York: Avon, 1966.

——. *A Beggar in Jerusalem.* Trans. Lily Edelman and E. Wiesel. New York: Random House, 1970.

——. *The Oath.* Trans. Marion Wiesel. New York: Random House, 1973.

CRITICAL AND HISTORICAL LITERATURE

Adams, Robert Martin. *NIL: Episodes in the Literary Conquest of the Void During the Nineteenth Century.* New York: Oxford University Press, 1966.

Adorno, Theodor W. "Engagement." *Noten Zur Literatur.* Vol. 3. Frankfurt: Suhrkamp, 1963.

——. *Negative Dialectics.* Trans. E. B. Ashton. New York: Seabury Press, 1973.

Aldinopulos, Thomas. "The Holocaust in the Stories of Elie Wiesel." *Soundings* 55 (1972): 200–15.

Alexander, Edward. *The Resonance of Dust: Essays on Holocaust Lit-*

erature and Jewish Fate. Columbus: Ohio State University Press, 1974.

Alter, Robert. *After the Tradition: Essays on Modern Jewish Writing*. New York: Dutton, 1971.

———. *Defenses of the Imagination: Jewish Writers and Modern Historical Crisis*. Philadelphia: Jewish Publication Society, 1977.

———. "Deformations of the Holocaust." *Commentary* February 1981: 48–54.

Alvarez, A. *Beyond All This Fiddle*. London: Lane, 1968.

Améry, Jean. *At the Mind's Limits: Contemplations by a Survivor of Auschwitz and its Realities*. Trans. Sidney Rosenfeld and Stella P. Rosenfeld. Bloomington: Indiana University Press, 1980.

———. *Radical Humanism: Selected Essays*. Ed. and Trans. Sidney Rosenfeld and Stella P. Rosenfeld. Bloomington: Indiana University Press, 1984.

———. "Asthetizismus der Barbarei: Über Michel Tourniers Roman 'Der Erlkönig.'" *Merkur*, 297 (1993): 73–79.

Appelfeld, Aharon. "After the Holocaust." *Writing and the Holocaust*, ed. Berel Lang. New York: Holmes and Meier, 1988, pp. 83–92.

Arendt, Hannah. *The Origins of Totalitarianism*. New York: Harcourt, 1951.

———. *Eichmann in Jerusalem: A Report on the Banality of Evil*. New York: Viking, 1963.

Aronson, Ronald. *The Dialectics of Disaster: A Preface to Hope*. London: Verso, 1983.

Artaud, Antonin. *Le Théâtre et son double*. Paris: Gallimard, 1938.

Avisar, Ilan. *Screening the Holocaust: Cinema's Images of the Unimaginable*. Bloomington: Indiana University Press, 1988.

Band, Arnold, ed. and trans. *Nahum of Bratslav: The Tales*. New York: Paulist Press, 1970.

Barclay, Craig R. "Schematization of autobiographical memory." *Autobiographical Memory*, ed. David C. Rubin. Cambridge: Cambridge University Press, 1986, pp. 71–81.

Base, Ron. "Jerzy Kosinski: His Writing Imitates his Life." *Boston Sunday Globe* 21 February 1982:83+.

Basse, Wilfried. "Notizen zu einem fast vergessenen klarsiker des Deitschen Dokumentarfilms." *Liebe, Tod, und Technick: Kino des Phantastischen 1933–1945*. Kraft Wetzel and Peter A. Hagerman, eds. Berlin: Verlag Volker Spiess, 1977.

Bell, Pearl K. "Sterile Diversion." Rev. of *The Ogre* by Michel Tournier. *New Leader* 19 February 1973:13+.

Benjamin, Walter. *Illuminations*. Trans. Harry Zohn. New York: Harcourt, Brace and World, 1968.

Berenbaum, Michael. *The Vision of the Void: Theological Reflections of the Works of Elie Wiesel*. Middletown, CT: Wesleyan University Press, 1979.

Berkovitz, Eliezer. *Faith After Auschwitz*. New York: Ktav, 1973.

Bettelheim, Bruno. *The Informed Heart: Autonomy in a Mass Age*. Glencoe, IL: Free Press, 1960.

———. "Eichmann; the System; the Victims." Rev. of *Eichmann in Jerusalem* by Hannah Arendt. *New Republic* 15 June 1963:23–33.

———. *Surviving and other essays*. London: Thames, 1979.

The Black Book: The Nazi Crimes Against the Jewish People. New York: Nexus, 1946.

Blanchot, Maurice. *The Writing of the Disaster*. Trans. Ann Smock [L'Ecriture du désastre]. Lincoln: University of Nebraska Press, 1986.

Blumenthal, Nachman. "On the Nazi Vocabulary." *Yad Vashem Studies* 1 (1957):49–67.

———. "Magical Thinking Among the Jews During the Nazi Occupation." *Yad Vashem Studies* 5 (1963):168+.

Bosmajian, Hamida. *Metaphors of Evil: Contemporary German Literature and the Shadow of Nazism*. Iowa City: University of Iowa Press, 1979.

Boyarin, Daniel. *Intertextuality and the Reading of Midrash*. Bloomington: Indiana University Press, 1990.

Boyarin, Jonathan. *Storm from Paradise: the Politics of Jewish Memory*. Minneapolis: University of Minnesota Press, 1992.

Boyers, Robert. *Atrocity and Amnesia*. New York: Oxford University Press, 1985.

Brewer, William F. "What is autobiographical memory?" *Autobiographical Memory*, ed. David C. Rubin. Cambridge: Cambridge University Press, 1986, pp. 25–49.

Brombert, Victor. *The Romantic Prison: The French Tradition*. Princeton, NJ: Princeton University Press, 1978.

Brown, Michael. "Metaphor for Holocaust and Holocaust as Metaphor: *The Assistant* and *The Fixer* of Bernard Malamud Reexamined." *Judaism* 29 (1980):479–88.

———. "Biblical Myth and Contemporary Experience: The *Akedah* in Modern Jewish Literature." *Judaism* 31 (1981):99–111.

Camus, Albert. *Le Mythe de Sisyphe*. Paris: Gallimard, 1942.

———. *Carnets, janvier 1942–mars 1951*. Paris: Gallimard, 1964.

Canetti, Elias. *The Human Province*. Trans. Joachim Neugroschel. New York: Seabury, 1978.

Cargas, Henry James. *Henry James Cargas in Conversation with Elie Wiesel.* New York: Paulist, 1967.

Cargas, Henry James, ed. *Responses to Elie Wiesel.* New York: Persea, 1978.

Caruth, Cathy. "Introduction." *Psychoanalysis, Culture and Trauma,* ed. Cathy Caruth. Special issue *American Imago* 48 (Spring 1991)1:1–12.

———. "Introduction." *Psychoanalysis, Culture and Trauma,* ed. Cathy Caruth. Special issue *American Imago* 48 (Winter 1991)3:417–24.

———. "Unclaimed Experience: Trauma and the Possibility of History." *Literature and the Ethical Experience. Yale French Studies* (1991)79:181–92.

Cayrol, Jean. *Lazare parmi nous.* Neuchâtel: Editions de la Baconnière, 1950.

Clerval, Alain. "Entretien avec Pierre Gascar." *La Nouvelle Revue Français* 279 (1976):72–75.

Cloonan, William J. *Michel Tournier.* Boston: Twayne Publishers, 1985.

Coale, Samuel. "The Cinematic Self of Jerzy Kosinski." *Modern Fiction Studies* 20 (1974):359–70.

———. "The Quest of the Elusive Self: The Fiction of Jerzy Kosinski." *Critique* 14.3:25–32.

Cohen, Arthur Allen. *Thinking the Tremendum: Some Theological Implications of the Death Camps.* New York: Leo Baeck, 1974.

Corngold, Stanley. "Jerzy Kosinski's *The Painted Bird*: Language Lost and Regained." *Mosaic* 4 (1973):153–67.

Corry, John. "Seventeen years of Ideological Attack on a Cultural Target." *New York Times* 7 November 1982. Sec. 2:1+.

Cunningham, Lawrence S. "Elie Wiesel's Anti-Exodus." *America* 27 April 1974:325–27.

Dawidowics, Lucy. *The War Against the Jews: 1933–45.* New York: Holt, 1975.

Dawidowics, Lucy, ed. *Living After the Holocaust: Reflections by the Post-War Generation in America.* New York: Block, 1976.

Des Pres, Terrence. *The Survivor: An Anatomy of Life in the Death Camps.* New York: Oxford University Press, 1976.

———. "The Dreaming Back." *Centerpoint* Vol. 4, No. 1 (Fall 1980), pp. 13–18.

———. "Terror and the Sublime." *Human Rights Quarterly* 5 (1983): 135–46.

Dicks, Henry V. *Licensed Mass Murder: A Socio-psychological Study of Some SS Killers.* New York: Basic, 1972.

Dobroszycki, Lucjan, ed. *The Chronicle of the Lodz Ghetto, 1941–1944.*
    New Haven, CT: Yale University Press, 1984.
Donat, Alexander. *The Holocaust Kingdom.* New York: Holt, 1965.
Dvorjetski, Mark. "Adjustment of Detainees to Camp and Ghetto Life
    and Their Subsequent Readjustment to Normal Society." *Yad
    Vashem Studies* 5 (1963):193–220.
Eagleton, Terry. *The Rape of Clarissa.* Minneapolis: University of Min-
    nesota Press, 1982.
Ellman, Mary. Rev. of *The Ogre* by Michel Tournier. *Yale Review* 62
    (1973):465–67.
Engel, Marion. Rev. of *The Ogre* by Michel Tournier. *New York Times
    Book Review* 3 September 1972:7+.
Engelmann, Bernt. *In Hitler's Germany: Everyday Life in the Third
    Reich.* Trans. Krishna Winston. New York: Random, 1986.
Erikson, Erik H. *Childhood and Society.* 2nd ed. New York: Norton,
    1963.
———. "On Totalitarianism." *Identity: Youth and Crisis.* New York:
    Norton, 1968. 74–90.
Esh, Shaul. "Words and their Meanings: 25 Examples of Nazi Idiom."
    Yad Vashem Studies 5 (1963):133–68.
Esslin, Martin. *The Theater of the Absurd.* New York: Doubleday, 1961.
———. *Antonin Artaud.* Harmondsworth: Penguin, 1976.
Estess, Ted L. *Elie Wiesel.* New York: Ungar, 1980.
Ezrahi, Sidra DeKoven. *By Words Alone: The Holocaust in Literature.*
    Chicago: University of Chicago Press, 1980.
Fackenheim, Emil. *From Bergen-Belsen to Jerusalem: Contemporary
    Implications of the Holocaust.* Jerusalem: World Jewish Congress,
    1975.
Feder, Lillian. *Madness in Literature.* Princeton, NJ: Princeton Uni-
    versity Press, 1980.
Fein, Esther B. "Inventing a Life, Then Living It: At the Office with
    Louis Begley." *New York Times* 14 April 1993, p. C1+.
Feldman, Yael. "Whose Story Is It, Anyway? Ideology and Psychology in
    the Representation of the Shoah in Israeli Literature." *Probing
    the Limits of Representation: Nazism and the "Final Solution.*
    Ed. Saul Friedlander. Cambridge, MA: Harvard University
    Press, 1992, pp. 223–39.
Felman, Shoshana, and Dori Laub. *Testimony: Crises of Witnessing in
    Literature, Psychoanalysis, and History.* New York: Routledge,
    1992.
Felstiner, John. "Translating Celan's Last Poem." *American Poetry
    Review* 11:4 (1982):1+.

————. "Translating Paul Celan's 'Du sei wie du.'" *Prooftexts* 3 (1983): 91–108.

————. "The Biography of a Poem." *New Republic* 2 April 1984:27–31.

Ferderber-Salz, Bertha. *And the Sun Kept Shining . . .* New York: Holocaust Library, 1980.

Filipovic, Zlata. *Zlata's Diary: A Child's Life in Sarajevo.* Trans. Christina Pribichevich-Zoric. New York: Viking, 1994.

Fine, Ellen S. *Legacy of Night: The Literary Universe of Elie Wiesel.* Albany: State University of New York Press, 1982.

Fisch, Harold. *A Remembered Future: A Study in Literary Mythology.* Bloomington: Indiana University Press, 1984.

Foley, Barbara. "Fact, Fiction, Fascism: Testimony and Mimesis in Holocaust Narratives." *Comparative Literature* 34 (1982):330–60.

Foucault, Michel. "The Discourse on Language." *The Archaeology of Knowledge and the Discourse on Language.* Trans. A. M. Sheridan Smith. New York: Pantheon Press, 1972.

————. *Discipline and Punishment: The Birth of the Prison.* Trans. Alan Sheridan. New York: Vintage, 1979.

Frankl, Viktor E. *Man's Search for Meaning.* Trans. Ilse Lasche. New York: Simon and Schuster, 1959.

Freedman, Samuel G. "Bearing Witness: The Life and Work of Elie Wiesel." *New York Times Magazine* 23 October 1983:32+.

Friedlander, Albert, ed. *Out of the Whirlwind: A Reader of Holocaust Literature.* New York: Schocken, 1976.

Friedlander, Saul. *Reflections of Nazism: An Essay on Kitsch and Death.* New York: Harper & Row, 1984 [*Reflets du Nazisme.* Paris: Seuil, 1982].

————. "The 'Final Solution': On the Unease in Historical Interpretation." *Lessons and Legacies: The Meaning of the Holocaust in a Changing World.* Ed. Peter Hayes. Evanston, IL: Northwestern University Press, 1991, 23–35.

Friedlander, Saul, ed. *Probing the Limits of Representation: Nazism and the "Final Solution.* Cambridge, MA: Harvard University Press, 1992.

Freud, Sigmund. *Totem and Taboo.* Trans. James Strachey. London: Routledge and Paul, 1950.

Frye, Northrop. *Anatomy of Criticism.* New York: Atheneum, 1969.

Gerber, Frederick. "The Art of Elie Wiesel." *Judaism* 22(1973):301–28.

Gilman, Sander L. *On Blackness without Blacks: Essays on the Image of the Black in Germany.* Boston: Hall & Co., 1982.

————. *Difference and Pathology: Stereotypes of Sexuality, Race and Madness.* Ithaca, NY: Cornell University Press, 1985.

———. *Jewish Self-Hatred: Anti-Semitism and the Hidden Language of the Jews*. Baltimore: Johns Hopkins UP, 1986.

Girard, René. *The Scapegoat*. Trans. Yvonne Freccero [*Le Bouc émis-saire*, by Bernard Grasset, Paris: Editions Grasset, 1982]. Baltimore: Johns Hopkins University Press, 1986.

Glenn, Jerry. *Paul Celan*. New York: Twayne, 1973.

Gottlieb, Freema. "A Talk with Aharon Appelfeld." *New York Times Book Review* 23 November 1980:41+.

Gould, Eric, ed. *The Sin of the Book: Edmond Jabès*. Lincoln: University of Nebraska Press, 1985.

Green, Arthur. *The Tormented Master*. Woodstock, VT: Jewish Lights Publishing, 1993.

Green, Mary Jean. "Witness to the Absurd: Elie Wiesel and the French Existentialists." *Renascence* 29 (1977):170–84.

Gussow, Mel. "Focusing on History Through Interviews." *New York Times* (25 January 1995), pp. C13, C15.

Guthrie, Ramon. Introduction. *The Other Kingdom* by David Rousset. New York: Reynal and Hitchcock, 1947. 10–25.

Haas, Peter J. *Morality After Auschwitz: The Radical Challenge of the Nazi Ethic*. Philadelphia: Fortress, 1988.

Haft, Cynthia. *The Theme of Nazi Concentration Camps in French Literature*. Mouton: New Babylon, 1973.

Hallemish, Moshe. "Nahman (ben Simhah) of Bratslav." *Encyclopaedia Judaica* Vol. 12. Jerusalem: Keter, 782–84.

Halperin, Irving. "Spiritual Resistance in Holocaust Literature." *Yad Vashem Studies* 7 (1968):75–82.

———. *Messengers From the Dead: Literature of the Holocaust*. Philadelphia: Westminster, 1970.

Harel, Isser. *The House on Garibaldi Street*. New York: Viking, 1975.

Hartman, Geoffrey. "The Response to Terror: Some Introductory Notes." *Human Rights Quarterly* 5 (1983):113–15.

———, ed. *Holocaust Remembrance: The Shapes of Memory*. Cambridge, MA: Basil Blackwell, 1994.

Hassan, Ihab. *The Dismemberment of Orpheus: Toward a Postmodern Literature*. New York: Oxford University Press, 1971.

Hayes, Peter, ed. *Lessons and Legacies: The Meaning of the Holocaust in a Changing World* (Evanston: Northwestern University Press, 1991).

Hindus, Milton. *The Crippled Giant: A Bizarre Adventure in Contemporary Letters*. New York: Boars Head, 1950.

Hirsch, David. *The Deconstruction of Literature: Criticism after Auschwitz*. Hanover, RI: Brown University Press, 1991.

Hoffman, Frederick. *The Mortal No: Death and the Modern Imagination*. Princeton, NJ: Princeton University Press, 1964.

Horowitz, Sara R. "Rethinking Holocaust Testimony: The Making and Unmaking of the Witness," *Cardozo Studies in Law and Literature* (Spring/Summer 1992) 4.1:45–68.

Howe, Irving. "Auschwitz and High Mandarin." *The Critical Point: On Literature and Culture*. New York: Horizon, 1973.

Hueston, Penny. "An Interview with Michel Tournier." *Meanjin* 38 (1979):400–5.

Hull, David Stewart. *Film in the Third Reich: A Study of the German Cinema 1933–45*. Berkeley: University of California Press, 1969.

Huxtable, Ada Luise. "Totalitarian Tools of Seduction." *New York Times* 27 October 1980. Sec.2:1+.

Huyssen, Andreas. *Twilight of Memories: Marking Time in a Culture of Amnesia* New York: Routledge, 1995.

Hyman, Paula E. "New Debate on the Holocaust." *New York Times Magazine* 14 September 1980:65+.

Idinopulus, Thomas. "Betrayal of the Spirit: Holocaust, Horror and Literature." *Centerpoint* 4 (1980):96–100.

Insdorf, Annette. *Indelible Shadows: Film and the Holocaust*. New York: Vintage, 1983.

Johnson, Phyllis and Brigitte Cazelles. "L'Orientation d'Abel Tiffauges dans *Le Roi des aulnes* de Michel Tournier." *Rocky Mountain Review of Language and Literature* 29 (1975):166–71.

Kahler, Erich. *The Tower and the Abyss: An Inquiry into the Transformation of Man*. New York: Viking, 1957.

Karpowitz, Stephen. "Conscience and Cannibals: An Essay on Two Exemplary Tales—'Soul of Wood' and *The Pawnbroker*." *Psychoanalytic Review* 64 (1977):41–62.

Katz, Fred E. "A Social Perspective to the Holocaust." *Modern Judaism* 2 (1982):273–96.

Katz, Steven T. *Post-Holocaust Dialogues: Critical studies in modern Jewish thought*. New York: New York University Press, 1983.

Keppler, Carl Francis. *The Literature of the Second Self*. Tuscon: University of Arizona Press, 1972.

Klein, Dennis B. "History versus Fiction." *Dimensions: A Journal of Holocaust Studies* 8 (1994)1:2.

Knopp, Josephine. "Wiesel and the Absurd." *Contemporary Literature* 15:212–20.

Koppel, Gene. *Elie Wiesel: A Small Measure of Victory*. Tuscon: University of Arizona Press, 1974.

Kosinski, Jerzy. *Notes of the Author on 'The Painted Bird' 1965.* New York: Scientia-Factum, 1967.

Kraemer, David Charles. *Responses to Suffering in Classical Rabbinic Literature.* New York: Oxford University Press, 1995.

Kristeva, Julia. "Oscillation between Power and Denial." *New French Feminisms: An Anthology.* Eds. Elaine Marks and Isabelle de Courtivron. New York: Schocken, 1981.

Krystal, Henry. "Integration and Self-Healing in Post-Traumatic States: A Ten Year Retrospective." *Psychoanalysis, Culture and Trauma,* ed. Cathy Caruth. Special issue *American Imago* 48 (Spring 1991)1:93–118.

Krystal, Henry, ed. *Massive Psychic Trauma.* New York: International Universities Press, 1968.

Kuper, Jack. *Child of the Holocaust.* New York: NAL, 1967.

Kurrik, Maire Jaanus. *Literature and Negation.* New York: Columbia University Press, 1979.

LaCapra, Dominick. *History and Criticism.* Ithaca, NY: Cornell University Press, 1985.

Lang, Berel. *Act and Idea in Nazi Genocide.* Chicago: University of Chicago Press, 1990.

Lang, Berel, ed. *Writing and the Holocaust.* New York: Holmes and Meier, 1988.

Lang, Jochen von. *Eichmann Interrogated: Transcripts from the Archives of the Israeli Police.* Trans. Ralph Manheim. New York: Farrar, Straus and Giroux, 1983.

Langer, Lawrence. *The Holocaust and the Literary Imagination.* New Haven, CT: Yale University Press, 1975.

———. *The Age of Atrocity: Death in Modern Literature.* Boston: Beacon, 1978.

———. *Versions of Survival: The Holocaust and the Human Spirit.* Albany: State University of New York Press, 1982.

———. *Holocaust Testimonies: The Ruins of Memory.* New Haven, CT: Yale University Press, 1991.

Lanzmann, Claude. *Shoah.* Paris: Fayard, 1985.

———. "Seminar with Claude Lanzmann, 11 April 1990." *Literature and the Ethical Experience. Yale French Studies* (1991)79:82–99.

Laub, Dori. "Truth and Testimony." *Psychoanalysis, Culture and Trauma,* ed. Cathy Caruth. Special issue *American Imago* 48 (Spring 1991)1:75–91.

Leibowitz, Herbert. *Fabricating Lives: Explorations in American Autobiography.* New York: Knopf, 1989.

Leiser, Erwin. *Nazi Cinema*. Trans. Gertrud Mander and David Wilson. New York: Macmillan, 1974.

Leitner, Isabella. *Saving the Fragments: From Auschwitz to New York*. New York: NAL, 1985.

Lejeune, Philippe. *On Autobiography*. Trans. Katherine Leary. Minneapolis: University of Minnesota Press, 1989.

Levi, Primo. *Survival in Auschwitz: The Nazi Assault on Humanity*. Trans. Stuart Woolf. New York: Collier, 1969.

——— . *The Periodic Table*. Trans. Raymond Rosenthal. New York: Schocken, 1984.

——— . *The Drowned and the Saved*. Trans. Raymond Rosenthal. New York: Summit, 1986.

——— . *Moments of Reprieve*. Trans. Ruth Feldman. New York: Penguin, 1987.

Levin, Harry. *Gates of Horn*. New York: Oxford University Press, 1963.

Levy, Claude. *Betrayal at the Vel d'Hiv*. Trans. Inez Bushnaq. New York: Hill, 1969.

Lewis, Stephen. *Art out of Agony: The Holocaust Theme in Literature, Sculpture and Film*. Montreal: CBC Enterprises, 1984.

Lifton, Robert Jay. *Death in Life: Survivors of Hiroshima*. New York: Random, 1968.

——— . "Beyond Atrocity." *Saturday Review* 27 March 1971:23+.

——— . *The Nazi Doctors: Medical Killing and the Psychology of Genocide*. New York: Basic Books, 1986.

——— . *The Future of Immortality*. New York: Basic, 1987.

——— . "Interview with Robert J. Lifton." With Cathy Caruth. *Psychoanalysis, Culture and Trauma*, ed. Cathy Caruth. Special issue *American Imago* 48 (Spring 1991)1:153–75.

Lind, Jakov. *Numbers: A Further Autobiography*. New York: Harper, 1972.

——— . "John Brown and His Little Indians." *Times Literary Supplement* 25 May 1973:589–90.

——— . *The Trip to Jerusalem*. New York: Harper, 1973.

Lottman, Herbert R. *The Left Bank: Writers, Artists, and Politics from the Popular Front to the Cold War*. Boston: Houghton, 1982.

Lowenthal, Leo. "Terrors Atomization of Man." *Commentary* 1 (1946).

Lustig, Arnost. "Auschwitz-Birkenau." Trans. Josef Lustig. *Yale Review* 71 (1982):393–403.

Mandel, Barrett. "Full of Life Now." *Autobiography: Essays Theoretical and Critical*. Ed. James Olney. Princeton, NJ: Princeton University Press, 1980.

Marrus, Michael R. *The Holocaust in History*. Hanover, NJ: University

Press of New England, 1987.

Marrus, Michael R., and Robert O. Paxton. *Vichy France and the Jews.* New York: Basic, 1981.

Mason, Ann. "Günter Grass and the Artist in History." *Contemporary Literature* 14 (1973):347–62.

———. "Nazism and Postwar German Literary Style." *Contemporary Literature* 17 (1976):63–83.

Matis, David. "Films of the Holocaust." *Yiddish* 1 (1973):23–33.

Middleton, Drew. "Why TV is Fascinated with the Hitler Era." *New York Times* 16 November 1981. Sec.2:1+.

Miller, Karl. "The Cyclopean Eye of the European Phallus." Rev. of *The Ogre* by Michel Tournier. *New York Review of Books* 30 November 1972:40–43.

Mink, Louis O. "Narrative Form as a Cognitive Instrument." *The Writing of History: Literary Form and Historical Understanding.* Eds. Robert H. Canary and Henry Kozicki. Madison: University of Wisconsin Press, 1978.

Mintz, Alan. "The Rhetoric of Lamentation and the Representation of Catastrophe." *Prooftexts* 2 (1982):1–17.

———. *Hurban: Responses to Catastrophe in Hebrew Literature.* New York: Columbia University Press, 1984.

Monès, Phillipe de. "Abel Tiffauges et la vocation maternelle de l'homme." Postface in *Le Roi des aulnes* by Michel Tournier. 587–600.

Mortimer, Gail. "Fear Death by Water: The Boundaries of the Self in Jerzy Kosinski's *Painted Bird." Psychoanalytic Review* 63 (1976):511–28.

Mosse, George L. *Nazi Culture: Intellectual, Cultural and Social Life in the Third Reich.* Trans. Salvator Attansio et al. New York: Grosset, 1966.

———. "The Embourgeoisement of the Holocaust." Brandeis University, 15 September 1982.

Murdoch, Brian. "Transformation of the Holocaust: Auschwitz in Modern Lyric Poetry." *Comparative Literature Studies* 6 (1974):123–50.

Neher, André. *L'Exil de la parole: Du silence biblique au silence d'Auschwitz.* Paris: Editions du Soleil, 1970.

Nora, Pierre. "Between Memory and History: Les Lieux de Memoire." *Representations* 26 (1989).

Oberski, Jona. *Childhood.* New York: NAL, 1978.

Ornstein, Anna. "The Holocaust: Reconstruction and the Establishment of Psychic Community." *Reconstruction of Trauma, Its Significance in Clinical Work.* Ed. A. Rothstein. Madison, CT: International Universities Press, 1986.

Ozick, Cynthia. *The Cannibal Galaxy*. New York: Knopf, 1983.
————. *The Messiah of Stockholm*. New York: Knopf, 1987.
Peli, Pinhas H. "In Search of Religious Language for the Holocaust." *Conservative Judaism* 32 (1979):3–24.
Petro, Patrice. "From Lukacs to Kracauer and Beyond: Social Film Histories and the German Cinema." *Cinema Journal* 22 (Spring 1983) 3:47–70.
Pinsker, Sanford. "Fictionalizing the Holocaust." *Judaism* 29 (1980): 489–96.
Porat, Zipporah. "Ha-zavo'ah ha-zohek [The Laughing Hyena]." *Mo'oznayim* 32:190–99.
Preudowska, Drystyna. "Jerzy Kosinski: A Literature of Contortion." *Journal of Narrative Fiction* 8 (1979):11–25.
Pryce-Jones, David. *Paris in the Third Reich: A History of the German Occupation, 1940–1944*. New York: Holt, 1981.
Rappaport, Ernst A. "Notes on Blindness and Omniscience: From Oedipus to Hitler." *Psychoanalytic Review* 63 (1966):281–90.
Rawson, C. J. "Cannibalism and Fiction: Reflections on Narrative Forms and 'Extreme' Situations." *Genre* 10 (1977):677–711.
Reik, Theodor. "Die psychologische Bedeutung des Schweigens." *Wie Man Psychologe Wird*. Leipzig: Internationaler Psychoanalytischer, 1927. 101–26.
Richter, David H. "The Three Denouements of Jerzy Kosinski's *The Painted Bird*." *Wisconsin Studies in Contemporary Literature*. 15.3:37–85.
Ricoeur, Paul. *Symbolism of Evil*. Trans. Emerson Buchanan. Boston: Beacon, 1967.
Ringelblum, Emmanuel. *Notes from the Warsaw Ghetto: The Journal of Emmanuel Ringelblum*, ed. and trans. Jacob Sloan. New York: Schocken, 1974.
Rosen, Robert S. "The Holocaust in Theatre and Film." *Modern Jewish Studies Annual II* (1978):84–88.
Rosenfeld, Alvin H. "Jakov Lind and the Trial of Jewishness." *Midstream* February 1974:71–75.
————. *A Double Dying: Reflections of Holocaust Literature*. Bloomington: Indiana University Press, 1980.
————. "The Holocaust in American Popular Culture." *Midstream* 29.6 (1983):53–59.
————. *Imagining Hitler*. Bloomington: Indiana University Press, 1985.
————. "Popularization and Memory: The Case of Anne Frank." *Lessons and Legacies: The Meaning of the Holocaust in a Changing World*. Ed. Peter Hayes. Evanston, IL: Northwestern University

Press, 1991, 243–78.

Rosenfeld, Alvin H., and Irving Greenberg. *Confronting the Holocaust: The Impact of Elie Wiesel.* Bloomington: Indiana University Press, 1978.

Roskies, David G. "The Holocaust According to the Literary Critics." *Prooftexts* 1 (1981):209–13.

———. "Sholem Aleichem and Others: Laughing Off the Trauma of History." *Prooftexts* 2 (1982):53–77.

———. *Against the Apocalypse: Responses to Catastrophe in Modern Jewish Culture.* Cambridge, MA: Harvard University Press, 1984.

———, ed. *The Literature of Destruction: Jewish Responses to Catastrophe.* Philadelphia: Jewish Publication Society, 1989.

Roth, John K. *A Consuming Fire: Encounters with Elie Wiesel and the Holocaust.* Atlanta: Knox, 1979.

Rousset, David. *The Other Kingdom.* Trans. Ramon Guthrie. New York: Reynal and Hitchcock, 1947.

Rubenstein, Richard L. *After Auschwitz: Radical Theology and Contemporary Judaism.* Indianapolis: Bobbs, 1966.

———. *The Religious Imagination: A Study in Psychoanalysis and Jewish Theology.* Boston: Beacon, 1968.

Rubin, David C., ed. *Autobiographical Memory.* Cambridge: Cambridge University Press, 1986.

Samuels, Maurice. *In Praise of Yiddish.* New York: Cowles, 1971.

Sartre, Jean-Paul. *Réflexions sur la question juive.* Paris: Gallimard, 1943.

Satner, Eric. *Stranded Objects: Mourning, Memory, and Film in Postwar Germany.* Ithaca, NY: Cornell Univrsity Press, 1990.

Scarry, Elaine. *The Body in Pain: The Making and Unmaking of the World.* New York: Oxford Univesity Press, 1985.

Scholem, Gershom G. *Major Trends in Jewish Mysticism.* New York: Schocken, 1946.

Seh-Lavan, Yosef. *Aharon Appelfeld.* Tel Aviv: Or-'Am, 1978.

———. *Sifrut ha-sho'ah* [Literature of the Holocaust]. Tel Aviv: Or-'Am, 1978.

Sewell, Ernestine P. "The Jungian Process of Individuation as Structure in *The Painted Bird.*" *S. Central Bulletin* 38 (1978):160–63.

Shattuck, Roger. "Why Not the Best?" Rev. of fiction of Michel Tournier. *New York Review of Books* 28 April 1983:8–15.

Sherwin, Byron. "Elie Wiesel on Madness.' *Central Conference of American Rabbis Journal* June 1972:24–32.

Shmulewitz, I. "Our Obligation to Remember." *Yiddish* 1.3 (1973–1974): 49–54.

Short, K. R. M., ed. *Film and Radio Propaganda in World War II*. Kent: Croom Helm Ltd, 1983.

Sissman, L. E. "Obversities." Rev. of *The Ogre* by Michel Tournier. *New Yorker* 30 December 1972:68–71.

Sloan, James Park. "Kosinski's War." *New Yorker* (10 October 1994): 46–53.

Sokoloff, Naomi. *Imagining the Child in Modern Jewish Fiction*. Baltimore: Johns Hopkins University Press, 1992.

Sontag, Susan. *Under the Sign of Saturn*. New York: Vintage, 1981.

Spendal, R. J. "The Structure of *The Painted Bird*." *Journal of Narrative Technique* 6.2 (1976):132–36.

Sperber, Manès. Rev. of *A Beggar in Jerusalem* by Elie Wiesel. *New York Times Books Review* 25 January 1970:1+.

Steinberg, Theodore L. "Isaac Bashevis Singer: Responses to Catastrophe." *Yiddish* 1.4 (1975):9–16.

Steiner, George. *Language and Silence: Essays on Language, Literature and the Inhuman*. Harmondsworth: Penguin, 1969.

———. *Extraterritorial: Papers on Literature and the Language Revolution*. New York: Atheneum, 1971.

———. *In Bluebeard's Castle: Some Notes Towards the Redefinition of Culture*. New Haven, CT: Yale University Press, 1971.

———. *After Babel: Aspects of Language and Translation*. London: Oxford University Press, 1975.

———. *On Difficulty and other essays*. New York: Oxford University Press, 1978.

———. "A Conversation Piece." *Proofs and Three Parables*. London: Granta Books, 1992, pp. 99–114.

———. "The Long Life of Metaphor: An Approach to 'the Shoah.'" *Encounter* (February 1987):55–61.

Spiegelman, Art. "A Problem of Taxonomy." Letter to editor. *New York Times Book Review*. 29 December 1991:3.

Steinsalz, Adin. *Beggars and Prayers*. New York: Basic Books, 1979, pp. 148–70.

Stern, David. "Imagining the Holocaust." *Commentary* July 1976:45–51.

———. *Parable in Midrash: Narrative and Exegesis in Rabbinic Literature*. Cambridge, MA: Harvard University Press, 1991.

Stern, Ellen Norman. *Elie Wiesel: Witness for Life*. New York: Ktav, 1982.

Stille, Alexander. "Primo Levi: Reconciling the Man and the Writer." *New York Times Book Review*. 7 May 1887:3.

"Superhuman Prospectus." Rev. of *Le Roi des aulnes* by Michel Tournier. *Times Literary Supplement* 23 October 1970:1214.

Swirsky, Michael, and Sharon Pucker Rivo. "The Holocaust in Films."
    unpublished paper.
Szklarczyk, Lillian. "Le Juif démoli en quête de soi." *Ethique et esthé-
    tique dans la littérature française du XXe siècle* ed. by Maurice
    Cagnon. Saratoga, CA: Anima Libri, 1978. 133–46.
Teichman, Milton. "Literature of Agony and Triumph: An Encounter
    with the Holocaust." *College English* 37 (1976):613–18.
Timerman, Jacobo. *Prisoner Without a Name, Cell Without a Number.*
    Trans. Toby Talbot. New York: Knopf, 1981.
Tournier, Michel. *The Wind Spirit: An Autobiography.* Trans. Arthur
    Goldhammer. Boston: Beacon Press, 1988 [*Le Vent Paraclet.*
    Paris: Gallimard, 1977].
Touster, Saul. "Comments on Des Pres' 'Terror and the Sublime.'"
    Human Rights Quarterly 5.2 (1983):147–50.
Traubner, Richard. "The Sound and the Fuhrer." *Film Comment.*
    July/August 1978:17–23.
Tuchman, Barbara. *A Distant Mirror: The Calamitous 14th Century.*
    New York: Knopf, 1978.
Van Delft, Louis. "Les Ecrivains de l'exode: Une lecture d'André
    Schwarz-Bart." *Mosaic* 8.3 (1975):193–205.
Van der Heuvel, Pierre. "Parole, Mot et Silence: Les Avatars de l'Enun-
    ciation dans *L'Etranger* d'Albert Camus." *Revue des lettres mod-
    ernes* 10 (1982):53–88.
Vidal-Naquet, Pierre. *Assasins of Memory: Essays in the Denial of the
    Holocaust.* Trans. Jeffrey Mehlman. New York: Columbia Uni-
    versity Press, 1992.
Watts, James F., Jr. "Nahman (ben Simhah) of Bratzlav." *Encyclopae-
    dia Judaica* Vol. 12. Jerusalem: Keter, 784–84.
Weisberg, Richard. "Avoiding Central Realities: Narrative Terror and
    the Failure of French Culture Under the Occupation." *Human
    Rights Quarterly* 5.2 (1983):151–70.
Wiesel, Elie. "Eichmann's Victims and the Unheard Testimony." *Com-
    mentary* December 1961:510–16.
———. "Everybody's Victim." Rev. of *The Painted Bird* by Jerzy Kosin-
    ski. *New York Times Book Review* 31 October 1965:5+.
———. "For Some Measure of Humility." *Shma* 5.100 (1975):1+.
———. "Art and Culture After the Holocaust." *Auschwitz: Beginning of
    a New Era?* ed. Eva Fleischner. New York: Ktav, 1977.
———. *Souls on Fire: Portraits and Legends of Hasidic Masters.* Trans.
    Marion Wiesel. Jerusalem: Keter, 1979.
White, Hayden. *The Content of the Form: Narrative Discourse and His-
    torical Representation.* Baltimore: Johns Hopkins University
    Press, 1987.

Worton, Michael J. "Myth-Reference in *Le Roi des aulnes.*" *Stanford French Review* (Winter 1982):299–310.

Wyman, David S. *The Abandonment of the Jews: America and the Holocaust 1941–1945*. New York: Pantheon, 1984.

Ya'oz, Hannah. *Sifrut ha-shoah b'ivrit: ke-sifrut historit ve-transhistorit* [Literature of the Holocaust in Hebrew: As Historical and Transhistorical Literature]. Tel Aviv: Eked, 1980.

Young, James. *Writing and Rewriting the Holocaust: Narrative and the Consequences of Interpretation*. Bloomington: University of Indiana Press, 1988.

————. *The Texture of Memory: Holocaust Memorials and Meaning* (New Haven, CT: Yale University Press, 1993).

Ziolkowski, Theodore. "Versions of the Holocaust." *Swanee Review* (1979):676:85.

Index

absence
  of past, 13
  of memory. *See* memory
  as testimony. *See* testimony
abstraction
  and values, 113–14, 118
  and violence, 19, 31, 115, 165,
    189, 214
absurdist writing
  influence of, on Elie Wiesel, 139
  laughter in, 140
  silence in, 139
  and World War II, 139, 237 n.20,
    n.23
Act and Idea in the Nazi Genocide,
  17–18
Adams, Robert, 115
Adorno, Theodor, 8, 16–18
Aichinger, Ilse, 115
Alexander, Edward, 26
Alter, Robert, 134
Améry, Jean, 31, 99, 174, 214
  At the Mind's Limit, 172–74
  criticism of Tournier, 202
Amis, Martin, *Time's Arrow*,
  193–94
amnesia, 49, 73
  See also forgetting
anti-Semitism, 85, 111, 130–31, 146,
  193, 184
aphasia, 38, 49, 92
  See also muteness

Appelfeld, Aharon, 16, 18, 24, 89
  Tzili, 135
Arendt, Hannah, 19, 158
  Eichmann in Jerusalem, 158–59
  The Origins of Totalitarianism,
    207–9
art (artistic imagination)
  appropriation of, 211, 243 n. 24
  and atrocity, 15–18, 182, 211–13
  crisis of, 182
  and fiction, 6, 12
  history, 6–7, 12, 17–18
  as implicated in Nazi ideology,
    182
  inadequacy to represent
    Holocaust, 145, 182
  as interpretation, 6
  and invention, 3
  Maus as, 2–6
  Shoah as, 2–6
  and testimony, 5–6
"Art and Culture, " 120, 130
At the Mind's Limit, 172–74
atrocity, 39
  and aesthetic pleasure, 215
  and art, 15–18, 182, 211–13
  effects on culture, 111
  effects on faith, 111, 169–70
  effects on morality, 111
  and ethical behavior, 112
  and memory, 72
  and moral chaos, 110

atrocity *(cont.)*
 and muteness, 72
 poetics of, 17, 25, 73
 psychological effects of, 71–72,
  99–100, 111
 and speech/language, 72
Auerbach, Rachel, 51
 Yizkor, 1943, 47
autobiography, 11, 28
 autobiographical memory, 2–3, 5,
  12
 and Holocaust survivors, 12
 and trauma. *See* trauma
 and fiction, 2, 5, 8, 11, 12, 24
 See also testimony

Baudelaire, Charles, 203–4
Becker, Jurek, *Jacob the Liar*,
  67–68, 162
Beckett, Samuel, 141
 Happy Days, 140
A Beggar in Jerusalem, 121, 124–25,
  133, 138–39, 141–43, 144, 147–52,
  155
Begley, Louis, 1–2, 8–9, 24
 Wartime Lies, 8–11
 The Man Who Was Late, 8
Benjamin, Walter, 194
Bettelheim, Bruno, 74, 87
biography, and fiction, 2–3
Blanchot, Maurice, 48, 103–4, 106, 107
 The Writing of the Disaster, 17,
  117, 223
blindness
 and collaboration, 90, 201
 and muteness, 87–90, 199–200
 and sight, 87–91, 199–201
Blood from the Sky, 78, 102–4,
  106–7, 118–19
Blumenthal, Nachman, 164, 171
Borowski, Tadeus, *This Way to the
  Gas, Ladies and Gentlemen*, 26
Bosmajian, Hamida, 27, 195
Bratzlaver Hasidim, 143
 and absence, 143
 See also Nachman of Bratzlav

Brecht, Berthold, 172
Brombert, Victor, 117

Camus, Albert, 141, 144, 222
 Le Mythe de Sisyphe, 139
 The Fall, 140
Canetti, Elias, *The Human Province*,
  12–73
cannibalism, 182, 186
 in Holocaust literature, 240 n.8
 and identity, 188
 as metaphoric replacement for
  speech, 186
 as symbol of Germany, 187, 207
 as symbolically expressed
  muteness, 188–89
Caruth, Cathy, 49
Celan, Paul, 31, 123, 173–74, 179
Chaplin, Charles, *The Great
  Dictator*, 175
chronicles. *See* testimony
commix, 2
complicity. *See* guilt
"A Conversation Piece," 178–80
Culture
 appropriation of, 171, 210–11
 German. *See* German culture
 in ghettos. *See* ghetto
 identity. *See* identity
Czerniakow, Adam, 52–54, 56, 60

Death in Life, 105
defecation
 as fetish, 192
 and dehumanization, 195, 241 n.14
 as refused memory, 189, 191–93
 as symbolic expression of
  muteness, 189–91
Delbo, Charlotte, 30, 40, 41, 54, 62,
  98, 100–1, 107, 110, 189, 202
diaries. *See* testimony
Dickinson, Emily, 106
Difference and Pathology, 86, 208
The Drowned and the Saved, 23,
  47–48, 62, 99, 101, 104, 218–20,
  223, 225–26

Eagelton, Terry, 190
eating (ingestion)
    as communion, 186–87
    as memory, 189, 193
    as metaphoric replacement for
        speech, 185
Eichmann, Adolf, 158–59, 177–78,
    180, 196
Eichmann in Jerusalem, 158–59
Eichmann Interrogated, 159
"Eichmann's Victims, " 137
Elder [Erl] King, 206–7, 211, 242 n.19
    See also Goethe
Erl King. *See* Elder King
Esh, Shaul, 157–58
Esslin, Martin, 237 n.20
An Estate of Memory, 112–13
The Exile of the Word, 17–18
Extraterritorial, 214
Ezrahi, Sidra DeKoven, 28

fact and fiction. *See* fiction, and fact
The Fall, 140
A Farewell to Arms, 114
Felman, Shoshana, 6, 48, 98
Felstiner, John, 174
fiction
    and art, 6
    and autobiography, 5, 8, 11–12, 24
    and fact, 2–3, 227 n.8
    and history, 1–2, 5, 7–8, 12–18,
        20, 28, 37–38, 102–3, 106, 229
        n. 29, n.30
    of the Holocaust, 23–24, 37–40, 103
    as muteness, 39
    and lies, 1, 9, 12–14
    and meaning, 43
    as self-critique, 29, 39–40
    as self-conscious discourse, 29, 44
    and testimony, 5, 8, 147
fictionalized autobiography. *See*
    autobiography, and fiction
Filipovic, Zlata, 230 n.34
Fink, Ida, 8, 15, 21, 32, 40
    A Scrap of Time, 8, 217–26
    The Journey, 8

"A Spring Morning, " 13–14
"Traces, " 224–25
"The Table, " 225
"Night of Surrender, " 226
Foley, Barbara, 27
forgetting, 36, 40, 68, 196, 215, 229
    n.28
    See also memory
Fortunoff Video Archives for
    Holocaust Testimonies, 21, 231 n.6
Foucault, Michel, 72
fragmentary nature
    of testimony, 94, 97, 220, 223–24
    of writing, 44
Frankyl, Victor, *Man's Search for
    Meaning*, 151
Freud, Sigmund, 190
    Totem and Taboo, 186
Friedlander, Saul, 25
    criticism of Steiner, 176–79
    criticism of Tournier, 202, 239
        n.2, 340 n.3
    *Probing the Limits of
        Representation: Nazism and
        the "Final Solution"*, 18–19
    Reflections of Nazism, 176–79
Frye, Northrop, 118
Fuks, Ladislav, *Mr. Theodor
    Mudstock*, 85

The Gates of the Forest, 121, 125–39,
    141, 144–47, 151–55
German
    culture, 183–84
    Nazi appropriation of, 171,
        210–11
    and Nazi ideology, 211
    and Romanticism, 211
    language, as lost, 172–73
    as tainted, 171–74, 175, 178
ghetto writing, 30, 47–49, 51–69, 101
    compared with fiction, 48, 67
    compared with survivor writing,
        30, 48, 56, 59, 61–63, 67
    and contemporary readers, 67
    and everyday life, 54, 63

ghetto writing *(cont.)*
  and history, 52
  as historical writing, 58
  and imagined audience, 50, 53,
    60–62
  incompleteness of, 53, 56–57
  and Nazi falsification, 60
  numbing in, 50
  prevalence of death in, 63
  as resistance, 51, 59–60
  and trauma, 50
  use of historical models in, 61,
    64–65
  use of religious paradigm in, 60–61
  See also testimony
ghetto, cultural life in, 65–66
Gilman, Sandor, *Difference and
  Pathology*, 86, 208
Glatstein, Jacob, 123–24
Gobineau, Count Arthur de, 209
Goethe, Johann W. von, 175, 206–7,
  211, 213
Goldin, Leyb, 58–60
Göring, 183, 192, 195, 196, 224
Grass, Gunther, *The Tin Drum*, 181
The Great Dictator, 175

Haggadah, 22–23, 68
Halpern, Irving, 26
Happy Days, 140
Harel, Isser, 177–78
Hart, Kitty, 95–98, 100–1, 104, 107,
  189, 195, 221, 223–24
Hartman, Geoffrey, 162
Hassan, Ihab, 115–16
Hemingway, Ernest, 118, 157
  A Farewell to Arms, 114
  A Moveable Feast, 114
Heydrich, Reinhard, 224
Hilbert, Raul, 221, 224
Himmler, 158, 196
Hirsch, David, 20
historical analogue, inadequacy of,
  65
historical revisionists. *See* Holocaust
  deniers

history
  angel of, 194
  and art, 12, 17–18
  facticity of, 20
  false opposition of, and literature,
    24, 44, 230 n.38
  and fiction, 1–2, 5, 7–8, 12–18, 20,
    28, 37–38, 102–3, 106, 229
    n.29, n.30
  forgetting of, 196, 215, 229 n.28
  and imagination, 22
  and literature, 37, 150, 240 n.2
  and memory, 13, 18, 229 n.23
  and myth, 38, 80, 188
  and narrative, 44
  and redemption, 194
  as ruptured, 38, 150
  and storytelling, 150
Hitler Youth, 158, 187
Hitler, Adolf, 158, 176–98, 175, 180,
  182, 184, 187–88, 197–98, 207
Hoban, Russell, 242 n.19
holocaust deniers, 12, 20
holocaust narrative
  sense of failure in, 43
  as ethical, 3
  writing as a subject in, 44
*The Holocaust and the Literary
  Imagination*, 25
*Holocaust Testimonies: The Ruins of
  Memory*, 21
Hosea, 154–55
Howe, Irving, 25
Huberband, Shimon, 53, 55, 60–61, 64
Huckleberry Finn, 102
The Human Province, 12–73
Hyman, Paula, 105
hyperfluency, 181–82
hyperverbiage
  as evasion of responsibility, 167
  as muteness, 31
Hyssen, Andreas, 230 n.38

identity
  cultural, 55
  false, 9

Jewish, 9, 74, 125–26, 148, 170–71
and voice, 10
If Not Now, When, 25
imagination
limitations of, 101
as testimony, 13–14, 96, 224
"In the Midst of Life, " 113–14

Jacob the Liar, 67–68, 162
Jarry, Alfred, 28, 237 n.23
Job, 139, 153
Johnson, Samuel, 91
The Journey, 8

Kaddish, 154–55
Kaplan, Chaim, 52, 64
Karmel, Ilona, *An Estate of Memory,* 112–13
Keneally, Thomas, 227 n.8
King Lear, 88–91
Kitty: A Return to Auschwitz, 95–98, 223
Klementynowski, Josef, 52
Korczak, Janusz, 52
Kosinski, Jerzy, 8, 119, 202, 228 n.9
"Notes of the Author of *The Painted Bird,* 79, 92, 110
The Painted Bird, 8, 30, 71–94, 106, 110, 126, 139, 167–68, 187, 189, 197, 200
Kraemer, David, 122
Kristeva, Julia, 72
Krystal, Henry, 49, 50, 51, 72, 105, 111, 195

LaCapra, Dominick, 229 n.29
Lamentations, 123
Lang, Berel, 20, 22–23
Act and Idea in the Nazi Genocide, 17–18
Langer, Lawrence L., 19–21, 25, 28, 88, 224
The Holocaust and the Literary Imagination, 25

Holocaust Testimonies: The Ruins of Memory, 21
Versions of Survival, 20
language
and atrocity, 72
choice and muteness, 174, 215
of collaborator, 213
and complicity, 115–16, 129, 135
as "corrupted, " 120
crisis of (crise de), 115–16
as "damaged, " 118
deterioration of, 166
and difference, 73–74, 87
displacement of, 28
and ethical values/moral concepts, 114
exilic, 31, 172, 195–96
as facilitating atrocity, 115–16, 157
fragmented, 167
function of, 178
inadequacy of, 42, 54, 101, 111, 113–14, 196, 198, 202
Jewish reliance on, 133, 135
and knowing, 199
limitations of, 37, 98, 101, 115
lost, 172–73
and meaning and interpretation, 87, 93, 114, 123, 202
metaphoric replacements for, 185
mistrust of, 31, 114, 117
and moral obfuscation, 157, 178
muteness of, 116
and Nazi ideology, 203
power of, 75, 177, 204
and propaganda, 157
and responsibility, 202
rules (Sprachregelung) of Nazi Deutsch, 157
and rupture, 102
and self-definition, 85, 87
and silence, 43, 73, 138
as tainted, 171–74
and testimony, 96, 120
Language and Silence, 19, 73, 118, 173–74, 211–12

Lanzman, Claude, 6–7, 12–13
  Shoah, 6, 13, 221, 224
  as "esthetic" project, 6
  as *pensée*, 13
The Last of the Just, 168–71
Laub, Dori, 49, 50, 51, 98, 231 n.5
laughter
  in absurdist writing, 140
  as alternative to muteness,
    140–41
  in Beckett, 140
  in Camus, 140–41
  and madness, 142
  "metaphysical, " 142
  and Nachman of Bratzlav, 142–43
  in Wiesel, 140–41
Leibowitz, Herbert, 12
Leiser, Erwin, 158
Lejeune, Phillippe, 12
Levi, Primo, 30, 40, 67
  The Drowned and the Saved, 23,
    47–48, 62, 99, 101, 104,
    218–20, 223, 225–26
  If Not Now, When, 25
  Survival in Auschwitz, 98, 101
Levin, Harry, 27–28
Lifton, Robert J., 49, 91, 231 n.4, 232
    n.3
  Death in Life, 105
  Nazi Doctors, 105, 166, 193
  healing-killing paradox, 166
  on *hibakusha*, 51
Lind, Jakov, 26, 31, 17, 215, 238 n.4
  Soul of Wood, 26, 31, 159–68
literary paradigms (models), 43
  inadequacy of, for Holocaust,
    115–17, 133
  prison poetry as, 117
  nineteenth century, 115–16
  of the void, 115
literature of the Holocaust, 16–18,
    25–27
  and atrocity, 179
  ethical boundaries of, 16
  false opposition of, and history,
    24, 44, 230 n. 38

and history, 37, 150, 240 n.2
  power of, 43
Lodz Ghetto, 57, 59, 63–65, 67–68
Lodz Ghetto Chronicles, 51, 52,
    54–60, 63
The Long Voyage, 24, 29–30, 33–37,
    41, 42, 73, 81, 96–97, 112, 117–18,
    223
Lustig, Arnost, 16, 98, 100–1
Lyotard, Jean-François, 99

madness, 47
  and laughter, 141–42
  and sick memory (*la memoire
    malade*), 141–42
  and testimony, 142–43
Mandel, Barrett, 5
The Man Who Was Late, 8
Mann, Klaus, 171
  Mephisto, 182
Mann, Thomas, 171
Man's Search for Meaning, 151
Martryology [*Eileh Ezkerah*], 124
Maus, 2, 16
  as art, 2–6
  as literature, 5
  as nonfiction, 2, 4–6, 227 n.2
  as testimony, 4
memoir. *See* testimony
memory
  absent, 3–4, 7, 24, 193
  abuses of, 26
  accuracy of, 100, 217–19
  and atrocity, 72
  autobiographical, 2–3, 5, 12
  avoidance of, 214
  collective, 25
  compulsion of, 41
  constructed, 21
  and disparity with present, 34,
    95–96, 100
  distrust of, 3
  as eating, 189, 193
  and experience, 29
  futility of sharing, 36
  and history, 13, 18, 229 n.23

Holocaust fiction as enacting, 39
and imagination, 20, 96–97, 150, 224
limitations of, 98
memory novel, 29
memory place (*lieu de memoire*), 19–20
and narrative, 37, 136
and omission, 222
refused, 189, 215
ritualization of, 23
ruptured, 38, 102
and seeing, 89
and self, 5, 12, 100
sick memory (memoire malade), 141–42
survivor, 2, 12, 21, 36, 221, 225, 242 n.20
as "tainted, " 225
and testimony, 3, 37, 96, 219–20
traces, 97, 224–25
and trauma (pain), 3, 5, 24, 41, 49–51, 155
undisclosed, 218
unreliability of, 39, 62
Mengele, Josef, 68
Mephisto, 182
midrash, 22–24
on Akeda, 179–80
and history, 23–24
as moral discourse, 22
Steiner, 179
Mintz, Alan, 235 n.4
moral discourse 22, 24
Morley, Peter, *Kitty: A Return to Auschwitz*, 95–98, 223
Mosse, George, 19, 171
A Moveable Feast, 114
Mr. Theodor Mudstock, 85
mute characters, 38, 40, 71, 116, 119, 159
mute witness, 29, 30, 49, 73, 88, 98, 110, 167
muteness
and animals, 79–81, 168, 198–99
and atrocity, 72

and blindness, 87–90, 199–200
as condition of the survivor, 31
and the dead and death, 31, 91–92, 138, 149, 152
divine, 139
and discontinuity, 39, 74
and displacement, 38
as evasive practice, 198
feigned, 74, 113, 126, 232 n.4
in fiction, 38
and genocide, 39
and helplessness or loss of agency, 10, 159
of Holocaust survivors, 91
and hyperfluency or hyperverbiage, 31, 181
idea of, 38
and inability to love, 152
impenetrability as, 179
imposed or enforced, 33, 51
interplay of unspoken and spoken, 44, 49
as "invisible writing, " 116
in *King Lear*, 88–91
and language choice, 174, 215
and loss of faith, 77–78
and loss of identity, 10
and meaninglessness or meaning, 31, 38, 75, 77–78
and narrative voice, 30, 144
and Nazi jargon, 158–60, 167, 180
of onlookers, 120
radical, 4, 14
and reality, 200–1
as rupture, 75, 78
and speech, 43, 155
and storylessness, 87
symbolically expressed as cannibalism, 189
symbolically expressed as defecation, 189–91
and testimony, 6, 40
textual gaps or muteness, 32, 38, 39–40, 43
in torture, 72

muteness *(cont.)*
    trope of, 1, 24, 29, 38, 48, 98, 156
    and trauma, 11, 30, 49, 232 n.3
    and untold stories, 4, 149, 152
    of victim, 31, 202
    as witness, 72
    See also silence
myth
    and history, 38, 80, 188
    and ideology, 210–11
Le Mythe de Sisyphe, 139

Nachman [Nahman] of Bratzlav,
    142–44, 156
    and laughter, 142–43
    and muteness, 143–44
    and the paradox of faith, 142–44
    Sefer ha-Nisraf (Burned Book),
        143
    "Seven Beggars, " 144
    and storytelling, 144, 156
    in Wiesel, 142
naming and namelessness, 127–28
narrative (storytelling)
    absent, 3–4, 11, 32
    as artifice, 43
    and ethics, 139
    and factuality, 44
    and history, 44
    inadequacy of, 36, 98
    and memory, 37, 136
    as an ordering process, 115
    and rupture, 43
    self-conscious, 3
    as self critique, 39
    self-referentiality, 44
    spaces or gaps, 23–24, 72, 221
    as telling and not telling, 103–4,
        221
    truncated, 222
    work of, 137
Nazi
    biomedical vision, 165
    deception, 49, 57, 65, 81
    discourse, 197, 204–5, 207
    duplicity, 58, 66

ideology, 207–8
imagery, 200
language. *See* Nazi jargon
physicians, 165–66
propaganda, 54, 85, 157–58, 171,
    193, 211
Nazi Deutsch. *See* Nazi jargon
Nazi Doctors, 105, 166, 193
Nazi jargon (Nazi deutsch), 31, 157,
    159, 160, 163–64, 170–71, 173,
    177, 181, 196
    abstractions of, 161, 165
    as deception, 161–62
    medical metaphors, 163–65
    and moral obfuscation, 157–59,
        162–65, 168, 171
    and muteness, 158–60, 167, 180
    special treatment, 160, 162–63,
        166
Neher, André, *The Exile of the Word*,
    17–18
Niederland, William, 111
New York Times Book Review, 2–6
Night, 112, 123, 134
"Night of Surrender, " 226
Nora, Pierre, 19–20
Norkus, Herbert, 211
"Notes of the Author of *The Painted
    Bird*, 79, 92, 110
Notes from the Warsaw Ghetto, 52,
    53

Oedipus Rex, 88–89
The Ogre, 31, 181–215
On Difficulty, 179
Oneg Shabbes, 51–53, 57, 67
The Origins of Totalitarianism,
    207–9
Orwell, George, 171
Ostrowski, Bernard, 52
The Other Kingdom, 27–28

The Painted Bird, 8, 30, 71–94, 106,
    110, 126, 139, 167–68, 187, 189,
    197, 200
paradigms of meaning, 43, 117

Peretz, Y.L., 135
phylactories, 154–55, 238 n.33
The Portage to San Cristobal of A.H., 175–79
posttraumatic stress, 49, 72
"Precis, " 117
Probing the Limits of Representation: Nazism and the "Final Solution", 18–19
psychic numbing, 49, 51, 79, 105–6, 231 n.4

Rabbi Nahman of Bratzlav. *See* Nachman of Bratzlav
rabbinic literature, 121–25
See also midrash, suffering
racial thinking, 85–86, 209–10
and Romanticism, 209
racial purity, 85, 91, 164, 201, 203, 205, 209
metaphors of, 164–65
and racial laws, 175
racial doctrines, 208–9
Raw, 2
Rawicz, Piotr, 30
Blood from the Sky, 78, 102–4, 106–7, 118–19
reader as witness, 9
Reflections of Nazism, 176–79
representation
inadequacy of, 18, 44, 62
limits of, 5, 145
Ringelblum, Emanuel, 55–60, 63, 65–67, 160
Notes from the Warsaw Ghetto, 52, 53
Romanticism, 203, 206–7
and Nazi atrocity, 206
and Nazi discourse, 204
and prison poetry, 17
and Racial thinking, 209
Rosenfeld, Alvin, 28
Rosenfeld, Oskar, 52
Roskies, David, 48, 111, 133–34
Rousset, David, 237 n.23
The Other Kingdom, 27–28

Rozewicz, Tadeus, 111–12, 113, 118, 121
"In the Midst of Life, " 113–14
"Precis, " 117
"The Survivor, " 41–42, 109–10, 121, 156
Rubenstein, Richard, 131
Rumkowski, Chaim, 56, 64–65, 68

Sachs, Nelly, 25, 73
Sartre, Jean-Paul, 85
Scarry, Elaine, 51, 72
Scholem, Gershom, 151
Schwarz-Bart, André, 31
The Last of the Just, 168–71
A Scrap of Time, 8, 217–26
Semprun, Jorge, 25, 40, 43, 100, 120
The Long Voyage, 24, 29–30, 33–37, 41, 42, 73, 81, 96–97, 112, 117–18, 223
Seven Beauties, 77, 189
Shoah, 6, 13, 221, 224
Sholem Aleichem, 133–35
sight, metaphoric connotations, 199–201
silence (muteness)
and absurdist writing, 120, 139
and agency, 121
and collaboration, 31, 120
communicating with, 120
and complicity, 120
and the dead, 129, 136–37, 149
and the final solution, 179–80
of God, 31
and love, 151–53
as meaninglessness, 140
of onlookers and bystanders, 31, 120, 122
of perpetrators, 120, 122
and the impossibility of testimony, 30
and mysticism, 120
and narrative, 138
as penance, 129
in Semprun, 29–30, 112–13, 120

silence (muteness) *(cont.)*
  as sign, 222
  and speech/utterance, 12, 17, 116,
    148, 150
  as speech act, 138
  of survivors, 3, 6, 73, 112–13,
    121
  as tainted, 136
  and trauma, 152–53
  of victims, 73, 120–22, 136–37,
    168
  in Wiesel, 31, 112, 119–20, 122,
    236 n.14
  See also absence, muteness,
    narrative gaps
Singer, Isaac Bashevis, 232 n.4
Singer, Oskar, 54, 63
Soul of Wood, 26, 31, 159–68
Souls on Fire, 142, 143, 144
speech, metaphoric replacements for,
    185–86
  See also language
Speer, Albert, 178
Spiegelman, Art, 2–8, 13, 15
  Maus, 2, 16
    as art, 2–6
    as literature, 5
    as testimony, 4
    as nonfiction, 2, 4–6, 227 n.2
  New York Times Book Review,
    2–4, 6
  Raw, 2
  "The Road to Maus" exhibit, 227
    n.2
  and Anja Spiegelman, 2–5
  and Vladeck Spiegelman, 2–5, 12,
    13
"A Spring Morning," 13–14
Steiner, George, 19, 31, 229 n.28
  "A Conversation Piece," 178–80
  On Difficulty, 179
  Extraterritorial, 214
  Language and Silence, 19, 73,
    118, 173–74, 211–12
  *The Portage to San Cristobal of
    A.H.*, 175–79

story, told and untold or truncated
    or absent, 3–4, 14, 38–39, 103,
    218
storytelling
  and history, 150, 155
  and Rabbi Nachman. *See*
    Nachman of Bratzlav
  as testimony, 147–51, 155
  in Wiesel, 147–50
  See also narrative
suffering
  as affliction of love, 122–24, 130,
    153
  and faith in God, 111, 153
  and Jewish liturgy, 124
  in *The Last of the Just*, 168–71
  meaninglessness of, 124
  traditional Jewish explanations
    of, 121–25, 154
Survival in Auschwitz, 98, 101
"The Survivor," 41–42, 109–10, 121,
    156
survivors, Holocaust
  experiential gap between, and all
    others, 36
  and memory, 2, 12, 21, 36, 221,
    225, 242 n.20
  muteness of, 91
  as not "true witness," 99
  paradox of, writing, 54
  silence of, 36, 73, 112–13
symbolic systems, 181–82, 187–88,
    196, 202, 204–8, 215
symbol-making, 19, 214
symbolic imagination, 31

"The Table," 225
testimony, 98, 116
  absent, 4, 11, 32, 98–99
  and art, 5–6
  boundaries of, 4
  constructed, 21
  and "crisis of witnessing," 48
  of or for the dead, 98–99
  and evidence, 222, 224–25
  and experience, 4

and fiction, 5, 8, 32, 44, 144, 147
fragmentary nature of, 94, 97,
220, 223–24
of ghetto writers compared to
survivors, 48
and imagination, 13–14, 96, 224
as imperative to survive, 48
impediments to, 62, 98–101
impossibility of, 14, 30, 34, 43, 48,
100
inadequacy of, 95
incompleteness of, 99, 101, 221
and interpretation, 40–42
and invention, 8, 12–13
and language, 96, 120
limitations of, 98
listener response to, 3, 24, 28,
96–98, 100, 145, 225–26
and madness, 142–43
and memory, 3, 37, 96, 219–20
as moral, 17–18, 41, 100, 226
multiple versions, 3, 147
and muteness, 6, 30, 40, 88
and narration, 41, 144, 197
as narrative, 121, 147
"privileged, " 219–20
by "proxy, " 223
reader response to, 28, 104
reading as, 224
and seeing, 89–90
silent, 73, 102
as storytelling, 147–51
transmission of, 224
and trauma, 5
truncated, 221
videotaped, 21
withholding, 113
See also autobiography, ghetto
writing
textual muteness. See narrative,
gaps
*This Way to the Gas, Ladies and
Gentlemen*, 26
Timerman, Jacobo, 111, 121, 126
Time's Arrow, 193–94
The Tin Drum, 181

torture
as enforced muteness, 72
psychological effects of, 51, 72,
99–100, 111, 121
and voice, 51
Totem and Taboo, 186
Tournier, Michel
The Ogre, 31, 181–215
criticism of, 239 n.2, 240 n.3
cannibalism in, 182, 186–89,
207
defecation in, 189–92
eating in, 185–87, 189, 193
hyperfluency in, 181
The Wind Spirit, 183–84, 205,
210, 211, 214, 240 n.4
Touster, Saul, 177–78
The Town Beyond Beyond the Wall,
112, 116–17, 120–21, 139
"Traces, " 224–25
trauma, 42
and cognitive constriction, 30, 50
and cognitive void, 49
effects of, 11, 30, 50–51, 105
and loss, 152
and love, 151–55
and memory, 3, 5, 24, 41, 49–51,
155
and muteness, 11, 49
and primary repression, 49
reconstruction of, 49
and religious faith, 111
and repression, 51
and silence, 152
and survival of self, 24, 49
and testimony, 5, 51
Twain, Mark, *Huckleberry Finn*, 102
Tzili, 135

U.S. Holocaust Memorial Museum,
105

Van der Heuvel, Pierre, 223
Versions of Survival, 20
Vidal-Naquet, Pierre, 6, 13, 229
n.230

violence and abstraction, 19, 31, 115,
165, 189, 214
voice
for the dead, 152
death as extinction of, 11
and identity, 10
loss of, 9–10
search for fictional, 37, 146
and self-definition, 10
voicelessness, 11. *See also*
muteness
void
in literature, 114
psychological, 49, 72

Warsaw Ghetto, 47, 51–52, 55–60,
64, 66–67
See also ghetto writing
Wartime Lies, 8–11
Wertmuller, Lena, *Seven Beauties*,
77, 189
White, Hayden, 12
"Why I Write," 119, 122, 128–29
Wiesel, Elie, 15–16, 31, 40, 119–21,
198, 202, 215
"Art and Culture," 120, 130
A Beggar in Jerusalem, 121,
124–25, 133, 138–39, 141–43,
144, 147–52, 155
"Eichmann's Victims," 137
The Gates of the Forest, 121,
125–39, 141, 144–47, 151–55
Night, 112, 123, 134
Souls on Fire, 142, 143, 144
*The Town Beyond Beyond the
Wall*, 112, 116–17, 120–21, 139
"Why I Write," 119, 122, 128–29

and absurdist writing, 139
and classical rabbinic literature,
121
and divine muteness/silent God,
121, 139, 136 n.14
and Jewish explanations for
suffering, 122–25
and Jewish texts, 148, 150
laughter in fiction of, 140–42,
144
mute characters in fiction of, 116,
119, 121, 128–31
mysticism in works of, 150–52
and Nachman of Bratzlav, 142–44
relationship between God and
Israel in, 153–55
review of *The Painted Bird*, 139
and silence, 119–22, 136–38,
148–50
and storytelling, 138, 147–50
theology in, 152–55
The Wind Spirit, 183–84, 205, 210,
211, 214, 240 n.4
Witness
crisis of witnessing, 48
Holocaust as an "event without,"
50–51, 98–101
mute, 29, 30, 49, 73, 88, 98, 110,
167
privileged, 33
witnessing. *See* testimony
Writing of the Disaster, 17, 117, 223

Yizkor, 1943, 47
Young, James, 229 n.30

Zilokowski, Theodor, 19